DER KAPITÄN

U-BOAT ACE HANS ROSE

MARKUS F. ROBINSON AND GERTRUDE J. ROBINSON

AMBERLEY

Dedicated to German men and women, past and present, who have served their country with honour and distinction on the field of battle.

First published 2018

Amberley Publishing
The Hill, Stroud
Gloucestershire, GL5 4EP

www.amberley-books.com

British Library Cataloguing in Publication Data.
A catalogue record for this book is available from the British Library.

ISBN 978 1 4456 7560 2 (hardback)
ISBN 978 1 4456 7561 9 (ebook)

Typesetting and Origination by Amberley Publishing.
Printed in the UK.

Contents

COAT OF ARMS REDESIGNED BY HANS ROSE At the top Rose's redesign has *U 53* dancing proudly on the waves. At the bottom, Rose's *Ordre Pour le Mérite* lies on a field of grey. In the space to the left a single red rose is all that remains of the original, officially recognized version of Rose family crest. On the right a white mare rears on a field of red. The horse symbolized Hros, the Germanic origin of the name 'Rose' and a deity identified with the goddesses Rhiannon and Epona, who are represented by a white mare. A white mare rearing in a red field is also the heraldic crest of German Lower Saxony (Niedersachsen) from which the Rose family hail. Above the heraldic shield, a blue crest with a medieval silver helmet amid leafy flourishes completed Rose's design. The German Imperial College of Heraldry turned down Rose's redesign and informed Rose that such crests were reserved for nobility. Redrawn by his son Christian. [Rose Family Archives]

Introduction

Knight *n*. 1. In medieval times, a gentleman bred to the profession of arms, and admitted with special ceremonies to honourable military rank, including an oath to protect the distressed, maintain the right, and live a stainless life. 2. A military champion and gentleman having the qualities of bravery, courtesy, honour, and gallantry toward women.

This is the story of one such gentleman; Hans Rose, a knight in modern times.

American Ambassador Walter H. Page described it as 'the most formidable thing the war has produced – by far.'[1] British Lord Beaverbrook stated that it threatened the British Empire 'with absolute and irremediable disaster'.[2] Both men were referring to the German U-boat. In WWI it almost won the war for Germany, and in the process it fundamentally transformed naval warfare.

The disaster that Lord Beaverbrook was referring to was the unlimited German U-boat campaign against Allied shipping. In April 1917 alone, it sent 875,000 tons of shipping to the bottom. Outbound, one in four British merchant vessels were being sunk. Only six weeks of grain remained in Great Britain.[3] First Sea Lord Admiral Jellicoe predicted an Allied surrender by 1 November unless something could be done to stem the tide.[4] Something was done; the armed convoy system was introduced, and the German attack was blunted.

This weapon, which over the course of the war destroyed 6,394 merchant vessels totalling almost 12 million tons, and which threatened to bring the British Empire to its knees, was a rapier which at its sharpest counted only 134 U-boats.[5] But 'Ships don't wage war, men do!'[6] Writing in 1930, British Rear Admiral S. S. Hall, leader of the British Submarine Service for much of WWI, noted:

Germany had some four hundred submarine captains during the war, but over sixty per cent of the damage they did was accomplished by but twenty-two of these four hundred officers... The one and great difficulty in submarine warfare is to find a sufficiency of officers ... who will rise superior to the incidental intricacies of these complicated vessels, who will make their opportunities and take advantage of them when found under conditions of hardship and acute discomfort.[7]

The top five U-boat commanders, Germany's most successful submarine aces, accounted for 13.3% (1,589,011 tons) of all Allied mercantile war losses. Hans Rose was one of those commanders. Remarkably, he sank 17.6% of all ships destroyed while travelling in convoy to and from Great Britain; a success no other U-boat commander in WWI came close to duplicating.

Hans Rose served Germany with distinction in both World Wars. Having become a national hero as a U-boat captain in WWI, honoured with Germany's most prestigious military award, the *Ordre Pour le Mérite*, Rose was recalled to duty at the outset of WWII to serve his beloved navy and country once more. Between these two great conflagrations and in their aftermaths, Rose and his family shared the trials, tribulations, and personal disasters faced by the German people as a whole. On at least one occasion, following a confrontation during the occupation of the Ruhr, Rose's stature as a national hero and his international renown saved him from a long prison term. Later it made him a figure courted by the Nazi Party, causing him to cross paths with Adolf Hitler several times.

This biography considers Hans Rose's life within the context of a tumultuous epoch defined by both World Wars and the passage of the German state from monarchy, through republican government, then fascist dictatorship, to modern democracy. Where possible, drawing directly from Rose's copious writings, it allows Rose to speak directly to the reader.

We chronicle Rose's remarkable military career, including his duty at the court of the Turkish Sultan at the turn of the 20th century, his role in the 1913 rescue of the Ottoman Sultan Abdülhamid II, his exploits as commander of a destroyer at the start of the war, and then as captain of *U 53*. Rose was only thirty-one years old when, by voyaging to the United States, he more than doubled the longest solo voyage ever accomplished by any submarine. We trace Rose's military service during WWII, first as a liaison officer in Krakow, then as commandant of the U-boat training school in Plön, and finally as Sea Commander in Trondheim during the German occupation of Norway; an important post with 'thousands of soldiers... under [his] command'.[8] Yet the German Navy chose not to deploy Rose in a manner that would have optimized his military contribution.

We trace Rose's struggle to rebuild a life for himself and his family in the interwar Weimar period that saw the occupation of his homeland, economic collapse, and the rise of the totalitarian Nazi regime. The story continues through the second wrenching period for German citizens following their country's defeat in WWII, and ends with Rose as an elder statesman.

As a national naval hero, Rose would win his place in the German pantheon of what was best in German martial service. But he was also a very complex man with human frailties. Cerebral and classically educated, he was a polymath, multilingual and a talented artist, an excellent writer, an effective speaker, and a gifted teacher. Throughout his naval career he paid great attention to establishing and burnishing his reputation.

Rose was a quintessential 'gentleman',' an old school naval officer, and a man with a gallant appreciation of the fairer sex. He was a man who meticulously weighed all decisions. He was a Social Darwinist, a romantic, an idealist, and a man able, most of the time, to maintain tight control of his emotions. He knew how to play his role to perfection but struggled with an inferiority complex. Sensitivity to rights and equality were a leitmotif in his thinking. Yet he exhibited a substantial territoriality that manifested itself politically as pan-Germanic romantic narrow nationalism. While he exhibited sentimentality, he was a tenacious warrior who was as lucky militarily as he was chivalrous.

Throughout his life, Hans Rose demonstrated a democrat's recognition of the contributions of men from all walks of life, both famous and unsung, giving orders or following them. He was quick to acknowledge the contributions of his crew, without which he could not have been successful. Yet his choice of a military career reflected his authoritarian predisposition. The chain of command was, for him, an absolute, to be obeyed unquestioningly, whether the ultimate leader was a man of knightly virtues, an unscrupulous U-boat commander, the German *Kaiser*, or Adolf Hitler.

Rose was truly a contemporary knight, though one called upon to play his chivalrous role at a dark time in German history. In this context, careful emphasis is placed upon a study of the interwar years, the rise of the Nazi Party, and how the economic and socio-political challenges of the epoch combined to influence him. This illuminates his views, actions and relationship to the Nazi Party, and the ways Rose, when possible, opposed the abominations of the Nazi regime.

This biography is based upon archival materials from German, British, French, American and Norwegian sources, original naval logs and war diaries, and unfettered access to the Rose family records. These include Hans Rose's considerable public and private papers, and interviews with his children and stepchildren.

Dozens of people from Germany, Norway, France, England, Canada and the United States contributed their knowledge. Although the conclusions are the authors' alone, without their many generous contributions this book could not have approached the completeness it has attained. We owe a debt of gratitude to Christian Rose, Donald Chisholm (Stephen B. Luce Professor of Naval Strategy, Joint Military Operations Department, Naval War College), Alan Walker (British Royal Navy Rtd), Beren and Wendy Robinson, all of whom comprehensively reviewed the manuscript. Alan Walker made a contribution that only a naval rating could, showing the authors how atypical and extraordinary an officer Hans Rose was. He taught us what Hans Rose meant by saying, 'Authority is not synonymous with gold braid, authority has to be re-established daily.'

We particularly thank Hans Rose's son Christian, Rose's stepson Rudolf-Eduard Brickenstein, Bernd Molter a.D., retired submarine commander and Commanding Officer of the 3rd Submarine Squadron of the modern German Navy, and Beren Robinson for their invaluable contributions.

Chapter 1

An Extraordinary Act of Chivalry:
the *Jacob Jones*

STANTON KALK ASSISTS SURVIVORS OF THE JACOB JONES F. Luis Mora's painting depicts Lieutenant Kalk rendering conspicuous and gallant services after the ship sank by helping men from one raft to another to equalize the weight on the rafts. He died of exposure and exhaustion in order to save others and was posthumously awarded the Distinguished Service Medal. [U.S. Naval Historical Center (Washington D.C.)]

It was 6:40 p.m., 6 December 1917 and the North Atlantic was cold. On land and on sea, more than three years of carnage had bled Europe white. Yet the war dragged on. At his post aboard *Emeline* escorting a coastal convoy north to England, wireless operator Fass suddenly dropped the knife he was sharpening his pencil with and copied an incoming message into the ship's log:

> GLD DE UZAG – Destroyer *JACOB JONES* sunk 49° 25′ N., 6° 22′ W. Survivors on three rafts still at large. UUU.[10]

GLD designated Land's End, England. *DE*, Germany. *UZAG*, a U-boat's call sign. A German submarine was sending an uncoded message directly to the enemy. Wireless operator Wickliffe Rose wondered aloud:

> 'The *Jacob Jones* came into Brest with the troop convoy ... she must have been on her way back to Queenstown. But if she was running without any ships to worry about, how on earth did a sub ever hit her?'

'The message might be a fake,' Fass argued, 'I've heard of instances where subs send out false distress calls to lure ships to the vicinity and then sink them.'

'Well, then,' responded Rose, 'why did this one address his message to the shore station at Land's End instead of sending an SOS? And why did he use the call *UZAG*, which evidently is his own, instead of adopting one that resembled ours?'[11]

Six years later, Hans Rose, captain of the German U-boat, provided the answer:

A bright day and a still sea… In spite of our experience with submarine warfare, what followed was new to us all – the boom of big guns rolling over the sea without a vessel in sight. Visibility was good except to the southwest, where a light mist made it impossible to see more than about six miles. Accordingly we steered in that direction at top speed.

We had not gone far when the flash of guns and the sound of reports emerged from the mist once again. But still no sign of a ship. It must be small. At 3:30 p.m., presuming a submarine was engaged in battle, we wired: 'Are you in action? Please give us your location. *U 53.*' But there was no answer.

A few minutes later … the outlines of a small craft could be dimly seen. It stood end on to us at first, but soon turned, materializing into an American torpedo-boat destroyer with four funnels.

At the command 'ready for action' the men sprang to their battle posts, the diesel engines stopped and driven by her two powerful electric motors *U 53* raced ahead at undiminished speed.

Another quick order, 'Submerge!'

The lookout and the officer of the watch went below and I followed them after a last glance around, closing the hatch cover as the air began to hiss from the diving tanks. *U 53* disappeared gently beneath the surface. Only the wrist-thick end of the periscope made a light wake on the surface. The torpedoes were readied and in two or three minutes everything was prepared for the work ahead.

I stood at the periscope and followed the movements of our opponent. The ship was cruising at low speed in a zigzag pattern. At times she appeared to almost stop. I could not see what she was firing at. Behind me stood the chief navigator, equipped with protractor and stop-watch. Minute by minute we tracked our position and that of the enemy ship on his chart table to determine the speed and course of our protagonist.

… The hum of the motors brought us steadily closer to the unsuspecting enemy. The destroyer turned north and we altered course to intercept her at almost right angles. As we were almost three miles distant from our prey, it was still too soon to shoot. When the destroyer suddenly increased her speed the distance diminished rapidly.

Except for brief seconds, I kept the periscope submerged. These were tense moments. The men below, their ears to the speaking tubes leading to the tower, awaited the next orders.

At 4:20 p.m., at a distance of 1,000 metres, I fired my fastest and strongest torpedo. Because the torpedo was not very deep, it broke surface frequently, racing along in full sight; a very dangerous situation. If the enemy kept a close watch and had any kind of luck, he would see the danger and save himself with a sharp turn.

In that event we would become the pursued instead of the pursuers. Depth charges were unpleasant and very dangerous.[12]

The torpedo sped towards *Jacob Jones*, headed for a point about amidships. A lookout spotted it and shouted 'Torpedo!' Officer-of-the-deck Lieutenant Stanton Kalk immediately put the rudder hard to port and rang up emergency speed on the engine room telegraph. Hearing the alarm Captain Bagley rushed to the bridge and five seconds later again rang up emergency speed.[13]

Submerging about fifty or sixty feet from the ship, the torpedo hit *Jacob Jones* at 4:21 p.m. striking her fuel oil tank starboard between the auxiliary room and the after crew quarters. The explosion caused massive damage, blowing the deck open fully twenty feet athwartships.

On deck, Ed Dismukes and three gunners simply vanished. George Bryan was killed in the explosion, as was James Cummings, blown to the top of the aft deckhouse. Coxswain Donat Marchand was swept off the ship. In the Chief Petty Officers' compartment, Martin Nee died when his head struck the heavy iron beam under the gun. Both James Sweeney and Archie Leedy were killed in their bunks when the oil tank bulkhead blew in. In the washroom John P. Murphy was cut in two. Walter Morrisette died in the provisions room. They were a few of the many men killed by the explosion.[14]

Those not stunned by the detonation scrambled for the relative safety of the deck. Commander Bagley immediately tried to send a wireless SOS but the mainmast had been carried away, the antenna collapsed, and all electric power failed. The aft compartment, fuel oil tank, auxiliary room, and engine room immediately flooded. There, David Carter watched helplessly as the bulkhead gave way and the water overwhelmed George Pote.

The explosion immediately flooded the ship's deck to just forward of the rear deck house. Then, less rapidly, *Jacob Jones* continued flooding until the deck abreast the engine room hatch was awash. Gunnery Officer Lieutenant John Richard realized the new catastrophe this represented. The depth charges in the stern chutes were set on 'ready' and would explode as soon as they reached their prescribed depths. He rushed aft to disarm them but could not reach them. Lieutenant Norman Scott, the Executive Officer, ordered the steam from the fireroom to the engine room shut off, and then fired two shots from the No. 4 gun in the hope of attracting the attention of some nearby vessel.

With the ship mortally wounded, crewmen turned their attentions to saving themselves, desperately struggling to launch rafts and boats. The motor dory, hull undamaged but engine out of commission, floated off, and the punt and wherry also floated clear, though the former was wrecked beyond usefulness. Gustave Eulitz saw Ralph Williams trying unsuccessfully to lower the aft fall of the whaleboat but then disappear, pulled into the auxiliary room by the suction of water flooding that compartment. Patrick Burger fought unsuccessfully to free the large motor sailer from the tangle of rigging and twisted wreckage. It would have held twenty or thirty men. He continued 'at the risk of almost certain death'[15] until the suction from the sinking *Jacob Jones* pulled him under. Still, while other crewmen swam for their lives, Laurence Kelly and Howard

Chase, under Lieutenant Scott's direction, remained aboard until the last possible moment, cutting adrift splinter mats and life preservers.

Seeing his ship rapidly settling, Captain Bagley ran along the deck ordering everybody he saw to jump overboard. Some, like William Donovan, could not swim and sank with the ship. But most of those not killed by the explosion had already got clear and were on rafts or clinging to wreckage. The frigid sea around the ship was dotted with swimming men, and a few, having probably jumped overboard almost immediately after the ship was struck, were at some distance from the rafts.

Less than eight minutes after the torpedo struck her, *Jacob Jones* gave up. As Captain Bagley jumped overboard the ship sank stern first, turned turtle, and 'twisted slowly through nearly 180 degrees as she swung upright'.[16] Bagley recalled that 'from this nearly vertical position, bow in the air ... she went straight down.' The depth charges, now at detonation depth, exploded, destroying what was left of her. Captain Bagley, Lieutenant Kalk and several others were stunned into insensibility, while many of those aft of the ship died. As the disaster overwhelmed them and the ship sank, some, like cabin cook Dock Johnson, lost their heads, swam towards the ship instead of away and were drawn under by the suction.[17]

Immediately after launching his torpedo, Rose dove to fifty metres to minimize the danger from depth charges. He abruptly veered west so that any oil trail *U 53* might leave would be more difficult to see in the setting sun. He ordered, 'Close the water-tight compartments! Get the emergency lights ready!' With the U-boat's five compartments sealed off, the Chief Engineer no longer had complete control of all apparatus. But from long experience, the crew could be counted on to do what was necessary in an emergency. Rose's precautionary measures reflected battle tactics that would keep him and his crew safe where others, less cautious, died.

Rose recalled the effect the torpedo's explosion had in the submarine:

> Suddenly a heavy detonation broke the silence. Nobody who has not experienced it can conceive of its violence. The untried men in the crew tumbled against the walls, their eyes staring at this new horror. Our veteran chief pilot, utterly unmoved, looked at his stop watch, made a rapid mental calculation and announced laconically: 'Forty-nine seconds, equivalent to a range of 960 metres.' The men cheered, 'We've got him! Hurrah!' 'Not so fast,' I called down to them: 'That may have been a depth charge.' The time was right, but you never can tell.[18]

Far from hunting *U 53* however, the crew of *Jacob Jones* was now engaged in a more unequal contest between frail bodies and the killing cold of the North Atlantic in December. Where the ship had been moments before, men calling for help now bobbed among the floating debris. Those that could, made their way to the splinter mats, the Carley rafts and float, the damaged whaleboat, motorless motor dory and the leaking wherry. Few made it. Treading water and hanging onto a life-buoy, Simon Steiner made it to within twenty yards of the Carley before he drowned, exhausted.

Under the direction of the officers, others, like stunned Captain Bagley and Lieutenant Kalk, were pulled aboard the boats and rafts. It was essential to get men out of the water as quickly as possible. But they had to make desperate choices. Reggie Fisher was seen in the water *in extremis* with blood coming out of his mouth. Gustave Eulitz thought he wouldn't last a minute longer, yet it was impossible to assist him.

The ship's officers had fixed the position of *Jacob Jones* just before the explosion of the torpedo; they were twenty miles from the nearest land. But unable to send a signal before the ship sank, one of the life boats would have to pull towards land for assistance.

Submerged, *U 53* sped on into the setting sun frequently changing course to complicate any pursuit. When, eight minutes later, the terrific explosion from the detonation of the sinking *Jacob Jones'* depth charges came rumbling through the ocean, Rose assumed that he had missed the destroyer and they were now being pursued. The first explosion must have been a depth charge, and now here were more. But when after a further ten minutes there were no additional detonations, Rose cautiously rose to periscope depth:

> The periscope disclosed no enemy – nothing but sea and sky. I searched the horizon carefully once more, then we came to the surface. Still nothing to see. We turned squarely about and went back toward the place where we had fired the torpedo. No; we were not being followed. There, ahead of us, a vast field of wreckage; a quarter of a mile across, a great spot of oil stretching over the sea, and, strewn about it, boards, pieces of spars and other objects, with men clinging to them. In the middle of the field two lifeboats, jammed full with survivors.[19]

There had been three lifeboats when *Jacob Jones* went down. Frank Chappie and Maurice Costigan hauled themselves aboard the damaged whaleboat after the depth charges went off, only to have it capsize shortly afterwards, drowning both men. Now only the motor dory and the damaged wherry remained.

About fifteen minutes after *Jacob Jones* had sunk a ragged cheer went up from the men on one of the rafts. They had sighted *U 53* two or three miles away bearing down on them. Thinking it was a friendly vessel, they assumed rescue was at hand. The U-boat approached to within about 800 yards of the men. They watched as a survivor was thrown a line and pulled aboard. Then submerging, the U-boat disappeared.

Kapitänleutnant Rose recalled his U-boat's short time among the struggling survivors:

> Ordinarily I permitted the crew to come on deck in such cases, to reward them for their enforced confinement below, where they could see nothing. On this occasion, however, I left them below to spare them the sight of this terrible human misery. I only summoned two sailors on deck. We threw lifebelts and rings to several of the survivors, without even a piece of wreckage to cling to, and pulled two others with no support aboard *U 53*. But I could not save more. There was no place for

them but on deck, and all would have been lost the first time we had to submerge. I went away with a heavy heart.[20]

The rescued men were Albert C. DeMello, Seaman 2nd class, a youth of about eighteen of Portuguese descent, and the middle-aged Ship's Cook, second class petty officer John Francis Murphy.[21]

As Rose prepared to submerge, he took a last look around:

> A few yards from *U 53* a man was struggling against death. I can see him yet. He looked over toward us, gave no cry for help, no cry of anguish, none of fear. Silent, resolute, heroic, he went down as we passed, dead for his country.[22]

As one of the rescued men was brought up to the conning tower, he told *Kapitänleutnant* Rose: 'You had better get out of here. We sent off a message and destroyers will probably be here shortly.' Later though 'he admitted that he was not definitely informed concerning the transmission of the signal.'[23] Subsequently Rose would remark: 'This was not cowardice. It was an instinctive, involuntary reaction to the horrors just passed through. The man wanted no further acquaintance with torpedoes.'[24]

Below decks the two prisoners were separated. Strong tea was proffered to clear their throats of any sea water and fuel oil. The men were stripped of their wet clothing and put to bed in the forecastle. *Kapitänleutnant* Rose and Lieutenant Stein each donated underwear to them. Though neither man suffered any lasting injury from their immersion, Rose noted that 'the shock from the two explosions must have been terrific.'[25] A short while later, after the men had recuperated somewhat, they were escorted to Rose's cabin, where they sat on his bed and identified *Jacob Jones*. But now, having collected their thoughts,

> ... they could give no details about the alleged wireless message for help of which they had spoken. They were inclined finally to believe that none had been given, and that the crew had merely been told that one had been sent to quiet them.[26]

It was now almost two hours since the destroyer had been sunk. Without an early rescue there was little chance any of their crewmates would survive. After reflecting a few moments Rose ordered a German-language message be wirelessed to Land's End. At 6:40 p.m. the message intercepted by the *Emeline* was twice transmitted.

In 1930, Albert DeMello recalled:

> The operator was pounding the key. I turned to Captain Rose and said, 'notifying your sister ship of your victory?' His answer word for word was, 'No I am sending a S.O.S. to Land's End for the remainder of your shipmates, as I have no more room for more of you aboard.' I'm quite sure that he spoke the truth.[27]

For his part, Rose declared:

> Such an action was doubtless unusual during this murderous war, and I debated
> with myself whether I could accept the responsibility for it before the souls of
> German submariners gruesomely killed by the enemy. I wavered for a while, but
> finally decided to let mercy prevail and bring some chivalry into the conflict.[28]

There can be little doubt about Rose's humanitarian concerns. But they may
not have been his sole motivation. The notation in *U 53*'s war diary next to the
radio message sent to Land's End states:

> I sent out this radio message because our surfaced boat had moved slowly among
> the survivors. [I] hoped to widen the discontent between the British and American
> sailors, which one of the prisoners had alluded to.[29]

Or perhaps he felt the need to justify his action to higher command. Later that
evening at 8:50 *U 53* intercepted a message from Land's End:

> UZAG on Land's End. USS *Jacob Jones* torpedoed 4925 9622 at 8 p.m. Survivors
> on board three rafts still at large.[30]

Rose's call had been heard and heeded.

After *Jacob Jones* sank, Lieutenant Scott pulled the badly stunned Captain
Bagley aboard the motor dory, where despite his condition, he immediately
took command. Not having been able to issue an SOS, the officers recognized
how desperate their situation was. None of the rafts or boats left afloat had
any navigational equipment, and there was no way to signal in the dark. Bagley
ordered that with the exception of a half bucket of water and some emergency
rations, all the dory's supplies and medical equipment were to be left with the
rafts and the wherry. Then with four crewmen he struck out for the Scilly Isles
steering by the stars and the direction of the sea and wind.

The three remaining rafts could not be rowed efficiently. But the wherry
might be navigated although the boat was leaking so badly that about half the
men aboard had to bail full-time to keep her afloat. With the seas still calm, the
men decided to try to pull for shore. They were never seen again.

What remained of Bagley's crew was now clustered in and around the
rafts. Despite his weakened condition after the explosion of the depth
charges Lieutenant Kalk swam from raft to raft shepherding men to them
and helping distribute the men as equally as possible. Seaman Edward W.
Fenton with a deep wound in his scalp was rescued, as was seaman Chester
B. Lane. But the survivors reported that ten or fifteen minutes of heavy sea
sweeping over men in the water seemed to take the heart out of them. Finally
Kalk himself was pulled aboard the Carly raft. Exhausted from his efforts,
he died around 11 p.m. The Carley survivors would later recall that 'he was
game to the last.'[31] Posthumously he would be awarded the Distinguished
Service Medal.

Through the long night the freezing cold and the men's wet clothes gradually took their toll. As each man died he was stripped of any warm clothes he was wearing and dropped overboard to lighten the rafts. Still, except for the dead, the long night could not last forever. Though sixty-four of their crewmates had died, in addition to the two men taken prisoner aboard *U 53*, forty-four men survived the night.

The first men to be rescued were aboard one of the small Carley rafts which drifted away from the others. They were picked up by the SS *Carolina* at 8:00 p.m. The remaining survivors on the rafts were picked up the next morning by the sloop-of-war HMS *Camellia*. Captain Bagley and the men in the motor dory continued to row for help for another four and a half hours. They were finally picked up six miles south of St Mary's at 1 p.m., 7 December by the small patrol vessel HMS *Insolent*.

'He Played his Desperate Game with a Certain Decency'

Germany's U-boats proved to be its most potent weapon in the war at sea. Once Germany unleashed its campaign of unlimited U-boat warfare against merchant ships, Britain's very survival became so precarious that at its worst, only six weeks of grain reserves remained in the British Isles.

Demonization of the enemy is as old as warfare itself. Propaganda dehumanizing the enemy while portraying one's own soldiers as heroic and unbeatable serves to maintain martial fervour and mobilize each combatant's population. The portrayal of German U-boat captains as murderous pirates became a staple of Allied propaganda despite the reality Vice Admiral William Sims, commander of American Naval Forces in European waters, acknowledged: 'Speaking ... as a seaman speaking of other seamen ... the [German] submarine commanders generally acted in a humane manner.'[32]

In 1918, in the immediate aftermath of the war, the British accused eighteen German U-boat commanders of war crimes; many of them simply for having attacked merchant vessels without warning. By 1920 that number was reduced to only three U-boat *Kommandanten*; Wilhelm Werner (*U 55*), Helmut Patzig (*U 86*), and Karl Neumann (*UC 67*). Karl Neuman would be cleared of all charges having 'in no way exceeded the orders which he had received'.[33]

The vast majority of WWI German U-boat commanders operated well within 'the laws and customs of war'.[34] Nonetheless, the British persisted for decades in portraying the German U-boat commanders as heartless pirates. A 1930 request by the U.S. Navy for confirmation of reception of *U 53*'s message by the British Admiralty brought the following response: 'there is no record of the reception by Land's End of any message from *U 53*.'[35]

There is however, no doubt that their American allies were awake at their receivers. Three hours and twenty minutes after Rose sent his radio message, American Commander-in-Chief Lewis Bayly cabled about measures taken by the Americans to save their drifting comrades. Asserting that *Jacob Jones* had been torpedoed, Bayly cited Rose's communication about location and crew status exactly, and reported that he had already dispatched a number of ships to search.

Unlike the British, Vice Admiral Sims explicitly acknowledged Rose's chivalrous act:

> Indeed, the personalities of some of these German officers ultimately took shape with surprising clarity; for they betrayed their presence in the ocean by characteristics that often furnished a means of identifying them. Each submarine behaved in a different way from the others, the difference, of course, representing the human element in control. One would deliver his attacks in rapid succession, boldly and almost recklessly; another would approach his task with the utmost caution; certain ones would display the meanest traits in human nature; while others – let us be just – were capable of a certain display of generosity, and possibly even of chivalry.
>
> We acquired a certain respect for Hans, because he was a brave man who would take chances that most of his compatriots would avoid; and, above all, because he played his desperate game with a certain decency. Sometimes, when he torpedoed a ship, Rose would wait around until all the lifeboats were filled; he would then throw out a tow line, give the victims food, and keep all the survivors together until the rescuing destroyer appeared on the horizon, when he would let go and submerge. This humanity involved considerable risk to Captain Rose, for a destroyer anywhere in his neighborhood, as he well knew, was a serious matter. It was he who torpedoed our destroyer *Jacob Jones*... On this occasion Rose acted with his usual decency. The survivors of *Jacob Jones* naturally had no means of communications, since the wireless had gone down with their ship; and now Rose, at considerable risk to himself, sent out an 'S.O.S.' call, giving the latitude and longitude, and informing Queenstown that the men were floating around in open boats.[36]

Chapter 2
'The Things of Tomorrow are Beyond Us'

Sounding a warning in the first issue of his new scientific quarterly *Submarine Navigation Past and Present*, published in London in July 1901, Alan H. Burgoyne, wrote: 'Our minds are made for today and for today only – the things of tomorrow are beyond us.'[37]

Nowhere was Burgoyne more prescient than in the technological developments that shaped the naval conduct of WWI. Around 1865, American Vice Admiral Samuel Francis Dupont declared: 'Submarine boats have no other mission than rendering it dangerous for the enemy to blockade a friendly port.'[38] For the next fifty years, admiralties the world over seemed incapable of contemplating any alternative use.

At the turn of the 20th century British First Lord of the Admiralty George Goshen declared: 'The submarine boat, even if practical difficulties attending its

'FIAT EXPERIMENTUM!' – TORPEDO Britannia. "Allow me to introduce a young gentleman who has just made his debut on the Danube, and to whom you and I will, I rather think, have a good deal to say." *Punch*, or the *London Charivari* – 9 June 1877. [Author's Archive]

use can be overcome, would seem ... to be eventually a weapon for Maritime powers on the defensive.'[39]

Lieutenant L. H. Chandler, USN, speaking at the United States Naval Academy in 1902, asserted: 'the submarine has not yet developed far enough to be of any practical use in warfare.'[40]

Chandler's opinion echoed that of Admiral Alfred von Tirpitz, 'the most brilliant naval man of his time'.[41] In 1900, as Secretary of State for the Imperial German Navy and architect of Germany's naval buildup, he declared: 'The U-boat is, at present, of no great value in war at sea.'[42] His position had not changed in 1902 when he again asserted: 'Germany does not require such a "purely defensive" weapon.'[43]

It is no surprise therefore that, through the first weeks of the war, German naval strategy ordained a primarily defensive role for its U-boats.

Limited speed and range of the early submersibles were not the only problems the new submarine weapon had to overcome. Highly constrained conditions aboard, coupled with dangers inherent in a new form of sea-going vessel, imposed extraordinary demands upon the sailors who went to sea in them. While conditions aboard Imperial German Navy U-boats in WWI were generally better than those of their adversaries, life aboard was anything but pleasant.

WWI U-boats were relatively small and slender vessels that the surge, swell and storms of the open ocean pitched about with shocking ferocity. Crewmen were often seasick in the early days of a mission. The majority of a U-boat's compact volume was consumed by the machinery necessary for surface and submerged travel. Unlike surface vessels, submersibles required two forms of motive power; a pair of huge diesel engines for surface operation and electric motors for submerged navigation. The former demanded large reserves of diesel fuel. The latter, a massive bank of batteries. Diving and surfacing required a plethora of tanks and compressed air vessels. Necessarily limiting the habitable area, these were located outboard the pressure hull that protected the crewmen from the crushing weight of the ocean around them. What area remained was largely consumed with the equipment required to operate the ship, keep men alive, and wage war. That area was cramped and poorly ventilated.

Men were rarely warm in the north Atlantic. German submariners were issued heavy woollen undergarments and leather clothing to combat temperatures inside a U-boat that dropped as low as four degrees centigrade (39° fahrenheit). Condensation on steel surfaces left bedding and clothes damp. In all but the calmest conditions, any hatch kept open for ventilation leaked volumes of water. Voyages in warmer climes generated stifling conditions compounded by the huge amount of heat generated in the diesel engine compartment. While sweltering conditions in that compartment might provide temporary respite from the cold, it came at the expense of a sailor's eardrums. The noise was so loud that a man had to shout to make himself heard by a crewmate next to him in the cramped passage between the two engines.

The atmosphere inside the U-boat could never really be cleansed of the oily reek of the diesel engines. By the end of a voyage, the stench was multiplied by spilt fuel, food scraps, cooking fat, vomit and excrement mixed with sea water sloshing about in the bilges. During voyages in warmer climes, heat exacerbated the fetid odors of unbathed bodies swathed in unchanged clothing. Both were blackened by the end of a voyage.

These unpleasant creature comforts paled when compared to the ever-present danger that came from trespassing in an alien environment. Any mistake compromising the modest positive buoyancy that kept a U-boat shallowly submerged quickly turned fatal. If a U-boat plunged deeper than the maximum depth at which its supply of compressed air could purge its diving tanks, the boat's pressure hull inevitably imploded.

The batteries produced hydrogen gas. While not deadly to breathe, it was explosive when concentrated and had to be regularly vented from the boat. But if a battery's sulphuric acid mixed with seawater, deadly chlorine gas resulted. Any accident or enemy activity that kept the U-boat submerged quickly degraded the breathable environment.

While human beings become desensitized to stench and extreme conditions over time, the best living conditions possible maximized naval efficiency. German ingenuity was brought to bear in myriad ways to address these challenges. Nonetheless, 'life aboard the submarine was a continuous cycle of foul air and dangerous gases when submerged, and sodden misery when travelling on the surface.'[44]

For all these reasons, service in the submarine arm of any navy was almost universally voluntary, and submariners received higher pay, better food, and often better accommodations when ashore. A. J. Hill reflects upon these issues:

A WWII Submarine Commander once remarked that only individuals with 'a certain psychological attitude' were suited to the submarine service... In addition to mental stresses like claustrophobia, crowding, and lack of privacy, early submariners had to endure levels of physical discomfort that most people would find unbearable ... it is unlikely that material benefits alone made up for the drawbacks of the submarine service. There had to be something else about it, something intangible.

Pride certainly played a role. To join the submarine service was to become an adventurer into a new and unknown world, a world of stealth and secrecy. Submarines could go where other ships dared not, strike where other ships could not, and slip away undetected to strike again. Here was power and prestige of a sort for those willing to pay the price.

The pride of the undersea service had a personal dimension, too, because everyone on a submarine from the captain down to the lowest enlisted rating had to master a great deal of sophisticated technology in order to do his job. There was no room on a sub for the old-fashioned ordinary seaman, qualified only to chip paint or pull on a rope's end. Submariners had to be smart and capable...

The informality aboard subs may have been a factor in their esprit... Living arrangements in subs contributed to the informality. Especially in the earliest boats ... the close proximity led to a degree of familiarity between officers and enlisted men that would have been unthinkable in other branches of the tradition-conscious navy.

Of all the ties that bound submariners together, however, danger was probably the strongest. The sea is notoriously unforgiving, but it reserves its harshest penalties for those who venture beneath its surface. A mistake that might be embarrassing or even humorous on a surface ship was often fatal – instantly fatal – in a submarine and not just for the sailor who made it, but for every one of his shipmates too. These were dramatically illustrated by the number of peacetime fatalities that occurred during the early years of the service.[45]

Hans Rose understood that danger, remarking: 'There is only one other profession which provides the same kind of training: that of the collier, the miner deep under the earth.'[46]

Discarding the 'Purely Defensive' Mindset – and Enter Krupp

The German Admiralty's initial, primarily defensive strategy for U-boats was almost immediately modified by the demands of war, and especially by its increasingly confident and imaginative U-boat commanders. As early as 5 August 1914, one day after Great Britain declared war on Germany, *Korvettenkapitän* Bauer, commander of the 1st U-boat Flotilla based at the island fortress of Helgoland, ordered the first offensive war patrol. It was a reconnaissance sweep 350 miles northwest of Helgoland to determine the limits of the British patrol lines and to 'attack all battle-cruisers, cruisers and light cruisers, which may be encountered.'[47]

On 22 September, less than seven weeks later, the British Empire was stunned by the loss of three armoured cruisers in a single engagement. Using six torpedoes, Otto Weddigen's *U 9* sank *Aboukir*, *Hogue* and *Cressy* and killed 1,459 men.

From Bauer's first patrol, German U-boats were demonstrating a capacity to execute increasingly long unaccompanied ocean-going voyages. An international stir was created on 22 June 1916 when *U 35* delivered a personal message from *Kaiser* Wilhelm to King Alfonso of Spain. The *U 35* made the 1,500-mile trip to Spain without stopping to resupply, rendering its skipper Lothar von Arnauld de la Perière a national hero.

Then only eighteen days later, on 10 July 1916, lightning from an electric storm over Chesapeake Bay etched the lines of a U-boat steaming towards Baltimore, Maryland. As the submarine ploughed through the tumbling whitecaps at the end of a voyage of 3,806 miles, searchlights from steamers crowded with gawkers threw her darkly painted hull into stark relief against the blackness of the rainy night. Painted on each side of her bow was the name *Deutschland*, 'Germany'.

Less than a week before, the 4 July editorial of the *Baltimore Sun* had quipped: 'The alleged German merchant-submarine is as ubiquitous and intangible as the ghostly *Flying Dutchman* of maritime mystery and legend.'[48]

American naval officers and marine experts derided the idea as a hoax. While recognizing the daring of German sailors and navy officers, few believed 'even a Teuton U-boat'[49] would attempt a trip of four thousand miles. At the Brooklyn Navy Yard, several of the officers made wagers that it would never appear on the American side of the Atlantic. They were blissfully ignorant of advances in German submarine technology.

Friedrich Krupp founded his Cast Steel Works in 1811. His son Alfred turned it into the greatest industrial empire in Europe and the largest armaments colossus in the world. Then Friedrich's grandson, Friedrich Alfred, transformed it into a preeminent manufacturer not only of guns, armour and shells, but also warships.

In 1895 despite Germany having become the second most important trading nation in the world, its navy ranked fifth in the world after Italy. Leaping at the opportunity, Krupp retooled his Gruson works to produce battleship armour, organized his factories in Annen, Rheinhausen and Magdeburg for naval construction, and began work on nine ships. Most important, in 1896, he bought *Germaniawerft*, a shipyard in Kiel.

But it was Friedrich Alfred's fascination with what lay below the surface of the sea that led him to become the builder of Germany's first military submersible, *U 1*. In cruises off Naples, Salerno and Capri, he had identified thirty-three new species of 'free-swimming animal forms'[50] as well as other aquatic life forms. To jump-start submarine expertise at *Germaniawerft* at the beginning of 1902, Krupp hired the Spanish engineer Lorenzo d'Equevilley. Krupp instructed *Germaniawerft* engineers to design improved equipment for deep-sea dives. Within the year, his first experimental submersible, the *Forelle*, was launched. Krupp was convinced that submarines were practical, and in 1906 *U 1* slid off the ways. By the end of WWI, *Germaniawerft* had built eighty-three more U-boats, including Hans Rose's *U 53*.

Gustav Krupp did not share his father-in-law's appreciation for submersibles, but he understood their non-military applications. The merchant U-boat *Deutschland* and her sister ships were officially the property of the Deutsche Ozean-Rhederei G.M.B.H. In fact, the company was a subsidiary of the North German Lloyd shipping company with Krupp a prime mover behind the scenes. For its wartime manufacture at home, Gustav Krupp needed access to his foreign-sourced nickel, tin and rubber. Seven unarmed merchant U-boats were scheduled to be built at his *Germaniawerft* shipyard for the express purpose of breaking the Allied naval blockade of Germany and bringing critical war supplies back to Germany. The crews of *Deutschland* and her sister ships *Bremen* and *Oldenburg* were trained by the German Navy and largely comprised of naval reservists.

The British had not been dismissive of German submarine technology but despite their naval blockade of the North Sea and the approaches to Germany, U-boats were largely voyaging with impunity. If a U-boat were to select an American port, Baltimore would be a natural candidate; it would be hard to patrol effectively. Though British and French cruisers from the North Atlantic squadron in Halifax appeared and began patrolling along the coast, *Deutschland* slipped past them undetected.

In fact the Allied surface blockade could not be effective against a fleet of merchant U-boats. It was a point the Germans trumpeted. The day *Deutschland* arrived in America, the Managing Director of the North German Lloyd Company in America stated: 'I have been informed that six large super-submarines are being constructed in Germany and that a weekly service will be started, leaving from Bremen and some port in the United States on the same day.'[51]

To drive home the point, *Deutschland*'s captain König affirmed the imminent arrival of a second commercial submarine, *Bremen*:

> It may arrive within eight weeks or less... It marks the beginning of regular international commerce by means of submarines. We have proved that their range is practically unlimited, that the British blockade, so called, cannot hinder them, and that they are economically feasible.[52]

Nonetheless, although the British and French had been unable to blockade *Deutschland* inbound to America, they promised to sink her on her return voyage. And they made plans to waylay *Bremen*.

Their trans-Atlantic accomplishment made *Deutschland*'s Captain König and his crew darlings of the American and German presses. Even Germany's enemies, while minimizing the strategic importance of the voyage, had no alternative but to show grudging admiration. The 11 July London *Morning Telegraph* wrote: 'The voyage is interesting as an illustration of the success with which physical science is triumphing over obstacles that were regarded, comparatively recently, as insurmountable.'[53]

The same day the *Manchester Guardian* editorialized: 'We are quite ready to join in the laugh against ourselves and to applaud the skill and daring of the Captain, who appears to us as a sportsman and has earned his laurels cleanly.'[54]

The London *Daily Graphic* lauded the feat declaring: 'The submarine trip does credit to German enterprise and seamanship.'[55] The French press echoed the sentiment, describing the expedition of *Deutschland* as an '*incident dramatique*'.[56]

Three weeks after her arrival in America, at 5:38 p.m. on 1 August, the mooring lines were thrown off and *Deutschland* began her homeward voyage. She submerged, easily evaded the British blockade hunting her, and docked in Bremen twenty-three days later. With this first trans-Atlantic voyage, a German U-boat had set a new solo submarine distance record and Gustav Krupp had found a way to get critical war materials. Neutral America awaited the imminent arrival of *Bremen*, while Germany's enemies, Great Britain in particular, made new plans to thwart her.

The scene was set for Hans Rose's arrival on the world stage.

Chapter 3

The Making of a Hero – *U 53*'s Voyage to America

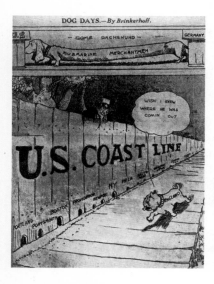

SOME DACHSHUND – 'WISH I KNEW WHERE HE WAS COMING OUT' German-American propaganda deriding Britain's incapacity to locate Krupp's merchant submarines. [Author's Archive]

Hans Rose was not yet a household name in Germany and still unknown abroad. But he had been active behind the *Deutschland* scene. During the second winter of the war, he trained the captains and crews of the merchant U-boats *Bremen* and *Deutschland*. When *Bremen* departed Helgoland towards the end of August, Rose stood waving at the end of the quay, close enough to call out: 'Hail Schwartzkopff, hail Liebermann! Have a safe journey and do everything right.'

Schwartzkopff, *Bremen*'s commander replied: 'Will do! And thanks for your training.'

Caught up in the spirit of the moment Rose shouted back: 'I'll follow you.'[57]

His next voyage was however much more prosaic; taking *U 53* to Wilhelmshaven to repair steering gear damaged during his last mission off the English coast. Then the following Sunday morning, on 3 September 1916, while the majority of his crew were on leave during the refit, Rose received a summons to meet with *Fregattenkapitän* Hermann Bauer, U-boat Force Chief.

In his memoir *Auftauchen! – Kriegsfahrten von U 53*, 'Surfacing! – Wartime Missions of *U 53*', written in the third person, (hereafter *Auftauchen!*) Rose

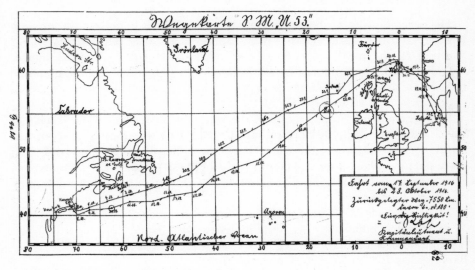

MISSION MAP TO AMERICA Hand-drawn by Rose and signed, it was inserted into *U 53*'s *Kriegstagebuch*. [Bundesarchiv – Militärarchiv (Freiburg)]

would observe: 'Throughout his life, Sundays had played a fateful role in the commander's major decisions.'[58]

Aboard *Hamburg* moored in Wilhelmshaven harbour, Bauer reviewed his decision to hand-pick Rose for a mission. He had a reputation as a meticulously prepared campaigner, he was captain of one of the newest U-boats in the German fleet, and he already had the eye of his superiors. Received immediately for the interview, Rose found himself alone with the *Fregattenkapitän* who, with a rare smile, asked: 'Do you have the confidence to sail your boat to America?'

That was unexpected. After a pause Chief Bauer continued: '[*Deutschland*'s] Captain König suggested to the *Kaiser* destroying British cruisers abroad. The Chief of the Admiralty supported the idea and I was asked to make a U-boat available for this purpose.'[59] Their intention, Bauer explained, was to try to 'blow a path through the screen of British destroyers for the merchant submarine *Bremen*'.[60] He continued: 'I know this task is beyond the rated capacity of your U-boat, and perhaps your crew, which is the reason I do not command, but request your approval.'

Rose was assured that the mission was the first act of a larger play, and that

…in the immediate wake of my appearance in America, the submarine weapon would be freed of its shackles and unrestricted submarine warfare would be declared. Truly my heart beat faster at this news. For more than a year, ever since the *Kaiser* circumscribed our actions after *Kapitänleutnant* Schwieger's *U 20* sank the *Lusitania*, all German submarine commanders had been praying for this order.[61]

Rose responded: 'Commodore, the task is very appealing, may I think about it?'
'Yes,' Bauer replied, 'I'll give you thirty hours.'

He ordered Rose to begin immediate preparations if he felt the mission feasible. With a warm hand-shake, Captain Rose was sent on his way.[62] Rushing to the local post office Rose telegraphed *U 53*'s Chief Engineer Henning Möller to join him that afternoon. Möller's first words as he prepared to race aboard *U 53* to examine charts and tables were: 'Whatever it takes, we've got to make this happen.'

Rose responded: 'Stop, let's think the situation through first. We'll have to travel a distance of 8,000 nautical miles, which would require 80 tons of fuel under the best of circumstances... That's not sufficient... I'll come back with more detailed plans after consulting with the [boat's] designers... Remember, even the most reliable men can't be confided in. Our success depends on keeping our destination secret.'

Möller agreed: 'We'll have to throw them off the scent.'[63]

Twenty-four hours after his initial interview with Bauer, Rose reported back: 'Commodore, Sir, I am prepared.'[64]

Bauer ordered: 'You leave in two weeks' time.'

Returning to Möller, Rose instructed him to let *U 53*'s other two First Lieutenants, Stein and Wacker, in on the secret.[65]

Anticipating 'Extraordinary Strain'

At 8 knots, assuming perfect sea conditions, *U 53* had a theoretical range of 9,400 nautical miles. But cruises of anything more than about 5,000 miles had not been anticipated during the U-boat's design. And the longest mission the *U 53*'s crew had previously completed lasted only nine days. The German Admiralty believed they had to plan for a voyage of 8,000 miles requiring fifty days. It would require extra provisions of fuel oil, drinking water and food, and be extraordinarily demanding on the crew, especially the engineers.

The designers of *U 53* recommended that the two middle diving tanks III and IV be converted into fuel tanks. This would allow the U-boat to carry 150 cubic metres of fuel; sufficient to travel 11,000 nautical miles in calm seas. 'Not exactly a lot,' Rose reflected, wondering 'How will that affect the sea-worthiness of the boat?' The fuel would be sufficient if turbulence in front of the bow was not too severe. But due largely to increased fuel oil, outbound *U 53* would draw forty centimetres (sixteen inches) more water than she was designed to, very seriously impairing her sea-keeping qualities and reducing her buoyancy by half. Möller warned: 'In heavy seas we'll take on a great deal of water.'[66]

Post-mission, subsequent to entering a laundry-list of mechanical failures and breakdowns in its *Kriegstagebuch* (KTB), the boat's war diary, Rose provided qualified praise: 'Otherwise, the boat has worked excellently in all weather conditions, *after* [authors' italics] the usual weight status was restored.'[67]

Rose decided to add two engineers to the complement increasing *U 53*'s normal crew of 34 to 36. Considering the needs of the crew, the men increased the supply of drinking water by filling the two rear torpedo tanks with fresh water. Two of the four trim tanks were filled with another three tons of fresh water bringing the total to 7,000 litres. This was barely sufficient, providing each crewman with only 1.03 gallons (3.9 litres) of water a day; precious little for both consumption and hygiene. Reflecting concerns about supplies, Rose's pre-mission instructions to his crew underlined maximal conservation of electric power, the washing of dishes with sea water, and even the retention of undrunk tea and coffee. He instructed his engineering personnel to keep close watch on fuel consumption and as a health measure to keep all bilges well drained. The entire crew was instructed to boil all water before drinking it.

In 1966, fifty years after his historic cruise, Rose said he chose to carry extra torpedoes:

> We loaded six torpedoes, which was two more than the design called for. One of the extras was secured beneath my bunk. In two weeks we got everything stowed away and ready for departure. But we knew the vessel would react sluggishly, and that the deck would be awash for most of the outbound trip.[68]

In fact, *U51*-class boats were designed to carry up to six torpedoes forward and four torpedoes aft. Overloading of the boat probably explains the decision to only carry forward torpedoes. As Rose's youngest son Christian remarked, 'My father knew how to spin a good yarn.'[69]

It is difficult, from calculations of fuel and quantities of supplies, to appreciate just how dangerous and demanding this voyage was. Not only had the boat not been designed for such a long-distance voyage, the crew would be at sea for more than twice the eventual average twenty-day length of a WWI mission of *U51*-class boats.

The *Deutschland*-class merchant U-boats had been specifically designed for such long distances. They were more than twice the size of *U51*-class boats, so their sea-keeping qualities were not extraordinarily taxed by such a voyage. In addition, they only needed to bring fuel and supplies for a one-way voyage, not the anticipated round-trip without resupply in the United States that was demanded of *U 53*. Most of the first half of the mission would be carried out under extraordinarily overcrowded and over-loaded conditions. From a psychological perspective, the crew was being called upon to do something previously considered unthinkable.

U 53 was scheduled to leave Helgoland on 15 September, eleven days after Rose declared the mission possible. The work necessary to modify *U 53*, the unusual trial runs and tests, the secret meetings and conferences made the time fly. But the modifications to the U-boat and the frenetic preparations were sure to arouse curiosity. To throw off enemy agents, Rose and Möller leaked out that *U 53* was headed south towards warmer seas. As word got around, some of the crew slipped bathing suits into their kits.[70]

Rose was ordered aboard the flagship *Friedrich der Große* to receive his sailing orders. These were handed to him personally by Captain von Throta, the ship's commander and officer of the Naval Staff in Berlin. Rose was surprised to learn that he was ordered to visit the Newport Naval Harbor. His precise orders were to cross the Atlantic and

> ...attack and seek to destroy as many British warships as I could off the American coast, then make an unannounced dash into the Newport, Rhode Island naval port

to hand over for internment any British prisoners I might have made, and return to Germany. On the home-bound voyage, I could engage commercial vessels carrying contraband, under normal Prize rules.[71]

Von Throta moreover provided Rose specific oral instructions on the political objectives of the mission:

The naval staff hopes that you will not show up over there before October 5. Your appearance off the American coast and an eventual attack on British warships should coincide with the arrival, scheduled for early October, of our troops in Romania.[72]

The Admiralty and the German Foreign Office had debated the merits of the proposed mission and the messages it should deliver. Romania's entrance into the war was a blow to the Central Powers. America's continued neutrality was at risk, and the outcome of the upcoming presidential elections could be decisive. How would the United States react to an attack three miles off their eastern seaboard in international waters? The navy and the Foreign Office decided that the United States must be made to understand that Germany had the capacity to expand its U-boat campaign against merchant shipping across the entire North Atlantic. Having concluded that the mission was worthwhile, it was preferable that the U-boat not resupply in America and under no circumstances be placed at risk of being interned. Nonetheless, Rose was instructed to allow American naval personnel on board to inspect the boat and appreciate first-hand the technology and personnel they would confront if they went to war with Germany.

As Threatening and Unfathomable as the Sea

In 1806, Sir Francis Beaufort, an Irish-born hydrographer developed the scale that bears his name. The Beaufort Scale standardizes the description of sea conditions into thirteen categories from zero to twelve. At Force Zero the sea is 'like a mirror' and all the sails of a British man-of-war would be deployed with a result 'just sufficient to give steerage', while at Force Twelve, conditions would be such that 'no canvas sails could withstand [them]'.[73] The scale became the standard for the Royal Navy in 1830, and was gradually adopted worldwide. It remains the standard today.

Beaufort Forces 8 and 9 describe gale conditions, Forces 10 and 11 storm conditions, and Force 12 a hurricane. Throughout *U 53*'s voyage, the average for each day's worst conditions was Force 6, winds of 25-31 m.p.h. (22-27 knots) with waves 9.5 to 13 feet tall. For half the mission, they would prove to be considerably worse, with Force 9 and 10 winds recorded on six days.

Delayed two days by inclement weather, *U 53* departed the Helgoland naval base on Sunday 17 September 1916, setting off on a northern circumnavigation of the British Isles. In the interests of secrecy, the routine farewell ceremonies and even the Flotilla Chief's traditional goodbye were dispensed with. High above the departing U-boat, dirigible *L-17* shadowed them, watchful for enemy vessels and submarines. Although the airship and the U-boat exchanged radio messages, Rose noted that the dirigible could not have proffered much aid in the event that the boat struck a mine or was torpedoed. Nonetheless he recalled, almost plaintively: 'Human nature felt comforted knowing there was someone to bear witness.'[74]

The weather was propitious. But it would not remain that way. Later in the day, with developing rain squalls, *L-17* was ordered to return to base and *U 53* was on her own. Almost immediately Rose and his crews got a foretaste of the nightmare that lay ahead. Heavily loaded with a following sea, waves broke constantly over the stern, despite relatively mild winds. Rose recalled that the boat 'lay in the water like an ironing board'.[75] The first evening of their voyage, Rose annotated the ship's log with 'one breaker covered the tower's protective cowling and filled it with water, almost pulling the watch overboard.'[76] He didn't identify the men at risk; Navigator Schroeter and himself.

The next day, Christian Petersen, Senior petty officer, engineering service, keeping a diary of the voyage wrote:

Sept. 18th: Bad weather rising. Voyage is carried out with one [diesel] engine. Sea state becoming so heavy that water pours in through the air in-take funnel into the engine room. – Can't even keep the engines dry![77]

It was the start of increasingly bad weather that would plague *U 53* on much of its outbound voyage. The KTB for the 18th reported that sea conditions had deteriorated to 6 on the Beaufort Scale, with gusts of 8 to 9 generating waves between 19 and 33 feet tall; a significant sea swell for a boat as small and overloaded as *U 53*. At 11:40 in the morning Rose was unable to radio the U-boat's position because the antenna mast was damaged:

The commander had other things on his mind. The barometer fell, the winds increased and the heavily loaded boat performed badly... The watch had to attach itself to the tower with steel cables ... because the waves rolled not only over the ship, but also the conning tower... The watch could have been swept overboard, if the cables had not held... In a few hours the wind increased to 9 and the barometer had dropped 20mb – an unusually high drop for the time of the year – it was a bad night for everyone.[78]

As men were bounced about the boat, Rose remembered hearing the first swearing of the voyage. The *Zentralmaat* (the Control Room Mate) smashed his head against a control room valve screw; 'the latter,' Rose opined, 'having proved tougher than the former'.[79] In addition two of the men would become so seasick that they became bedridden and did not recover until the boat entered calmer waters six days into the voyage. With the arrival of dawn however,

The wind dropped to nothing and the starry skies above became visible – the boat seemed to be drifting in the centre of a lull... By 9am the course could be re-established and the first storm lay behind [us].[80]

That evening, as the boat travelled along the Norwegian coast, Rose recalled the night

...was beautiful. The sea was smooth as a mirror, and a golden strip of small fluorescent animals formed on both sides of the boat, bubbling along the hull, where they turned into foaming, glistening curls. The stars were reflected as shining points in the sea.[81] 'Are we a comet?' dreamily inquired petty officer Thomas.[82]

The next day, 19 September, things deteriorated again. Still in the North Sea, a new storm roared down from the north. *U 53* laboriously crossed 60° north, the latitude of the Shetland Islands. The U-boat's bow crashed repeatedly down through the high swells, pummeling the axles of the forward hydroplanes, and forcing Rose to alter course and reduce speed to 3.5 knots in an attempt to relieve the stress. Finally with sea conditions ranging between 6 and 7, the boat was no longer able to make headway. Rose commented, 'Let's try from below, what we cannot accomplish above the seas.'[83] He dove to protect the boat and continue forward progress. The crew breathed a sigh of relief, silence reigned in the boat once more, and forward progress resumed. Nonetheless, sea conditions were so rough that it was impossible to accurately determine their position. Worse still, Petersen recorded: 'Port engine, which had been in operation, fails. One piston overheated and has seized up. Voyage is carried on with the starboard engine.'[77]

The complete breakdown of the port diesel, only three days into the mission, was an extraordinarily serious development. Petersen's very cryptic diary entries provide only the barest account of how serious the problem was. The next day, 20 September, he wrote:

Installation of the spare piston unsuccessful, damaged piston cannot be removed! Cylinder has to be withdrawn. But it is jammed so that all efforts to pull it out fail... Repair with resources available in the boat appears impossible. Finally a spark of genius. In the emergency, a small file comes to the rescue and serves very well.[77]

On 21 September, Petersen could write, 'After hard work, port engine again ready.'[77] Hard work indeed. In his post-mission analysis of technical issues, Rose reported that the repair had taken seventy-two hours of continuous work. When the revolutions of the port diesel suddenly fell off on the 19th, investigation revealed that one of the compressed air pump pistons had broken and damaged the piston cylinder. The piston was jammed in the damaged cylinder, and the engineers had no idea how to dislodge it. Such a repair had not been anticipated at sea.

There is no record of who came up with the idea of using a file to cut away bit by bit at the interior of the piston in order to remove the broken piston ring from the inside. But after all other alternatives had been exhausted, the strategy proved successful and twenty-four hours later the piston had been replaced with a spare. But the replacement piston also failed, further damaging the cylinder. After another twenty-two hours a second spare piston was installed. This repair also failed, and the file was again used to remove jammed bits of the piston ring. Another twenty-hour effort ensued in a third attempt at repair. Finally, after a further six hours of testing, the engineering staff could report that the port diesel was once again ready for use.

As *U 53* ploughed through the North Sea and up around Scotland between the 19th and the 21st the meteorological conditions under which this round-the-clock repair of the diesel were carried out were daunting. On the 20th, as *U 53* approached Muckle Flugga, the northern point of the Shetland Islands above Scotland, the winds reached Force 7, near-gale conditions, with seas approaching eighteen feet in height. Heavily overloaded, *U 53* was making very slow progress with heavy breakers constantly passing over the boat. As soon as winds reached Force 4, the waves regularly washed over the conning tower and the watch had to be clipped to the conning tower with steel cables lest they be washed overboard. Since the top of the conning tower's protective cowling rose 3.8m (12.5ft) above the waterline of the overloaded boat, and Force 4 waves do not exceed 5 feet, one gets some idea of how much the *U 53* was pitching and rolling in even moderate seas while these repairs were underway. In Force 7 conditions, *U 53* would have been sliding into troughs between waves, whose peaks rose well over a metre above the top of the conning tower. To ride out the storm and complete repairs, Rose again had to alter course.

From a description of conditions in *Deutschland*'s engine room under similar stormy conditions, one gets some idea of the conditions under which *U 53*'s engineering personnel carried out these repairs:

> [Outside] it was an inferno, pure and simple. But this was nothing compared to the hell down below, especially in the engine room. This ferocious sea had naturally forced us to keep all openings battened down. Even the hatch in the turret could only be kept open at intervals. It is true that two large ventilation fans were going continuously, but the fresh air they sucked down from the carefully protected ventilation shaft was immediately devoured by the greedy diesel engines. Out of sheer ingratitude, these hungry monsters returned us nothing but heat – a heavy, oppressive heat, saturated with a frightful smell of oil, which the ventilating fans kept whipping and whirling through all compartments of the boat.[84]

The problem with the port diesel's piston was the first of a long list of mechanical failures that would test *U 53*'s engineering personnel.

Considering how difficult, drawn-out and remarkable the repair was, coupled with Rose's habit of acknowledging the contributions of his crew, it is surprising that he omits this critical failure from everything he ever wrote about the voyage to America. Its omission from *Auftauchen!*, published in 1939 by Essener Verlagsanstalt, the Nazi Party publishing house,[85] cannot be divorced from the political context of the moment; the martial mobilization of the German nation for war. Rose actively participated in efforts to promote popular enthusiasm for the German navy and particularly its submarine service as an adventuresome avocation. Perhaps he decided that the failure of *U 53*'s port-side diesel engine, critical to the warship's effectiveness, should not linger in a sailor's subconscious.

The near-gale conditions that prevailed during the repair of the port diesel piston were not, however, the most wretched *U 53* would encounter. Still heavily overloaded, *U 53* proved 'totally unsuitable'.[86] What little living space normally available aboard was consumed by the extra supplies stowed in every conceivable location. Additional stores were packed on the upper deck where the battering of the seas threatened to tear them off. With the U-boat constantly riding so low in the water, everything was damp. It was impossible to keep bedding dry. Ventilation was inadequate. To prevent oxygen deprivation Rose resorted to releasing pure oxygen into the ship for five minutes every half hour. With the sea-keeping qualities of the boat compromised by its reduced buoyancy, diving manoeuvres performed during the first two weeks of the voyage became 'occasions for great anxiety'.

Shortly before midnight 20 September *U 53* entered the Atlantic Ocean. On the 21st *U 53* finally cleared the British blockade, passing a patrol vessel submerged.

Conditions had improved to Force 2 on the 21st, but they deteriorated again to Force 6 on the 22nd. Rose concluded: 'Forward progress in the face of frontal seas of Force 6 is impossible.'[87]

During the night of the 21st waves constantly crashed over the deck and flooded the conning tower. When the four hour watch came off duty Lieutenant Wacker and the other crewman were frozen from having stood in water up to their hips. Wacker's rubber suit was filled with ten litres of water. Subsequently the lookouts cut holes in the soles of their boots to allow the water to drain out.

Safely out into the Atlantic, Rose called the crew into the control room to make an announcement demonstrating just how completely the mission's objectives had been choreographed prior to departure:

We are now in the Atlantic. We have been ordered to travel to the United States. Before entering Newport, Rhode Island, if possible we will seek and attempt to destroy British warships, which are searching for *Bremen*, now en route to New London [Connecticut]. We will attack and destroy wherever possible, and take prisoners. I will attempt to set off these prisoners in Newport. After leaving Newport, we will move to the vicinity of the Nantucket lightship and intercept commercial vessels according to the rules of Prize warfare. I expect every man to do his duty carefully and competently because our mission is important and could be decisive to the outcome of the war.[88]

Rose recalled his crew's reaction:

The men returned to their posts quickly and quietly. But then they began an incredible palaver. The whole ship echoed with it. Every man was chattering about the surprise [mission], and wondering whether he was going to see wild red Indians or streets of gold. Only one fellow [Bernhard Wandt the cook] had ever been in an American port and he was the most popular man aboard, letting his imagination run wild as he told fabulous stories of the United States. The men debated heatedly about how the Americans would react to us, some were certain we would be wildly welcomed, others worried that we might be interned.[89]

Everyone inquired at once what the place looked like. 'Well,' [Wandt] responded, 'Over there the white women paint themselves even more than the red ones'... That was surely an exaggeration, but an interesting manifestation of the 'voice of the people'.[90]

Rose spent hours poring over weather reports, sailing handbooks and sea charts as he reviewed what route to chart across the Atlantic. Finally he instructed navigator Schroeter:

> We will follow the most northern circle route to the Newfoundland Bank, even though it will be cold and unpleasant. The path of the barometric low is located from south of Cape Hatteras to the southern tip of Ireland. West winds are rarely found north of this route.[91]

But headwinds from the west were the least of his problems. Two days later, on the 23rd, Peterson's brief, dry, engineering-centric diary entry notes: 'Exhaust pipe of the starboard engine has become leaky. Pipe is taken off and rendered water tight. Also fuel bunkers in the aft section are made tight, while seas pass over [the boat].'[77]

Multiple perils remained unspoken. Along with working on deck or being suspended over the side in heavy seas was the danger of leaving a trail of oil in the U-boat's wake. That not only wasted *U 53*'s precious fuel supply but also acted, in the words of the erudite, classically educated captain, as 'a kind of "Ariadne's Thread"'[92] for enemy submarine trackers. Rose had tried unsuccessfully to staunch the leaks two days before. Finally the efforts were successful. In the boat's log, Rose acknowledges Petty Officer Mazurimm and Able Stoker Schröder, who 'must spend one hour in 12° water'[93] effecting the repairs.

The next day, though it began well enough, brought yet another serious mechanical failure:

> Next morning at the change of the watch at 8:00 o'clock, officer Wacker and his watch companion climbed up the tower, turned east with raised arms and called out: 'Hail to the gods of the day,' while his companion turning west intoned: 'Hail to the gods of the night...'
> After a while the commander inquired: 'What were you up to Wacker?'
> Wacker, coming to attention responded: 'That was our morning greeting to the gods of Valhalla – an old prayer from the "Edda".'

Emerging from the conning tower hatch with his sextant to take a bearing from the sun, chief navigator Schroeter inquired:

> 'Have you studied the "Edda" and its Germanic belief system, Wacker?'
> 'Not really, but the language of the "Edda" is so close in spirit, so distinct, so clear and formidable, and as threatening and unfathomable as the sea, on which we sail.'
> A half hour later it cleared up and the sun came out.[94]

Suddenly, chief navigator Schroeter called out: 'Right forward, a boat.' Peering through his binoculars to try to make it out, he declared, 'It's a sailing vessel.' Staring at the distant object, Rose disagreed: 'Definitely not. It's also not a ship or a fishing boat... it is something much more dangerous: It's Rockall islet.'[95] Rose recalled, 'We were heading directly toward the rock.'

Had *U 53*'s lookouts been less attentive, the result could have been catastrophic, for suddenly, where it shouldn't have been, Rockal Felsen, Rockall Islet, had appeared dead ahead, 'looking like a sugarloaf',[96] a 21-meter-tall monolith, jutting up out of the mid-Atlantic. Coincidentally Chief Engineer Möller emerged from the hatch to report that both the mother and daughter compasses were reading 30° out of true. They had been following a course of 230° rather than the 260° charted. The boat's compasses were malfunctioning.

Lieutenant Wacker, in response to Chief Engineer Möller's announcement, replied laconically: 'We don't need your instrument. We know exactly where we are.'

Later, when Möller announced that thereafter the compasses would be inspected every hour and their condition noted in the engineering log, Rose raised his hand in acknowledgement: 'It's no use thinking about the dangers we've survived, because that interferes with our actions. It is far more important to make sure that the breakdowns are not repeated.'[97]

Where Rockall Islet juts from the Atlantic, the ocean's bottom is relatively shallow. The waters are more moderate, and Rose took advantage of the conditions to execute the required repairs to the antennae and the leaking fuel tanks. The calmer seas were also beneficent for the two seasick crewmen who First Lieutenant Stein ordered on deck to breathe the fresh air. They were fed sandwiches and tea and then sent back to their bunks for more sleep. Awakening they were cured and Rose reported seasickness was 'banished from the boat for this trip'.[98]

But then, with only 1,224 nautical miles behind them, a third of the outbound voyage, another storm blew up for two days. Petersen recorded that the winds were Force 9 and they were 'making little or no headway'.[77] The ship was taking a terrible pounding and once again, to better ride out the storm, the boat had to deviate from its optimal course.

In bad weather the boat crashed into the sea with full force, and the forward diving hydroplanes hit the water like giant splayed hands. The groans of the axle terrified us. Chief Engineer Möller and I spent hours sitting in the bow compartment, expecting a fatal disaster at any moment. The only confidence we had at the time was in our construction materials. And that, thank God, was justified.[99]

The radio antennas had to be repaired daily, but the bow hydroplanes posed the greatest risk. Insisting that he be immediately notified if either bearing box began leaking, Rose ordered a crewman stationed in the forward compartment around the clock to monitor their condition during bad weather. He insisted that everything necessary for emergency repairs be close to hand: a crowbar, wrenches, sledge hammers, rags, wooden wedges and the like. To alleviate pressure on the hydroplane axles the fins were tilted down, so they entered the water more cleanly with every drop of *U 53*'s bow. This fin position reduced the forward speed of the boat. But Rose argued that it could not be helped since breaking an axle would force abandonment of the mission.

The voyage's delays left Rose increasingly concerned. Faced with Force 10 seas, his 24 September annotation in *U 53*'s log states:

The destination must be reached no later than October 7 [1916]. If henceforth the weather improves, this can be achieved with daily runs of 185 Sm [*Seemeile*]. If however there is another delay, the mission will have to be aborted.[100]

185 nautical miles at an average speed of 7.7 knots was well within the capacity of the boat if weather conditions accommodated. However, on the 25th, Petersen's diary entry noted:

Weather shows no signs of improvement, rather, becoming worse. Slave gyro-compasses fail. At noon officers' grand council of war, whether to return or to carry on. Unanimously decided to carry on, irrespective of weather conditions. This was affirmed with a bottle of wine.[77]

Needing to vent his concerns somehow without affecting morale, Rose consigned his thoughts to the ship's log: 'Help, oh gods of Valhalla, we are in dire straits.'[101]

On the 26th, to save time, Rose cancelled the normal daily practice dive. Tardily, the gods seemed to hear Rose's plea, and the winds shifted north. On the 27th Petersen recorded the status of equipment repairs including to the WT (Wireless Telegraphy or Wireless Telephone, the radio):

Half of the distance to America completed, time 8.30. Two springs broken in the air-intake valve of the port engine. Damage repaired in three hours. Also WT equipment can be repaired because of steadily improving weather conditions. Weather becomes fine. Calm sea for the first time. Gulls and diving Great Crested Grebes visible. Dolphins circling around the boat.[77]

Then on the 28th, for the first time since the start of the voyage a week and a half earlier, conditions improved enough to allow the crew on deck. Möller produced an invention constructed prior to departure. Warm sea water sprayed out and, starting with the commanding officer, the crew was able to shower. That evening, until late into the night, the off watch sang on deck. Rose recalled:

The trip's hardships were forgotten. The antennas and telegraph masts were repaired. In the nick of time, to forestall future catastrophes, all cables were checked. The fuel in the middle tanks was used up; they could now be blown out. As a result, the boat had twenty-five tons more buoyancy. Its engines worked more efficiently, and the boat took on less water and responded to the sea better. This increased its speed. It was a well-deserved day of celebration. Clothes, mattresses and covers were dried in the light breeze. The crew sat beaming and enjoyed a tastily prepared dinner. Afterwards, with their bunks finally dry, everyone slept deeply.[102]

On the 28th, sufficient oil had been consumed that several of the outer diving tanks could be restored back to their original purpose. Rose's log entry noted: 'Boat's movement noticeably rougher but less water is taken in and speed increased.'[103]

The good conditions didn't last. The evening of the next day, with steep heavy seas, and wind force 7, *U 53* must again temporarily heave-to. On the 28th and 29th, Rose had to dive twice to avoid being seen by merchant vessels. On 1 October Rose again dove twice to avoid steamers, and once to avoid a British destroyer. But conditions had once again moderated, and finally the off duty watch could venture on deck. On 3 October, with additional diving tanks reconverted from fuel-bunkers, the boat returned approximately to her normal draught. From that day forward, the weather cleared for the remainder of the voyage west across the Atlantic.

Still the strain and days of horrific weather had taken their toll. By the beginning of October, at the end of the second week of the voyage, seven crewmen have fallen victim to the flu. Wandt, the cook who had some rudimentary medical training, became the de facto ship's doctor. Rose recalled:

> On arrival at the Newfoundland Bank, a remarkable thing happened. Stein reported to the commander that one petty officer and two sailors were sick and Möller reported the same about three petty officers and a stoker. The commander himself felt drained as though his head had been transformed into a diving helmet. Everyone had a terrible headache and some suffered from vomiting. The commander and Stein tried to find the cause of the illness in the medical manual, but none of the descriptions fit... 'What can we do Wandt, to help get the people back on their feet?'... He replied: 'It's Newfoundland fever. I've heard about it. We'll give them a strong grog and if that doesn't help, a second and a third.'... Next day everyone felt better... Later the commander discovered that the crew's symptoms coincided with the influenza epidemic that had raced around the world.[104]

On the 24th, seven days out from Helgoland *U 53* passed beyond radio contact with the Admiralty and the magnitude of Rose's responsibilities struck him:

> There I was, a 31-year-old German naval officer, with powers equivalent to those of an ancient Roman proconsul, heading my submarine for Newport naval harbor, while no one really knew just how neutral those American destroyers would be.[105]

Though he might have the powers of a Roman proconsul, Rose remained accessible to the men under his command. Rose recalled a comic example of this as they entered the Atlantic on the 22nd. Lieutenant Stein, 'always concerned with the men's well-being',[106] inquired whether crewmen would be able to smoke in the boat, since the extreme weather had frequently made smoking on the conning tower impossible. Rose considered the pros and cons, finally concluding that smoking inside the boat was not advisable. However he decreed smoking hours topside midday from 11:30 to 13:30, and in the evenings from 17:30-19:30. Ten minutes later, Chief Petty Officer Schroeter, the navigator, made a show of marking their location on the map. Rose enquired: 'Is it as expected?'

'Yes, within two nautical miles.'

'Well done.'

There was a pause, and then Schroeter, 'with the most innocent face in the world',[107] continued: 'May I suggest that we turn the ship's clocks back a half hour daily, while we pursue our westerly course?... Perhaps each noon at 13:00 hours?'

Rose agreed to the suggestion, only realizing later that he had been manipulated into adding a half hour to the midday smoking schedule. Having extended the daily smoking period, Rose recalled that Stein and Schroeter were 'the heroes of the day'.[108] Rose noted that henceforth whenever practicable 'the tower was full of people happily smoking as though they were being paid for it.'[109]

After eleven days at sea *U 53* was no longer able to reliably pick up the German radio station at Nauen, 2000 nautical miles away. Partial reception of a noon transmission from Nauen seemed to indicate that *Bremen* had arrived in the U.S. Although they would still be able to receive signals from the Eiffel Tower and Poldhu for another day, Rose ordered the radio operator to monitor American broadcasts for reports of *Bremen*'s arrival. Almost immediately, on 28 September he picked up a report from Sayville, Long Island, reporting that *Bremen* had been sunk. Rose wrestled with his next move:

> I knew that even if they were lying about it being sunk, the report meant at least that *Bremen* hadn't arrived in New London on schedule, and that I might not find any British warships to engage. I spent several days arguing with myself about going into Halifax, firing my torpedoes and heading back out to sea. But the British might trap me by closing the narrows and I would either be captured or have to blow up my ship. I would be disobeying my orders, and was that justified? One prime condition of the mission was that I return home safely. I finally decided against Halifax.[110]

On 4 October, now over the Newfoundland Banks, Rose makes a toneless entry into the ship's log: '9:30 a.m. Test dive. Starboard exhaust vent closes imperfectly. Vessel therefore can be submerged only in emergency. Halt in order to repair the trouble.'[111]

It is both a masterful example of understatement and somewhat misleading. In order to avoid other vessels, Rose had been travelling north of the Atlantic trade routes. But now the lookouts had spied a French ship and the Captain ordered a crash dive:

> Almost immediately, I noticed a list to starboard. I yelled a warning, but it only got worse. At a depth of forty-five feet, the list had increased to seven degrees. A mate reported water pouring into the starboard engine. I ordered all tanks blown and we popped to the surface. The Frenchman apparently hadn't seen us, so I went looking for the defect. I discovered that Stoker Erich Gensch had reported 'ready for diving' before he had gotten the exhaust vent closed, and it had locked open. In another minute or two and with another couple of degrees of list, the battery fluid would have spilled, and we would have suffocated before drowning.[112]

It was a very serious matter. Rose convoked the entire crew on deck. The mission (perhaps the outcome of the war?) had been endangered by the carelessness of one man. And now, unable to submerge, delicate repairs would have to be undertaken. The Captain ordered the miscreant to help with the repairs and then announced that when they were completed the man would be placed under arrest for the remainder of the journey awaiting court-martial back in Germany. It would take Gensch and three other crewmen, suspended over the side of the submarine, four hours to repair the problem.

In the somewhat sentimental version of events described to Wellington Long in 1966 when he was eighty-one years old, Rose recounts how that night, still angry, he had taken his dinner of soup in his cabin with the curtain closed. Outside, the sounds of sniffling could be heard. It appeared to be another sick crewman. When the noise didn't stop, an irritated Rose threw open the curtain to discover Stoker Gensch crying in the passageway. Inconsolable, Gensch explained that he liked to be the first crewman to flash his signal light 'ready for diving' and had done so after disengaging the diesel clutch but before closing the exhaust vent. Rose recalled:

> ... he told me it had always worked before. But he now realized what a terrible thing he had done. He wished he could atone for it. He would never do it again. I put my hands on his shoulders, and told him we would consider the matter closed. I almost cried myself.[113]
>
> ... thankfulness was reflected and thankfulness was demonstrated in the remaining twenty months of shared seafaring. Tears in a man's eyes in such a situation are not a sign of weakness, but a sign of the depth of his earnestness and of the depth of his soul.[114]

The Gensch episode epitomises Rose's attitude towards discipline and punishment. In general Rose sought to minimize the lasting impact of disciplinary actions on the men under his command. This approach was clearly important to him, and he referred to this incident and two similar ones which occurred in Norway during WWII in the various unpublished versions of his autobiography as well as in several articles he wrote about the voyage to America. The end result of each incident is either no lasting or limited punitive action.

In his short unpublished biography, *A Life Portrait*, Rose wrote:

> It was policy of the Captain never to have physical contact with the crew. On this occasion he laid his hand on Erich's shoulder: 'It's alright, Erich, we shall remain friends.' Both did many trips on *U 53* during the succeeding years and they are still in contact with each other despite the passage of half a century.[115]

It is difficult to imagine that Rose, having throughout his military career developed an arms-length relationship with the men under his command, would be brought almost to tears by an errant stoker with whom he had still been angry only moments before. Further, Rose glosses over his angry exchange with Chief Engineer Möller, unfairly holding him responsible for Stoker Gensch's error. Rose was most comfortable in situations where he had absolute control over his environment. In this situation, Gensch's error left him feeling powerless and he lashed out at his Chief Engineer. In Rose's account to Wellington Long decades later, there was an element of emotional redefinition. Clearly there was an iron fist inside the velvet glove.

In the New World

Rose recalled that on the evening of 5 October a glorious aurora borealis – 'belts of colour glowing in the west: green, red, purple and gold, fading in seconds in the east'[116] – flashed for hours above Newfoundland, announcing their arrival off the coast of the New World. Moved by the experience, Petersen described it in his diary:

> Oct. 5th Beautiful weather. Packs of dolphins bustling about in the ocean. Sea calm as a mirror. Smell of seaweed in the air. The weather here is like ours at home during high summer. In the evening we saw a tremendous aurora borealis.[77]

Monitoring American radio traffic, Lieutenant Wacker brought Rose the report: 'German commercial submarine *Bremen* destroyed by the Allies – A second boat with the same name is on the trip across the ocean.'[117]

The report could not be verified and unsure of the fate of *Bremen*, Rose was again forced to reevaluate his orders in the context of *Bremen*'s absence:

> What did that mean? One thing was clear... U-*Bremen* had not yet reached New London. The ship was already at least ten days over-due. This was the moment where the commander had to decide for himself what to do. He thought long and hard about whether to abort the trip to Newport, where there was probably nothing to be had anyway, or to creep into the Canadian harbor of Halifax ... and destroy everything in sight: warships, ships and docks and then steal away under the cover of night... What, he thought further, if as a result of mines, shell fire or navigational difficulties, he would not find the way out of the harbour and had to surrender, or choose the praise-worthy heroic death? No, he decided, such a plan was wrong. If it failed, the German U-boat weapon and Germany itself would be open to the enemy's scorn and derision.
>
> He himself would be accused of disregarding a clear command. He discussed his ruminations with the officers and concluded: 'We will carry out our mission as ordered.'[118]

In preparation for their upcoming inspection by the American navy, 'Brushes, brooms, floor mops, paint brushes and paint saw the light of day and within a short time the seamen turned the ship into a showpiece. The boat's interior too was finally aired and dried out.'[119]

On 6 October, the penultimate day of their outbound journey, Petersen noted:

> My birthday – In the morning arrived in the area of our destination in the latitude of New London. Fog coming up, getting so thick that we can't proceed. Voyage becoming dangerous. We let go anchor. In closest vicinity strong, lively English WT-traffic can be heard, most likely coming from enemy ships.[77]

The elements prevent any possibility of attacking the enemy and before dawn on 7 October *U 53* arrives off Martha's Vineyard. Scanning the charts, Rose noticed an island marked as 'No Man's Land'. Several of the crew suggested that they row ashore, plant the German flag and claim it in the name of the *Kaiser*: 'It would have been a fine joke, but we didn't have time for jokes.'[120] Rather, in preparation for a possible visit to Newport, Rose anchored in twenty-three metres of water and ordered that the entire crew wash, shave and dress up:

> The crew donned clean new clothes. The sea boots and newly greased leatherwear sparkled. Everyone was shaved. Hands and faces had been cleaned with soda. The gold and silver labels on the caps sparkled and their ribbons fluttered cheerfully in the sun. The boat's stern surged pure white with a brand new war flag, the staff was decorated with a shining copper crown.[121]

Rose carefully trimmed his goatee and moustache and put on dress blues. To Rose's surprise Able Seaman Gerd Noormann appeared with teeth polished to a brilliant white. When the Captain inquired after the motivation for this unusual preparation, Noormann, with a huge grin, replied: 'After all, we came over here to show the Americans our teeth, to give them something to think about.'[122]

So prepared, Rose weighed anchor at sunrise and began searching for British warships. Initially running surfaced, as daylight grew and he drew in close to New London Rose dove to periscope depth. But search as he might, the British navy was nowhere to be seen. Just before noon a disappointed Rose concluded: 'It was obvious we were going to be unable to carry out the most attractive part of our assignment. There was nothing left to do but to bluff.'[123]

Rose gave the order to surface, signalled full speed ahead and broke out *U 53*'s war ensign. At 11:50 a.m. under a brilliant sun in a cloudless sky, the U-boat crossed into American waters.

The watch sighted several American destroyers miles off, headed into Newport to join the thirty-seven already anchored there. No British ships appeared to be among them. The almost idyllic conditions were suddenly shattered however when one of the ever-vigilant lookouts sighted a periscope to starboard: '*Donnerwetter*,' Rose thought 'the damned English are going to sink me right here within American territorial waters.'[124]

Throwing his ship hard to port to narrow his silhouette and present as little a target as possible, Rose ordered his gun crew to the deck: 'I had to be prepared for anything, because the British were quite ready to violate the rules of war.'[125]

As quickly as the danger materialized it disappeared. The other submarine surfaced and a crewman ran aft raising the American flag. Rose relaxed and ordered 'ahead slow'.

Chapter 4

Visiting Newport and Raiding Nantucket

American submarine *D-2*'s routine patrol off Newport Rhode Island harbor was interrupted shortly before 2 p.m. Saturday 7 October 1916 when Hans Rose's *U 53* was sighted. There was an initial flurry of activity when the U-boat suddenly steamed away to port, but when *D-2* surfaced and a crewman ran aft to raise the American flag, *U 53* slowed. Commander of *D-2* Lieutenant G. C. Fulker brought his submarine up close on a parallel course to convoy the U-boat. As the submersibles reached Brenton Reef Lightship the Captain of the German boat requested permission to enter port. Fulker granted it. Rose called back by megaphone: 'I salute our American comrades and follow in your wake.'[126]

As the two submarines approached the Newport naval harbor, Fulker sent a coded message to Rear Admiral Albert Gleaves, commander of the Atlantic Fleet destroyer force, apprising him of the situation. A few minutes later, her crew lined up at attention and her German War ensign and commission pennant proudly flying, *U 53* entered the harbor. Destroyer crews rushed to the rails to stare. Rose recalled: 'A duty officer from the Station Chief came aboard immediately. His question whether the boat wanted to be interned was denied with a laugh.'[127]

Almost immediately a small motor launch bumped up against the U-boat and a reporter repeated the question: 'Have you come here to be interned?'

Yelling down from the conning tower, Rose replied: 'No. But I've brought a letter for the German Ambassador. Will you mail it for me?'[128]

ROSE AND HIS LIEUTENANTS IN NEWPORT Aboard ship Hans Rose (left) and his officers Lieutenant (command & operations) NR Stein (centre) and Lieutenant (radio operator) Wacker host American Naval visitors. [British Records Office]

Rose handed him a slim official envelope. It contained nothing more than a personal greeting from Rose to Ambassador Bernstorff, but would give rise to wild rumours in the press that it contained the *Kaiser*'s new conditions for peace.

Harbor Master Thomas Shea came alongside. Informed that the submarine would only remain in harbour several hours, and that the crew would not disembark, he notified the health officials who waived inspection as impractical in the time available. Rose requested the loan of a boat to pay his respects. One was furnished and at 3 p.m. *Kapitänleutnant* Rose called first on Rear Admiral Austin M. Knight. Rose meditated later on the uniqueness of his circumstances:

> The commander was thinking about the diverse life of a seafarer. Last night, [he was] full of murderous thoughts on the filthy tower. This morning [he stood] at the dripping periscope, dressed in oily fatigues. And now as a German representative in a spotless uniform with a chest full of medals, [he was] on the way to see the Chief of the American Naval Forces. Strange existence.[129]

Rose recalled the encounter:

> Admiral Knight received me in his office... He began the conversation with the words 'Where is *U-Bremen*?'
>
> I shrugged my shoulders and thought 'Well, it seems poor *U-Bremen* has not arrived.' The conversation was formal.
>
> 'Would you like to be interned?'
>
> 'No.'
>
> 'Would you like to transfer sick crew members ashore?'
>
> 'No, my crew is completely healthy.'
>
> 'Then perhaps you want to make repairs to your boat?'
>
> 'No, the boat is in perfect shape.'
>
> 'So what are you doing here anyway?'
>
> 'I am simply making a formal visit *Herr* Admiral.'
>
> 'Would you like water, food, or fuel?'
>
> 'No, thank you. I have all of those things.'
>
> 'Ah hah, that's good, because I would not have been allowed to give you anything anyway.'
>
> 'Why not Admiral? In accordance with international law, you would be required to supply these things if I had asked you for them.'
>
> Embarrassed silence. I got up, bowed and departed.[130]

A quarter-of-an-hour later Rose was piped aboard *Birmingham* to visit Rear Admiral Albert Gleaves, commander of the destroyer flotilla based at Newport. Rear Admiral Gleaves requested that while in port, no use be made of the submarine's radio apparatus. Then, for fifteen minutes, Gleaves and Rose exchanged pleasantries.

It was a decidedly more comfortable and fruitful conversation for both parties. Rear Admiral Gleaves questioned Rose closely about his Atlantic crossing. Rose informed him that he had left Wilhelmshaven, touching at Helgoland. The trip had been made on the surface without incident passing to the north of the Shetland Islands and along the coast of Newfoundland. The crossing from Helgoland to Halifax had required seventeen days. They had encountered considerable fog and on one occasion, during a heavy gale, had been forced to submerge for four hours. Many steamers had been sighted, though none had sighted them. Rose stated that he practised submerging for fifteen minutes daily. The Rear Admiral produced several photographs of mutual acquaintances in the German Navy and Rose offered news about each of them. Gleaves apologized for being unable to offer Rose a drink, citing regulations that kept American ships 'dry'. Rose proudly declared that his vessel was a man-of-war, armed with guns and torpedoes. He then reiterated that he had no reason for entering the port except to pay his respects; that he needed no supplies or assistance. He proposed to go to sea at six o'clock that evening.

Rear Admiral Gleaves recalled that Rose was wearing three decorations, and with his little goatee and moustache, closely resembled an officer on duty at the nearby Naval War College. Formalities aside he enquired as to Rose's decorations. Rose described them as the Order of the Majedia, presented to him by the Sultan of Turkey for services rendered in the war between Greece and Turkey; the Oldenburg medal; and an Iron Cross Second Class, awarded for his participation as commander of a destroyer in the Yarmouth-Hartelpool raid. Rose added that he was not wearing a second Iron Cross, of First Class grade, for sinking a British cruiser, commenting that he didn't know the cruiser's name. He had attacked her at night, sinking her in a few seconds with two torpedoes.

Rose had begun delivering the German Admiralty and Foreign Office's carefully scripted propaganda message overstating the military threat posed by German U-boats. His assertion that *U 53* had travelled from Helgoland to Halifax was pure fiction. So was his claim that he possessed a second Iron Cross awarded for sinking a British cruiser. His later assertions that *U 53* had 'food and all necessary supplies to keep us going for three months' and that *U 53* had lain off two other American ports were also exaggeration and misinformation. *U 53* did not come anywhere close to Halifax, and had travelled straight through to Newport. First Lieutenant Wacker later embroidered upon the Halifax tale when he told American officers that the U-boat had lain off Halifax for three days 'looking for enemy ships'. All demonstrate that before meeting the Americans, the Germans had coordinated their campaign of misinformation designed to overstate the military threat posed by German U-boats.

Then, to Admiral Gleaves's surprise, Rose stated that he would be pleased to have officers visit his ship and would show them around. The Americans took the bait. It was an opportunity not to be missed.

No, I Speak American

During Rose's absence visiting the two rear admirals, *U 53*'s deck had become crowded with civilians:

Our submarine was surrounded by a most unbelievable flotilla of curious boats. Eventually I was incapable of interfering with a group of ladies that stormed the boat. It was the signal for the general attack. After a few seconds nobody on board could move a limb. Everyone was wedged into the tiniest space, pressed between talking, gesticulating and gasping bodies.[131] [Officers and men alike] received countless invitations for tea, for dinner, to go dancing etc. Unfortunately, none of these could be accepted.[132]

Members of both rear admirals' staffs and a number of officers from the Destroyer Force immediately returned Rose's courtesy and boarded *U 53*. A short time later both rear admirals arrived. The crew and officers at the gangway received them with full naval honours. Drawn up at attention was the U-boat's full complement of officers and her crew of thirty-two men. Rear Admiral Knight paid the shortest courtesy call that protocol would allow. But the much more affable Rear Admiral Gleaves arrived with his wife and twenty-year-old daughter. After giving them a tour of the ship, Rose returned to his cabin, sat down, and offered them German champagne and cake from Wilhelmshaven: 'The pretty daughter put the cake into her charming little mouth, while her mother, typically American, stowed it in her handbag "as a keepsake".'[133]

In the course of the conversation the young lady asked to see his battle station. Rose, enthusiastic, especially as concerned the fairer sex, acquiesced. Rose later wrote:

> The daughter, following the conversation silently with half open lips, suddenly asks:
> 'Captain, where do you stand during a battle?'
> 'When we are under water, at the conning tower.'
> 'Captain, would it be possible for me to look through the periscope?'
> 'Of course, if your parents will excuse us for a moment.'...
> The commander let her use the periscope, where she saw her father's flagship and the beautiful parkland behind... The commander enlarged the view. She was entranced. Her cheeks glowed and the slender figure trembled slightly.
> 'Captain,' she stared at him 'Do you look through this periscope all alone?'
> 'Yes,' he replied... at which she lowered her graceful head and whispered,
> 'No one but I have seen the world through your eyes.'[134]

Remembering the visit years later, Rose recalled: 'As she left, she said she admired my popeyes. I still don't know for sure whether she was referring to the periscope.'[135]

Familiar with conditions aboard their own submarines, yet aware that *U 53* had just completed a trans-Atlantic crossing, the Americans were surprised by the demeanour of *U 53*'s crew. One visitor remarked that the officers 'presented a very natty appearance in their naval uniforms. They looked as though they had just come out of a bandbox, their linen being spic and span, white and starched.'[136] All hands were very military in deportment, but more surprising still, all the officers and men appeared in robust physical condition.

While one or two observers thought that the Captain seemed 'serious and rather weary'[137] all agreed that the other officers and the crew 'seemed entirely happy and gave no indication that they considered themselves engaged in any undertaking involving hazard or responsibility'.[138]

Morale and discipline were clearly excellent; whenever a man moved about the deck on duty he went at a run. But appearance was not the only surprise. The Captain, officers, and a large percentage of the crew spoke English. Asked if he spoke English, Marine Engineer Möller replied, 'No. I speak American.'[139] The freedom with which officers and crew conversed with visitors, and their willingness to show their guests throughout the ship were startling. An elegantly lettered visiting card read

> *Hans Rose*
> *Kapitänleutnant*
> *Kommandant von U 53*

The first thing that struck the visitors was that there was no trace of foul air anywhere. Every valve, switch, door and appliance was labelled and everything was explained. Although there were a dozen or more visitors circulating below decks without apparent restriction, there were only three or four German officers and men below at any time. The engine room log, lying on a desk, showed that the vessel had been at Wilhelmshaven in July and August, in the North Sea and Atlantic Ocean during September, and in the Atlantic Ocean during October. The deck log was also open, as was the boat's Visitor's Log, to which a number of the Americans contributed their business cards. While guiding his guests through his small stateroom, Rose showed them a book containing 'a silhouette of every battleship afloat'.[140]

The visit was sensational. Within an hour of *U 53*'s arrival, the local press and more than a dozen civilians, including several women and a German governess, all boarded the U-boat and were shown around. The Germans announced to officers and civilians alike that 'they were willing to tell all that they knew and to show all that they had.'[141] A number of German-Americans conversed freely with the crew in their native tongue. The atmosphere was almost festive; all hands except officers and men showing visitors through the boat were on deck, where the crew was playing a phonograph.

To the untutored eye, the U-boat was a marvel. Visitors viewed surrounding points of Newport through the U-boat's periscope. Descending the long iron ladder through the conning tower hatch, visitors glimpsed the Captain's and officers' quarters; two staterooms for their use, 'very cleverly designed', with hardwood finished lockers, 'upper berths folded up as in sleeping cars' and 'nice little writing desks'.[142] Hanging on the sides of the officers' quarters were paintings of the *Kaiser*, General Hindenburg and some of the noted field marshals of the German army. There were pictures, cushions and 'signs of long and comfortable habitation in all quarters'.[143] One was struck with the completeness of the Captain's 'office', a 'veritable *Multum in parvo*' (much in a small place).[144] Between the companionway and officers' wardroom was the galley 'where all cooking is done by electricity'.[145] The quarters of the men forward included bunks, which closed up with iron pipe frames. A 'powerful wireless'[146] was located just below the conning tower at the bottom of the periscope.

Conversation with the civilians was friendly. When asked if he needed stores *Kapitänleutnant* Rose repeated, 'We have food and all necessary supplies to keep us going for three months.'[147] To questions about the trans-Atlantic crossing, he replied 'We had some rough weather but the greater part of the voyage was good.'[148] He acknowledged the good health of his crew. When asked 'Did you see any foreign warships?' he answered. 'Not one, are there any here about?'[149] Wacker received a small Irish republican flag; green, white and orange. Accepting it he declared, 'the first British ship we sink, we will hoist this flag in honour of Ireland.'[150] It flew as the submarine departed.

Still, there was no escaping the war. Rose requested that the *Newport Herald* be sent to Wilhelmshaven so that news of their safe arrival might reach the German Admiralty and relatives of the officers and men in Germany. Asked about the latest war news he responded, 'You do not get the real news in this country, believe me.'[151] But when asked when he expected to reach home, Rose replied, 'maybe never'.[152] Members of the crew were very optimistic about the arrival of *Bremen* and said the stories about *Bremen* being captured were 'all rot',[153] asserting that *Bremen* would dock at New London before the week was out. When asked if they had sunk any ships on the way across, one of the crew said no but added that the submarine would start in on her return trip.

The visit was an intelligence bonanza. This was one of the most modern U-boats afloat, launched just eight months earlier. Destined for both Washington and London, officers and civilians alike produced photographs of the submarine's exterior, detailed notes and drawings from tours of the interior and quotes from conversations with the crew.

While most of the civilians were only allowed as far as the compartment at the foot of the periscope, the various military officers were given complete tours of the submarine and had extensive conversations with the crew. Commander H. B. Price, captain of USS destroyer tender *Melville*, reported:

> Four officers of *Melville*, and I visited the German Naval Submarine no. 53 during her stay in this harbor this afternoon. We were courteously received... The officers spoke our tongue with careful correctness, though not fluently, and answered all questions except when we asked their names, which they courteously declined to give. We refrained from seeming too inquisitive.[154]

Clearly, the Americans were impressed and the reports included statements such as: 'the vessel is much larger than our L-class providing sufficient stowage space for three months' supplies'[155] and 'the Captain stated with pride that his engines were almost noiseless and made absolutely no smoke except when first starting.'[156]

> They stated they carried six weeks provisions and had a cruising radius of ten thousand miles. When this latter was questioned it was repeated and emphasized. They said they could remain on the bottom, submerged, for four days, theoretically, but two days was the longest they had ever remained submerged.[157]

Claiming that he could travel about 450 miles on his batteries, 'the engineering officer stated to me that he could make 18 knots on the surface, 10 knots submerged.'[158]

Engineering Officer Möller told one of the Americans that they could hear Germany from 2000 miles away. According to first officer Wacker, *U 53* had lain off Halifax for three days 'looking for enemy ships'. He continued that they 'could have sunk a number of other ships but that is not what we are after'.[159]

Rear Admiral Albert Gleaves passed on one of the more blatant attempts by the Germans to overstate the capacity of their boat.

> It was stated that this [deck] gun could be sighted from below by periscope, and that it also could be trained, elevated and loaded from below. The loading gear... was a chain belt arrangement. This gear was not shipped and this statement could not be verified.[160]

Then, as quickly as she had arrived, *U 53* departed. A sudden visit by the harbor master precipitated events. He announced that the Station Chief, Rear Admiral Knight, had requested that since the port doctor had not yet approved land traffic that it cease immediately. When Rose responded, 'You are wrong, the port doctor was on board, the quarantine has been lifted,' there was an awkward silence before the harbor master replied 'Yes, yes, but the Station Chief insists on stopping the traffic.'[161] Rose interpreted the order as a warning that *U 53* might be interned by force:

> This behaviour was a clear indication to me of what to make of the American government's so-called 'neutrality'. Apparently, instructions had been received from Washington. Since the purpose of our visit had been fulfilled and forcible detention had to be avoided, we weighed anchor and hurriedly left the harbour accompanied by the 'hurrahs' of the American torpedo boat crews, the cheers of our displaced visitors, and much cap waving. All told we had spent exactly two-and-a-half hours in America, of which I spent a quarter-of-an-hour on land.[162]

At 5:17 the submarine weighed anchor and by 5:30 the U-boat stood out to sea. As the boat left the harbour the crew once again stood to attention on deck. Facing the naval vessels they passed they saluted *Melville*. As they passed the last destroyer officers and crew waved their caps. A flotilla of small craft, including a boat chartered by the Associated Press, followed the U-boat. At 7:10 p.m. about a mile east of Brenton Reef Light Vessel the long-range wireless outfit was stowed and the crew went below. The vessels still crowded about were warned by megaphone that the submarine was about to make a quick practice dive. The submersible disappeared in fifty-two seconds. Then with her officers and one or two of the crew on the bridge, *U 53*'s running lights gradually disappeared in the gathering dusk.

The only tangible evidence of her visit remaining was one of the U-boat's life buoys, marked with its distinctive 'SM *U 53*'. Having been forgotten on the conning tower it had floated free when the U-boat submerged.

Before sleep at the end of this momentous day Rose thought of

> ...*U-Bremen* whose passage had been unsuccessful in spite of the fact that it had been specifically designed for the trip and was three times the size of his own boat.

At the threshold of success, the ship with its crew went missing and was soon forgotten... How differently yesterday and today would have been, if it had been a more successful voyage... The commander went to sleep with a sigh on his lips.[163]

Recalling his voyage to America, Hans Rose remarked:

Our experiences on the eighth of October 1916 were so numerous and so extraordinary that it is impossible for me to put them in narrative form. I can render them best by repeating the very words that I found written in my diary when I returned.[164]

The main North Atlantic shipping lane stretching along the American east coast makes a wide bend off Rhode Island skirting the Nantucket shoals. The Nantucket lightship warns vessels of the danger of the shallows and marks the intersection with the great trans-Atlantic shipping lane. There, well outside the neutral zone of American territorial waters, Hans Rose and *U 53* spent Saturday night.

Targets

The previous morning at 10 a.m. Captain John Smith's American freighter *Kansan* departed New York, bound for St. Nazaire and Genoa by way of Boston where she would take on a cargo of horses. Her hold contained 6,500 tons of iron and steel for munitions manufacture. Both the horses and scrap metal were destined for Germany's enemies. Besides carrying the American flag *Kansan* had a ten-foot-long American flag painted on her sides, with the name of the ship in large letters, followed by 'U.S.A.'. At 4:35 Sunday morning, three miles south of the Nantucket lightship, a shot reverberated through the ship. A Morse code message was received instructing the merchant vessel to halt and Captain Smith ordered *Kansan* stopped. But before the engines could be brought to a halt a second shot was fired. As *Kansan*'s momentum fell away, off her bow the silhouette of a submarine was glimpsed through early morning haze. *U 53* approached and 'a youthful officer' hailed *Kansan* from the deck of the submarine asking where *Kansan* was bound and what her cargo was. The Americans were requested to bring their ship's papers over to the U-boat. For more than half-an-hour Hans Rose examined those papers.

Perhaps because the proffered papers only indicated a cargo of soda destined for Genoa, or because the ship flew the American flag and in compliance with some unrecorded verbal instruction from the Admiralty not to sink American vessels, Hans Rose chose to ignore the cargo of iron and steel and the lay-over in enemy France. Neither is recorded in *U 53*'s log. Rose signalled that *Kansan* could proceed.

The British merchant steamer *Strathdene*, bound from New York for Bordeaux, was the next to heave into view. She was investigated two miles south by east of the Nantucket Light Vessel. Though her captain refused to bring Rose the ship's papers, the ship was clearly British, and so she was fair game. Signalling 'Abandon Ship' he waited for the two lifeboats to pull away, fired a torpedo into her aft cargo hold, and turned to his next target.

Rose's next victim, the tanker *Christian Knudsen*, flew the neutral Norwegian flag, but she carried a cargo of contraband gasoline from New York to London. Preoccupied with the still floating *Strathdene*, Rose instructed the Captain to wait his turn while the *Strathdene*, which had not succumbed to the torpedo fired into her, was sunk by shell fire. Then with yet another steamer approaching, Rose sank the *Christian Knudsen* with two torpedoes.

Strathdene and *Christian Knudsen* had been compliant victims, going to their graves quietly. Sighted on the horizon, some ten miles south of the lightship, Hans Rose's next target proved less docile. In response to warning shots across her bow, the British steamer SS *West Point* immediately began broadcasting a distress signal.

To stop the warning, Hans Rose ordered the ship shelled. With her radio silenced, the work of dispatching *West Point* became routine. Captain Hansen ordered the ship abandoned and calmly officers and crew collected their personal effects and rapidly launched two life boats. But the alarm had been sounded. At sea, *Kansan's* wireless operator picked up the message and Captain Smith reversed his engines to go to *West Point's* assistance. Once safely away, Rose sank the ship with gunfire.

Ashore at Newport, the radio reports were electrifying. In addition to *West Point's* SOS, a radiogram from *Kansan* telling of the submarine's appearance in the vicinity of the lightship had been received. By 12:55 in the afternoon Rear Admiral Gleaves was apprised of the situation and ordered all available destroyers out to rescue survivors. To attract the attention of liberty men ashore, a cacophony of hooting broke out as ships sounded their whistles and fired up their boilers. Black smoke belched from the stacks. Ashore, sailors and civilians were infected with the excitement. Men and women ran down Thames Street towards Government Landing. It appeared that 'the vessel which had been in the day before and paid a friendly call was running amok outside amid shipping.'[165] The first destroyer cast off only twenty-nine minutes after the SOS was received by Gleaves. It was *Jarvis*, which was to have remained in harbour in reserve. There was so much smoke from the fleet that observers mistakenly assumed *Jarvis* had laid out a smoke screen as it darted out to sea obscuring recall signals sent after her. Then, one after another, the destroyers steamed from the harbour, many under-manned. Rear Admiral Gleaves had not taken the situation lightly; twenty destroyers were mobilized. Commanding Officer Price aboard the destroyer repair ship *Melville*, who had visited *U 53* the previous day, acted as the senior officer afloat while Gleaves remained in harbour aboard *Birmingham* directing operations by wireless.

It would still be almost four hours before the destroyers could reach the scene of the action. During that time several ships were warned of the German U-boat and avoided the area. Hans Rose stopped the neutral Norwegian vessel *Kaspana* but allowed it to proceed. He also took time to ensure that the crews of the sunken vessels were able to reach safety.

The Game Changes

Throughout the day *U 53* had roamed at will across the sea-lane stopping ships and sinking three. Then in the late afternoon, as clear sky and bright moonlight promised the opportunity to continue operations into the evening, the rules of the game suddenly changed. Hans Rose moved a little to the westward and at dusk three miles south of the lightship stopped the Dutch tramp passenger steamer *Blommersdyk*. She was bound from New York for Rotterdam with a hidden lay-over in Kirkwall on the British Orkney Islands. The *Blommersdyk* was hailed and ordered to produce its papers.

Then a destroyer arrived. Hans Rose was in international waters. But what was the destroyer's nationality? If it was American, would it respond aggressively to his attacks against enemy commerce so close to American shores? For protection Rose dove to decide his next move. It was a moment of great delicacy. Breaking off the attack would prevent American complications. But it would also indicate that Germany's enemies were safe under the mantle of American protection. After the war Rose reflected:

> Years have passed since all this happened, but my heart still skips a beat when I think of the terrible risks that we ran. I understood that I was responsible for whatever happened. I had to decide one way or another, and when I think the matter over today I still believe that in similar circumstances I should again do just as I did at the time. The most difficult decision was whether we should remain submerged when the American destroyers first approached us. Had we stayed under water we should have run less risk of immediate conflict with the United States, but we should also have surrendered the whole purpose of our journey.[166] So I surfaced. Everything went off as it should have, and so my decision was the right one.[167]

Rose's decision to surface and continue attacking in the presence of American destroyers is indicative of something more. Destroyers do pose 'terrible risks' to submarines and yet Rose took them here. Why? Not only was Rose an extraordinarily aggressive warrior, but driven by his rigid ethical credo he was also driven by a sense of the justice of his mission. To back down would have been unthinkable for him. Later in the voyage he would be consumed with self-doubt, agonizing over his decision and wondering whether by tweaking the American nose he might have precipitated her entry into the war.

The political implications of Rose's next move were critical. He describes the *Blommersdyk*'s fate in his personal journal:

5.30 p.m.
We surface. Great number of destroyers approaching from Newport. The first apparently has taken on the crews of all the steamers sunk in the morning. The Blommersdyk *sends its boat out again with papers.*

5.40 p.m.
Before the boat has reached us another steamer appears from the east. In order to prevent its coming closer, we shoot across its bows from a distance of three miles, and stop the distress signals from the Blommersdyk, *whose papers we now look over. We find that the* Blommersdyk *is fully laden with cargo, partly contraband, and is ostensibly headed for Holland. In none of the ship's papers is the destination Kirkwall given. The officers who are sent also do not give me any such information.*

Only from the health papers and the American certificates on board can I learn that the Blommersdyk *is for that port in the Orkney Islands. Considering all the circumstances, I reach the conclusion that the capture depends on my estimate, as the regulations would permit either capture or release. In normal circumstances I would have taken the milder course. But the situation here was that, in order to protect American feelings, I wanted to let the passenger steamer, whose nationality I had not yet been able to determine in the dusk, pass without hindrance after inspecting its papers. But I have to be careful lest I give the impression to all participants that the presence of the American destroyers has caused me to adopt a weak position of complaisance and renunciation of my rights. I decide on a stern attitude and, while lying about 500 metres to the side of the* Blommersdyk, *raise the signal 'Abandon Ship'. The preparations relating to* Blommersdyk *have already been well advanced.*

5:45 p.m.
In the meantime, in addition to the two steamers and U 53, sixteen American destroyers have gathered in a small area, so that one could manoeuvre only with the greatest care. As I tow the boat which brought the officer with the papers from the Blommersdyk *back towards his ship, U 53 comes so close to the destroyer NR. 53 that I have to reverse both engines in order to prevent a collision. We manage to get clear of each other at a distance of about fifty metres. In reversing, I cut loose the tow, so that its crew does not stop at* Blommersdyk *but continues directly to destroyer NR. 53. I have told the officer I would give the crew 25 minutes to abandon ship – until 6:30, but that to ensure no one is injured he should lower the flags as a sign that everyone has left.*[168]

The second steamer, the British passenger liner SS *Stephano*, rounded the east end of Nantucket and following *U 53*'s warning shots halted. Only three years old, launched by the Red Star line in 1913 at a cost of $400,000, she carried a cargo of codfish oil valued at $150,000 consigned to parties in the United States and South America. But more importantly she carried 104 passengers and crew, 47 of whom were Americans; men, women, children and a two-month-old infant.

On the bridge of *Stephano*, Captain John Smith, a New Yorker, lost no time. Before any instructions beyond the original order to heave to were sent by *U 53*, he broadcast the wireless message to the surrounding destroyers disclosing the presence of American passengers aboard and requesting, 'Please take off our passengers.'[169] Destroyers *Ericson* and *Balch* were close by. The *Balch* was sent alongside, but before she could arrive, Captain Smith issued the order to abandon ship and all but two of the lifeboats were launched.

The next morning Miss Mary Griffin told reporters:

We had just had dinner and most of the passengers were below when we heard shots and ran on deck and saw a submarine a short distance away. A Unites States destroyer was in sight. The submarine fired three shots from one of her deck guns. She appeared not to be trying to hit *Stephano*, but the third shot was so close that we felt the jar. There was a little confusion as the boats were lowered, but officers and crew quieted the excited ones, and we all got into the boats O.K. There were five boat-loads. About thirty women and children were on board the ship. We were in the small boats about fifteen minutes before being picked up.[170]

Fearing the worst, *Stephano*'s Second Officer William James secured a gun which he took aboard the lifeboat as a precaution. Dr Andrews declared that the Germans gave the ship 'proper warning' and then stood by until all the passengers had been taken off. He noted that 'officers of the United States torpedo boat destroyer which had arrived in time to take care of the passengers of *Stephano* visited the steamer to make sure that all the passengers and crew were safe.'[171]

It was an extraordinary scene. Two commercial steamers, sixteen destroyers, and *U 53* clustered together so closely that collision was a danger. Later, officers of the *Benham* reported that Rose was plainly visible in the moonlight and that both the *Benham* and *McDougal* received Rose's request for manoeuvring room. Crowded at the rails of various destroyers passengers and crews from the ships attacked by Rose watched. Transferred aboard a destroyer, D. Andrews described the *Blommersdyk* standing a short distance away as 'a steer waiting to be slaughtered'.[172] Aboard the *Benham* the cabin boy of the *Blommersdyk*, a bright lad of about fourteen, clattered around the deck in his wooden shoes. Totally undisturbed by events he explained that this was the third time that he'd had the experience of being aboard a torpedoed ship. Rose fired two torpedoes. The second torpedo buckled the *Blommersdyk* amidships and she triangled into the depths. Rose remembered a lost requisition:

…the situation had an element of the comic about it. In one evening we had suddenly run into two steamers. Although we were glad to let one of them go free, both had been left, with all lights going, by everyone on board. Wacker, one of my officers, entered the dining-room of *Stephano* and found a marvellous array of food from the Indies on the table. He quickly filled a sack with bananas, pineapples, ducks, pullets, ham, grapes, roast chicken, lobsters, and fresh vegetables, and jammed it into our little tender. But as he was going back he noticed that the boat leaked badly, and in order to keep it from sinking he had to throw the whole business overboard just twenty yards before he reached *U 53*. When he boarded us he wept aloud.[173]

Mr and Mrs Hurlburt watched as *U 53* went alongside *Stephano* and sent men on board. The next day they reported that the ship was 'searched and ransacked, articles apparently being taken from the liner to the war vessel'.[174] They counted twenty-eight explosive shells fired at the ship without any sign of material damage and then described the climax: 'The submarine drew off a little distance and fired a torpedo. The ship was lighted from stem to stern... There was a great commotion of water, the ship seemed to break in two, settled in the water and plunged to her ocean bed.'[175]

Off the Nantucket Lightship the only reminder of the day's extraordinary events were a set of small black marking buoys the destroyers placed over the spots where the ill-fated merchantmen were last seen afloat. Overnight, three British destroyers arrived from Canada and began to sweep the area for *U 53*. But Rose was long gone, having, in just under seventeen hours, sunk five merchant vessels without taking a single life.

Homeward Bound through 'the Watery Desert of the Atlantic'

Immediately after sinking *Stephano* on Sunday night Hans Rose headed for home:

> The crew were all delighted, and I too was relieved, to feel that we had seen the shackles fall from the German submarine campaign. But I was greatly worried during the next few days, wondering whether I had done right, and whether war with the United States could be averted.[176]

At 3 p.m. on 10 October, travelling northward up the coast, *U 53* joined first the coal-black waters of the Labrador Current, and then with an eye to increasing the boat's speed home, the warm waters of the Gulf Stream. As they moved into it the temperature rose ten degrees. 'The air in the boat was moist and sultry, and though we went around in our shirt-sleeves sweat ran out of all our pores. Water clustered in beads on the sides of the ship.'[177]

The warmer conditions wouldn't last. On the 14th, off Newfoundland, the heavy seas returned for twenty-four hours. A severe storm struck. Its engines throttled back to 155 rpm, the *U 53* could only proceed slowly. One of the crew recalled:

> Eight or ten hurricanes must have struck us at once, and they raised an enormous sea. When we went over these mountainous waves our bow pointed up at an angle of sixty degrees, and the forward part of the ship stood clear of the water beyond the conning tower. Then we would crash down and the stern of the boat would stick up so far that the propellers were in the air ... our ears rang with the vibration. During this time, we did not move forward an inch, as our lightened vessel was the sport of the elements.[178]

On the 17th they were again able to pick up radio messages from home. Four days later WT from Nauen informed them that *U 55* would meet them off the Faroe Islands to offer assistance if needed. The same day the U-boat encountered a British auxiliary cruiser, but without torpedoes could not engage. During their return *U 53* encountered a number of merchant vessels. But they were all headed towards neutral ports and were allowed to proceed.

Not only had *U 53* expended all her torpedoes and the greater part of her fuel, but her crew had also long since consumed the store of fresh produce. Provisions now consisted chiefly of barley, prunes and lard, which Rose remarked 'all tasted the same'.[179] As conditions deteriorated crewmen fell ill. The machinist's mate developed boils, which officers Stein and Rose lanced with a razor blade sterilized over a spirit lamp. The ship's ad-hoc barber became increasingly pale and thin, requiring medication three times a day. Gerd Noormann, 'the man with the laughing white teeth', developed terrible stomach cramps and Rose feared appendicitis. For a week, until his condition improved, Rose nursed him at his berth with condensed milk. When he finally recovered the ship's crew celebrated with macaroni spiced with nutmeg and fried bacon. When Rose complained that perhaps 'you've put a little too much nutmeg in,' the cook thundered, 'The flavour of the nutmeg must prevail, *Herr Kapitänleutnant!*'[180] Rose suffered the loss of most of one of his 'chief pleasures'[181] when his personal container of jam smashed to the floor. He spent hours meticulously removing the shards of glass to save the delicacy.

Eventually the barometer rose again and for a week *U 53* steered eastward through the Gulf Stream and a light wind. During the day the autumn sun shone down and the nights were alive with a beautiful sea of stars. During the evening those not on watch formed small groups about the conning tower singing to the accompaniment of seaman Göthling's harmonica and the 'musical sweet potato', an ocarina. From time to time the rejoicing crew would break into the last verse of ship's unofficial anthem, the *Pirate Song*, 'dearest to the German sailor's heart'.[182]

> Like an arrow wildly speeding through the air,
> At the enemy's ship we fly.
> Our muskets crash, our cannons roar
> While we, our boarding axes ply.
>
> The enemy falls, the heavens resound
> To our cries o' victory.
> Long live the life of the roaring deep!
> Long live sea piracy![183]

October 22 was Empress Auguste Victoria's birthday. Rose honoured her in a speech to the crew in which he commended them for having accomplished the work of 'a third of a year'[184] over the forty-three-day mission. It also marked the first time on their return voyage they reestablished contact with home. *U 53* met *U 55* in the Hebrides at 1:45 in the afternoon, waiting to provide any necessary aid. Petersen:

> Meet *U 55* off the west coast of England (Faroes). A warm welcome. They have brought us our mail from home. Also a small packing-case filled with many pleasant things. One of the guys receives a letter from home with a newspaper article about the arrival of *U 53* in America. As *U 55* has to move on, we exchange additional good wishes from boat to boat, mutually calling a 'see-you-again at home' and then disappear in the watery desert of the Atlantic.

Stoker Kulgatz cheered when he was handed a postcard from home. Passing it around he exclaimed, 'Wow, we're famous!'[185] But to what end? To Rose's great disappointment, in response to his call upon meeting *U 55*, 'Hail Werner, has unrestricted U-boat war been declared?' *U 55*'s captain simply replied 'It has not.'[186] Rose recalled that his 'whole structure of proud hopes fell in ruins'.[187]

The same day, shortly after separating from *U 55*, the crew of *U 53* were startled by a tremendous knocking coming from the boat's bow. Petersen recalled that being near the British coast their first thought was that the U-boat had been caught in a British anti-submarine net. That could not be the problem because the boat was still able to manoeuvre. The LI checked the hydroplanes which had been so sorely tested on the voyage, but they too were operating correctly. Rose slowed the boat and the knocking declined. He stopped it and the knocking ceased. The riddle was solved. Each of the bow hydroplanes was protected by a horseshoe-shaped guard enclosing the fin, protecting it from entanglement from nets and mine cables, and acting as the fin's outboard pivot. One of these guards had snapped off forward and was now flopping at the end of the fin. Since the boat could no longer dive, it was a perilous situation with British naval vessels in the vicinity. In the gathering dusk Rose sent Stein and two seamen to the forecastle where secured to the railing they attempted to disconnect the guard from the fin. But after an hour the men returned to the conning tower cold, thoroughly drenched, and defeated: 'We can't make it work,' Stein groaned, 'It's too cold, we don't have the strength to grab it.'[188]

To revive their spirits, Rose plied them with hot grog. It was out of the question to have lights on deck, so resumption of repairs would have to await daylight. The next morning at daybreak they returned to the task, finally managing to haul the guard up, unscrew it, and store it inside the boat. A practice dive confirmed that the boat was once again fully operational. Nonetheless Stein later remarked to the boat's assembled officers: 'From a design perspective, the two front hydroplanes are the weakest link in the boat.' Rose replied:

> What the boat has endured is remarkable ... and it's surprising that the diving guard did not break during the first days of the trip. I think, gentlemen, we have had enough of this voyage to America. Steward Göthling, let's have some port.

Raising his glass he toasted: 'Our thanks and best wishes to *Germaniawerft*.'[189] Underway once more, they skirted Shetland and that night entered the North Sea. The temperature plummeted and a storm developed. Conditions deteriorated so badly that it became impossible to remain in the conning tower. *U 53* was forced to dive to 120 feet (36.6m) before the navigator could maintain an even keel. They ran submerged for an entire day before surfacing to recharge their batteries and then resubmerging. Still, they were close to home. While most of the crew slept and Rose lay awake in his berth 'Papa Stein' played Schubert on the flute in the officer's room and the LI enjoyed a few shots of cognac. Wacker had the helm and Bode tended his engines.

From America, You Ape

At Horn's Reef *U 53* was hailed for the password by a German naval picket vessel disguised as a fishing trawler. Informed that *U 53* had been at sea so long that they did not know it the guard trained his cannon on the U-boat and demanded, 'Where do you come from?' The answer came: 'From America, you ape!'[190] He lowered his guns. It was a well-used German slur.

At noon, with Helgoland in sight on the horizon, the boat's compass suddenly failed at the very moment it became superfluous. It was Saturday 27 October, nineteen days after the incredible day near the Nantucket lightship. *U 53* entered Helgoland harbour to the sound of a brass band, companies of coastal artillery, and boat crews lined up to salute them. Rose's crew was lined up on the forward deck once again singing the *Pirate Song*. Letters sent to the crew of *U 53* from throughout Germany awaited them, praising them for their extraordinary voyage. That evening aboard the flagship of the fleet they regaled their compatriots with stories of their voyage as they were fêted to a dinner of 'good food and better wine'.[191]

The next day, *U 53* departed Helgoland for Wilhelmshaven amid more band music, cap waving and choruses of hurrahs. As the short voyage progressed more and more boats swarmed around shouting their greetings and blasting their horns. By the time the U-boat docked the entire crew was hoarse. In Wilhelmshaven harbour two brass bands played the national anthem and an enormous crowd of people strained to see them. Rose and his crew were greeted by the commander of the fleet, Admiral Scheer, and his staff. The Admiral personally awarded each member of the crew the Iron Cross. Later Rose received the House of Hohenzollern's Order of the Knight's Cross with Swords signed personally by the *Kaiser*. That night for the first time in six weeks Rose and his crew slept ashore.

Three weeks before, closing six columns of front-page coverage of *U 53*'s 'Errand of Destruction' off Nantucket Lightship, the *Newport News* had waxed poetic:

> No legendary *Flying Dutchman* ever was the center of so much mystery or the cause of so much speculation or lived so true to the tradition of being the fore-runner of marine mishaps as German war submarine *U 53*, which dropped so dramatically into Newport harbor Saturday.[192]

Rose's voyage was by far the longest and most demanding any submarine had achieved. The challenges the captain and crew faced rendered the accomplishment all the more extraordinary. While the larger merchant U-boat *Deutschland* made the same round trip, she did it in two voyages. Her crew spent three weeks ashore and were completely resupplied prior to returning to Germany. Rose's crew never set foot ashore and the U-boat received no supplies in America.

It is pure dumb luck not to be destroyed by the vicissitudes of war. Submarine aces who survived the war exhibited these characteristics:

- a high tolerance for discomfort
- structured thinking framework for situational analysis
- mastery of the technical and tactical complexity of submarine warfare
- tactical flexibility
- understanding of the importance of the human element in battle
- ability to forge their crew into a high-performance team through definition, training, motivation and reward
- aggression, but not to a foolish degree
- meticulous preparation
- risk minimization, particularly through preventive measures
- emotional detachment in crisis situations
- pragmatism and opportunity creation

Hans Rose was one such ace.

Chapter 5

The Icon and the Man

During the Great War, over the course of fifteen missions in command of *U 53*, Hans Rose became Germany's fifth most successful U-boat ace, sinking at least eighty merchant vessels totalling 220,051 tons, along with the American destroyer *Jacob Jones*. During their round-trip crossing of the Atlantic Rose and his crew overcame formidable challenges and more than doubled the longest solo voyage ever accomplished by any submarine. These accomplishments earned Rose Germany's highest military honour, the *Ordre Pour le Mérite*. His chivalric comportment also earned him the admiration and respect of such knowledgeable enemies as US Vice Admiral Sims, commander of American Naval Forces in European waters and the French Comte de Varennes, who administered the occupied Ruhr in 1923. During WWII, this time in occupied Norway, Rose would earn the admiration and respect of his enemies yet again.

Icons are made, not born. The official biographies, like the soliloquies delivered after his death, almost always come to a close with the end of WWI when Hans Rose was still only thirty-three years old. What went unsaid in the funerary testimonials? What role did Rose play in that second great calamity, WWII? What was his relationship to the Nazi regime that instigated it? What life did Rose craft for himself and his family? What did he believe? Who was Hans Rose the man?

HANS ROSE in 1898, age 13.
[Rose Family Archives]

Johann (Hans) Eduard Friedrich Rose, the third of five children and the middle son, was born in Berlin-Charlottenburg on 15 April 1885, but grew up in Berlin. His fondest childhood memories revolved around the Weser River and nearby Hameln, where both of his parents were born and where he spent many of his summer holidays when he was not vacationing in the Bavarian and Tirolean Alps. Reflecting his strong affinity for the natural world Rose recalled Berlin was 'a pile of stones devoid of all nature'.[193] Throughout his life Rose pursued a keen interest in gardening and a particular interest in the natural sciences. He would consider it very important that his children have gardens of their own. Later, as a naval officer, having some feeling for nature's 'mood' and signals, this affinity made him comfortable with the sea. He respected it, leveraged it to his advantage, and ultimately used it to summarize his world view in his essay 'What We Learned from the Sea.'

Rose grew up in a well-to-do cosmopolitan family living at the political centre of the German state in a historical epoch and political context defined by the Victorian era. That era was characterized by the rise of nation states, the rapid industrialization of German society, and a morality emphasizing the primacy of the male in the external world and the female in the family setting and child-rearing domains. Becoming a man with a gallant appreciation of the fairer sex, Rose developed into a 'quintessential gentleman'.[9]

Gifted with superior intellect reinforced by the Prussian classical education system, Rose's upbringing nurtured his structured thinking process. As an adult it allowed him to carefully weigh his decisions. Rose was, on the whole, a pragmatist. At the same time he was a quiet and somewhat delicate child who loved verse and was enchanted by the Hameln legend of the Pied Piper. During childhood he also developed a 'Nordic fascination'[194] that would express itself both as racial kinship with the people of the region during the WWII occupation of Norway and as an important foundation of his political nationalism. Developed early on, his appreciation of verse, legends and nordic mythology represent the romantic side of his personality. Philosophically, these themes, expressed later as pan-Germanic romantic narrow nationalism, are consistent with the early romantic nationalism of German philosophers who embraced the concept of naturalism and asserted that to be legitimate a nation 'must have been conceived in the state of nature'.[195]

Rose developed both an interest in and a talent for the hard sciences: physics, mathematics, chemistry, and especially astronomy. A high school teacher tried to convince him to become a mathematician. Though he

>...toyed with the idea of studying astronomy, [Rose] felt that he would probably not be able to endure the everlasting problem of unsolvable questions arising from the concept of the infinity of time and space.[196]

It is an early indication that Rose had a somewhat rigid world view and was not particularly comfortable with uncertainty. It could also be an indication of feelings of insecurity common to many intellectuals, and a recurring theme in Rose's life. Such a self-image, believing he could not become a sufficiently gifted scholar to address these challenges, is inconsistent with son Christian's assertion that 'he could have been a professor in a number of fields.'[197] Later, though impassioned by architecture as a mature adult Rose would reject it as a career option feeling that comparison with the great architectural masters left him wanting.

A cerebral young man, Hans Rose worked constantly, 'his mind always on the go, only letting go when he slept'.[198] Quiet and quite reticent about almost everything, he had 'an incredible desire to be perfect'.[199] Rose became a polymath and linguist. As foundations for his classical German education, he mastered Latin and Greek in addition to his native German. He read and spoke French and English. During the occupation of Norway during WWII he became fluent in Norwegian. He could speak a little Italian, and some Spanish. During the interwar years, to facilitate his business pursuits, he studied Russian. Christian Rose recalled that his father frequently counselled his children, 'When in Rome, do as the Romans do.'[200]

Language facility is linked by some with intelligence. It is also arguably indicative of respect for diversity, other peoples and cultures. No doubt Rose drew upon this perspective when confronted with Nazi xenophobia and anti-Semitism.

Rose had a decidedly romantic, idealistic and at times naive world view. Some of his romanticism expressed itself through a developed aesthetic for how things should be positioned, through painting spare and gifted water-colours, a love of poetry, and in writing at least one romantic short story. Another manifestation was a certain impracticality around the house. He never learned to cook. Both Christian and sister Helga recall that their mother was 'much more practical'.[201] And yet, Rose's stepson Rudolf Brickenstein recalled that Rose 'believed there were two sins in life; to wish without acting and to act without a goal.'[202] He would become a superb warrior.

Be Noble, Be Considerate – Ancestry and Obligation

Hans Rose was proud of his lineage. Blood-lines, wealth and achievement conferred status in Victorian-era German society. Following WWII, Rose would express this status by redesigning the family coat of arms to highlight his accomplishments. Had the German Imperial College of Heraldry accepted his petition, it would have represented an external validation of his ideals and life story.

Through his mother, Marie Louise 'Lilli' Rose, née Kroseberg, the family traced their descent back ten generations to Hermann Kroseberg, who died in 1591. Hermann was the Fire Marshal and Keeper of the Seal of the City of Hameln. As far back as the family tree can be traced, the Krosebergs had been citizens of the city. Lilli's father, grandfather, and great-grandfather were manufacturers in the snuff, tobacco, and brewing industries. Further back her paternal ancestors were master cobblers, burghers of Hameln, and members of the Brewers Guild.

Rose could trace his paternal heritage back seven generations to Tobias Rose, merchant and citizen of Walstrodt, born in the 15th century. But there the documentation stopped; Tobias' birth records and those of his ancestors were lost when the village church was destroyed during the Thirty Year War. In contrast to the majority of the population who remained serfs, Tobias and his sons were craftsmen and free citizens of the city, exercising voting privileges.[203] Rose's paternal grandfather was both a Senator and a Superior Court Judge in Nienburg. Further back the family members were master shoemakers, brewers, and tanners. The family's strong tradition of independent success was no doubt a dinner table theme passed down the generations.

Rose's father, Heinrich Otto Ludwig Rose, was Director General of the European division of the Germania Insurance Company of New York and Berlin. That career, and Heinrich Otto Ludwig's rise to become the company's top officer in Europe, guaranteed the family a window on the world. Family and friends lived in the United States, the West Indies and Mexico. Rose remembered that as a child, dinner table discussions with his parents were always very cosmopolitan.[204] Such exposure to cultural diversity certainly stoked Rose's interest in languages and his demonstrated respect for diversity at the same time that the German political context, bookended by its role in the two world wars, contributed to the development of his pan-Germanic narrow nationalism. Neither Heinrich Rose, nor the fruits of his four-decade career in Germania's European division would survive the war. Hans Rose's father died in 1918 and as an enemy-alien of the United States all of his Germania stock was confiscated.

Rose's parents were Protestants but Rose himself appears to have developed few significant religious inclinations. While Rose and his wife Anne-Marie were formally Christians, and 'there were prayers before each meal'[205] neither were active church-goers. Christian Rose recalled his father remarked: 'I do not need a priest to tell me that I am a sinner – I have sufficient difficulty coping with my inferiority.'[206] The family's narrative of successful men coupled with the extremely high standards Rose set himself may have contributed to that sense of inadequacy. Later in life, writing on the occasion of his youngest stepson's confirmation, Rose advised Hans-Joachim: 'Very quietly there is a God that speaks in your heart. Very quietly but insistently he will indicate what is to be avoided and what you should do.'[207]

Rose's assertion demonstrates a bedrock conviction with respect to individual ethics. It was a viewpoint sufficiently empowering eventually to allow him to confront even the *Kaiser* despite the fact that Rose was a strict authoritarian. Christian noted that his father 'was a man who could cut a person down to size without him ever knowing it,'[208] and that he 'really had very little tolerance for bureaucracy, absolutely no patience [for it]'.[209]

Rudolf Brickenstein stated that honesty was a theme that ran throughout Rose's life.[210] Hans-Joachim Brickenstein agreed:

> Rose was a man of his word and he assumed that other people were likewise men of their word, and would stand by what they said – Rose was a hero in 1918 … after WWII he was a different person. He didn't polish his image after the war. He was a proud man, and an honest man. If someone would doubt his honesty, he would go through walls... I don't know anyone as honest as Hans Rose. Maybe he was too honest sometimes.[211]

Rose contested those in authority (including those with command over him) when he felt strongly that they were not acting in the best interest of his beloved navy and country. He displayed intolerance for fools and bureaucrats, a considerable confidence in his own opinions, and warlike combativeness. Rose's propensity for speaking his mind to his superiors proved damaging in both his military and civilian careers.

Rose inherited a world view about family and society characterized by duty, Victorian social hierarchy, and the key role of the individual. Families with a long history of 'important people' tend to reinforce the idea of the individual as the weaver on the loom of time. This can encourage an individual rather than collaborative management and leadership style, and a sense of obligation born of duty rather than empathy. Nonetheless, while Hans Rose embraced the traditional German national sensitivity to hierarchy, rank and order, he leavened it with a strong sense of personal rights. Christian noted that his father had a 'profound consciousness of rights and equality above all. That was definitely a leitmotif in his thinking. He tried to be extremely fair all the time.'[212] While it appears that his family history comprised of successful independent ancestors, a childhood framed by internationalist parents and friends, and an affinity for empowering stories of Nordic achievements all contributed, Rose appears to have explicitly modelled his leadership style, including his impartiality, on the superb naval officers who trained him as a cadet and young officer.

Rose credited his mother Lilli for his world view, writing to his fiancée that 'the worship of those who gave us life and raised us in selfless devotion ... constitutes the unshakable foundation of life.'[213] For Rose, his mother became the spokesperson for the family's sense of obligation and duty. Son Christian remarked that his father's motto might have been 'Be noble, be considerate.'[214] It is a Victorian sensibility defined more by charge and less by familial love. Perhaps having missed that in his nuclear family upbringing, he would be drawn to the fellowship offered by what was to become Rose's first love and second family.

Rose first found collegial fellowship and learned the value of cooperative effort in the Imperial German navy. These were provided him within the comforting confines of a rigid hierarchy that rewarded heroic individuals and leaders. At the same time his training of naval recruits, and the essential role every crewman aboard a U-boat played, reinforced Rose's appreciation of the contribution of the common man. Rose's acknowledgment of the contributions of his crew, without which he could not have been successful, was genuine. He would declare that 'in comparison to man, weapons are almost unimportant'[215] and translated that belief into a passion for teaching in the navy. And though he maintained a formal, paternalistic and distant relationship with his naval subordinates, he also consistently sought to minimize the lasting impact of disciplinary actions on the men under his command. These behaviours generated respect and helped create happy, highly effective teams that served Rose well as captain.

Rose's choice of a military career reflected his authoritarian predisposition. His desire to become a naval commander, a role that sets the captain apart from the rest of the crew, meshed well with his tendency to be a loner and his adherence to a generally rigid relationship with those subordinate to him. Christian Rose recalled:

There was a softness in him, and sentimentality almost to a fault, at the same time, there could be this extreme aggressiveness. He manifested a substantial territoriality... If you came into his territory and didn't toe the line, he would be on you.[216]

That territoriality was something Rose exploited at sea very effectively where his role as commander of a hierarchically organized crew gave him the 'Powers of a Roman Proconsul'.

As mentioned earlier, Rose's 315-page WWI memoir *Auftauchen!*, printed in 1939, is written in the third person. Relatively muted emotionally, it depicts him as a loner; intensely private, and somewhat self-effacing. The image portrayed, while incomplete, may have been an astute marketing tool for legacy and posterity. Son Christian described the figure that that emerges as the 'Humanist admired by everyone and certainly good for public relations'.[217] As a cerebral, internally focused adult, Rose aristocratically set himself above the common man.

In general, whenever Rose writes about his naval career, he does so either in the third person, or using the acronym 'Haro', a contraction of HAns ROse. Only his account of his personal affairs during the interwar period is written in the first person. With rare exceptions he does not comment on his emotions. For example, he makes no mention of how the death of his older brother, in the first months of WWI, affected him. Nor does Rose say anything personal about the death of his oldest son during WWII. Rose limits himself to a comment about how Heinz's death would have affected his wife Anne-Marie, had she remained alive to learn of it.

Rose does record his emotions following several exceptional military incidents, and during his hospital visits to his dying wife Anne-Marie. And his autobiography contains a set of intimate, revelatory letters, written to her when he was twenty-seven. One of those letters, written 25 July 1912, demonstrates that Rose intimately referred to Anne-Marie as 'Mara' while she referred to him as 'Haro'. When he wrote his autobiography years after her death, Rose's use of Haro to identify himself can only be a reflection of the deep and heartfelt feelings he retained towards his first wife.

Rose could maintain tight control of his emotions when the situation demanded it. This and his pragmatism were essential skills in the extremely dangerous arena of submarine warfare, allowing him to be both calm under pressure and tactically flexible. Key factors facilitating his pragmatism and his emotional control included his rigid sense of *noblesse oblige*, his structured thinking, and his selection of roles, such as naval instructor and ship's commander, which situated him as the ultimate arbiter able to control his environment. It is clear that he saw his actual paternal role with his children in a similarly authoritarian and hierarchical fashion.

Christian noted that whilst his father

...always strove to be represented as in calmer times ... there was the other persona. It was the person with a very short fuse, very forceful, irritable at the slightest thing [that] caused major outbursts when his body would shake with physical irritations.[217]

In addition to these familial outbursts, there are indications that Rose experienced such irritations as a civilian businessman, and on occasion in the military hierarchy below and above him in the chain of command. In every case where Rose succumbed to an emotional outburst, the context is one where he did not have ultimate control over the environment in which the events played out. There was a certain rigidity of perspective when flexibility would have been more productive, considerable confidence in the validity of his own opinions and convictions reinforced by his role in positions of authority, his territoriality, and paradoxically what Christian termed his father's 'big inferiority complex'.[218] 'He had a great deal of self-doubt.'[217] Yet Rose did not flinch from stating his opinions to anyone, regardless of his relative position in the pertinent hierarchy. When Rose believed the situation called for it, he adopted a certain 'damn the torpedoes' attitude.

The antithetical divide between the self-effacing humanist and the explosive critic may reflect the coexistence of the exceedingly high personal and moral standard Rose set for himself and his inferiority complex, perhaps a difficulty in forgiving himself. That profound paradox caused tensions that Rose held in check most of the time. But when something happened to overwhelm that check, the internal tension between these two aspects of his personality manifested itself.

These behaviours are particularly problematical, becoming barriers to advancement, in such highly hierarchical social structures as the military and traditional business management. In addition, interpersonal modalities that operate well in a military context are frequently not nurturing in nuclear family relations.

Despite Rose's view that his mother was primarily responsible for his development as a human being, with his birth children Rose appears to have replicated the emotionally distant and apparently less important relationship he had with his father. However, later relationships with the stepchildren of his second family appear far more successful. Rose eventually recalibrated his parental responsibilities in light of his life experience.

When he was twenty-eight and she twenty, Rose married Anne-Marie Siemers. Although he and Anne-Marie loved each other profoundly, he was very careful to choose a wife from a family whose blood-line would be a social asset. He agonized for months over the decision to propose to her.

Cultured and beautiful, Anne-Marie was a talented watercolourist and played the piano. She was also a very strong and determined woman. Between 1920 and 1930, she would bear Rose four children: Heinz Viktor, Gerd, Helga and Christian. Anne-Marie, his intellectual equal, provided Rose with emotional support, love, a person to confide in, and the freedom to pursue his naval passion without having to worry about the home front, which she managed with love and empathy. Daughter Helga remarked, 'My father was a nationalist and an idealist ... he always had his head in the clouds. My mother was the right wife for him, because she could keep his feet on the ground.'[219]

Tragically, she would die of cancer in 1943. Her illness and death were devastating for Hans Rose whose familial priority had always been his wife.

The portrait of Rose that emerges is that of a multifaceted man of considerable complexity and remarkable opposites. Rose was undeniably successful as a warrior and leader of men under his command. He became an 'old school' naval officer whose world view and ideas of duty reflected both a sense of *noblesse oblige* and an admiration for Germany's old aristocracy. He was a respected community leader and an admired national hero. He was a talented artist, an excellent writer, an effective speaker, and (reflecting his humanism) a gifted instructor. And yet, he suffered from an inferiority complex and bouts of depression.

Throughout his life, Hans Rose demonstrated a democrat's recognition of the contributions of men from all walks of life. Though he was capable of accepting the imperfections in others, Rose had neither forbearance for fools nor for bureaucrats, and he had difficulty forgiving himself. Philosophically, Rose evolved into a Social Darwinist, asserting the ethical correctness of the concept of survival of the fittest. Politically, this manifested itself in his conviction that globally, the English were infringing upon Germany's sphere of influence. Nonetheless, Rose's stepson Peter asserted that while his stepfather was a nationalist, he was not nationalistic. His friends were Norwegian, French, American and English; all the more so as he grew older.[220]

Rose's viewpoint often focused on 'great men' as the makers of history, at the same time that he valued men over machines as the tools of war. He was demonstrably comfortable in his roles as teacher, military leader, and father. It is significant that all these positions have clearly defined social power relationships where Rose exercises overarching authority. With the exception of his relationship with his wife Anne-Marie, he seemed to have kept himself outside of these interpersonal relationships, looking in rather than leaning in. He was proud of his leadership style, which acknowledged contributions and human merit. This made him quite unusual as a military leader. Not only was Hans Rose the personification of the German military concept of *Auftragstaktik*, leading by mission, but at a human level Rose's leadership style demonstrated that true authority only comes through the respect that the men under an officer's command accord him.

Despite frequently modern and progressive social perspectives, it appears that Rose was somewhat backwards-looking, embracing older, receding social structures and constructs rather than exploring new ones. Until the end of his days, Rose retained a profound admiration for Germany's old aristocracy, and an extraordinary admiration for the Hohenzollern family. His desire to recreate his family coat of arms and have it legitimized is instructive. In private life Rose hated the bureaucracy that encumbers modern life. He was unable to become a successful entrepreneur. Rather, he was most happy and effective in the rigidly hierarchal German navy. Still, without succumbing to Nazi barbarism, his strength of character, perseverance and credo of personal honour, devotion, and duty allowed him to survive two World Wars and forty of the most extraordinary years that anyone could experience. Rose romantically considered himself an anachronism, a German knight.

Chapter 6

Training for Knighthood

SAILING FRIGATE SMS *STEIN* Laid down in 1879, *Stein* became an officers' training ship crewed with 450 men. Rose was a cadet aboard in 1904. [Das Bundesarchiv Koblenz]

On 1 April 1903, Hans Rose, a newly minted sea cadet, class of '03, entered the service of the Imperial German Navy. Eighteen years old, he had just completed his studies at the famous *Kaiserin Augusta Gymnasium* in Charlottenburg (1896-1902). Believing he did not have a seaman's constitution Rose's high-school classmates advised him not to go to sea; but his innate determination, cosmopolitan upbringing[221] and the temptation to 'Join the navy and see the world' won the day. His godfather, Herman Rose, a Freemason who founded the Hanseatic Association to aid shipwreck survivors in Bremen,[222] no doubt approved.

Rose recalled that the first weeks of basic training ashore were 'almost unbearable' with rifle drills 'a repulsive chore'.[223] Early on, the training officers were less than complimentary of his abilities. Rose's pride suffered and 'he was often tempted to make a complaint'.[224] It was an early sign of his willingness to contest authority. But he kept his mouth shut, persevered and it was noted that he improved. Basic training completed, Rose put to sea aboard sailing frigate SMS *Stein*, a naval officer training vessel where the skills of practical seamanship were taught alongside daily lectures. By the time *Stein* returned to Germany in spring 1904, the sea cadets had become, in Rose's words, 'tough men'.[225]

Following another year of academic training at the Marine-Schule, the Navy Academy (1904-05) in Mürwik, the 1903 class of sea-cadets were posted to naval vessels for further training and a practical course in weaponry. Rose reported to the pre-dreadnought ship-of-the-line SMS *Hessen*,[226] where he encountered 'all the difficulties ... of get[ting] one of the newest battleships up and running'.[227] Not only had Rose to master *Hessen*'s motors, engines, and technical apparatus, and 'learn how to rotate the heavy artillery turret so that shots would hit their intended target[228] but he had also to contend with 'the new crew ... made up of disparate components of old and new cadres, not to mention bosses and subordinates who did not know each other and had no common experiences.'[229]

Almost immediately, however, Rose was sent ashore to the old fort at the entrance of Kiel harbour, where new recruits destined for *Hessen* were given preliminary rifle training. Rose 'noticed the devotion with which the young men applied themselves and his love for Germans who came from less well-off homes, grew'.[230]

Clearly Rose had a talent for teaching, since he was assigned to the Recruitment Division for the next few months before returning to *Hessen* to continue his own training. Upon returning he and the other ensigns continued their apprenticeship 'under the stern eye' of Lieutenant Bruno Kater: 'a temperamental, elegant officer, who made fast, clear and impartial decisions... a leader, who was able to inspire his subordinates, he was their idol.'[231]

Since striking out from his family and increasingly comfortable in his new one, the German navy, Rose having turned twenty began to understand the mysteries of duty. 'The training was strenuous; one had little rest day or night. The more work, the higher the spirits of the ensigns.'[232]

Rose recalled that night watch was 'often boring,' and that 'walking around deck [on watch] induced a kind of dream', since the young officers were forbidden to sit down. Through the long hours, sometimes target practice until midnight, often followed by anchor manoeuvres, and then duty during the 'middle watch' until eight a.m. the next morning, Rose 'learned self-discipline'.[233] The young ensign's dreams of command found immediate fulfilment when charged with steering the ship's sixteen-ton steam launches with their five-man tender crews. 'Here one functioned like a commander and felt accordingly. Those who did not roar around at top speed were considered wimps.'[234]

Rose notes that as an ensign aboard *Hessen*, he was privileged to be assigned the responsibility of replacing the vacationing Adjutant to the First Officer. This made him responsible for the control of secret documents. This was an extraordinary reflection of the navy's confidence in Rose's developing trustworthiness, competence and leadership skills, since it would have been highly unusual that an ensign could have replaced the adjutant on board a ship-of-the-line.[235]

Rose reports that these secret Imperial Navy documents fell into four categories:

- The least secret termed 'ND-property' were kept in green folders and marked 'for official use only.' They were, Rose remarked, 'relatively harmless'[236] and included a directive governing 'beard styles' which specified that 'the chin beard must reach to the ears and be three millimetres long on the cheek.' For Rose it was 'paternalism gone a bit too far'.[237]
- The 'G' or 'Secret' documents in red folders were one degree more secret than the ND-properties. Rose noted that 'they were off-limits for ordinary eyes and had to be protected like a chick by its mother hen.'[238]
- More secret were the 'GG' or 'Top Secret' documents which Rose noted were best not touched but consigned to the safe until the Adjutant's return. 'If it was necessary to give an officer one of these secret monsters, one had to keep it on a "mental leash", in order to avoid the accusation of having lost it.'[239]
- Most secret were the so-called 'highest decrees'; 'something that was equivalent to the Gospel.'[240] Rarely publicized or revealed to other countries, 'the 'highest decrees' were only read behind locked doors.[241] Naturally Rose derived 'a quiet pleasure' leafing through them.[242]

It was a period in the development of the German navy that saw rapid change, as the entire navy developed and honed the skills, strategies, and tactics essential to becoming a formidable high seas fleet. This larger context for his own training was not lost upon Rose:

In April 1906 *Hessen* joined the squadron group led by Admiral [Max] v. Fischel. He was a person who commanded respect and trust... Too bad for Germany that [Fischel] was born a few years too early... The Admiral would surely have seen to it that the high seas fleet was used differently than it was in the first few years of WWI. He initiated varied training for the different squadron groups at a time when these [roles] were not yet well understood and the North Sea was considered unsuitable for practice. Through ongoing training, the strategic role of single ships and the squadron were clarified and the utilization of different ships' types, as well as the artillery and torpedo weapons were explored... Flotilla commander Admiral [Hans] v. Köster was highly valued, but also feared for his sarcasm...[243]

The May and summer voyages, as well as the fall manoeuvres were very useful for the professional development of the ensigns. Most of these took place in the North Sea.

At the end of the fall manoeuvres, the whole fleet steamed past the flagship *Kawezwo*. All crews were lined up on deck and bade farewell to Admiral v. Köster, who stood on his bridge and waved.[244]

Rose's account of 'these wonderful months'[245] interweaves three themes: the larger context of the Imperial Navy's development, his own experiences, and frequent observations about the role and the responsibilities of command.

Recounting life in the mess hall, Rose intertwined the boisterous nature of youth and the requirements of leadership.

> The ensigns had a mess hall to themselves... The cook didn't really know how to cook so as a result they skipped hot lunch for weeks on end in favour of sandwiches... washed down with beer. In spite of that there were no signs of drunkenness... Haro was probably the tamest of its denizens... Guests were particularly delighted to try out the mess hall's special drink: champagne with port wine... The accounts of the mess hall were consequently in disarray. One person was the [primary] cause of the deficits. Over time he sank deeper and deeper into drunkenness and debt that even his relatives could no longer cover... Finally after two years he left the ship... Perhaps it is good for a young person to spend a year free of control... The way this played itself out on *Hessen* however went too far. Guidance by older comrades would have prevented some of the mischief that occurred.[246]

On 29 September 1906 the sea cadets were promoted to *Säbelfähnriche*, Sabre Ensigns. Hans Rose was twenty-one years old.

> In the morning they reported to the Station Chief and at noon they returned to the commander wearing their white dress uniforms with gold stripes. A whole battery of champagne glasses was emptied and the new lieutenants saluted with hands to their caps, which a wind gust blew over board... Haro was ordered to the Recruitment Division... It was a great pleasure for him to guide young men from all parts of Germany into the navy.[247]

Auftragstaktik

Having barely assumed his role as a trainer of new recruits, Rose unexpectedly found himself ordered back to Mürwik near Flensburg to take a three-month Torpedo Officers course. Rose 'loved the nautical and military sciences and related issues, which enthralled him for the rest of his life.'[248] The course was Rose's chance to pursue his 'longed-for torpedo weapon'.[249]

Rose's 'Flensburg Interlude'[250] was academically challenging: 'Day long [the] young gentlemen sucked fantastic atrocities into their brains about engine blocking pistons, jammed pendula, gyro momenta, Trinitrotoluol and the addition of specific chemical ingredients.'[251] But they spent their evenings joyously together in Flensburg:

> Everyone got together at night in Flensburg and indulged in cheerful camaraderie. Two different fraternities were usually present: the 'Schlickatia' and the 'Butjadingia'. The former, where Haro was an inductee, wore yellow caps. The night he was inducted as a 'fellow' after an evening with lots of beer, the group sent a telegram to *Vater* [father] *Sens* in Berlin. It said: 'Son Haro has received "*floreat Schlickatia*."' Father *Sens*, obviously thrilled by the midnight interruption, replied by sending the requisite amount of money to support the new honour.

All of Flensburg's energy and endurance during this affluent time manifested itself in the citizens' love for grog. Haro remembered walking home one evening after downing ten grogs… when a Flensburg citizen, having spent half an hour trying to find the key hole, all the while murmuring 'how come that this house has no door?', asked Rose for help unlocking his front door. Another evening an older comrade caused a commotion in the main street by asking Haro to drag him along while he played a drunk babbling 'leave me alone, Constable. I did not butcher the young lady.' That the pretty blonde Flensburg girls received the kind of attention they deserved goes without saying.[252]

Despite being the youngest officer in the group Rose seized the opportunity, receiving high grades. As a result Rose fully expected 'the honour of a transfer to the torpedo boat flotilla.'[253] 'To everybody's surprise'[254] Rose's dream was not immediately fulfilled and instead of being transferred to the torpedo squadron at the conclusion of the course he was ordered back to his training duties.

Rose's assessment here is similar to his favourable analysis of his accomplishments as a young trainer. Rose, young and ambitious, may have been 'surprised', but clearly the navy believed he would benefit from additional seasoning before assuming such important responsibilities.

Since the 19th century, *Auftragstaktik*, or *Führen mit Auftrag*, leading by mission, has been a core doctrine of the German military's tactical realization of strategic objectives. Empowering leaders at all levels of the military to act with initiative and creativity, *Auftragstaktik* was one of the key factors making the German military such a powerful adversary. To be successful *Auftragstaktik* demands that commanders at every level of the service delegate responsibility for the tactical execution of strategic objectives. At the same time, in order that a subordinate commander is able to take initiatives that will contribute to the realization of strategic objectives he or she must have the capacity to analyse whether the initiative being contemplated is consistent with those strategic objectives.

On 1 April 1907 Rose was transferred to the newly modernized and recommissioned training ship SMS *Freya*. As a freshly minted midshipman it was his first command over rank-and-file sailors. Rose would apply the doctrine of *Auftragstaktik* at arm's-length, 'the importance of maintaining distinction between military ranks was to him[self] self-evident.'[255] Yet Rose was determined 'not to train uninventive robots, but rather men with personality and initiative'. It was a responsibility to which, Rose asserts, he applied himself with 'fierce enthusiasm and great success'. He 'felt himself completely a mentor'.[256]

Aboard *Freya* Rose served as the *Rollenofficier*, essentially an Adjutant to the First Officer (IO) nicknamed 'the Raccoon' 'because his beard completely covered his face'.[257] Rose compared him unfavourably to SMS *Stein*'s superb IO under whom he had trained as a cadet assigned to BBI, *Backbord Eins* (Portside One), reflecting the distribution of a navy ship's crew into port and starboard watches:

The duties of the First Officer are all encompassing. He is in charge of organizing the service operations for the whole ship. He is responsible for wake-up calls;

stowing of hammocks; laundry; breakfast; for the ship's routine; the watches etc...
He is in charge of rectifying smaller infractions; and for the appearance of the ship
and its crew. The tone in the mess hall is dependent on him. He leads the anchor
and line manoeuvres on the port side; he lowers and raises the boats; he is in charge
of damage control. In short he is responsible for everything. The ship is judged by
him, and he by the ship. If he has a heart, temperament and character, the ship and
crew are capable of high performance. If he is listless, without a social conscience
or even untruthful, even an excellent officers' corps is unable to ameliorate these
defects. The First Officer of a ship is the crucial personality in peace time. The
crew's as well as the individuals' mood and perceptions depend upon him...

On *Stein*, the men of BBI had the good luck to serve under an ideal I.O. He never
had a personal exchange with the cadets; yet, in spite of this they loved and admired
him. He formed his charges' young souls and laid the foundations for a serious and
resolute professional approach. He was exemplary and his example proliferated
a hundred fold. The personality of the 'Raccoon' left behind a much weaker
impression. Most likely the cadets of *Freya* do not even remember his name.[258]

Later, as a commander Rose would emulate the leadership style of the *Stein*'s I.O.,
remarking that it was the 'policy of the *Kommandant* never to have physical contact
with the crew.'[259] Though only twenty-one years old Rose's attitude already reflects
both his democratic recognition of every man's contribution, but also his somewhat
aristocratic attitude. Years later he would admonish his children to recognize the
implicit nobility of the trade professions, while at the same time being fond of
saying *Schuster bleib bei deinem Leisten* – 'cobbler stick to your shoes,' (i.e. stick
to what you know).[260]

Newly converted, SMS *Freya* was the first sailless, steam-powered, sea-cadet
training vessel in the German Imperial Navy. This required that its training
curriculum be overhauled. It was a task that devolved to Rose:

New 'roles' had to be designed for different training tasks. Haro devoted himself
with great zeal to this voluminous work. In his attempt to cover every aspect, he
possibly went a bit too far. But his First Officer usually signed his proposals, giving
them the power of the law. When these commands were however to be executed,
this or that division officer might have objections and beguile the First Officer to go
back on his signature, not telling his Adjutant about this change of mind. When the
latter then complained, the 'Raccoon' would stutter: 'Well, yes... no... I thought it
over.' Why he had 'thought it over' the Raccoon did not reveal. As a result one did
not know where one stood.[261]

Reading Rose's account of his time aboard this 'floating *Gymnasium*'[262] one is
left with the impression that had he been in command, *Freya* might have been
run as a tighter ship.

The commander of *Freya* was a gallant gentleman, whose name was *Walzerfranz*
(Waltzing Franz). He viewed his pleasant command as a kind of 'gift' and
represented Germany in an endearing manner abroad. His motto was: let's be
relaxed. He was a *grand seigneur*.[263]

At the end of *Freya*'s nine-month voyage,

> ...the atmosphere was affected by the dread inspection that awaited them on their return. The inspection turned out well. The likeable commander remained on board for another year, while nothing more was heard of the First Officer, who had been unable to create a cohesive context for those who had been part of this remarkable trip.[264]

Rose provides a detailed account of the *Freya*'s voyage starting with the cruise's first waypoint which left 'a deep impression on Haro and effected his development'.[265] Unsurprisingly, it was the land of the Vikings:

> [In] the deep Sognefjord, *Freya* anchored close to Balholmen. On these coasts the Vikings arrived with their dragon boats... and built their huts.[266] Dragon boats with one sail still ply the waters of the fjord and carry on coastal trade... When *Freya* anchored during the warm summer nights with their starry skies, the sound of voices carried far and wide from the light Norwegian boats close by... It was difficult to say goodbye to this enchanted landscape and its endearing people.[267]

Proceeding westward:

> Iceland, the next destination, came in sight.[268]... On the invitation of the German Consul, small ponies were made available to the crew, to ride inland to the hot springs surrounded by craters and lava fields.[269] Haro's youthful Germanic dreams were made reality in this setting... The Norsemen are self-satisfied on their island and preoccupied with commerce.[270]

As *Freya* sailed south towards the Mediterranean, Rose contracted rheumatic fever and for six weeks was confined to his berth below, unable to enjoy the passage through the Strait of Gibraltar towards Corfu. Though able to do some sightseeing, the classically educated Rose remarked that 'he not only had difficulty walking across St. Mark's Square in Venice ... but was also unable to view St. Mark's ceiling paintings, because he could not lift his eyes above the horizon without excruciating pain.'[271] Travelling into Corfu's interior:

> One feels as though transported into another world... During *Freya*'s visit, the festivities for the 'Holy *Spiridon*', the island's protector were in full swing. The holy mummy, brown and leathery, was carried through the streets in a glass sarcophagus, while the inhabitants sank to their knees... *Freya* stayed in Corfu for weeks enjoying the Homeric landscape.[272]

Asia Minor:

> In Smyrna the ship entered another continent... In the bazaars ... international currencies prevailed[273]... and learning how to bargain became a fine art... Haro was particularly impressed by a performance of dancing Dervishes and their deep

religiosity… The next stop was Alexandria in Egypt, where *Freya* moored at a pier opposite the Khedive's palace.

Keen to show his erudition:

Alexandria represented the 'educational centre' of the antique world. It was home to world-renowned libraries, as well as the Pharaonic lighthouse that sent its red light thirty miles out to sea. Here the chariots of the old Egyptians competed and Cleopatra led her luxurious life.[274]

He and his cadets travelled to Cairo by train… where they could see the distant pyramids of Gizah and Sakkarah and the Nile winding its way through the desert. In the Cairo Museum, Haro looked at the leathered mummy face of Pharaoh Rameses II. He was impressed by the classical profile and overtaken by the thought of his audacity at gazing down [on the sacred body.] He stepped back in awe… Haro mounted a camel to ride over to the foot of the Cheops pyramid.[275]

Still debilitated by his bout of rheumatic fever, 'the descent from the top was a ghastly and long, drawn-out experience…'[276] The group then took a boat trip up the Nile to Memphis, Sakkarah, etc. 'Next stop Palestine, where Haro was in charge of organizing the Christmas celebrations aboard.'[277]

Then the Island of Malta. This island must be viewed as the most secure base of the British fleet (just as Helgoland for the Germans).[278] One evening the German officers were invited to a reception at Admiral Prince von Battenberg's palace, where both groups mutually appraised each other. Haro was of the opinion that the Germans did not come out too badly in the comparison. It had been different in Cairo… where the English and Scotch aristocracy, all tall and thin, had outshone them.

The trip continued on to Messina and Barcelona. In Port Mahon, Spain, a storm overtook *Freya* 'generating an awkward night'.[279] Rose was ordered to determine the quantity, location and calibre of artillery guarding the harbour entrance, and so was 'introduced to the excitement associated with espionage work'.[280] Several times Rose crawled around among the rocks, keeping out of sight of the Spanish guard. Unfortunately 'the fruits of the exercise were incommensurate to the psychological pressures involved.'[281]

Returning to Germany at the voyage's conclusion, Rose was accorded a two-month furlough to Wiesbaden to cure his rheumatic fever. Formally, he was assigned to be a Company Officer, 11th Shipyard Division in Wilhelmshaven, but his duties for the remainder of the summer of 1908 were reduced to working every second day as a lifeguard. He read voraciously the rest of the time recalling that 'if it is true that human understanding can only be developed in leisure time, then this summer was probably one of the most useful periods of [my] life.'[282]

Unfortunately the legacy of his rheumatic fever lingered, and 'in spite of this [period of rest], when the weather changed, he continued to suffer severe pains for years to come. Climbing stairs was torture.'[283]

Germany's New Naval Monster – and Promotion

On Sunday 8 March 1908 under the lurid page-two headline 'Germany's New Naval Monster', and the subtitle 'Other Giant Battleships Being Constructed', the *Salt Lake Herald* reported that Germany had launched SMS *Nassau*, her answer to the British Dreadnought.

> The launch of the giant battleship *Nassau* inaugurates a new era in the German navy. In size, armament, speed and installation, she will be superior to any warship hitherto built in Germany.
> DIMENSIONS KEPT SECRET
> The *Nassau* displaces 17,960 tons and is built entirely of hardened [Krupp] steel...
> A twin ship in every respect [the *Westfalen*] is to be launched soon from the Weser yard at Bremen. Two other battleships are also to be laid down this year, and [each of] these are, it is believed, to displace over 20,000 tons.[284]

For Britain and her allies, the *Nassau* and her sister ships were indeed a surprise. Paid for by the Naval Bill of 1908, *Nassau* was laid down on 22 July 1907 amid absolute secrecy assured by detachments of soldiers guarding the shipyard and the yards of the ship's suppliers. All three of her sister ships were also laid down in 1907 prior to the Reichstag vote that funded their construction through the Supplementary Naval Law of 1908.

The first of four dreadnought battleships of the Imperial German Navy, the *Nassau* precipitated the 1908-1909 'Naval Panic' in Great Britain. Coupled with the Bosnian crisis and the 1908 First Balkan War these naval and political developments formed the ominous backdrop for Rose's return to the Imperial German fleet.

On 15 July 1908, Rose was promoted *Leutnant zur See*, Lieutenant-at-Sea. Two-and-a-half months later, at the beginning of October, he reported aboard the battleship SMS *Wettin* where he became Adjutant to its commander, Vice Admiral Souchon, who would become the future leader of the Ottoman fleet. Since his last appointment to a ship-of-the-line two years earlier things had changed dramatically:

> The demands had substantially increased. Everyone was involved in bringing the fleet's striking power to the highest perfection. If they were not on extended squadron trips that kept them away from their home harbours for weeks at a time, the ships were out to sea from Monday to Friday. Night exercises frequently continued into the early morning.[285]

The High Seas Fleet was commanded by the *Kaiser*'s brother,

> ...the wiry Prince Henry of Prussia, to whom all of the younger officers looked up with admiration. He was an excellent, personally courageous seafarer. However, his interests were occasionally diverted from the navy by princely duties at which the brotherhood turned up its nose.[286]

Often Rose buttressed his assessments of individuals with examples of their behaviour:

> In heavy fog, during the fleet's practice run in the Baltic Sea, *Wettin* was rammed by the next ship astern. Its sharp prow with the bronze torpedo tube hit *Wettin*'s stern. A few of the ship's aft quarters filled with water. The fleet anchored immediately. Just as some semblance of peace was restored, a cutter rowed by fourteen sailors emerged from the fog. It was the Fleet commander. In fairly heavy swells, the boat came alongside and the Prince climbed the rope ladder to the deck. He wanted to assess the damage with his own eyes. Haro was impressed by this solicitousness. He was proud to be part of an organization in which every superior was fully engaged in protecting the personnel and materiel entrusted to him.[287]
>
> ...Haro became aware that resistance to the storm remains as fragile as the soul of a woman one has offended. The immediate effect of the ramming was that Haro's interest increased in everything connected with the under-water war.[288]

Wettin was the sixth ship-of-the-line in the Second Squadron under the command of Admiral Henning von Holtzendorff, who 'sported a wide, grey beard, almost like Santa, but his comportment was full of temperament and youthful energy.'[289]

Vice Admiral Souchon, *Wettin*'s commander, was

> ...a far-sighted man, who knew how to treat everyone correctly. He gave everyone freedom, as well as the opportunity to show initiative... When the ship was at sea Haro as Signal Officer was usually stationed on the bridge, close to his highly admired commander.[290]
>
> ...In the summer of 1908 the High Sea Fleet set out for the Atlantic Ocean. A seaman died of a heart attack while swimming in Ferrol Bay. It was extremely hot when Haro, following his commander, climbed up the steep path to the cemetery. The Spanish minister murmured the usual Latin prayers and dropped earth on to the sarcophagus. The atmosphere was anything but solemn... at which point the commander stepped to the grave side and found the right words of farewell, so that everybody walked away both moved and elated. The return march from the high cemetery to the city turned into an impressive expression of German military tradition.[291]

Later during WWI, when Souchon was given command of the Turkish fleet, Rose recalled that he would become known as 'Ghazi Souchon Pasha'.[292]

Wettin's First Officer, Captain Otto Lans

> ...was equally insightful and led the officer corps in duty and in the mess hall with humour and comradeship. No wonder that there was not a single dissatisfied officer. This atmosphere was passed on to the crew and it can be said that they all served together on what may be called a 'sunny ship'. As a result of its excellent leadership the ship won the *Kaiser*'s prize in artillery and torpedo target practice; in boat service, flag signalling and in telegraphy. It was always in the right place during manoeuvres; it was an exceptional ship.[293]

Returning to the fleet's preparations for war, Rose noted:

> The fleet's tactical plans were developed under Admiral von Köster, while the
> Prince refined the overall use of the fleet. The training was carried out with
> tireless industry. The over-arching understanding of how to operate followed
> Nelson's dictum that officers and crew had to become a 'band of brothers'. Haro's
> experience convinced him that the German High Seas Fleet learned this by 1908. It
> had acquired it through devoted dedication to Germany's highest mission.[294]

Vice Admiral Souchon, *Wettin's* commander, developed novel ways to improve
the ship's performance under battle conditions. He assigned Rose a key
responsibility in the procedure, stationing him on the bridge and tasking him
with being an observer during 'combat undertakings'[295] such as squadron
engagements mounted against a designated ship steering a particular course at
a given speed. Afterwards Rose was to 'write up a [set of] so-called "disruption
notice[s]" to help the crew to know what kinds of disasters might occur during
battle'.[296] Later the disruption notices were distributed to the officers and men
responsible for the operation's execution. Following individual review they were
brought to evaluation discussions where each recipient rose, read them out loud,
and explained what action he had taken during the combat undertaking: 'In this
way, when more than one person spoke up, invisible connections were revealed.
An excellent result.'[297]

Assessing the value of his role, Rose remarked:

> The preparation of these paper attacks occupied Haro, the Adjutant, many days
> and nights, but since their effectiveness was so obvious, his zeal and enthusiasm
> were boundless. Haro's 'note war,' which had been suggested by the commander,
> was transmitted from ship to ship.[298]
>
> ...His frequent duty on the bridge, his responsibility for the 'technical orders'
> and secret staff rules, coupled with his manoeuvre duties, taken together, created
> an excellent preparation for the training of young officers.[299]

It wasn't all war games. That summer of 1908, the German High Seas Fleet
returned from strategic exercises off Quessant in the Atlantic. As the fleet
approached the south coast of England, the signal 'clear for action' was
broadcast from ship to ship along with the admonition not to swivel the ships'
artillery.

> Political tensions were particularly high in these weeks. The fleet command
> believed that, as they had with the Spanish Armada in the past, the British
> would use the opportunity to destroy the entire German fleet off the English
> coast. The tension grew to its highest when a British destroyer fleet left
> Portsmouth and approached close to the Germans. Had the artillery not been
> instructed not to swivel their artillery, how easily a cannon might have gone
> off, precipitating the war that Germany did not want. Thousands breathed
> a sigh of relief when the destroyers turned away showing their white water
> screws.[300]

Rose characterizes the period between April 1903 when he joined the Imperial Navy and the autumn of 1908 when he became Adjutant to Commander Souchon as covering his apprenticeship as a squire before knighthood:

> Until his transfer to *Wettin*, Haro had been 'absorbing'; a student open to everything that the world had to offer and the navy thought worth knowing about. The years in the High Seas Fleet solidified his practical experience and anchored him in his profession. He was no longer merely on the receiving end, but felt co-responsible for everything that happened to the fleet. Over time he had grown and become one of those who could pass on his knowledge to the younger recruits. Haro now viewed himself as one of the building blocks constituting the foundation upon which the German state rests. Whether his particular block was seen, respected or paid attention to, was not important... The tall and slender youth had turned into a determined man, for whom devotion and sacrifice were natural. He had *mutatis mutandis* developed into a German knight.[301]

Rose here demonstrates a very particular form of introspection. Referring to himself in the third person is in itself revealing and slightly disconcerting for the reader; Rose is creating his own story for posterity. Passing in silence any questions of self-doubt, a recurring struggle he alludes to elsewhere, Rose describes himself as an increasingly confident young man who has become a knight.

Chapter 7

Mistakes, Chance and Unexpected Consequences

SMS *AUGSBURG* passing under the Levensauer High Bridge while transiting the Kiel Canal. Rose served aboard as First Lieutenant. [Author's Archive]

The summer of 1909 found Rose and the battleship *Wettin* visiting northwest Spain and 'Norway's beautiful Trondheim'.[302] Rose 'particularly loved the dome [of the cathedral] with its interior decorations'.[303] Thirty-one years later, during the German occupation, he would visit Nidaros Cathedral again when, in July 1940, he assumed his responsibilities as Sea Commander of Trondheim.

Rose begins his account of 1909 with another review of the chain of command. Once again he provides an example of the leadership style he will emulate as a commander. Vice Admiral Souchon, *Wettin*'s commander 'who had captured everybody's heart',[304] was transferred to other duties in the fall of 1909. 'The officers rowed him to land in his gig while the crew stood at the railings waving good-bye.'[305]

The commander that replaced him, Admiral Paul Behncke, later Supreme Commander of the German Navy

>...had a difficult act to follow. However, his comprehensive understanding, his sincerity, the depth of his knowledge, quickly won him the admiration of the crew. He was a bit hesitant in his decision-making... and relied more on administrative rules, but he showed great concern and was always fair. He supported his subordinates strongly in trying to avoid a negative judgment or in reversing it. This became most evident in the case of a squadron honour proceedings. Night after night, the commander worked on a clear and logical written justification that was also full of human understanding. It served the accused as a justification, a learning experience and a healing remedy.[306]

Rose was promoted from Adjutant to commander of the battleship's light artillery. In this role he assisted the First Officer in the artillery control centre as well as being responsible for the night-time operation of the ship's searchlights. His promotion also made him a division officer responsible for 120 men including 'two dozen ordinary seamen, these were young people who had completed time as cabin boys and were now being trained for such careers as: gunner, pyrotechnician and signal mate etc.'[307] The importance of training and Rose's aptitude as a teacher are recurring themes in his autobiography:

>He gave a lecture to the sub-officers and specialists about the recently terminated Russo-Japanese war. He seems to have been able to hold their interests because no one fell asleep and no one coughed. The most important insight that Haro had garnered from his week-long preparations was that a leading soldier needs to know more than weapons and their use.[308]

In 1910 *Wettin* received a new commander, Hermann Nordmann, and Rose was promoted to command of the rear 24-cm. 'battle tower'[309] which housed two of the battleship's four main guns. The promotion completed his training across the entire range of the ship's artillery: light, middle and heavy. Coupled with his promotion, he was responsible for the training of new recruits: 'There was no better task in Haro's opinion than to participate in the training of Germany's young people. His engagement bore fruit; there were visible changes in the group from week to week.'[310]

In March 1911, immediately prior to being transferred from *Wettin*, an excess of zeal almost proved disastrous during Rose's last official duty. Rose was charged with demonstrating the operational efficiency of his battle tower during the yearly combat readiness inspection by the 1st Squadron's Chief, Vice Admiral Hugo von Pohl. Impatient to demonstrate that 'there was "action" in Haro's tower,'[311] Rose signalled 'start' to the bridge, before Admiral Pohl had finished climbing into the massive turret. The turret immediately began turning, causing the Admiral to lose his footing and fall against the turret's armoured wall. Furious, the Admiral thundered: 'Who gives the orders here? Do you say "start" or do I say it?'[312] Rose, frozen in salute with hand to cap, said nothing. He described the episode's denouement:

Well then 'start' the Admiral ordered, concluding the one-sided conversation. 'Frumm,' once again the tower swung around and our smart battle drill commenced with demonstrations of breakdowns, gas masks, fires, and jams. The Admiral's brow unclouded. After a quarter of an hour he climbed back on deck. The critique was remarkably mild in the light of the initial disaster. Haro could be proud and the fifty tower crew men smiled from ear to ear.[313]

It was his last hurrah aboard *Wettin*. Rose had been informed that immediately after the inspection he was to transfer to the small cruiser *Augsburg* for a few weeks before moving on to teach at the Torpedo School in Mürwik near Flensburg.[314] Rose was posted to SMS *Augsburg* during the idyllic spring and summer of 1911. Rose

...loved returning to the most beautiful part of Germany's coast, the Flensburg Bay. In one of the sunniest summers that the twentieth century had given the German people up to that time, it was wreathed with light green beech forests.[315]

The Imperial Navy's torpedo boat flotilla had only been created the previous autumn, so there was much to develop, learn and perfect during the spring manoeuvres:

The small cruiser *Augsburg* was one of the newest ships that could manoeuvre at much higher speeds. It was captained with great elegance. And since it was much smaller there were no pre-set routines as on the battleships. One worked more spontaneously... One travelled independently on the small cruisers, fully occupied with learning about the new torpedo weapon... The attack-and-reconnaissance exercises lasted far into the night.[316]

Rose's 'new command was, to use an expression of the time, "pure joy."'[317] He was teaching again, and 'the *Fähnriche* (ensigns) were of the highest calibre that the navy had to offer.'[318]

Every morning, he cheerfully stepped before his attentive *Fähnriche*. He was delighted with their progress even though some of them confused machine-locking pistons with water impact dampers and did not understand the interdependence of a pendulum and a pressure device. Haro often gave his exams shortly before the end of class, starting with those that were the weakest and couldn't concentrate. Then, when the bell rang, he'd say: 'Well, young men, you will have only yourselves to blame if you fail.'[319]

Known to them as 'Uncle Kulle',[320] *Augsburg*'s commander, Johannes August Karl Franz von Karpf, was a close intimate of the German royal family. In addition to commanding *Augsburg*, von Karpf was commander of the 'royal and beautifully appointed'[321] racing yacht SMY *Iduna* 'which was at the disposal of the *Kaiser*'s wife'.[322] During a tour of the *Iduna*, von Karpf spoke intimately about the royal family, giving Rose the impression that 'the Hohenzollerns were motivated by the same human frailties and desires as other people.'[323]

In a short story Hans Rose will write in Constantinople, a key character comments, 'I have much for which to thank fate.' One finds frequent references to providence in Rose's autobiographical writings. While Rose himself was 'deeply opposed to passively submitting to fate', two unanticipated occurrences during the period March to May 1911 play a pivotal role in his life. The first, precipitated by events aboard *Augsburg*, likely prevented his premature death.

Rose found his *Fähnriche* attentive when seated in the classroom, but not always so at their posts in the ship:

> At times it was not easy to teach the *Fähnriche* when they had other things on their minds and failed to pay attention. This was dangerous in the flitting torpedo boats where reaction times demanded split seconds. If a *Fähnrich* on the bridge was inattentive Haro impatiently shifted his weight from foot to foot and commanded 'back rudder.' The ensuing backward movement [of the ship] was pedagogically more effective than long explanations.[324]

Mistakes happened. During torpedo target practice one morning one of Rose's *Fähnriche* accelerated against orders while Rose, at the back of the bridge, was looking up something in the Torpedo Exam Book. The young man's error compounded that of a *Fähnrich* on another light cruiser that, also against orders,[325] was cutting across the bow of Rose's ship. With a loud crack Rose's ship hit the bow of the other ship. Her bow filling with water, the other ship immediately began to sink. To make matters worse 'the two ships were interlocked like two fighting stags and could not be disentangled.'[326] The weight of the sinking ship began pushing Rose's ship underwater. Rose reports, somewhat testily, that 'the damned *Fähnriche*'[327] were off-loaded to other ships while a third ship was brought up to support the impaled ship from the other side of its bow. Then 'one of the strangest sea voyages that Haro had ever experienced'[328] began as together the three ships made for the *Germaniawerft* shipyard in Kiel. Arriving at nightfall, 'the great crane heaved the bow of the sinking ship up and Haro's ship finally escaped its pernicious embrace.'[329] Luckily Rose's ship was undamaged while the impaled ship was repaired 'with a few new frame ribs and metal plates'.[330]

Rose recounts the story of a second accident in much greater detail 'because it was decisive for Haro's future comportment'.[331] A *Fähnrich* posted to the engine room telegraph on *Augsburg*'s bridge appeared to be daydreaming. Rose, in an angry voice,[332] snapped: '*Fähnrich* Thiel, you need a few slaps around the ears because you have endangered the ship.'

Thiel, 'who was the son of a well-known general, looked offended'.[333] Later that afternoon Thiel was again stationed at the engine room telegraph. Arriving on the bridge Rose demanded, 'Please pay attention *Fähnrich* Thiel.'

'Yes, First Lieutenant.'[334]

A second *Fähnrich* was steering *Augsburg* as it approached the dock. That *Fähnrich* gave the order: 'Engines stop,' Then, with Thiel repeating 'Engines stop,' he telegraphed the order to the engine room. With engines disengaged, the ship began to glide silently towards the pier.

'Slow power back' commanded the *Fähnrich* at the helm. Daydreaming Thiel set the telegraph to the 'Slow power ahead' position. Haro screamed: 'He said BACK!'

The ship continued to move forward.

'Back!' screamed Haro once more:

'*Fähnrich* Thiel, full power backwards!'

Thiel opened his mouth, stared at Haro with childish eyes and jammed the telegraph to the 'Full power ahead' position. The ship jumped forward like a tiger, ramming the exploding pier as far as the bridge, at which point [she] was stuck fast. Horrified and white as a sheet, Thiel stared... Haro's face was red as a turkey hen... It took many hours with axes and saws to free the ship.[335]

Once ashore 'Thiel staggered to his room. One could see how embarrassed he felt.' Following Thiel, Rose thought 'A future disaster has to be prevented.' Finding him leaning against the wall, he said: 'Now Thiel you have seen the outcome of inattention. If you had received the slaps this morning, the trouble would not have happened... Take comfort and do better in the future. The mistake is easy to repair.'[336]

Perhaps the mistake was easy to repair but the punishment, in Rose's view, didn't seem to fit the crime.

> Thiel was disciplined for the 'accident' (but very lightly), by being given nothing more than a 'reprimand'. Haro thought about this outcome for two days and then, against the advice of some comrades, launched a formal appeal. This went to the Chief of the Baltic Sea Naval Station, Rear Admiral Souchon... Haro's appeal was accepted and the 'reprimand' was converted into a 'mistake' with much greater career consequences.[337]

Here is a signal example of Rose's penchant for contesting higher authority when he felt it appropriate. Unexpectedly, the mistake had much greater consequences for Rose as well. His decision to appeal the ruling of a superior officer had not sat well and his next promotion was rescinded. Rose recounts unflinchingly that Rear Admiral Souchon admonished him:

> Son, you filed an appeal and were vindicated. However that was not wise. You were slated to become Flag Lieutenant with von Spee in East Asia. Because of your appeal you have lost this excellent command. Please remember the following: sensibility is the strength of great souls, touchiness is the weakness of small souls. Promote and develop your sensibility and fight against your touchiness.[338]

Rose's action appears paradoxical. On the one hand, after admonishing him, Rose comforted Thiel and minimized the import of the ensign's mistake. On the other hand, he filed an appeal that Thiel had received an insufficiently severe punishment. Perhaps Rose was offended that the powerful protect their own; in this case the son of a general. And Rose had screamed at Thiel, not once but twice during the incident, a reaction, in the moment of crisis, that could only have further shattered Thiel's composure at a moment when he urgently required the calm guidance of a mentor. Perhaps by increasing the responsibility the navy accorded Thiel for the mishap, Rose sought to minimize his own.

Vice Admiral Count Graf Maximilian von Spee was in command of Germany's East Asiatic squadron. Flag Lieutenant to the squadron would have been a plum promotion indeed. But fate is fickle. Had the promotion gone through, Rose would almost certainly have been killed in December 1914 during the Second Battle of the Falklands. That battle ended in a decisive victory for the British, the destruction of the majority of Count von Spee's outgunned ships, and the one-sided loss of 2,200 German seamen.

When the news reached Germany, Rose recalled:

> When the *Scharnhorst* and *Gneisenau*, with the heroic Count Spee and his two sons, as well as most of the crew died near the Falkland Island in the icy waters of the South Atlantic [Rose] bowed his head, deeply moved. *Fähnrich* Thiel had probably saved his life, and certainly given a new dimension to his being.[339]

Still it remained in the best interests of Germany's new navy to further the career of such a promising young officer. Only a few weeks later, in April 1911, Rose was told that his next promotion would be to First Officer on the German consular Station Yacht *Loreley* in Constantinople. With French the international consular language of choice, Rose requested a three-month language training leave. During that leave, in the winter of 1911/12, Rose enrolled as an *Etudiant des lettres* in Grenoble. While there, he lived with the family of an officer of the Alpine troops where 'French and German were spoken alternately for an hour at a time.'[340]

With the autumn 1911 graduation of his crew of *Fähnriche* training on *Augsburg*, Rose assumed new teaching duties in Wilhelmshaven in the 11th Shipbuilding Division at the Torpedo School in Mürwik and aboard the School-ship SMS *Württemberg*. Without saying goodbye[341] Rose left *Augsburg* to take up his new duties:

> One hundred and twenty young people were recruited to become engineers. They were divided into two groups of sixty each. Haro became the instructor for one of the groups. The head of his company was an excellent athlete. Ordinary people stretch and yawn after waking up. *Kapitänleutnant* von Luck, however, performed giant swings on the cross bar, forwards and backwards in full uniform. Then he began his daily service. His example, of course, fired up his company... The Admiral arrived for the final review just before Christmas 1911 and the whole company demonstrated its athleticism – officers, petty officers and the engineering recruits demonstrated somersaults over the vaulting horse, without a single mistake – it was a huge pedagogical success.[342]

Anne-Marie

No doubt contributing to his satisfaction was the second chance event that 'changed his life':[343]

On a sunny May [1911] day there was a charity party in the 'Harmonie' [near Mürwik]. Everyone that was anyone was there. The officers from the Torpedo School were invited as well. A young woman offered Haro a choice of cakes from her platter... When Haro thanked her looking into her eyes he knew that his destiny was being decided. He followed her with his gaze as her white dress with the long pink bow disappeared into the crowd. Then he went in search of her and asked for a dance. Weeks later he and some of his friends were invited to her parents' farm estate located north of Gravenstein. Here she wore a pale blue dress. She impressed him by her open and yet tactful spirit, her natural grace and the lightheartedness of her appearance, as well as her companionable nature. When the officers returned to Mürwik under the starry skies, he was silent among the happily gossiping comrades, thanking that fate had brought him here.[344]

The young woman was Anne-Marie Siemers. In his autobiographical papers he refers to her as Mara.

He wrote to Mara, and now began the feverish anticipation for the daily mail... that kept Haro in agitation. The terrible restlessness interfered with any other joy he might feel... Even in Paris, which he visited at the beginning of March 1912... While there he wrote to Mara whether he could come for a visit. A few days later he was there and drove through the fields with her in a buggy, wandered through the meadows, inspected the cattle barns and was in a condition of exaltation near his beloved girl. On the day before his departure he told her that he would always be there for her if she so desired. And she desired it. It was 11 April 1912. Now, in one fell swoop, Haro's life changed completely. He was no longer responsible only for himself, but for another graceful, tender being, whose fate he had tied to his own.[345]

The decision to marry Anne-Marie had been agonizing. 'Weeks and months passed during which Haro was unable to make a decision.'[346] Then following his decision,

Should he have done that? Could he expect that a young girl would give him her whole being? Terrible doubts plagued him. These feeling are called 'inferiority complexes' today, but at the time Haro had no name for his condition, which made it worse.[347]

In April, Rose prepared for his departure for Constantinople and the Orient.

Some days with the chosen and her mother in Berlin provided solace and relaxation. The parting hour arrived too fast. Haro collected his men in Wilhelmshaven for transport on the Danube and arranged for a huge farewell party in the Casino. When he arrived at the Hotel Loheyde in the early morning hours his wallet was considerably lighter. When he got up to leave at six o'clock in the morning six of his comrades were there to see him off and offer the usual 'blood brotherhood' that cost fifty Pfennigs per person. Haro had to give up the last money he had in his pocket...[348]

Chapter 8

Under the Spell of the Levant

In 1912 Constantinople, seat of the Ottoman Empire, seethed with political intrigue and great power intervention. Russia, Turkey's enemy for a thousand years, schemed to take the city that guarded the exit of the Black Sea through the Bosporus and the Dardanelles. With its narrow 50-mile-long channel, the Dardanelles offered the Czar the only year-round western hemisphere maritime passage to his country. Losing the Crimean War, Russia was obliged to sign the 1856 Treaty of Paris which demilitarized the Black Sea coastline and made it neutral territory closed to all warships. The Treaty of Paris gave each signatory the right to permanently station a warship in the Bosporus (and thus in Constantinople). Until 1914 the lightly armed German consular station ship SMS *Loreley* was the only ship of the Imperial Navy posted to Constantinople.

Destabilization of the Balkan powder keg, once part of the Ottoman Empire's western province of Rumelia, reflected that empire's accelerating decay. The Balkans became fertile ground for the growth of national movements, the appetites of aggressive neighbours, particularly Austria and Serbia, and finally revolt at the heart of the empire itself. In 1905, opposing the Turkish autocracy, the Young Turk Movement comprised of students and army officers coalesced into the Young Turk Party. Hoping to forestall a partition of the empire

SMS *LORELEY* anchored off Tophane. [Author's Archive]

and to revitalize it, the revolution of the Young Turks coupled with a 1908 military uprising in Constantinople led by Enver Pasha overthrew the regime of Abdülhamid II. Under Enver Bey and the Committee of Union and Progress the revolution attempted to transform the Ottoman Empire into a constitutional state with equal rights and universal male suffrage. Transported by *Loreley* in 1909, Abdülhamid II was exiled to Salonika.

The other great powers, Hungary, Italy, and Russia directly, and Germany, France, and Britain indirectly, backed the various parties. At the outset of WWI, despite a century of having supported the Ottoman Empire, Great Britain would trade any possibility of alliance with Turkey for two battleships. But Germany, by transferring two of her own to Turkey, and having actively courted the Ottoman Empire at the beginning of the 20th century, won her as an ally.

Thus Constantinople, at the crossroads of Europe, Asia and the Middle East, with its 2,500-year history, seat of empires, hub of consuls flush with political intrigue and with great-power warships at anchor in her port, had much to offer. No wonder that Rose, learning of his upcoming commission to *Loreley* stationed there, wrote, 'This commission made up for the lost East Asian command.'[349]

In April 1912 Hans Rose was 27 years old, of average height and slender build, a young man recently engaged, who unselfconsciously described himself as 'very socially inclined … danced well'.[350] He was an up-and-coming lieutenant in the Imperial German Navy whose next posting, as First Watch-officer aboard the station-yacht *Loreley* in Constantinople, reflected the high hopes the navy had for him. It was Rose's first significant ship command. The First Lieutenant runs the ship. The posting, made possible by his facility with languages, entailed visits to ports in the Black Sea, Sea of Marmara, the Aegean Sea, the Adriatic and the Mediterranean, and the execution of various diplomatic missions. Other than the standard duties of a ship's First Officer, Rose's responsibilities would primarily be in the nature of social protocol at German Embassy events. It was an exciting time. Most of what we know about Rose's roughly year-long posting to Constantinople comes to us from the letters he wrote to his fiancée, Anne-Marie Siemers.

By this point in his career, *Loreley*'s First Officer had learned how to lead men and manage ships. The anecdotes Rose shares with Anne-Marie about his role aboard *Loreley* confirm what we already know about these talents. What Rose experienced in Constantinople, and more largely in the Levant, tell us more about the man. Largely absent elsewhere in his autobiographical writings, references to religion and spirituality are notable in his letters to Anne-Marie during this year in Constantinople, though he admits it is 'a strange world for me, for which I have no affinity'.[351] In love, his letters also explore the roles of husband and wife.

Reading these letters, one is struck by their intimacy, written in the first person. While in Constantinople Rose wrote at least one semi-fictional short story. Haro, the protagonist of that short story, is himself. Years later Hans Rose referenced that semi-fictional tale as he strove to construct a narrative about his place in history.

Rose's decision to include his letters to Anne-Marie without revision in an autobiography which otherwise largely reflects the analytical, emotionally restrained persona that he liked to project, is remarkable. Perhaps it reflects his core romanticism as well as a desire to maintain a deep and immediate connection to his lost first wife. By including these letters, Rose has given voice to two men; the younger man living the life that made him famous, and the older Rose, 'imprinted by the stamp of life',[352] reflective and seasoned by experiences.

The year in Constantinople is also a period when Rose's artistic talents are expressed in lovely line drawings, some of them coloured. Demonstrating Rose's considerable talent as a sketch artist, seven survive.

The first of Hans Rose's letters to Anne-Marie was written on 3 May 1912, the day after his arrival aboard *Loreley*.

> After a long and at times very boring trip on the Danube, we arrived in Galatz yesterday afternoon... *Loreley* is tied up at the pier. The reception by my predecessor was: 'Hello. There you are. Welcome. This morning breakfast with the German Consul, in the evening dinner at the Commander's.'[353]

Privately, Rose was unimpressed both with *Loreley* and his predecessor:

> The trip to *Cospoli* [Constantinople] was terrific – The '*Pontos Euxinos*' [the Black Sea], the unwelcome flood as the Greeks called it, demonstrated its worst... We pitched up to 35 degrees in each direction. I don't have much confidence in the Old Lore steam yacht, built in England in 1885 and later bought by the German navy. The ship's body is terribly rusty. I will concentrate on repairing it. Moreover, its wooden sheathing is full of bed bugs. I would never have expected such conditions on a German warship, even less here, because our trip is for representational purposes. The Greeks think that bedbugs bring luck – I shake out every piece of clothing washed by the Greeks. We have a tastefully wood-panelled mess hall with colourful leaded windows on both sides and a large concave ceiling that is also made of colourful glass. On the front wall there is a fireplace above which there hangs a large mirror. However, everything is pretty run down. Either my predecessors didn't understand the ship's worth, or they followed an erroneous ambition: to save money. I will use every penny I can lay my hands on to restore the ship.[354]

Conditions would not immediately improve. Fifteen days later he would write: 'When I climbed into my bunk yesterday, I was looking forward to a well-deserved sleep. But instead I was eaten alive by the bed bugs.'[355]

During Whitsuntide, around the beginning of June, Rose reported that the battle was still fully engaged:

> I am still carrying on my war against the vermin. To start with, I had all mattresses, bedclothes, hammocks and covers hung on deck to be sterilized by the sun and beaten with a carpet beater. Initially, whole armies of bed bugs appeared and the uncleanliness was disgusting. Now we are making progress.[356]

The physical condition of the ship was unnerving as well. In September, he wrote to his fiancée: 'In the bunkers I found a 20mm-thick layer of rust... I am worried about the possibility of a hole in the plating.'[357] Rose took his responsibilities for her condition seriously and proudly left her a year later in better condition than he found her. At the end of December Rose had the ship repainted 'so that we will appear white as a swan, when we return to Tophane at the beginning of the New Year'.[358] On 1 February 1913 *Loreley* sailed through the Marmara Sea to Trieste, where the ship was to be overhauled. Rose was with his fiancée for a couple of days in Rapallo,

> ...but was primarily concerned that the repair work progressed as smoothly as possible... Much money was saved, because the crew helped out. On 1 March 1913 Haro could report to the commander that the budget had not been exceeded, and that he had a five hundred Mark surplus in the till.[359]

The few comments Rose provides Anne-Marie about *Loreley*'s crew demonstrate the pride, attention and concern for his men's wellbeing that are a hallmark of his military career:

> I made an excursion with the ship's crew into the high mountains. I love to do this and I think they enjoy it as well. The mood and attitude of the crew is excellent. They look so clean and cheerful that one's heart smiles with pleasure.[360]

However, three days later *Loreley*'s First Officer had other preoccupations:

> On 11 July 1912, the day before our departure from Noworossisk, we were as usual invited out for dinner. When we returned to the ship about 1:30 a.m., we experienced a NE storm that the 'Sailing Handbook' described as strong enough to push small craft under water... I did not go to bed that night, because if we had drifted away from the Mole, which lay only fifteen metres behind our stern, we would have been smashed... I hope, Mara, to be spared such a fate as the loss of a ship... All day long it continued to blow forcefully... We set off in the evening... The wind soon abated as we glided past the Caucasian cliffs and I experienced three of the most beautiful sunrises... An example of the ongoing struggle between light and dark in the world.[361]

In September he described a premonition:

> I rarely dream, or remember what I have dreamed, let alone am awakened by a dream. This night I was dreaming that a cutter holding the crew was being lowered into the water, but that because of inattention, the rope had gotten tangled in the ship's side. I screamed and woke up before the dream disaster had taken place. We had planned a similar training exercise for this morning... and lo and behold, if the cutter was not hanging vertically in the air, with some of the crew afloat in the Bosporus. Do you believe in premonition?[362]

Accidents aside, *Loreley* seemed to be a happy ship and September ended with the addition of a new 'crewmate':

> On the recommendation of the commander, I bought a brown bear from gypsies for the ship. It is a lovely, playful animal. Some of the crew tried to tie it up and

muzzle it. Now it growls and tries to bite everyone, after previously licking my hand. Some people are foolish. I scolded the culprits sharply, who stood around me with pale faces. The bear's name is of course 'Albrecht'.[363]

Around the beginning of December 1912, Rose found himself rescuing a drowning crewman:

I heard a loud splash behind me. I turned around and saw one of our crew disappear in the Bosporus. I called to the man on the bridge: 'drop a buoy' and 'man overboard' and found myself in the water... Rockefeller too jumped to the rescue. We caught the man who could not swim and put a life preserver over his head and swam to the gangway. All three of us were happy to get back on board. The water was terribly cold and not too clean... The atmosphere after the rescue was really wonderful. I had not expected that I would automatically respond by jumping. That I did so, reassures me and gives me hope for the future.[364]

On New Year's Day 1913 Rose wrote to Anne-Marie of 'a small sign of Germanic generosity':[365]

A few weeks ago, Rockenfeller and I saved one of our crew from drowning, when he fell into the Bosporus. The commander dutifully notified the High Command in Wilhelmshaven. They are planning to give us the Lifesaving Medal in the near future.[365]

Sharing news of the holidays just concluded, Rose wrote:

Christmas is behind us. The people, it seemed to me, were overjoyed. We had prepared and decorated the ship beautifully... Took an hour's long walk with the crew. They sang loudly and jumped around like goats. I jumped with them, but refrained from singing in order not to undermine discipline. The weather is wonderful.[366]

Absorbed in Medieval Times – and Heroes

Loreley departed Galatz in Rumania almost immediately after Rose came aboard. The next day she had returned to Constantinople, mooring off the Dolma Baghtcheh alongside the naval vessels of the other great powers. They faced the Seraskerat, the Ottoman War Office buildings:

We are moored between the palace of Domabagt and the Eski Serail... The stern is tied to the shore. To the right is the Italian, to the left the Austrian post, followed by the Russian, the American, British and French. I am reading a lot of history in order to understand the times past which surround me.[367]

Nine days later Rose would write to Anne-Marie about the history of the metropolis that had become his new home port: 'This city has drunk floods of blood. In the Hippodrome alone, 30,000 people were killed in one day... We visited the Hagia Sophia, one of the most famous churches in the world.'[368]

Rose found himself 'absorbed in medieval times'.[369] Rose describes his visit to Stamboul, the oldest part of Constantinople:

Yesterday I drove past the old Byzantine city wall. One marvels at this edifice which the Roman king had built to protect his new residence... Stamboul is the old centre of Istanbul. Here you find the old Mosques, the War Ministry and the 'High Gate' where the Califs lived... Compared with the undemanding nature of the Moslems, the German worker constitutes the epitome of entitlement... There are things we can learn from the Muslims. Everyone here lives in his own world and their feeling of happiness is not dependent on property or the type of work they do. It consists of an inner balance that, in spite of external battles, shines its mild light over the people. The peace of God, which is higher than all understanding, keep our hearts and souls and be with us all. Good night Mara.[370]

A week later, on the 27th, he visits the great bazaar again:

Went to the bazaar to bargain for an old carpet. Over and over again the Turk claimed he would like to do a deal with me – but the bargaining went on until he finally asked me how much I was willing to pay. I answered:
  'Ten pounds.'
  'How about twelve pounds?'
  'Jamais, Monsieur, jamais.'
  I shrugged my shoulders and said: 'Too bad.'
  Suddenly he offered me two carpets saying: 'Take the two, Effendi for thirty pounds.'
  I finally bought the older carpet for twelve and a half pounds. It's a Farahan.[371]

In the Constantinople of 1912, with French the language both of diplomacy and commerce, Rose continued to hone his language skills: 'I have energetically re-started my French lessons, though the oriental torpor also affects the North German accustomed to work.'[372] In the same letter he told Anne-Marie:

Toward evening I had an interesting conversation in French with a Greek merchant. But the high point of the evening was a talk with a young married Greek lady, who reminded me of Scheffel's *Ekkehard*. I recommend you read this appealing German novel. You will be absorbed into medieval times ... which I am experiencing here.[373]

On 3 June 1912 Rose witnessed a huge fire which roared through Stamboul generating a three-quarter-mile swath of destruction that swept to the sea:

The railroad tracks were covered with the debris of houses, smouldering remains of a huge fire that destroyed the district of the Hagia Sofia. The southerly wind increased the speed of the fire by turning the copper nails anchoring the roof shingles into catapults, which in turn ignite other roofs as they fall to the ground. The roar and rattle was monstrous as all of Stambul disappeared behind dark clouds of smoke. On the square where the gleaming festivals of the Romans used to take place ... the belongings of the burned-out were thrown together into huge piles. In between, men and women crouched and gazed stone-faced into the flames. 'God gives and God takes away Inshallah.'

...Unbelievable confusion reigned in the direction where the prevailing wind pushed the conflagration. Carts rammed into each other, pedestrians, soldiers and firemen rushed around, but in spite of the chaos, everyone was polite, and provided passage for women and aided them in loading up their belongings. People worked together as one.

A small white coffin rested unprotected on a small rise in front of the Hagia Sofia. It bore a young girl who was to have been buried before the conflagration began. Now she was left in the protection of the temple while the family members dashed away to save what remained. The belongings of the burned out were guarded, bread and water were distributed, and tents were put up in the prefecture for the 15,000 homeless. More than 2,000 houses were destroyed – I have gone into so much detail because it was an event that will remain in my memory forever: huge, horrible and heart wrenching.[374]

In July during *Loreley*'s fifty-day circumnavigation of the Black Sea Rose referred without explanation to spiritual discomfort: 'My spiritual distress during the last two weeks has kept me from telling you about Batum, Sinope and Tiflis.'[375]

On New Year's Day 1913 Rose wrote to Anne-Marie about several almost incomprehensible religious practices he observed in Constantinople; among them Whirling Dervishes he'd first observed in Smyrna:

I also want to tell you about the dancing Dervishes and the Haida Pascha, a Persian celebration in Istambul. The dancing Dervishes are an order of monks who wear a high brown fez made of felt and whose rituals include spinning in place. In the company of other Germans I had watched this swirling uncomprehendingly. I was then invited by the Prior to share a cup of Turkish coffee. All of these activities take place in completely bare rooms. There is no distraction of any kind. The dancers have a gaze that is serious and unreal, completely turned inward. After this strange experience I had the need to be alone for a few hours and remain silent.

What I saw in the Persian festival can only be summed up as difficult to describe. Imagine the steep, bumpy streets of Stamboul rising and descending in innumerable curves, crowded full of people who stand, walk, kneel, squat, sit, ride, drive...

Louder and louder, swelling, we hear the monotonous rhythm of drums, this monotone song from many throats, soundless, toneless, only a rough, irresistible beat. Various religious orders pass, some fanatical, others deeply serious, yet more, transported. For a moment there is silence among the observers, then the babble of voices sets in again.

The olfactory senses are fully engaged: fish fried on the grill, mutton is boiled, chestnuts crackling in the pans, fritters scented, sweets are prepared and offered for sale.

New drum beats draw near in a narrow alley decorated with coloured paper. Dancing, howling dervishes pass by and large groups of men who, to the beat of the drums, beat their backs with rods, whips, and chains. Some bleed, but they feel nothing. Smack, smack, the scourge rushes over their backs. Woe to him who laughs or mocks them, he puts himself into great danger. – Gone!… A white horse appears followed by huge, black-haired men with shaven heads, wearing long white shirts, dangling to their toes. They roar deep and hoarse, in time with the music. They twirl around as they walk and at every fifth or sixth beat hit themselves on the heads and on the back with heavy swords. Some strike carefully, but others use full force. Their heads, beards and shirts are terribly besmirched with streaks of blood, and a great deal more blood -- All in honor of Allah, the Great, the Powerful, the All-knowing, who has preordained the destiny of every individual and who also knows that today you will hack up your scalp until you collapse in a corner with crazy eyes and frothy mouth, horribly defiled.

This religious self-flagellation is hardly unique in the world. If such madness infects an entire people, then it sweeps over the earth like a hurricane and has only the choice between complete victory or annihilation. I pinched my arms and legs again and again. Wondering whether I am still alive? Am I dreaming? Is this real? Are these people that pray to the all-powerful as I do?

Enough of these morbid descriptions.[376]

In September, Rose referred mysteriously to a new friend:

I have found a friend, a discreet heroic friend. He is engaged and his fiancée comes from Schleswig-Holstein. He is an officer and clearly articulates all that I would like to say. I am happy to have found a real comrade, who responds to large and small issues in the same way I do, and whom I venerate because he towers above others. His name is Moltke. Yesterday he gave me his letters to his bride and I am smitten by the texts… You too will be inspired by the letters.[377]

Three months earlier, on 2 June, Rose wrote a similarly adulatory comment to Anne-Marie about the departing German ambassador:

On Saturday the Ambassador Marshall von Bieberstein and his wife bade farewell to the German colony. He received the difficult diplomatic posting to London. When the tall gentleman, who is a head taller than I am, stepped up to the lectern, there was perfect silence. Have you ever heard a really 'good man' speak? One is overcome by a 'special feeling' when men who are weaving on the loom of time reveal what goes on behind the scenes. The ambassador also talked about women – as ideal figures – their sovereignty and their inspiration for our thoughts. At his departure there was a huge crowd of people at the railway station. There were the men from the German colony, the heads of the Osman authorities, the diplomatic representatives of all countries, and the Archimadrit of the Orthodox Church. All pressed forward to show their admiration.[378]

Reading these reverential descriptions leaves one with the sense that old, wise, 'good' and 'heroic' men play a special role in Rose's world view. Rose is 'smitten' by Moltke, and 'all pressed forward to show their admiration' for Ambassador von Bieberstein. Rose's view that the right individual at the right moment and place could shape history was naively demonstrated again years later. When speaking about Hitler, Rose would remark: 'If he had had a single intelligent and highly principled friend, world history would have developed differently.'[379]

Shipboard duties aside, Rose's responsibilities in Constantinople fall largely in the category of flag-waving protocol. His first day in the city:

> This morning, breakfast with the German Consul, in the evening dinner at the commander's. The breakfast was on a beautiful yacht, which belongs to the *Commission Européenne du Danube*... The current president is the German Consul General, our host. I sat beside his wife, an American. Had to get used to the contrast between her grey eyebrows and blond hair. Why do women disfigure themselves in this way? The conversation turned to the complicated power and economic situations in the Balkans.[380]
>
> ...The ship's doctor and I made our introductory visits to the consulates and then to German families, particularly those of the German reformers. I used up 120 visiting cards.[381]

Towards the middle of June, *Loreley* steamed up the Bosporus north from Constantinople and moored at Therapia on the European shore of the strait:

> This morning we arrived here in Therapia and are moored in a small bay. Behind us is the well-known Summer Palace Hotel and beside it in a wonderful park, the summer residence of the German ambassador.[382]
>
> There is a beautiful chapel in the Ambassador's park... Everyone who is part of the Embassy came together for a church service. The door to the park was wide open and the sunlight fell on the tiles. The pastor ... preached an inspiring sermon about human ideals ... and described the way forward in terms of the 'mutual understanding between husband and wife'. It was a thought-provoking speech, based on the bible text: 'Blessed are those who hunger and thirst after righteousness.' Everyone participated in the pre-dinner cocktail on *Loreley*, with the wives wearing their latest style hats.[383]

Rose continued his early August 1912 letter to Anne-Marie by presciently describing the political situation facing the Ottoman Empire:

> In the afternoon we males travelled across the Bosporus to receive the Turkish dignitaries, who were making their introductory visit to the Ambassador. The latter is about a head and a half taller than I am, and looked impressive in his uniform covered with 18 pounds of gold braid ... fighting off the afternoon heat with champagne. The much smaller Turkish ministers had trouble competing. However Mahmud Akar Pascha, the current Naval Minister pointed out in accent-less German that among them were important and world-wise men. He further noted: 'It would be dangerous to underestimate the current unrest in Macedonia, which is more like a revolution... We have reassuring news from Albania that their demands are fulfillable, except one ... if no one on any side commits a stupidity.' ... It would be wonderful if the responsible Turkish representatives were all like Mahmud Muktar and his father, the Grand Vizir, then I too would have faith in the rise of the half-moon. Yet, even though Turkey has been modernized in the last decades ... religion remains a hindrance

to development. For a number of centuries the Turkish state has lost parts of its empire. Particularly now, the Italians are actively engaged in border invasions and the Bulgarians will surely become restive, at which point the Greeks too will make claims, as will Russia, which for centuries has been wishing for access to the Golden Horn – In short, by the year 2000, no Turkish subjects may remain in Europe.[384]

Responsibility for these weighty matters did not lie on Rose's shoulders:

We are leading a healthy life. In the early morning we play one-and-a-half hours of tennis, and then jump into the wonderfully blue Bosporus to cool off and afterwards have breakfast. Then I concentrate on official business... In the late afternoon there is again tennis – this time with the ladies. Then I usually take a lone evening walk into the hills and after dinner there is dancing – which is what we are expected to do as representatives of our country. Almost every evening I either wear my tails or my smoking. Usually I am invited out to dinner, unless we ourselves are entertaining on *Loreley*.[385]

On one such occasion, over the 1912 Christmas holidays:

We gave a charming children's party on board. Little Marion v.H. whispered in my ear: 'I want to give you a kiss.' I ignored the request shamefacedly, but was eventually attacked from behind and got a juicy kiss on the cheek.[386]

In August Rose's older brother Ludwig, a *Jäger* (artillery) *Offizier*, visited *Loreley* and joined Rose during consular visits to Salonika and the Greek Island of Thassos in the Aegean Sea:

We left Salonika in the early morning and headed for Mount Athos, the 'Holy Mountain', where every nation of Greek-Orthodox faith maintains a cloister, of which there are twenty-three... The local monks told us that they are predestined from childhood to serve there. I do not approve of such a practice... It was picturesque on the 'Holy Mountain' but it remained a strange world for me, for which I have no affinity...

Thassos is desolate. We got to know it on a lengthy excursion on the backs of mules. Our staff surgeon was bounced out of his saddle when his mule bolted and thus initiated a race to corral the wild beast. We are here because there is an important mining business that belongs to the Speidel family... That night we were invited to the Speidels who live in a house overlooking the sea. The evening was idyllic because everyone knew some Faust, Wallenstein, Wilhelm Tell and Homer by heart... It was an unforgettable night. When I went to bed last night at 10 p.m., it was an 'ambrosian night' in Homer's words and continued to be moon-lit when I arose for the morning watch at 4 am.[387]

The visit to Thassos also demonstrated Rose's distaste for bureaucrats:

The local German Consul picked a fight with our commander and his Adjutant when he came aboard. That night he had a falling out with my brother Ludwig and me over a beer on land. Rarely have I encountered such a prickly civil servant. Men of his ilk are not good for our reputation abroad.[388]

Distinctly unofficial affairs also fill the time. In September Rose wrote:

What a disaster. Our doctor is in love with three young girls from the same family and doesn't know how to make up his mind. He therefore retires to the chapel in the Ambassador's garden where he pours out his feelings on the organ... How to find your way to bed on these moonlit nights? Especially since you might encounter a dog, cat or bear in your bunk, not to mention the small beasts, like bedbugs and mosquitoes. Consequently we usually sit on the terrace of the Summer Palace Hotel, discussing human, political, social and sometimes philosophical issues.[389]

That month there was an official example of the fraternization between the various navies represented in Constantinople. Rose was again remarkably prescient:

Today there was an international swimming competition between those nations based in the country. The Russians were way ahead. They are harmoniously proportioned men with stamina and quick in the water, like fish. Our own men are slim youths in comparison to them. No one knows the future of Russia with so much elemental strength among its people. Unfortunately, much blood will be lost before [we shall find out].[390]

But more casual fraternization also occurred. *Loreley*'s December visit to the port of Mudania midway along the southern coastline of the Sea of Marmara coincided with visits by the German battle-cruiser *Goeben* and the doomed British Cruiser *Hampshire*:

We are pleased to have the *Goeben* here. It is the most beautiful ship in the Bosporus and by far the strongest. Yesterday, I had tea on the British cruiser *Hampshire*. It was as always nice and companionable. Besides the Austrians, the British are the closest to us in the way they act... Their view of life is similar to ours, only simpler. The German sea officer is, as far as I have observed, more thoughtful and contemplative.[391]

Rose's lifelong love of peacocks dates from his role as Naval Attaché to the court of the last sultan of the Ottoman empire. Rose regaled son Christian with stories from the period[392] including the story of a diamond that became a family heirloom. At a reception hosted by Mehmed V, the last Sultan of the Ottoman Empire, Rose, the dashing young naval officer, recovered the false teeth of one of the Sultan's wives when they popped out of her mouth and skittered across the floor. Upon their return, the Sultan's wife told Rose that the teeth 'should go off and eat alone'.[393] The Sultan was somewhat more grandiose in his appreciation. He took a diamond pin from another member of the harem and presented it to Rose who for many years wore it as a tie pin.

My Life Has Been Enriched by You

Rose's letters to his fiancé, now nineteen, brimmed with love:

[27 May 1912] We took an idyllic excursion to the Prince Islands in our motor boat, which requires that one whisper a magic formula in its ear so it won't buck. The Marmara Sea was like a mirror and deep blue, dolphins jumped in groups out of the water and a sailboat glided by silently on the sparkling waters... I don't know what the others were thinking, but my thoughts went to the Flensburg fjord and looked deeply into two blue-grey eyes.[394]

[11 November 1912] Past Midnight: I spent the evening once again, with a small circle of friends at the Embassy and had a long conversation with MvW, the twenty-year old daughter from his first marriage... We stood by the wide open window-looking out on to a black sky punctuated by bright flickering stars. Lamps burned on the war ships... And do you know who I was thinking about on this fairy tale night? Do you know? I know it, which is the reason why I sat down in my smoking to write to you. Good night.[395]

[4 December 1912] We have returned to our moorings in Tophane. The war situation is unchanged. But our personal situation, I mean yours and mine, will be drastically changed – Read on and be surprised – We will probably go to Trieste for three weeks in February, to have our boiler checked. Wouldn't that be wonderful? Weren't you planning to go south? Couldn't you come to Istria, to Abbazia, Brioni or Portoroz? Think about it and come. The condition of the Queen Mother is of course crucial for a decision, my queen Mara. Hail to you.[396]

[9 January 1913] So, you are coming to Rapallo! – The blossoms, the scent, the sun, the sky, the blue ocean, the peace – May all these come together to give the Queen Mother back her health. But most of all, your company! In the sunny south, a Nordic, slender young maiden – that is like a peach melba.[397]

[22 January 1913] On your birthday, I filled my pocket with beautiful, golden Turkish pounds and went to the bazaar to exchange them for a colourful Shiraz carpet. Wandering on I found a small old silver light with angel's heads. I probably paid too much for it, but one has to make sacrifices if one wants to give a far-off betrothed angel heads.[398]

[4 & 11 August 1912] You inquire whether I continue to wear a beard as at our engagement? I removed the beard quite a while ago and got rid of the moustache just recently... One lady was unwilling to talk to me in my 'naked' condition, while another thought that it showed I was not vain. In fact, both of their opinions are wrong because the removal of my facial hair was a result of trying to get rid of a skin rash that has not only bothered but also disfigured me.[399]

Rose trusts Anne-Marie and appears completely frank. While occasionally paternalistic towards a woman almost eight years his junior, they reveal both his own insecurities and some of the clearest clues about the origins of his world view:

[3 May 1912] You are concerned that you will be unable to develop and learn hidden away in your country estate. I don't believe that is true. Art and sciences are stimulating, yet we draw our life force from holy nature. Those are the strong roots of our strength.[400]

[15 June 1912] Your mother wrote recently that the engagement of her daughter was a difficult sacrifice. I would like to respond that for me the worship of those who gave us life and raised us in selfless devotion ... constitutes the unshakable foundation of life. Your mother does not lose, she wins. Though she will have to reconcile herself to a spatial separation, our thoughts and letters will be hurrying to the parents whom we remember with devotion... Who told you that one should not marry in the year thirteen? Superstition must not paralyze action for a full year. Life is too short... Enclosed a picture of the cemetery in Ejub. The Muslims do not take care of their graves because they believe in predestination which is more paralyzing than the number thirteen. They do not thank their parents for their existence; they do not revere them because of what they have taught them. They do not complain when their houses burn down and they do not seem to be happy when there is a favourable turn in their life's circumstances. After all, they are convinced that their life's path is predestined in Allah's Great Book, before they even see the light of day in birth. How enervating and deadening to all aspirations this belief system must be.

I am deeply opposed to passively submitting to fate. For me the ideal is to master fate, to steer the ship of life through the storms of existence and by overcoming doubts, to develop the energy to pass on one's own convictions to others.

Goodbye my beautiful and fearless child, you my life's holiest pride. Tomorrow we begin our trip through the Black Sea.[401]

[8 July 1912] I am surprised how well you have been able to discern the unspoken and unmentioned aspects of my mother. I owe her care and my outlook on life. She is responsible for the fact that I ignore small life problems and that my heart yearns for higher ideals. I often wonder whether I can fulfil the expectations you have for your life's partner. I am not at all convinced of my excellence. Is it weak and unmanly to feel, or unwise to admit this? I am looking for truth and have no interest in crowning myself with false feathers.[402]

Counseling Anne-Marie about doubts and mood swings, Rose appears to share self-realizations:

[25 July 1912] I read your letters not just once, but many times and wonder about every word's meaning. I don't think this is difficult to decipher because throughout my life I have been able to understand people so well that I often handle subordinates too leniently as the mischief they make seems to be understandable and forgivable. It is particularly easy to understand your thoughts because we are soul mates. (I often have the impression that there is a kind of telepathy between us, though my reason resists this belief.) If a clear and rationally thinking person like you succumbs to mood swings, these are the result not only of longing, but also of uncertainty. You ask yourself whether it would not have been better to postpone the decision about our life together from last Easter to my return from the East, when in fact you primarily doubt yourself. I do not want to criticize these doubts, because they are the mark of a deeper, thorough, sincere and transparent nature. Why, Mara, do I have to cause you these sorrows? Can't one love each other without pain? I guess not. If the dark thoughts outweigh light ones, let me know. (And when I then read: 'Haro, I am still so young, I cannot solve these problems, let me live the way I have in the past,' then I will bow in silence to your wish and my esteem for you will not be diminished. We will have to fight to the limits of our capacities, in order to achieve the summit of happiness.) What a wonderful custom of the past, when the maiden gave the knight a rose after a successful jousting match. Today one fights with words and money. (A pathetic shopkeeper's existence.) My life has been enriched by you, Mara. Please write soon.[403]

[4 & 11 August 1912] We are, once again, more or less home and I am happy to find a letter from you in which you write: 'As a person from Schleswig-Holstein forever undaunted'. That will be the motto for our life together. A thousand thanks. I am so proud of you. You inquire about my family. We have frequently intermarried... I have often thought about bloodlines and used to believe that tradition and intermarriage was a good thing and for that reason had a high opinion of the aristocracy. Unfortunately, I had to re-assess these opinions, because I have met many representatives of aristocratic families, who are proof that intermarriage does not [guarantee] a higher spiritual, intellectual or moral level. I am sorry to make this discovery. I am proud of my family and want to make sure that the name that you will carry in the future will retain its reputation.[404]

[October 1912] That you are planning to take cooking lessons is a good idea. Men have the obligation to do their duty with the utmost conscientiousness; a wife has to know how to cook well and how to apply this knowledge... Though our ideals are not centred on the cook-pot, the stove is the foundation from which thoughts and feelings can rise to the heavens.[405]

On the home front, Rose's letters demonstrate his romantic ideal of motherhood. He worships the mother's role and declares his objective to live up to the standards his mother set for him. He references hearth and home as anchors for happiness and culture. In contrast to the traditional Muslim belief in predestination, Rose is modern in his unwillingness to accept fate and to struggle against it at all turns. The happier man distinguishes when it is productive to struggle with life from when it is not – perhaps the meaning of 'Inshallah' or 'God willing'. Rose appears to believe that he has no intrinsic right to happiness.

In the Land of the Cossacks

At the start of the 20th century, the Black Sea coastline was divided roughly in half with the northern half subject to the Russian Empire and the southern portion possession of the Ottoman Empire. Between 16 June and 4 August 1912 *Loreley* made its annual clockwise circumnavigations of the Black Sea, visiting ports and German communities of importance along the way. The first stop was cosmopolitan Odessa, the fourth largest city in the Russian Empire, described by the great Russian poet Alexander Pushkin as a city where 'the air is filled with all Europe, French is spoken and there are European papers and magazines to read.'[406]

The Germans we got to know here live like royalty. Most of them have a *datcha* or country house, situated on a steep bank with wonderful views over the deep blue sea... Most of the dinners start with caviar accompanied by lots of drinking, Russian style. The annual appearance of *Loreley* is viewed as the high point of the 'summer season' in Odessa. Most dinners are followed by a few hours of strolling through whatever park we were visiting, yet by midnight everyone is once again at the table ... until the heavens begin to turn rose colored. Evening after evening and night after night, this spectacle repeated itself. In the morning I took a tour of the historical museum with the well-informed wife of the German Consul... You want to hear more about Odessa? The city is modern and therefore architecturally uninteresting. In comparison to Cospoli, it is a world city... The contrast between rich and poor is magnified – and one finds drunks lying in the streets day and night – Terrible.[407]

Rose has little to say about *Loreley*'s second port of call, Nikolajev (present-day Mykolaiv in the Ukraine), which was the largest ship-building port in the Russian Empire, its third largest port in volume of foreign trade:

One gets to Nikolajev on the river Bug, which flows through fields of very fertile grain... The grain surplus of Russia's southern provinces is immense. Tax and other matters in Russia are complicated.... But everyone agrees that Germans are very well treated by the Russians, because they can protect themselves from encroachment through official diplomatic channels.[408] We were greeted with open arms... The unlimited kindness we were shown was not for us as men, but for our flag, of which every German travelling in a foreign country is very proud.[409]

By 4 July 1912, *Loreley* had reached Sevastopol on the Crimean Peninsula, home base of the Russian Empire's Black Sea Fleet:

The Russian fleet, close to which we are moored, makes a good impression. It seems as though they work hard. The same goes for the army. I regret that they have been so easily beaten by the Japanese. In a potential fight with the Turks (probably over Constantinople), the Sultan's troops will be defeated, just as the Russians were by the Japanese.[410]

Leaving the Black Sea, *Loreley* passes through the four-kilometre Kersh Strait and enters the shallow Sea of Azov for a brief visit to the heavily industrialized city of Rostov in the Ukraine, the 'City of Thieves'. Rose was struck by the city's frontier lawlessness and proposed a modern, liberal solution:

In Rostow all mail and bank transfers are protected by ten Cossacks with drawn bayonets and revolvers... In the last year alone, thirty robbers stormed the bank and after stuffing the money into sacks, disappeared into the mountains of the Caucasus... One asks oneself, how Russia, this empire of unlimited opportunities, can be healed? The cancer, it seems to me, is graft. This kind of illness cannot be conquered by penalties, the healing has to come from within – through education.[411]

Loreley then returned to the Black Sea and anchored in Novorossiysk. On 15 July *Loreley* became the first warship to visit Gagri, the almost feudal domain of Duke Alexander Petrovich of Oldenburg who was transforming the town into a resort for the well-heeled:

We arrived in Gagri about 11 a.m. and anchored a hundred metres away from land... there was a celebratory breakfast with a thousand vodkas, ten thousand 'hurrahs' and Russian and French national anthems; as well as young, very pretty girls as observers in the galleries. After this [reception], we sank into the waiting automobiles to survey the surroundings... In the evening there was, to use an interesting expression, a 'reunion'. The air, the atmosphere, the conversation was Russian and sultry.

...It is the first time that a warship calls at the small principality. The seventy-year-old prince is not present but maintains scrupulous order in his domain... People who do not obey are beaten and then taken to the boat landing, where any passing ship is stopped by cannon fire and the evildoer removed... Sunday morning we had a large cocktail on board ... and in the afternoon the surgeon and I went riding with a Cossack officer... It is surprising how skilful these small steeds are... I must admit that I am not a very competent rider.

...The next day we first rode through a landscape that looked like Thuringia, then through beech woods and finally through jungle... Suddenly the Lieutenant who was riding up front called something and a Cossack behind me jumped off his horse and squeezed past me with a drawn sabre. A whirring slash and the body of a snake hung from a branch, while its severed head with poisonous fangs flew a few metres away. Contentedly, the bloody sabre was wiped in the grass... The Cossacks made a huge fire and skewered lamb on to spits... We ate these delicacies with radishes and cucumbers, as well as bread and butter... We joined the Cossacks for a toast of wine poured into goblets consisting of rolled-up leaves. They threw us up into the air after saying 'thanks', a tribute which was as unexpected as it was impressive. No wonder it was difficult to return to the musty life of the resort town.[412]

Rose has little to say about *Loreley*'s last three ports of call, Batum, Tiflis, and Sinope, prior to her return to Therapia from her Black Sea circumnavigation. A rail-line linking Batum on the Black Sea with land-locked Tiflis and Baku on the eastern shore of the Caspian Sea began in 1883 and was completed in 1900. Apparently Rose took the train to Tiflis:

I don't know much about Batum, the ancient junction of the Levantine trade. Here the oil lines that lead from the Caspian Sea over the Caucasus to the Black Sea end... We stayed only a day and went on to Tiflis, which is Asiatic, and made up of many different races. It is a colorless city, covered by dust and fog that nearly obliterates the sunlight... Sulphur baths provide some respite after the heat of the day... Unfortunately, I was unable to visit the German settlements for lack of time... And Sinope too, is not worth mentioning. The only important landmark of this town of 3,000 souls is a huge decaying castle with high walls and inner courtyards that are presently used as a cemetery. It is the palace of Mithridates, the King of Pontus, who was an enemy of the Romans... It was so hot in Sinope that my excursion with the crew had to be prematurely terminated... and a Greek doctor whom we met in a café groaned with boredom in this awful hole.[413]

Earthquake

At 03:29 a.m. on 9 August 1912, five days after *Loreley*'s return to Therapia, the magnitude 7.3 Mürefte earthquake struck just north of the Sea of Marmara causing widespread damage in northwest Turkey, and as far afield as Greece and Bulgaria. Several days later Rose wrote to Anne-Marie that the German *Kaiser* was concerned:

> Yesterday a telegram from the *Kaiser* to the Ambassador was received inquiring: 'What is happening in the sea of Marmara?' The Ambassador responded by telegram: 'Deployment of *Loreley* desirable.' In Gallipoli, in Rodosto, in Myriophyto it is reported that people are fighting for a drink of water or a piece of bread. That may be exaggerated, but we will of course be happy to help with our presence.[414]

Soon after receiving the *Kaiser*'s telegram, *Loreley*, packed with relief supplies, quickly departed Constantinople on its mission of mercy.

> The sound of timpani and monotonous singing drifted across to us. Many thousands of voices were heard praising Allah, the Highest, in this holy month of Ramadan and fasting. A beguiling scent of oriental flowers wafted across from the Sultan's gardens at the tip of the Serail. The cypress forests emitted the buzzing, chirping and humming of vibrant nature. Above us the 'Big Dipper', the sinking half moon, the symbol of the Turkish empire, was reflected in the windows of the Hagia Sofia... Slowly Stambul, the fairy-tale city of *A Thousand and One Nights* disappeared from our view and thoughts.[415]

Down the northeastern coast of the Sea of Marmara, *Loreley*'s first stop was Rodosto, which had been largely spared by the initial quake though it would soon be devastated by the massive aftershock on 13 September: 'The destruction at Rodosto, where we arrived the next morning, was not great. We left some clothes and food for the injured on land.'[416] Travelling westward along the coast, *Loreley*'s next stop was Garos:

> In Garos the destruction was much worse. Boats rowed towards us and a huge number of people were waiting on shore. More people arrived on mules. The Greeks rowed us through the high surf without our getting wet and we were pulled over the rocky shore by a hundred men shouting cries of joy.
>   The small town was a pile of debris, below which many dead were still lying. Handfuls of earth had been placed where the dead were thought to lie, thus providing them with a traditional burial. Most of the survivors had bruised faces and bandaged limbs.
>   We left many sacks of food, canisters of water, woollen blankets and clothes, explaining that they had been sent by the German *Kaiser*. One of the men mistakenly explained to his compatriots: 'Oh, King George.' People thought we were British. It was not easy to correct the mistake, because I did not know the Greek words for '*Kaiser* Wilhelm' and 'German'. However, we finally managed to explain.[417]

Loreley travelled westward to Hora, Myriophyto and Sarkioi:

The next place we visited was Hora. Here the destruction was even worse. Many of the inhabitants were dead or badly wounded. There was not a single house which was still inhabitable. We left many provisions. On our return through the surf, we got soaked.

In Myriophyto the Kamaikam (District Governor) came out to meet us in a small boat. The surf was high and the boat danced up and down. The Kamaikam prayed to Allah over and over again. Then, suddenly two sailor fists grabbed him by the arms and pulled him on deck. On feeling his back, he noticed that he had gotten a huge tear in his pants. With the inbred dignity of the Osmans, he ignored the situation. Next morning some boats came to pick up the designated provisions.

In Sarkioi, because the little town lies behind a small headland, we found a relatively favourable landing place. We discussed their situation in a large tent with the doctors, religious and other dignitaries. Of the 1,280 houses, 1,000 were destroyed by the quake and 200 by fire, only 81 were still inhabitable. There were large numbers of dead and injured. People were angry at the Turkish government that had sent nothing but a single Turkish doctor. Some houses looked strange, because their roofs were completely preserved, while their horizontal cornerstones had disappeared. The church had lost its walls, but the ceiling was still intact and the eternal flame burned in front of the altar... The bell had crashed with its tower, but got caught in the branches of two trees and continued to call the believers to prayers. God gives and God takes away. Blessed be the name of the Lord. To see a whole city in ruin and to realize that this was the result of a few seconds, is truly shattering.[418]

Her relief supplies exhausted, *Loreley* continued west passing through the Dardanelles and on to Thassos and Salonika in the Aegean Sea:

After we had dispersed all of our provisions, we raised anchor and set sail for the Dardanelles. We passed Aigospotamoi, where the Spartans beat Athenians, as well as Gallipoli and passed Bbydos and Sestos. I saw the place where Leander swam over to Hero and mentally planted the tower at the most beautiful spot of the European coast, the Tower of Hero, from whose recessed alcove the call arose: 'And to the remote shores beyond, his be the star that shines throughout the night.'

It was a beautiful evening when we followed a Turkish torpedo boat through the narrows... In a cloudless sky Mount Athos was visible in the north, thirty nautical miles away. It was a calamity to many seafarers. The fleet of the Persian King Darius, in his first strike against Greece, found its demise here.[419]

In September, returning to Constantinople from Salonika, *Loreley* moored on the south coast of the Sea of Marmara to visit the inland city of Bursa. It had been an extraordinary year for a young, classically educated naval officer; replete with all the Victorian luxuries that a consular posting could offer. But *Loreley*'s visit to Mudania and Rose's calls aboard the German battle-cruiser *Goeben* and the British Cruiser *Hampshire* in late December 1912 coincided with changes in the political situation with which the Ottoman Empire and soon the rest of the world must contend. The hurricane of war was about to erupt, and Rose, aboard *Loreley*, had already begun to sail into it.

Chapter 9

The Gathering Storm

The Ottoman Empire was at war when Hans Rose arrived in Constantinople in May 1912. As his year there progressed his letters to Anne-Marie were increasingly peppered with military observations and the possibility that he and Germany might be drawn into the conflagration.

Three regional conflicts, all fought over the disintegrating Ottoman Empire, are the immediate precursors to WWI. The Turco-Italian War had entered its eighth month when Rose arrived in Constantinople. The ease with which the Italians defeated the Ottoman troops in Libya encouraged the growth of nationalism in the Ottoman Empire's Balkan provinces. Before the war ended the members of the Balkan League would launch their own attacks against the Empire initiating the First Balkan War. That war resulted in the loss of the Empire's second most important metropolis, Salonika, the conquest of almost all of its European territories and their partition among League members. Then, just as Rose was completing his posting to Constantinople, the Second Balkan War began. Bulgaria, unhappy with the previous war's partition of the Ottoman spoils, attacked Greece and Serbia. Seeing an opportunity, Romania invaded Bulgaria and marched on Sofia while the Ottoman Empire recaptured territory previously lost in Eastern Thrace.

Rose's first reference to the descent into military conflagration came in a letter to Anne-Marie written two weeks after his arrival in Constantinople. It described the battle in Libya between the Ottoman Empire and Italy and the interruption

GERMAN EMBASSY
AT THERAPIA [Author's
Archive]

of commercial shipping in the Dardanelles. In it he shared the attitude of one of the German officers who was helping train the Turkish military:

> One of the German Reform officers praised his Turkish officer cadets, yet in spite of this he commented on their lack of personal initiative and regretted the vulnerability of their sense of honour. The Turk loves his 'Kheef' – inaction. Their initiative and forceful action have been eradicated in the course of hundreds of years of despotism... Yesterday a Lieutenant from Saxony, who had been in Tripoli, where he fought on the side of the Turks against the Italians, visited us aboard. He noted that the Italians cannot make any headway because they are opposed by ruthless Arabs, who are paid fifty piasters by the Turks... We notice that a war is in progress by the interruption of ship traffic. Yesterday about two hundred ships were waiting for the opening of the Dardanelles. Today the Bosporus and the Golden Horn are virtually empty because the ships left for the Sea of Marmara from which they will sail for the Hellespont, which will be opened the day after tomorrow.[420]

But the war was far away and Rose's perspective was still a matter of strategy and tactics. In August he told Anne-Marie:

> The Turkish fleet was moored in Nagara with, constituting the nucleus, two ships of the 'Brandenburg Class' we sold to the Turks a number of years ago. One could imagine having arrived in Wilhelmshaven when the two well-known ships became visible. Close by there were a few torpedo boats, also German-made. If the Turks could decide to mount a sea attack the face of the [Italo-Turkish] war might change completely. Neither the Turks nor their Italian opponents can decide whether to engage in a sea attack. In a war nothing is worse than half measures. If the impressive defences at Tschanak were reinforced with some additional batteries the Dardanelles would at present be unassailable.[421]

In October, Rose embraced the idea of Ottoman military dictatorship while writing to Anne-Marie about the possibility of a European conflagration that could draw Germany and himself into battle:

> Just now Commander Count Welsersheim of Austria left the ship, informing us that Serbia and Bulgaria are mobilizing against Turkey... Since most of our food comes from Bulgaria, we will have to expect price increases... Greek ships have been captured by the Turks and suddenly travel under Russian or French flags... North of Therapia spotlights search the Bosporus at night. I don't believe this will turn into a conflagration involving the whole world... The Turkish government is powerless against the Albanian insurrection. Their troops have gone over to the side of the rebels... A return to a toppled absolutism is impossible and a constitution of the West European kind is impossible to conceive, consequently only a kind of military dictatorship seems possible... In my opinion Germany should support this solution... Will there really be war? Macedonian autonomy will surely be granted by the Turks in the near future, so why go to war? However, the peoples of the Orient have less than we and consequently less to lose in a war... The war enthusiasm of the Osmani people is not great, as evidenced by our Jewish manservant, Jacob,

for whom I was able to arrange German citizenship. The Serbs have just declared war and have invaded Turkish territory near Adrianople. That will bring the Bulgarians into the fray... I do not believe that this war will spread to Europe.[422]

Rose's letter continued:

Now we have war. One notices it everywhere and the arriving wounded demonstrate that the news about fighting at Adrianople is true... I spent a few hours in Istanbul and had the impression that 'war is a terrible and savage business'... We, Mara, will always prepare ourselves for war but will be happy if we need not engage in murder.[423]

Rescuing the Sultan

On 26 October 1912 the German Ambassador in Constantinople received a request from the Sublime Porte to rescue the Ex-Sultan Abdülhamid II from Salonika and return him to Istanbul. Four days before, the Greek Army of Thessaly had broken through the centre of the Ottoman lines and the beaten 8th Provisional Corps had retreated into the confines of the city.

Loreley's Captain von Arnim asserts that the rescue of the sultan was a secret affair negotiated by the German ambassador. Since the mission might have political consequences *Loreley* was to claim that it was concerned with the situation in Salonika:[424]

After a conversation with Military Attaché Major von Strempel we consulted with Nodadunghian Effendi who was in charge of the Dardanelles to request that *Loreley* be permitted to pass through without the usual permission and health clearance requirements. I was also advised to proceed to the Palais Dolma Bagdache and to consult with his Majesty's Chamberlain... [At] 5 a.m. 27 October 1912 we set sail for the Sea of Marmara. Next day the Osmanian Lloyd published a notice that *Loreley* had left for Rodosto carrying Red Cross supplies. Though we arrived at the entrance to the Dardanelles without difficulties around 6 p.m., three issues complicated our passage: the southern lights on Nagara Huk had been dimmed, its shallow waters were treacherous and warning shots rang out, which forced *Loreley* to enter the crowded bay to negotiate with the guard ship.[425]

Captain von Arnim observed here, as so often in the past: 'The Turkish officials promised more than they ever had any intention to deliver and ... it is not the [Turkish] government but Abdülhamid II's court that is interested in his rescue.'[426]

Lacking a pilot there were more delays and the final mine blockade was traversed in convoy. Several days later, after traversing the Aegean Sea *Loreley* steamed up the Thermaic Gulf and anchored in Salonika's harbour at 6 a.m. on 29 October.

Conditions in the large cosmopolitan city were tense. As the Ottoman troops retreated into Salonika panic began to set in among the majority Jewish Ottoman population. Many of the great powers, having consulates and expatriate communities in the city, had sent cruisers to calm their nationals and to prepare if necessary for evacuation:

Immediately after our arrival Captain von Arnim left the ship to consult with the German Consul and obtain information about the political situation. Though [the former] was absent the Vice-consul Dr. Schwörbel had received a telegram warning of a strong political backlash against Abdülhamid II... Meanwhile, the city of Salonika was in dire military straits. It was overrun by thousands of wounded and 30,000 refugees from the surrounding countryside who were camping on the streets and squares. The Vice Consul was concerned not only that a battle might be fought in the vicinity of the city but also that the German colony was looking for safe passage on *Loreley*. Yet a delay implied dangers for the sultan's rescue. The intention to call on the *Geier* to help the Germans had to be abandoned because the Turkish authorities forbid the sending of coded messages...

On the same evening Arif Hikmet Pasha informed [the Captain] that his Royal Highness would come aboard at 10 a.m. next day, 30 October 1912.[427]

On 31 October, the day before *Loreley* departed, the Greek Navy appeared outside the harbour, further contributing to the panic. During the night of 1 November a Greek torpedo boat entered Salonika harbour and torpedoed the Turkish corvette *Fethi Bülent* killing six crewmen. 'The Turkish gunship *Fethi Bülent* had been anchored right beside us. How would history have been changed if we had followed the Consul's request to remain for another night?'[428]

Captain von Arnim noted that in comparison to 1901, when he had met him for the first time, His Imperial Majesty the ex-Sultan Abdülhamid II, seventy years old at the time, looked relatively healthy and well. But the overall impression was one of a depressed and worried old man, an effect reinforced by his awkward behaviour and emotional tone: the Sultan 'pressed my hand in the companionway and asked me to thank the German *Kaiser* for the way in which he had taken care of his health'.[429]

Ending a relatively uneventful return trip to Constantinople, *Loreley* delivered Abdülhamid II to the Palace of Beylerbeyi where, still under house arrest, he spent his last four years with his nine sons and seven daughters.

A Mixture of Dream and Reality

Page eighty-nine of Hans Rose's autobiographical account of his year in Constantinople contains a 'note to the reader':

The description of the *Life of the Men of the Port Side* has, up to now, been based strictly on the facts... Though some of the opinions described might have been mistaken, it is exactly these mistakes that are interesting for the reader who reads these lines a few decades later... We will now interrupt Haro's account with another, a short story entitled *Under the Spell of the Levant*, based on a mixture of dream and reality.[430]

A short, semi-fictional story, based upon the rescue of the Sultan, it begins:

The young sea officer, Haro Sens stood thoughtfully at the quay of the Tophane Turkish Bosporus Steamship Company. The sun radiated from a cloudless summer sky on to the Golden Horn off to the right, where local kaiks, steam and sail ships were busily traversing the waters so that ships from all nations anchored in the Bosporus could receive or exchange their cargoes. It was a colourful, forever changing picture, full of life. The far side of the Golden Horn lay shrouded in the morning haze. The minarets and domes of the many mosques rose out of the crush of small wooden houses of Istanbul. Dark, straight cypresses and overhanging plantain trees reinforced the contrast between light and shade. The promontory with the old seraglio of the Sultan projected far into the Marmara Sea, seeming to dream about the past... Even today, in the year 1912, the fate of the Osman Empire was once again in jeopardy. The Italians were advancing in Tripoli where they were trying to conquer sections of North Africa from the Turks, and the peoples of the Balkans were arming to lay their hands on European portions of Turkey... How will the European super powers react, the young Sens wonders? Will they passively stand by? And what role will we be playing ourselves, we who are supposed to protect the people of the German embassy with our small ship *Loreley*?[431]

As the story unfolds, young Haro Sens travels to the old Turkish city of Brussa where he meets an ageing goldsmith, Ahmed Selih, who bemoans the loss of his thirteenth child, Senieh. The goldsmith explains that years before Senieh, 'the most beautiful and the smartest of them all', had been seized from him.

A few years ago men came to Brussa, who saw the growing girl and wanted me to give her up. I demurred, because Senieh was the sun of my old age... Yet, there was no way to prevail against them, because they had been sent by those in power. They said that refusal entailed exile for me and my family. Moreover they said Senieh would be well taken care of... I had to submit. The only thing I was able to give her as a keepsake, was a golden work of jewelry that I had made in happier times. It consisted of twelve little sapphires [representing the twelve other children] encircling a beautiful diamond... I gave it to her ... with the admonition to keep it sacred because 'It will bring you luck. Wear it and when you feel your highest happiness is achieved give it to the person who is offering you salvation. Then the blessing of Allah will be with you to the ends of your life.' I gave what was most precious to me and the men gave me a bag of gold in return. Is that compensation?... Slowly he continued: 'It is four years since my child left and I have never heard from her again. However, night after night Senieh appears to my soul as she was then'... The old man fell silent and counted his prayer beads.[432]

A number of weeks pass in Rose's 'mixture of dream and reality', and the realities of the First Balkan War drive the memory of the old man and his beautiful daughter out of Haro's mind, to be replaced by orders that *Loreley* travel to Salonika to pick up the ex-Sultan Abdülhamid II. One evening as *Loreley* sails towards Istanbul with the Sultan and his entourage, Haro encounters a nameless member of the harem whom he christens 'Hera'. Night after night, the young officer and the beautiful harem girl meet in secret, talking. 'Tender bridges of mutual understanding [grow] between the two young people.' On the last night of the voyage Haro and the lovely Hera, 'enraptured ... yield ... to the overflowing current of irresistible, timeless feeling'. The next morning when Haro awakes Hera has departed. Returning desolate to his cabin his eyes alight upon a 'small, glittering item'. It is a sparkling diamond, surrounded by small sapphires. 'Oh, Hera... you are Sanieh from Brussa.' Tragedy intercedes, and the two young lovers are not fated to meet again. If the tale reflects Rose's psyche, it can be interpreted as wish-fulfillment, the wish to be considered a saviour; albeit, one resulting from a set of external events, not by the protagonist's choice.

While the story of the goldsmith and his lovely daughter Senieh is fiction, it is set within the context of the rescue of Abdülhamid II. Presumably this is the 'reality' portion of the 'mixture'. If so, it provides us with an intimate picture of the ex-sultan and of *Loreley*'s return voyage carrying him to safety:

> *Loreley* was well suited for the task, for it had not only comfortable oak-lined commander's quarters, but also a tastefully furnished salon and a pretty sleeping cabin for the Ambassador and his wife. Haro's cabin was situated close-by... *Loreley* anchored in the harbour of Salonika... The crew was told that the Sultan would arrive at 10 o'clock next morning in *Loreley*'s life boats. The Sultan was the first to alight from the row boat and being suspicious, asked two of his retinue to climb up the rope ladder before him to test its strength. He and his party then settled in the prepared spaces. Three disgusting, bloated, cross-legged Eunuchs guarded the entrance to the mess that had been turned into a Harem.
>
> The Sultan himself usually spent his days at the companionway, where he smoked cigarettes and talked to his Turkish gentlemen. Occasionally he would play with his cute eight-year-old son, Prince Abbik, or the comical bear 'Albrecht'. He was seventy years old at the time and a frail old man, but had intelligent and agile eyes. He wore European but shabby clothes and a red Fez. He was friendly and depending on his knowledge of the topic, talkative. Of the twelve Harem ladies, the Germans officially saw nothing. Only the doctor was requested to attend to one of them, a rather corpulent one who had rheumatism.[433]

Following a description of Haro's fictional meeting with 'Hera', Rose's presumably factual account continues:

> The Sultan talked to Haro at length and told him about his daughter who had been operated on years ago by Professor Bergmann. When Haro inquired whether he had seen his daughter recently he answered haltingly in French: 'No, I never saw her again' and after a pause 'It is my destiny.' He inquired about the military and political situation and asked Haro for his fountain pen to make some notes... A Eunuch interfered stating that his Highness was not used to this and produced a quill and ink...
>
> Suddenly a group of three [Greek] destroyers led by *Nike* headed straight for *Loreley*, their guns were manned and the torpedoes swung out ready for action. The Turks were sent below and [we] broke out the colours of the German Imperial Navy at the gaff, upon which the Greeks turned tail and left.

... Dinner was served in the commanders' mess for the Turkish gentlemen... The Sultan's chef prepared Pilaf, the national dish, with lots of grease, which was not quite to the German's liking.[434]

Then, after another imaginary but blissful encounter between the fictional Haro Sens and the lovely Senieh, Rose again takes up the realities of the voyage of *Loreley*. On the final morning, 'The lighthouse's beams from Serail Point reached out for the ship... A half hour later, they anchored in front of the burned out Tschiragan Palace.'[435] Looking into the sun, across *Loreley*'s deck, Rose noticed the Sultan at prayer and snapped a photo:

There was the Sultan kneeling on his prayer rug, with his face turned toward Mecca... It was an embarrassing picture, because the woollen socks of the grandee were full of holes and the flannel shirt underneath his vest was patched. Haro was disgusted by the Turkish government's neglect of its previously omnipotent ruler of all 'True Believers'. He turned away and looked out over the sun-filled waters of the Bosporus. What kinds of secrets did these waters and its surrounding land hide? ... Birds sailed, fast as arrows above, each of them carrying the soul of a deceased.

A sailor knocked on the door: 'The boats are coming to pick up the Sultan.' The baggage of the Turkish guests has been loaded. The gentlemen from the retinue were conveyed into *Loreley*'s cutter, while the domestic staff followed in the baggage boat. Six ladies ... the two Eunuchs and the remaining participants entered the second Turkish ship... Haro helped the Sultan and his little son with their descent, followed by five ladies [and] the head Eunuch.[436]

Mission accomplished. The Order of the Majedia was presented to Rose by the Sultan of Turkey 'for services rendered in the War between Greece and Turkey';[437] presumably for the rescue of the ex-Sultan.

Mankind Deserves a Substantial Bloodletting

At the end of 1912 refugees were pouring into Constantinople as the First Balkan War drew to a close. The front contested with the invading Bulgarians was less than twenty miles west of the city. Rose encountered the misery of the refugees but waxed Darwinian about their fate:

The Bosporus is full of different nation's war-ships, an unusual picture. The European inhabitants who were worried about being massacred, calmed down. Complications among the major powers are not to be expected. Though the confrontation between Austria and Serbia could become serious there is no cause for alarm concerning the outbreak of a World War unless uncertainty leads to a loss of judgment. If that becomes the case, mankind deserves a substantial bloodletting. Though we don't want to provoke any dangers, they do not grow larger from talking about them... It is important that one observes and analyses them carefully... The Turks gave up their position without Bulgaria's doing anything, because the soldiers found it intolerable to remain in the trenches in the rain without food, even though there were herds of cattle near the battlefield and flour was plentiful... Both leaders as well as followers lack decision-making capabilities. According to the reformers, the relatively well-trained troops were demobilized and transferred to the reserves just before the outbreak of war... Officers lack a conception of responsibility for their troops, which provides the foundation for discipline in any army... I assume that the Bulgarians will first lay siege and conquer Adrianople and then aim to break through to the Golden Horn. Salonika has fallen without a blow... Our embassy has been turned into a hospital under the leadership of our ship's doctor. He is working devotedly and I rarely see him, although I have requested his presence on board to tell us what to do in case of a cholera outbreak...

This afternoon I walked over the Stambul bridge to soak up the golden beauty of the sunset... I went to see the Hagia Sophia that was supposedly blown up according to the Western press. No Osman would have undertaken such a deed. They don't go in for violent acts... In the garden of the Ahmed mosque there was wagon upon wagon of refugees pressed together, animals and people in close quarters... They all left their houses, driven by hunger and deprivation... Should one feel worry for them? Should their fate arouse pity? Doubtlessly, it is moving to witness the disintegration of a great empire. But that is what life is all about. The powerful win. The weak, the spineless perish... The dignified, high-minded Osman people, previously a warrior nation, have given up fighting... They are awaiting their destiny, whatever that may be.[438]

A week later, *Loreley* was posted to guard duty in Haidar Pascha on the Asian shore of the Bosporus. Cholera had broken out and the sound of artillery could be heard in the distance. Rose was struck by the juxtaposition of conditions confronting the Ottoman troops, refugees and commoners on the one hand, and the Empire's elite along with the gun-boat-guarded nationals of the *Grandes Puissances* on the other.

We are moored on the Asiatic coast to protect the Anatolian Railroad. If we had not been here protection might have been necessary, but since we are here we are not expecting any unrest. The refugees are happy if one leaves them alone... The artillery of the Tschataldscha line is easily heard and the troops have, in fact, contracted cholera... The men are dying like flies... Since Cospoli receives its drinking water from Derkosse, which is on the left flank of the battlefield, there are worries that the epidemic will infect the capital's population. The Bulgarians too are said to be suffering from the cholera. The Rumanians and Serbs are increasing their demands and their language toward Austria is haughty. The Bulgarians will soon attempt to make peace to avoid the other Balkan nations from interfering.

The directors of the Anatolian Railroad invited us to a champagne breakfast this morning to thank us for protecting their rail line. What kind of a world are we living in? Inside we are feasting in the magnificent spacious station building, while outside the refugee families are in rags and gnawing at bread rinds. The warships of the *Grandes Puissances* are floating In the Bosporus, colourfully decorated with flags for the Beiram celebration. In Stambul the soldiers with cholera are wrestling with their illness. In the Legation quarter the crews of the Western powers strut in smart uniforms protecting the local Europeans, while the battle thunder of two nations that are fighting for their lives resents everything that is happening. Is that fate? Is that right? Is that heartlessness or stupidity? One has a bitter taste in the mouth and shakes one's head.[439]

As 1912 drew to a close Rose summed up the ominous geopolitical situation left by the First Balkan War, concluding with a personal commitment:

What has been going on in this large world of ours during the last year? Morocco has been divided between France and Spain. Italy has conquered Cyrenaica and Lybia. Persia has been divided into Russian and British 'spheres of influence'. The Balkan Federation reduced the Turkish influence in Europe. In a word, almost everywhere the Islamic nations have lost their sovereignty... In the summer the major powers concentrated their interest on the Balkan states... The latter created a Federation (despite hundreds of years of enmity) and were able to keep it a secret from the whole world; a huge diplomatic victory. The Federation's purpose is to free their nations from the yoke of Muslim religious influences and to expel the Turks from Europe. At the last minute, Austria tried to put together a Major Power conference in order to control developments. The plan failed on Poincaré's objection. By the time the ambassadors agreed to cooperate, they were too late. Two hours earlier ... Montenegro had declared war on Turkey. A few days later, the Balkan states that were part of the Federation against Turkey followed with their declarations of war.

In the rush of events the Serbs conquered everything before them and reached the Adriatic at Durazzo... In the space of one month, the Balkan Federation's war plans were largely achieved. On 3 December 1912 all members except Greece signed a truce with Turkey and peace discussions began in London on 16 December 1912. Austria fared the worst of all Western nations. Its search for access to the sea has not been successful but rather permanently blocked. What next? At the end of the year one has to admit that the future does not look bright. The Balkan war, which is not finished, has clarified some issues and rectified some injustices. However, by and large the tensions have not been reduced. We cannot change these situations. We will do our duties and enter the New Year with eyes wide open, hoping it will bring us the fulfilment of our wishes.[440]

As 1913 dawned Rose bemoaned the ineffectiveness of half-hearted action, be it military or diplomatic, and recorded the outbreak of the Second Balkan War:

The delegates of both sides are taking their time in London... Vanity plays an important role among the leaders who have to decide on the fates of nations. It is also depressing to notice how 'high' diplomacy makes guesses and floats, instead of making decisions... While the warring parties continue to negotiate in London the Turkish fleet has decided to act and left the Dardanelles setting a course for Tenedos... The Greek fleet immediately left the Budros Bay with the battleship *Georgios Aweroff* in the lead, followed by *Hydra*, steering a southerly course. The Turks too turned south, with the *Medjidie* attaching itself to the battleships. Fire was opened at a distance of 9,000 metres and both sides concentrated on the key ships. After a half-hour battle, the Turkish fleet turned away from the enemy, with the Greeks following ... ending up about 7,000 metres distant from each other... I was unable to find out anything about the outcome because the wounded I consulted had dropped out [before the end]... The destruction on the Turkish ships was negligible... In all they incurred thirty dead and ninety-three wounded. And that is called a 'sea battle?' – No, it was nothing more than a tickle... Neither partner was really willing to engage.[441]

As imperial norms continued to fray, the military situation was deteriorating. Rose was witness to the unravelling of the Ottoman government. When its willingness to sacrifice Adrianople led to popular outrage the Young Turks movement seized additional power. On 24 January 1913 Rose wrote:

> Yesterday afternoon a cavalcade under the leadership of Enver Bey burst onto the 'High Portal'. Enver jumped out and rushed to the building with a few men. Some shots were heard and Enver returned with his faithful. What had happened? The War Minister Nazim Pascha and his adjutant had been shot, which led to the resignation of the Cabinet... Enver returned with the news that Mohamud Schewket Pascha would become Grand Vizier... This morning ... I drove to the Sultan's reception and waited with a number of other guests in the shade of the Dolmabagt Mosque's plantain trees. We were of course talking about the events of the previous afternoon when we saw an equipage drawn by two trotting black horses arrive. Enver alighted with his sabre rattling... After ten minutes more equipages arrived. Old Sultan Mehmed V, who looks rather puffy, emerged laboriously from the most beautiful carriage... No wonder the hot-blooded Arab nations do not wish to recognize the over-aged Sultan of Turkey as their 'Calif'.[442]

On 26 January a reception by the Director of the Anatolian Railroad became the venue for fiery German nationalism, and a call to arms:

> Last night there was a grand reception at (the mansion) of the Director of the Anatolian Railroad. About thirty people, from the Embassy, Navy, Finance, Consul General and the Reformers were present. The host, a well-read and knowledgeable man, made a fiery speech, primarily directed at us sea officers. He noted the demands that would be placed on our shoulders in the future, saying: 'Germany's honour is placed in your hands. Keep it safe! It will fall with you and will arise with you once more!' The speech finished with a 'hail' to Germany and the *Kaiser*... For us sea officers it implied the tacit renewal of a vow made a long time ago. On the morning of 27 January 1913 everyone in full dress or gala uniform came together in the Embassy and proceeded to church. An impressive picture... The preacher presented an important sermon for peace... He was probably trying to counteract the presence of so many colourful uniforms. The whole city was decked out in wafting German flags. It was impressive but perhaps also a bit insistent and provocative... We want peace but our expectation as professional officers is complete sacrifice in case our nation [takes up arms]. I am ready. This readiness is the foundation of the German officer's reputation.[443]

In February 1913 the mundane realities of ship maintenance took *Loreley* away from these concerns. The ship's boilers needed to be flushed and for much of the month a refit was carried out at a shipyard in Trieste at the north end of the Adriatic Sea. On the return voyage Rose had a last opportunity to entertain his classical interests.

The entire crew was happy when the time in the shipyard was behind them. This was because the 'bora', the winds that cascade down from the karst hills, blew so violently that jack lines had to be strung and hackney carriages tipped over in the streets. On the return trip the ship spent a few days in beautiful Ragusa [on the southern shore of Sicily] and then as a crowning glory, in Piraeus, the harbour of Athens. The get-together with the family of the German ambassador and the royal family with archaeologists, as well as the visit to the Acropolis, the Parthenon and the delightful Erechtheios, will remain in Haro's memory till the end of his life. His Humanistic dreams were fulfilled.[444]

The return to Constantinople again confronted Rose with approaching war. The desire of the Osmani to hold onto Adrianople notwithstanding, March brought the surrender of that city and with it a 'world situation ... more tense than ever':

In the second half of March the truce was cancelled and on 25 March 1913 Adrianople fell and the Bulgarian demands increased with their successes. The Russians supported the Bulgarians, Serbs and Montenegrins... Their goal (since Catherine's times) was the conquest of the Turkish strait. Would they pounce? The world situation was more tense than ever and a war between the European great powers moved into the realm of possibility if the governments lacked good will or wisdom.[445]

As international events unfolded in 1913 the tenor of Rose's comments about his last day posted to Constantinople reflect the tension between Rose the classically trained romantic and Rose the nationalist German:

On the last day of their stay in the Bosporus, the ship's doctor and Haro ferried across to Asia in order to visit Hannibal's grave, which for months they had hoped to do... [Though they missed the grave] the ship's doctor opined that 'Asia Minor was the goal of many German plans. We must not suffocate between the rivers Rhine [in the west] and Weichsel [in the east]. We have to escape from our confinement in order to expand and build on the energies of our hearty people.' Haro agreed anxiously. The next day there was a lovely farewell breakfast with the Ambassador's family after which everyone went across to Beikos... On the return trip across the Bosporus there was a last tea. It was an hour in which hearts were opened and the leave taking cast a poignant shadow.[446]

Rose was twenty-eight years old. Perhaps for the first time his year in Constantinople had confronted him with the reality that his chosen avocation of warrior meant commitment to that 'terrible and savage business'. It must have been a disturbing realization. As the year progressed it appears as though youthful naiveté gave way to a deepening appreciation of life's complexity. Detached attitudes like 'mankind deserves a substantial blood letting' and the attitude that the powerful win while the weak, the spineless, perish, began to coexist with an appreciation that through it all, leaders and the powerful would survive and do much better than common men. Rose was obliged to reconcile the lack of social justice with warfare. He was coming of age.

Chapter 10

Skirmishing – From Destroyers to U-boats

In early summer 1913 Rose returned to Germany from Constantinople. Under the heading *Spannung*, Tension, events in the following twelve months are covered in three short paragraphs. In the first he takes command of his own ship:

> After returning from Turkey Haro had become torpedo boat commander. As of October 1913 he was a commander of *S 15*, part of the Seventh Torpedo Boat Flotilla. It was led by *Korvettenkapitän* Gottlieb v. Koch, whose nickname was 'God Almighty.'

Prior to being given command of destroyer *S 15*, to familiarize him with that class of ship, he was initially posted First Officer aboard the destroyer *G 157*.

The second paragraph informs us, quite offhandedly, that Rose is now married, but then returns immediately to more martial affairs:

> We have heard that Haro and his young wife, as well as various colleagues from 'BBI' took part in the 1914 'Kiel Week' with the traditional party-on-board hosted by the British Flagship. Thereafter, fleet exercises were held in the Kattegat.[447]

DESTROYER *S 18* Like Rose's *S 15*, a V1-class torpedo boat. The *S 13*-class were the first ships of the fleet using modern steam turbines. They displaced 570 tons, had a length of 70.2 metres, beam 7.6 metres, draught 3.1 metres and could reach a speed of 32 knots. [Author's Archive]

Rose has already leapt forward to June 1914. In the meantime, on 20 September 1913, Rose had married Anne-Marie Siemers in St. Marien church in Flensburg. Rose discloses nothing further about the event, nor the start of their married life together. The third paragraph begins: 'Subsequently the German fleet was discharged to various Norwegian harbours despite serious political and military reservations.'[448]

With the exception of a single brief paragraph about working up *S 15*, Rose indicates that nothing much of interest occurred prior to Kiel Week at the end of June 1914:

> Following his duties in Constantinople Rose became commander of one of the most modern torpedo boats in the German fleet. In this position during manoeuvres by day or at night, in storm or fog, he had to develop all the energy, determination and flexibility stored within him. The position of the commander of the torpedo boat was the great desire of every naval officer. The training for warfare was exemplary, but how little the navy desired war can be seen from the fact that during their stay in Norwegian ports in July 1914 the ships did not have even half of their torpedoes on board.[449]

As Germany's naval aspirations grew Kiel joined Wilhelmshaven as one of the two main bases of the Imperial German High Seas Fleet. It was (and still is) the venue for *Kieler Woche*, Kiel Week, 'the mother and father of all sailing ship regattas'.[450]

Precipitated by the Balkan Wars and the destabilization of Turkey, international tensions were high in June 1914. Coupled with Germany's dramatic economic and naval expansion, mistrust between the political leaders of Britain and Germany had grown dangerously. As a result the upcoming participation of British warships was highly anticipated and carefully monitored for meaning. German Admiral Reinhard Scheer wrote:

> The visit of a British squadron for the Kiel Week in June 1914 seemed to indicate a desire to give visible expression to the fact that the political situation had eased. Although we could not suppress a certain feeling of doubt as to the sincerity of their intentions everyone on our side displayed the greatest readiness to receive the foreign guests with hospitality and comradeship.
>
> The opportunity of seeing great English fighting-ships and their ships' companies at close quarters had become so rare an event that on this account alone the visit was anticipated with the liveliest interest. All measures were taken to facilitate the entrance of the English into Kiel Harbour and make it easy for them to take up their station and communicate with the shore. And it goes without saying that they were allotted the best places in the line, close to the Imperial yacht. Accustomed as we were from early times to regard the English ships as models, the external appearance of which alone produced the impression of perfection, it was with a feeling of pardonable pride that we now had an opportunity of making comparisons which were not in our disfavour...
>
> While the time of the senior naval officers was fully taken up with official visits and ceremonies, the juniors largely made use of the facilities afforded them to visit Hamburg and Berlin by rail. Friendly relations were soon established between the

men, after the way of seafaring folk, and these were further promoted by games and festivities to their taste. The feeling of camaraderie which, as my experience went, had marked intercourse between German and English naval officers, as men of similar ways of thought and capacity, up to the year 1895, had now disappeared as a result of the attitude of hostility towards our progress which had been displayed by English statesmen, especially in recent years. Every attempt to sham a relationship to which our inmost feelings did not correspond would have compromised our dignity and lowered us in the eyes of the English. It is also easy to realize that there could be no question of making an impression by a full-dress muster of every possible ship. For this occasion only those of our ships were assembled at Kiel which were based thereon.[451]

Aboard his magnificent 120-metre royal yacht SMY *Hohenzollern II*, *Kaiser* Wilhelm II would offer the champagne and caviar personally. Significantly more portentous for naval affairs however, for the first time, the *Kaiser*, visibly impressed, stepped aboard one of his own U-boats.

Though concerns swirled around the political arena as the festivities commenced there was no reason to believe that war was about to begin. Since Kiel was home base to the Seventh Torpedo Boat Flotilla, Rose's *S 15* was present. Along with his wife Anne-Marie, Rose attended ceremonies aboard the British battleship *King George V*.

A German officer aboard SMS *Schlesien*, F. W. Joch, who, like Rose, would subsequently transfer to the U-boats, recalled: '...there were balls in most Kiel hotels and restaurants... This year there was also a British navy squadron of warships which were open to visitors. I went on board HMS *Ajax* and had fun watching their traditional sailor dances.'[452]

British Naval Attaché Henderson described the atmosphere of the festivities:

Count Reventlow, who, by the way, was not at Kiel, is quite wrong in accusing his countrymen of 'gush'. That was the one thing which we naval officers were agreed was conspicuous by its absence. The friendly press was friendly and appreciative without being gushing or sentimental.

The people whom we met (chiefly naval people) were honestly glad to see us. The attitude towards us, of the German naval officers, was the very opposite of that insincere toadyism and sickly sentimentality which we are not infrequently treated to elsewhere. It was the attitude of strong, healthy men; men imbued with a consciousness of equality with us, and who felt that they lost nothing in dignity or in the respect which they had a right to expect from us, by honest and straightforward behaviour towards us.

I talked with many of them, and cannot sum up the feeling of the German naval officers better than by quoting a story told me by one of them: 'It was only last year the officers of a British and German warship were dining together. The only toast given was a mutual one to the two "white" nations.'

It is in the subtle meaning of that word 'white' (a meaning which is well understood by German naval officers) that the interpretation of their feeling towards us is to be found.[453]

A Perfect Conflagration Was Set in Motion

As *Kaiser* Wilhelm was racing his yacht *Meteor*, news that would ignite the Great War spread:

> Monday 29 June 1914: The Archduke Francis Ferdinand of Austria, nephew of the aged Emperor and heir to the throne, was assassinated in the streets of Sarayevo, the Bosnian capital, yesterday afternoon. His wife, the Duchess of Hohenberg, was killed by the same assassin.[454]

F. W. Joch recalled:

> The murder of Archduke Ferdinand at Sarajevo on 28 June 1914 brought an abrupt end to these festivities. We left Kiel for manoeuvres in the North Sea and a week in Sognefjord, which were interrupted by orders to return to Kiel immediately. The date was 23 July 1914; the day Austria sent an ultimatum to Serbia, which alarmed Russia. 28 July Austria-Hungary declared war on Serbia, whereupon Russia mobilized and Germany declared war on Russia 1 August 1914. 3 August Germany declared war on France, 4 August Great Britain declared war on Germany and a perfect conflagration was set in motion.[455]

Hans Rose describes the unpreparedness for war of his Flotilla:

> The VIIth Flotilla sailed for Stavanger and immediately began to fill its bunkers with oil, in order to be ready for action. Unexpectedly, an orderly arrived informing Haro 'The Flotilla Chief would like to see you.' The Flotilla Chief looked extremely concerned and inquired:
>
> 'How many combat ready torpedoes does the Flotilla have?'
>
> 'A total of 55 torpedoes, of which only 21 can immediately be made clear for action.'
>
> 'Does the Chief consider the situation to be critical?'
>
> 'Yes, information about the British Fleet's demobilization has turned out to be incorrect. The opposite is true, their ships are lying at the ready in their originating ports.'
>
> 'Then God be with us,' Haro responded with a slight bow. He continued:
>
> 'Is there no way for our statesmen to come to an understanding with the British?'
>
> 'I don't think so, all of our wooing was in vain... the growth of the German economy seems to have persuaded England that war is inevitable... When the economy follows, instead of leading in a polity, then a military confrontation becomes inevitable. Please speed up refuelling.'
>
> In a cloudy, somewhat rainy night, the German fleet hurried towards home... Helgoland was greeted with happiness and after mooring in Wilhelmshaven refuelling was immediately begun.[456]

On 14 July 1914 Hans Rose was promoted *Kapitänleutnant*, Lieutenant Commander. War had begun. But for Rose it was proving unsatisfactory; he and *S 15* found themselves only indirectly involved in the fighting:

The dream of the life of daring rides of the Hussars on the waves of the sea did not become reality in WWI. The German Navy had incorrectly calculated; an attack on the German coast by the British Grand Fleet did not materialize. The British confined themselves to the Freedom of the Seas and the unsatisfactory long-range blockade. Night after night German torpedo boats made great advances in the direction of the English coast, but only very rarely did they meet enemy ships. The enthusiasm of the young commanders diminished rapidly.[457]

At the outbreak of the war, the relative sizes of the British and German fleets significantly favoured the former. Fearing to imperil his fleet, the *Kaiser* gave orders that no major fleet actions take place, though small groups of ships were permitted to conduct raids. As a result the German Admiralty pursued strategies designed to lure smaller groups of the British Grand Fleet into actions where superior German forces could be brought to bear. Raids along the British coast were one way of trying to do this. Since the British had adopted a strategy of keeping the greater part of the Grand Fleet together so as to maintain numerical superiority, the raids were intended to split groups of ships from the main fleet by obliging them to engage in coastal defence.

On 3 November 1914 the German Admiralty launched the first raid against Yarmouth across the English Channel from Cherbourg. Its objectives were to lay mines, attack lone ships and if possible entice a larger group of British vessels into giving chase, drawing them into a trap, with the German High Seas Fleet awaiting them in safer waters nearer Germany southeast of the Dogger Bank. The raid was not particularly successful. A single British submarine, the *D5*, was sunk by the newly laid mines as it steamed out of the harbour to give battle. But the German armoured cruiser *York* was accidently sunk on German mines just outside her home port. Rose, *S 15* and the rest of the Seventh Torpedo Boat Flotilla were detailed to screen the main body of the High Seas Fleet southeast of Dogger Bank, but did not see action. Nonetheless, the German Admiralty was sufficiently encouraged by the ease with which they had penetrated British naval defences to try again.

The second major raid, this time against the British seaport towns of Scarborough, Hartlepool, West Hartlepool, and Whitby, took place on 16 December. It proved far more dramatic than the earlier raid. Prior to the raid, *U 17* was sent on close reconnaissance and reported little in the way of onshore defences, no minefields, and a steady stream of mercantile shipping. Admiral Hipper led the raid. The towns were shelled, killing 137 and wounding 592, many of them civilians. The attack resulted in popular British outrage at the German navy for having attacked civilians, and at their own navy for not having prevented the attack. British propaganda would trumpet 'Remember Scarborough.'

There was considerable action by both navies and British shore batteries. A number of ships on both sides were damaged during the attack and subsequent withdrawal. But no ships were lost. As the Germans executed their withdrawal, elements of the Grand Fleet were dispatched and a series of inconclusive engagements followed. At one point in the ensuing actions, Admiral Ingenohl, commanding the High Seas Fleet, and under strict orders not to engage the

Grand Fleet, broke off an engagement that would have pitted twenty-two German battleships and a host of lesser ships against four British battlecruisers and six battleships. Had the engagement occurred the heavily outgunned British force could well have been wiped out – at one stroke evening the balance of power between the two navies. Later, Grand Admiral Tirpitz would state that Ingenohl had held the fate of Germany in his hands. Once again the Seventh Torpedo Boat Flotilla was detailed to screen the main body of the High Seas Fleet southeast of Dogger Bank and *S 15* was part of the action. But its role was too minor to merit any comment in Rose's memoirs.

On 22 December, *S 15* would participate in screening operations as defensive minefields were laid in the German Bight. Subsequently, through April, it would carry out other patrol activities.

Rose did not get the opportunity to engage the enemy directly. So despite believing it unnatural that men should try to live underwater,[458] he requested transfer.

Transfer to the Submarine Service

> I really was a destroyer commander, but I switched to submarines in 1915 because I was fed up with the *Kaiser*'s refusal to let the High Seas Fleet leave port and engage Britain's Grand Fleet in battle. The underseas boats were the only ones getting into the fracas, and that's where I also wanted to be.[459]

Written after the war, we do not know whether Rose's assertion reflects his view of the *Kaiser* at the time or his post-war judgement. Rose was a staunch authoritarian and royalist, and the *Kaiser* was the leader of the armed forces. Yet, through the *Fähnrich* Thiel affair, Rose had already demonstrated a willingness to contest higher authority. A year-and-a-half later, when Rose was received by the *Kaiser* after his voyage to America, he chose to question another of the *Kaiser*'s decisions. It is certainly possible that Rose could have held the *Kaiser* responsible for a tactical blunder of this magnitude that early in the war.

Heretofore, over the course of Rose's military career, he had been largely and understandably reactive to responsibilities assigned to him. Now, with a knight's yearning to do battle, he made his first major choice about how that would happen. In April 1915, Rose relinquished his command of *S 15* and enrolled at the *Ubootschule*, the U-boat-Forces School. Seven months later, on 5 November, with his own training complete, Hans Rose took command of the antiquated training submarine *U 2*, teaching at the submarine school until he could commission the new *U 53* on 22 April 1916.

Rose's posting to command *U 2* was another plum appointment. Many graduates of the Commanding Officers course aspired to become *Ubootschule* teachers, since the position offered them the opportunity to improve their practical knowledge and skills by getting more boat handling and torpedo firing experience prior to assuming their postings at the front. But few were selected.

The *Ubootschule* urgently needed teachers and Rose's reputation as a good teacher was already well established.[460]

The long months of training were not easy to take; however, they became highly rewarding because Rose received a new.assignment shortly after their completion. The new assignment was to prepare the two Lloyd-Captains for their difficult duty to command the merchant submarines *U-Deutschland* and *U-Bremen*. All participants were deeply involved in their secret task.[461]

Regardless of how talented a teacher Hans Rose was, he wanted to fight. As soon as *U 53* was ready, he happily relinquished his teaching duties and set about commissioning her.

In spring 1916 Rose put the glittering new *U 53*, built at the [Krupp] Germania dockyard, into service. The necessary trial-runs showed no defects in the mechanisms of the boat. On May 30th, the boat sailed through the Kiel Canal into the North Sea. Before the departure Prince Heinrich, brother of the Emperor Wilhelm, delivered a star of luck to the boat. On the afternoon of 31 May 1916, as the battle of Skagerrak raged, *U 53* reached the Helgoland naval base. Direct communications with the German fleet, which was hurrying to the Skagerrak, were disrupted. Fortunately *U 53* obtained news from a submarine commander who had participated in the early stages of the battle before returning to port because of damages. He reported that German and British armoured cruisers were involved in the battle.

'At last!' shouted Commander Rose with joy.

'At last!' rejoiced the crew.

'God of battle, is there a chance for our boat to get into the fight on this first day?'

Alas Fate would have none of it, and they did not succeed in catching a thread of her hem. Orders for *U 53* to leave port towards the northwest arrived too late: the British Grand Fleet had left the battle.[462]

Chapter 11

Impending Revolution

Shortly before the outbreak of war, British Admiral Sir John 'Jackie' Fisher made an uncomfortable argument in a memorandum to the British Cabinet. Since a submarine had neither the manpower to spare to sail a captured vessel to a friendly port, nor sufficient space aboard to accommodate captured merchant crews, effective use of submarines against merchant vessels could not be carried out under Prize Rules. 'I don't think it is even faintly realized the immense impending revolution which submarines will effect as offensive weapons of war.'[463] Fisher argued that the Germans would probably use their submarines against mercantile commerce and would not hesitate to sink them if they could not be brought into port as required under those rules.

Admiral Sir Percy Scott, a naval gunnery expert, issued a similar warning in a 5 June 1914 *Times* article stating 'Submarines and aeroplanes have entirely

U 53 VOYAGING AT SPEED
[Bibliothek für Zeitgeschichte
Stuttgart]

revolutionized naval warfare; no fleet can hide itself from the aeroplane's eye, and the submarine can deliver a deadly attack even in broad daylight.'[464]

Neither the First Sea Lord, Prince Louis, nor Winston Churchill, First Lord of the Admiralty, concurred with Fisher's warning. On 1 January 1914 Churchill called his memorandum 'brilliant and most valuable' but noted 'there are a few points on which I am not convinced. Of these, the greatest is the question of the use of submarines to sink merchant vessels. I do not believe this would ever be done by a civilized Power... These are frankly unthinkable propositions, and the excellence of your paper is, to some extent, marred by the prominence assigned to them.'[465]

Not surprisingly, at the time, the German Admiralty thought the same. At the start of WWI, despite at least one proposal to the contrary, it explicitly rejected the use of its U-boats to attack merchant vessels. The roles assigned were either primarily defensive or auxiliary to its surface fleet.

The brutality of war would change this for both sides.

Prize Rules were a set of 'customary rules' governing the seizure of 'prizes', vessels captured on the high seas in time of war. Developed initially in the age of sail, Prize Rules were codified in a series of international agreements including the 1856 Declaration of Paris and the Hague Conventions of 1899 and 1907. The Prize Rules stated that passenger and hospital ships could not be sunk, that the safety of crews of merchant vessels had to be assured, and that only belligerent warships or merchant vessels posing a threat to the attacker could be sunk without warning. It was explicitly understood that abandoning a merchant crew in lifeboats on the high seas was not a 'place of safety' unless the lifeboats were close to land or subject to imminent rescue.

Unfortunately, Fisher argued, 'there is nothing a submarine can do except sink her capture.'[466] What was more, in order to effect the capture under Prize Rules a submarine would have to surface, come to a halt, search and warn any non-military target before somehow shepherding it to port. All these actions negated the elements of stealth and surprise that characterized the new submarine weapon. And they would expose the relatively fragile submersibles to danger. Continuing his disturbing thesis he asked, 'What if the Germans were to use submarines against commerce without [these] restriction[s]?' Winston Churchill and the rest of the cabinet rejected Fischer's argument out of hand. Theirs was a sort of Victorian sensibility that all sides in the onrushing calamity would soon abandon as impracticable both on land and sea. For their part, until 1 February 1917 when they unleashed unrestricted U-boat warfare against merchant vessels, the German Admiralty insisted that its U-boat captains adhere to the Prize Rules. Article 112 of the German Naval Prize Regulations required that prior to sinking a vessel the belligerent status of the vessel's country of origin be established, and the safety of the merchant crew and passengers be assured.

Germany's U-boat campaign against merchant shipping can be divided into three fundamental stages. The first marked by adherence to Prize Rules. The second defined by their abandonment on 1 February 1917 in favour of unrestricted U-boat warfare against merchant vessels. The third and final period is defined by Britain's ultimately successful response to that unrestricted campaign, the institution of the convoy system in August 1917.

The development of Germany's U-boat strategy was operationally complex. There was early uncertainty about the best use to be made of the U-boat weapon. Within three months of the outbreak of the war Britain initiated a total embargo of all shipping destined for Germany. The embargo targeted all merchant vessels. Britain sought not only to seize contraband of war transshipped directly to Germany as allowed by prewar international agreements, but also agricultural fertilizers essential to maintain yields from Germany's generally poor agricultural land, and foodstuffs destined for its population. The British embargo applied to all merchant vessels regardless of whether they transshipped their goods through neutral third countries. It was a clear violation of international law. Faced with a strategy intended to starve Germany into submission members of the German Admiralty and the political leadership, as early as six months after the outbreak of the war, advocated a retaliatory unrestricted U-boat campaign against Great Britain's merchant shipping. Concern that such a strategy could induce neutral states, and in particular the United States, to enter the war against Germany resulted in a strategy that evolved in fits and starts, tailored to the different theatres of war, and initially highly reactive to American sensibilities. In addition, conditions around the British Isles where anti-submarine countermeasures were most intense differed radically from those in the Mediterranean theatre where counter-measures were never as effective.

Chapter 12

War in Patent Leather Shoes
(Missions 1–5)

HELGOLAND'S OBERLAND constituted most of the island's meagre attractions. 9 June 1918. [Naval Academy Archive Mürwik]

Cruising a total of some 64,426 nautical miles, the equivalent of three circumnavigations of the globe, Hans Rose commanded *U 53* for the first fifteen of its seventeen missions. During those missions he was at sea for 298 days. Five of Rose's missions occurred during the first stage of the U-boat campaign, four during the second, and six during the increasingly desperate and dangerous third.

Mission 1 – Working up *U 53* (1–3 May 1916)

Hans Rose commissioned *U 53* on 22 April 1916. For the next five-and-a-half weeks he worked her up and trained her crew. She was ordered to active service on 31 May 1916, joining the newly formed 2nd U-boat Half-Flotilla based at the tiny but impregnable island fortress of Helgoland in the German Bight. The next day Rose took *U 53* out on her first mission, an uneventful three-day North Sea 'work up' voyage from Helgoland to Horns Reef and back.

Decrying the exchange of Zanzibar, the German colonial possession off the coast of Africa, for Helgoland, a tiny North Sea archipelago only 1,800 yards long and 650 yards wide, Carl Peters, a German colonial politician, denounced it as 'Germany having traded a bathtub for three kingdoms'.[467] Peters was not a naval strategist.

Bismarck, however, was. In 1870-71, at the conclusion of the Franco-Prussian war, he asked his London ambassador to explore whether the island might be exchanged by the British for a French colony. The British declined. *Kaiser* Wilhelm II, whose diplomats finally secured the island in exchange for Zanzibar on 1 July 1890, was also a naval strategist. Commander Godfrey Herbert, D.S.O. British Royal Navy, provides a strategic appreciation of the value of this particular bathtub.

> The possession of Helgoland as a fortified outpost was one of Germany's greatest assets. A rocky formation rising at places to 200 feet, it was a useful observation post and a fortress of utmost strength. With wide views extending in clear weather to the German coast it also protected a roadstead capable of concealing a considerable fleet [as well as] its wireless station, [both] of the greatest strategic importance – in short the keystone of Germany's naval defences.
>
> ...Such then was the Bight of Helgoland, commanded in its center by this rocky island ... and in addition on the outbreak of war mined and protected by every means that German ingenuity could invent and the Teuton is ingenious.[468]

Helgoland rises like a red granite Gibraltar from the shallows of the North Sea. The island *Oberland* is a large flat plateau lying two hundred feet above the shoreline. The Germans intended to fortify it as massively as the British had their Gibraltar. So much granite was removed that the island's southern tip was extended by twenty hectares (50 acres) and two additional harbours, a large thirty-hectare (74-acre) outer harbour and five-hectare (12-acre) inner harbour were completely surrounded with breakwaters formed from the debris. During WWI the outer harbour sheltered torpedo boats and seaplanes while the inner harbour protected the High Seas Fleet U-boats. The fortress's largest guns were three groups of paired 12-inch double-barrelled long-range Krupp guns with revolving turrets capable of a maximum 27,000-metre (16.7-mile) radius of fire.

In addition to its long-range guns the island fortress bristled with heavy machine guns and cannons to repel invaders, antiaircraft guns, barracks and blockhouses, barbed wire and searchlights. No wall was less than 3 metres thick, and the miles of tunnels that connected one installation to the next ran under at least 15 metres (50 feet) of solid rock. There was a 1,800 PS (1,775 HP) coal-fired powerplant sufficient to meet the needs of the entire island, military and civilian. In the event a siege knocked out the distillation/desalination plant there were fresh water tanks sufficient to supply a garrison of 4,000 men for three weeks. If an enemy attempted a gas attack the entire underground facility could be sealed off and an electric clean air system activated. The infrastructure of an entire military city was built into the solid rock; a foundry, a bakery capable of producing a thousand three-kilogram loaves of bread a day, machine shop, hospital, infirmary, barracks, fuel tanks, and munitions bunkers, command posts, observation posts, signal lamps and a powerful radio transmitter. Helgoland would be Rose's home base for the duration of the war.

Claus Bergen describes the living quarters of the U-boat officers aboard the depot-ship *Sophie*:

> Helgoland, now evacuated by the population, and inhabited only by the Navy, was fully equipped as an advanced post in the war-zone. U-boats of various types

and sizes lay against the piers... A few grey torpedo-boats, too, were sojourning as guests in that U-boat realm. There, in the U-boat Harbour, lay old *Sophie*, which was used as living quarters by the U-boat officers [each] given a most friendly welcome on board the still smart-looking old vessel, and shown to a very bright and roomy cabin.

In the large and airy ward-room of *Sophie* the commanders and officers, modest men with much war experience, used to meet together. When, with the shining eyes of youthful enthusiasm, they exchanged their experiences in their own simple words or sat smoking and absorbed in stale illustrated papers at the long mess-table, it was hard to believe that this cabin housed the harsh reality of the mighty struggle. How much of the best of Germany's loyal, gay, confident youth had foregathered here! How many had left that peaceful-looking Harbour with their comrades and their trusty boats, and sailed away westwards and northwards – never to return![469]

One night, returning from a Helgoland tavern, Leading Seaman Knud Iversen encountered his crew mate Wireless Operator Haidt of the *U 54*. It was dark and windy, a good night for the heroics of young men. They joked together for a while but finally Knud Iversen clicked his heels, saluted and said, 'Yes, Sir; U-boat men under orders for the next world.'[470] Fatalism was rampant.

The romance of the place, garrisoned by some 4,000 men, was soon dispelled. *Leutnant* Frederick Joch, artillery officer of *U 52*, recalled:

While military service kept me occupied for a good part of the day, there was still much time left in Helgoland to pursue my own private interests. There were not many attractions on Helgoland since it was one large fortification. The whole island consisted of an enormous rock pierced in all directions by casements, ammunition chambers and underground walkways for communication with the various defensive stations. The colourful islanders had been evacuated at the beginning of the war and one had to wrack one's brains to generate some entertainment.[471]

Naval officers could however dine in the officer's club on the *Oberland*. Bergen recalled: 'Wonderful, indeed, is the atmosphere of the clear blue moonlit night on the terrace of the club, with its far-flung view across the glittering, sleeping sea.'[472] With that and relatively short walks around the *Oberland*, looking down the island's steep cliffs at the nests of seabirds above the crashing sea below, or going to church, Bergen, Iversen, Joch and Rose largely exhausted Helgoland's meagre attractions.

Mission 2 – *Calypso* (3–13 July 1916)

On 3 July 1916, Hans Rose conned *U 53* out of the U-boat basin at Helgoland for her first true wartime mission: a search for enemy naval vessels in the North Sea. It was a disappointing and fruitless search. The seas were vast, there was no radar, and in WWI a U-boat commander's field of vision was, with the exception of the rare radio report from another U-boat, the extent of his world. What he couldn't see he couldn't sink. What he and his crew did see was the huge extent of British maritime trade plying to and fro across the North Sea carrying wood, food and other supplies to Britain and her allies. However, out of fear that attacks on merchant shipping would alert the British to the locations of the U-boats stalking their fleet, the German Admiralty had explicitly forbidden its U-boat captains from initiating such attacks during the outbound portions of their missions. They were only permitted during their return to base. The only event in the first nine days of his eleven-day mission Rose chose to record was two exhausted seagulls that landed on deck. The crew took them below deck to feed and rest overnight, then released them the next day.

Then, just after midnight on 11 July in the Skagerrak, skirting the Norwegian coast off Lindesnaes, Rose detected a ship's silhouette. Since she was travelling completely darkened Rose assumed she must be a British auxiliary cruiser which could be attacked without warning. Submerging, he fired a torpedo at her:

> There was little to see in the twilight of the northern night and the torpedo missed.
> 'That's all we need. Surface! Both engines full speed ahead!'
> The enemy had two black funnels and its size was about 3,000 BRT. Sunrise was near and it was no longer possible to attempt an underwater attack. The course and speed of the ship had been determined during the long pursuit. There was no alternative but to attempt a surface attack.
> 'First torpedo tube, attention... shoot! Second tube, shoot!'
> Twice the boat rocked. The torpedoes' trails of bubbles were almost unnoticeable in the dawn – Will they hit? With forced calm the commander ordered 'Both engines slow ahead, turn hard to port to 270 degrees.'
> Will they hit? Will they hit? The navigator counted: 'forty seconds, fifty seconds, sixty seconds.'
> Will they hit? – The commander thumped his hand on the railing: 70 seconds, 80 seconds – will they? The commander stamped his foot – 90 seconds – Boom!
> 'Finally' the commander mouthed, relieved. A huge flame shot up to heaven, higher than the masts of the ship. Everyone gave a sigh of relief and another boom was once again heard across the sea. A second flame rose into the sunrise. And when the two columns disappeared, the sea was empty and surrounded by total silence.[473]

She was the British S.S. *Calypso*, the first merchant vessel ever sunk by surface torpedo shot, and Rose's first kill. She, her master and twenty-nine of his crew, now lay on the bottom of the sea. Rose, the philosophcal romantic, continues:

> The lights of Egerö and Listor go out. Pure, uninvolved and eternally beautiful, the sun rose behind the Scandinavian mountain range and shone in infinite grace over the blessed and fecund, yet awesome man-killing sea. Weeks later, a deserted boat drifted on to the Norwegian coast. That was the only thing that had remained of the British ship. It confirmed that the vessel had been under British sovereignty, which gave the commander a deep sense of satisfaction... The search for the enemy, taken as a whole, had been unsuccessful. Yet, one was still at sea, which meant that attention must not flag.[474]

The remainder of his voyage uneventful, Rose returned to Helgoland on 13 July 1916.

U 53 Dodges a Bullet

14 July 1916, the day after *U 53* returned from her second mission, she and sister ship *U 51* were ordered to Wilhelmshaven for routine refits. The short 42-nautical-mile trip to the rear was well behind German defensive lines and considered so safe that both U-boats had their tall, double-mast, long-range wireless antennae raised, preventing an emergency dive. *U 53* led and *Kapitänleutnant* Walther Rumpel's *U 51* followed. Rose described a banal voyage that ended badly:

> It was a beautiful summer day with a ruffled sea. The boats headed towards home at twelve knots. The commander led and *U 51* followed at a distance of about 400 metres. They had their masts raised in order to receive war news. The crewmen played their harmonicas and were making merry. When the outer jade lightship was still about four nautical miles away, ordinary seaman Gothling stuck his head out of the conning tower hatch. He waited patiently until the commander lowered his binoculars.
>
> 'Lunch is served.'
>
> 'What time is it?'
>
> 'Twelve-twenty. The off-duty group is ready to take on their shift.'
>
> 'I'm coming,' the commander replied. He turned to the navigator who was on watch-duty ordering 'Please inform me in twenty minutes, when we pass the outer jade.'
>
> 'What's for lunch?' he called to Gothling, who was climbing down the ladder before him.
>
> '*Speckerbsen*' (peas with bacon).
>
> 'Wonderful.'
>
> The commander had instituted the rule that he ate alone at his desk. He did not want to disturb his officers and was of the opinion that he needed to give them the opportunity to talk openly about anything during meals, including about him. They needed the opportunity to criticize and to let off steam. This would result in better discipline... The crew talked from table to table. The meal was delicious.
>
> Suddenly there was a terrific blast. The boat shuddered. The commander automatically consulted his watch: 12:35 p.m., then raced to the control room and up the tower to the bridge. He froze as he witnessed *U 51* sinking by the stern straight into the depths.
>
> 'Full speed ahead, zigzag course.'[475]

Lieutenant Cromwell H. Varley, captain of the British submarine *H5*, departed Yarmouth on 10 July and headed for Wilhelmshaven, Germany's largest naval base in the North Sea. Repeatedly dodging German patrols to sneak far behind enemy lines, Varley spent two nights and a day waiting for a propitious opportunity to 'initiate hostilities'.[476] At 11:55 a.m. he rose to periscope depth and sighted the two U-boats 700 yards off his starboard bow. Varley altered course to starboard, set two torpedoes to spread three degrees each, and fired his starboard upper and port lower torpedoes. One hit with a devastating explosion. The sound and shock wave from the explosion rolled over the men aboard *H5*. Before *U 51* disappeared, Varley observed through the periscope 'a large column of yellow smoke about one and a half times as high as the mast'.[477]

Viewed from the surface, by the men standing lookout atop *U 53*'s conning tower, the submarine seemed to rise vertically and then immediately sink. The torpedo struck just behind the U-boat's conning tower. Aboard *U 51*, men in the sub-officer's compartment felt a strong wave of air pressure that shot through the boat as it shook from the heavy explosion. The diesel engines immediately fell silent, the submarine began to cant steeply to stern, the lights failed, and she was plunged into darkness.

In the aft-most compartment three stokers were in their berths when the torpedo hit. Heard through the two water-tight doors, the explosion came with a muffled boom and a strong tremor, flinging the three men into the bilge. A jet of flame and sparks shot out of the speaking tube leading from the conning tower to the aft compartment. A bluish-white smoke smelling of petroleum filled the chamber. Almost immediately scalding water was forced into the compartment from a point near the main rudder motor, quickly filling it knee-deep. More water shot in from the speaking tube.

Kapitänleutnant Rumpel and the watch officer had been in the officer's wardroom when the explosion struck. With the men in the sub-officer's compartment they grabbed emergency lights and rushed towards the control room. But when the watch officer opened the bulkhead hatch a bright fire forced him to close it immediately. With water already ankle-deep in the compartment, and fearing that the water pouring into the boat's batteries and accumulators would generate chlorine gas and spark short circuits, the *Kommandant* ordered everyone to the forward compartment. As the ship sank and the bilge began filling with water, the air pressure began to rise. The increased air pressure made it difficult for the men to open the hatch to the forward section. By the time they succeeded it already contained half a metre of water.

With three men in the aft compartment and eighteen men in the forward one, two-thirds of *U 51*'s crew were still alive in the stricken vessel. The watch officer tried unsuccessfully to blow the ballast tanks. But resting on the seabed, 24 metres (78 feet) down, canted slightly on its side, *U 51* would not move again.

On the surface Rose took charge:

> The commander ordered a picket boat in the vicinity: 'Search for survivors and anchor at the accident site!'
>
> The 9th Torpedo flotilla passed. The commander informed them: '*U 51* sank here, please search for survivors. Beware of the enemy submarine.'
>
> Then the commander himself returned to the scene of the disaster, stopped, dropped a buoy into the whirlpool of bubbles and oil.[478]

Steaming towards harbour, *U 53* moored next to *Hamburg* where the FdU, *Führer der U-Boote*, the Chief of the submarine fleet, *Fregattenkapitän* Hermann Bauer asked for a detailed report, explaining, 'I have already telephoned to Eckernförde. Salvage-vessel *Vulkan* could arrive tomorrow evening at the earliest.'[478]

The remainder of Rose's *Auftauchen!* account of the rescue attempt is compressed and somewhat sanitized. Initially it was unclear why there had been an explosion. Nonetheless the 9th Flotilla and patrol vessels began searching the inner bay for an enemy submarine and active depth-charging continued throughout the day. Unfortunately *Korvettenkapitän* von Rosenberg-Gruszczynski, Senior Officer of the II Submarine Half-Flotilla, was predisposed to assume that there were no survivors aboard *U 51*. Coupled with the presumption that an enemy submarine was present an immediate rescue attempt was deemed too dangerous. As a result, little effort was made to effect a rescue.

Four hours after *H5*'s attack, the air in the forward compartment being consumed by eighteen men suddenly degraded alarmingly. Oxygen was added and the men were forced to use the available *Tauchretter*, emergency breathing apparatus, or, if they had none, to hold their noses and breathe through potash filters. One man began to retch, his face turning pale. Breathing laboriously, he fell asleep. Shortly afterwards, everyone fell ill. Machinist's Mate Msyk remembered it was 'as though they had breathed bad air'.[479] The men's faces turned chalk white, their cheeks sank and blue circles formed around their mouths. The men's breathing was forced, coming in short pants. Msyk and his companions began to suffer headaches, dizziness and ringing in their ears. Looking at the men around him, Msyk found each staring straight ahead 'as though insane'.[480]

Increasingly the men appeared stupefied, breathing very heavily. Several men let their mouthpieces slip and slowly suffocated. Though no additional oxygen had been added, some of the men began to fantasize that the air quality had markedly improved. They 'toasted each other with their mouth-pieces'.[481] Msyk thought the mood bizarrely happy, 'as though everyone was badly drunk and entirely witless'.[482] Realizing that no outside help would be forthcoming, everyone shook hands for the last time. Msyk recalled it was 'as though they were taking leave from each other on the sidewalk'.[483] The disconcerted helmsman inquired of those around him, 'Why is no one weeping?'[484] By evening, five or six men in the forward compartment were dead.

Eleven hours after the explosion the air was so bad forward, Machinist's Mate Msyk heard someone say, 'This can't go on, we have to get out of here.'[485] *Kapitänleutnant* Rumpel ordered the attempt. Machinist's Mates Piper and Msyk stood on the ladder below the hatch. Neither had a *Tauchretter* or a life-preserver. They were only wearing rubber vests. They loosened the toggles on the hatch and taking a last breath of air through their potassium filters, pushed the hatch out. Almost explosively the air in the U-boat shot out as water cascaded into the compartment. Forced through first, Msyk lost consciousness and both men shot to the surface surrounded by an enormous cloud of air bubbles. No one else made it out and only Msyk survived.

In the rear compartment of the mangled submarine the three stokers now had only corpses for companions. Still, with fewer lungs aft to consume the oxygen, the air remained good and the three men slept through the night relatively well. When they awoke however, the air had begun to deteriorate and it was clear that salvation would only come through their own efforts. They would have to flood the compartment increasing the air pressure. Twenty-seven hours after the attack, under extreme stress, breathing with difficulty, the escape had to be attempted. To equalize the pressure the men flooded the compartment up to their necks. Then they donned their *Tauchretter* and opened the hatch. The escaping air drew the three men out, but only two survived to be rescued.

Concluding his 'Missed Shot' account in *Auftauchen!*, Rose wrote: 'It was war, which demanded victims, even if it was occasionally fought in patent leather shoes. A beautiful boat and good comrades were lost. The men did not sleep well the next night.'[486]

But Varley hadn't missed. He'd chosen *U 51*. Rose had just been lucky.

Mission 3 – Shadowing the Grand Fleet (17–22 August 1916)

By staging naval raids on British military facilities at Sunderland, Admiral Scheer attempted twice to lure the British Grand Fleet across U-boat picket lines. For his U-boats, the first attempt at the end of May 1916 was a total failure. However, between 31 May and 1 June, in what became known to the British as the Battle of Jutland and to the Germans as the Battle of Skagerrak, it lead to a resounding tactical victory by Scheer's surface warships over Admiral Sir John Jellicoe's Grand Fleet. Strategically however *Skagerrakschlacht* did nothing to alter the situation imposed by Britain's naval blockade.

Hans Walther, captain of *U 53*'s sister ship *U 52*, explained the strategy:

> Experience taught us that we could not inflict significant losses on the enemy fleet using submarines alone. A new method had to be devised. The idea of operational collaboration between the fleet and submarines was obvious. Why not blockade the main home ports of the English fleet with submarines and then attack them with our fleet to force them to leave their hiding places? Certainly our submarines would get plenty of opportunities to attack the British battleships when leaving or returning to their ports. The first attempt at this strategy was made at the end of May 1916 and led to the battle of Skagerrak. But opportunities for submarine attacks didn't materialize. First the British fleet succeeded in leaving its ports at night unnoticed. Then, after the battle, most of our submarines, following orders, had already left for home by the time the English ships, some of them heavily damaged, returned.[487]

Walther describes Scheer's second attempt, launched 18 August:

> Other methods promising more success had to be developed. We decided to place mobile lines of submarines across the course the enemy must take leaving port. This operation required the German fleet to make an attack on Sunderland. German submarines received the order to form two picket lines – one north and one south of the attacking course of the German fleet. These two submarine lines stretched from near the English coast out eastward into the North Sea. This way, while approaching the English coast, the attacking German fleet was protected by its own submarines to the north and south. The enemy, coming from either direction, had to cross a line of submarines.[488]

On 19 August Walther scored one of the two minor successes of the operation, sinking the British Light Cruiser *Nottingham*. However, had Admiral Scheer given greater credence to reports from Hans Rose, the outcome of this second attempt could very well have been a major victory. *U 53*, assigned during the operation to act as a *Fühlungshalter* (scouting vessel), successfully shadowed the British fleet the entire day.

Having watched from his vantage point atop *U 53*'s conning tower, Rose described an early, chaotic start to the day, contact with the enemy before dawn, and a disappointing error:

At 320 degrees, a vessel. Indeed it seemed as though there were two. Headed in the opposite direction, they were following each other bow to keel; definitely warships.

'50 degrees to starboard please.'

'Holy devil,' Stein called out, 'at forty degrees, three dimmed vessels appearing, course approximately 100 degrees.'

The commander ordered 'Turn to 270 degrees please – crew ready to dive.'

As light and visibility increased by the minute the enemy was on both sides of the U-boat.

'Alarm!'

It was 4:45 a.m. The commander had found and attached himself to the enemy, thank God... Furthermore the submarine managed to remain unseen.

'We will steer 160 degrees.'

To the right, at approximately 12,000 metres distance, four small Aurora class destroyers following the same course made it impossible for the U-boat to launch an attack.

'Damn,' said Stein, 'this seems to be turning into a very important affair.'

'Yes,' answered the commander without taking the binoculars from his eyes, 'I agree...'

'The smoke in the west must be coming from a host of fat ships.'

'Hey Stein, can you believe it? The destroyers to the south aren't bothering us, nor is the defensive screen to the east.'

'Steer a southerly course at top speed please.'

From below, Wacker, the handsome blue-eyed boy from Ehrenbreitstein, called up to the tower 'Both engines top speed at 180 degrees.'

Wacker had given the necessary orders and the U-boat foamed through the sea. The commander admonished

'Carefully check in all directions please, especially the enemy's off-sides.'

'Then we might as well go to sleep,' Wacker joked, 'because they are all around us.'

'Quit your shenanigans, though you are essentially correct. I see a few three-masters, and I can count one, two, three, perhaps four British battle cruisers, and in front of them, many destroyers and behind them, perhaps even more ships... If fate is on our side, the ships might change their course and may, after all, come close enough for our torpedoes to sink them. For the moment we will continue to follow them.'

While the crew kept a stony silence, one of the ships was targeted. The torpedo missed at a distance of 350 metres. It was a humiliating operator error; the heading angle had been set for the wrong side. The slim destroyer slid past the U-boat unmolested.[489]

With a considerable portion of the British Grand Fleet surrounding him Rose became the eyes of the German fleet:

It is important to let the German fleet know that the British are heading towards them... Their general course was 140 degrees. With the help of his messages the commander hoped to lead the British into the fiery arms of the High Seas Fleet. He also counted on other U-boats receiving the signals and having greater luck than he had had in attacking them... The U-boat saw a group moving south and even further away a dirigible... At 14:30 o'clock, [*U 53*] report[ed] the smoky clouds, their location and their course to the Fleet leadership... Grinning the Chief Engineer stuck his head out of the tower hatch. The motors were running without any smoke showing. The keel waters were swirling...

'Look at these engines!!!' Chief Engineer Möller commented: 'A song of praise to MAN' [*Maschinenfabrik Augsburg Nürnberg*, the engine manufacturers]. It could be that world history is decided by our actions.

A battle cruiser became visible at the head of the slowly approaching formation. It was the *Minotaur*, behind it eight to ten capital ships. Wacker tried with the help of the Petty Officer Paul [Mohr] to contact the radio transmission intermediary, the destroyer *Ascona*, whose wavelength was blocked. Finally, he was able to transmit the following signal: '15:10 p.m., location 70 nautical miles east of Sunderland. The enemy unit consists of ten battleships.'

That the enemy had not yet attacked the U-boat can only be explained by the fact that they thought it was British. Using the periscope it became clear that behind the unit that passed the U-boat silently there were masses of other vessels. It seemed as though the whole Grand Fleet was heading towards an engagement with the German High Seas fleet. This realization was immensely important and would have to be transmitted to the Fleet Chief as soon as possible... The submerged run had taken nearly three-quarters-of-an-hour. Of the destroyer that had forced the U-boat underwater, now only a few weak smoke clouds were visible... He was following a zigzag course. The dirigible too had disappeared. Wacker brought the FT [*Funktelegraphie*] message from the commander of the U-boats: 'To all U-boats in location I, move east to location II,' which was north of the Dogger Bank.

'Our dirigibles are better off,' mused Wacker, 'A tremendously long view, excellent orientation and opportunity to withdraw into the clouds anytime.'

At nineteen hundred hours, Wacker once again climbed up the tower with a piece of paper: Radio signal from FdU: Return immediately to location I.

'O.K. turn around, let's go.'

But, for heaven's sake, what is going on? Lots of smoke clouds appear in the west and over them a dirigible. That can't be the German fleet? But how did the dirigible end up directly over the Grand Fleet? Moreover, it remains motionless. That isn't a dirigible; rather it is a balloon that the British are pulling with them. It suddenly strikes the commander that the situation was completely different from what he had thought. Moreover he realized that the U-boat radio signals had been particularly important [in describing conditions].

'Attack the enemy!'

'Dive and follow a course of 315 degrees please. Now or never!'

Two unequal enemies were facing off. On the one hand eight of the largest battleships in the world. On the other, a single U-boat with a crew of 36. But ten minutes later the squadron passed the periscope eye of the disappointed commander only 15,000 metres away, seemingly sneering... Because the wavelength was busy it took almost half an hour to send the message. The boat meanwhile headed toward the Firth of Forth looking for the enemy... In the deepest dark, shortly before midnight, all engines were stopped in order to re-charge the batteries that had been depleted by the six different underwater runs.[490]

The British battleships left the Firth of Forth on 18 August 1916. Rose intercepted their vanguard in the early hours of 19 August east northeast of Blyth, but diving at 4:45 a.m., missed sighting the battle cruisers for the first time 'unfortunately exactly the moment when the whole squadron doubled back'.[491]

At 8:45 a.m., for the second time, *U 53* crossed the screen of destroyers surrounding the larger battlecruisers. But once again they were too far away to be seen. At 9:54, having surfaced earlier, Rose sighted the 'prime targets' for the first time and dove for the attack. But the U-boat's submerged speed was insufficient to catch up with the British battleships, which executed a second about-face unobserved, leaving Rose with no choice but to launch his flawed shot against a smaller target; one of the British destroyers. At noon, Rose dove for the fourth time. For the remainder of the day, Rose shadowed the British fleet reporting its position to the high command. Shortly after 7 p.m., Rose was unable to close within striking distance of a line of eight battleships:

Finally, at 20 o'clock, destiny demonstrated to the German U-boat commander that successes must be viewed as favours and rare gifts. Once more the Grand Fleet sailed past in full splendour, however again in a formation that made attack impossible.[492]

Around 9 p.m. Rose lost contact with the enemy. Misinformed by reports from its dirigibles about the strength of the British Fleet arrayed against it, the German High Seas Fleet began its withdrawal in the early afternoon. The British Grand Fleet began its withdrawal about 5 p.m. Units of its fleet crossed the U-boat picket line around 8 p.m. when *U 52* sank *Nottingham*. The two reversals early in the morning had delayed the British fleet's southerly progress by about four hours preventing an encounter between the two fleets. Rose concluded: 'It is thus that the fates weave the thread that influences the fortunes of men and nations.'[493]

A day of great hopes and great disappointments had come to an end. Though the German Fleet Chief [Scheer] had decided to do battle, he had changed his position and veered south when a dirigible reported sighting heavy British armed forces. He had considered the information from the dirigible more reliable than that of the U-boat. He later expressed his regret to the commander... At the request of the commander, the F.T. *Gast*, who had transmitted the message flawlessly, was promoted to Sergeant. How differently things would have worked out if one had been able to transmit and receive signals from a submerged U-boat.[494]

In 1938-9, Rose would say of naval communications:

> Nowadays two belligerent fleets would surely not miss each other. Aeroplanes launched in squadrons from ships and special vehicles would provide the necessary reconnaissance for both sides and inform the adversaries of each other's fleet strength way ahead of their actual sighting. The supreme importance of an aggressive, nautically and technically trained naval air fleet is obvious.[495]

The following day, 20 August 1916, *U 53* was still in the vicinity of the previous day's excitement. Though the fleets had returned to their home harbours the vigilant scouts of the two navies remained. Throughout the day *U 52* reported that British sub chasers, some with sweeps deployed, were hunting for them. At 4 p.m. *U 52* noted *U 53* on the horizon and two British ships veered towards Rose's boat and attacked. The Commanding Officer of HMS *Gunner* reported the particulars of that engagement:

> At 3.15 p.m., still pursuing submarine, another submarine was sighted three miles on port beam, steering to the Westward, our position then being 55° 28'N., 00° 8'E...
>
> This shot also fell short, when range was increased another fifty yards, and the remaining shots, second, third and fourth were observed to be certain hits.
>
> After the second hit, an explosion showing fire smoke and steam was seen in the after part of S/M, and after third hit, S/M went down by head, stern plainly visible above water.[496]

The British Admiralty correctly considered the report improbable. Two days later, *U 53* returned to Helgoland, her third mission of the war over.

Uneventful Mission 4 (23–31 August 1916) and Mission 5's Strategic Outcome (17 September–28 October)

Between 23 and 31 August Rose and *U 53* conduct their fourth mission, an uneventful 560-nautical-mile patrol from Helgoland, through the German Bight west of Dogger Bank, and back to Wilhelmshaven. Unbeknownst to Rose a debate was raging within the Admiralty about the efficacy of sending a U-boat to America's east coast. Eventually that debate results in the decision to dispatch Rose and *U 53* on their fifth mission of the war; their trans-Atlantic passage to Newport Rhode Island.

Paul König, captain of the merchant submersible *Deutschland*, made written and oral reports to the Admiralty upon his return from America. Subsequently it was decided to send two military U-boats to the American east coast. After consultations with *Fregattenkapitän* Hermann Bauer, the Chief of submarines, Vice Admiral Reinhard Scheer, the Chief of the High Seas fleet, decided that the military situation only permitted allocating one. The Admiralty held a meeting on 8 September 1916 to discuss the mission. It established the mission's military objective: to demonstrate the capacity of German U-boats to carry the campaign against merchant vessels to the American coast. This would be demonstrated by making a short call in an American harbour without requesting assistance, followed by acts of war in compliance with Prize Rules. That these objectives were not divorced from the larger debate about the merits of an unrestricted merchant campaign is demonstrated by an exchange during the meeting in which a question about whether the mission might lead to complications with the United States was answered by the remark, 'It would finally start the ball rolling.'[497] Michael Wala asserts:

> The protocol of a conversation about the U-boat war in Plesz and the message of the Chief of the Admiralty to his representative at Headquarters permit the inference that the *Kaiser* himself supported the idea of this 'showing the flag' strategy.[498]

Despite the 'tactical advantages' the operation offered, the opportunity for political complications caused Scheer to insist that the order for the operation come not from his fleet command, but directly from the Admiralty. He insisted that 'all leading members of the military as well as the politicians be informed about the planned operation and register their consent for the plan.'[499] A document accompanying the request stated that the Chief of the Admiralty Henning von Holtzendorff did not share Admiral Scheer's concerns and that the *Kaiser* supported the mission.

After the mission the American Neutrality Board determined that *U 53*'s mission did not breach American neutrality because of the brief nature of Rose's stay in Newport and the lack of assistance given. In addition it noted that under conditions pertaining at the time it would not have been possible to refuse a request for reasonable aid. As a result the Neutrality Board further recommended that a general and universally applicable entry ban be instituted and that subsequently German U-boats not be resupplied if they visited American ports.

Nonetheless the political ramifications of the mission were felt even before Rose and *U 53* returned to Germany. 'Protests were mounted by the American government, diplomats of the Entente and the American public.'[500] President Wilson summoned German Ambassador Graf von Bernstorff, and in a sharp rebuke indicated that it was impossible to justify to the American public a campaign against merchant shipping so close to neutral America's shores. For his part Bernstorff immediately reported to Germany that he did not see the military value of the mission and communicated American displeasure at its occurrence.

After *U 53*'s return the *Kaiser* addressed a written message to the crew praising them and the importance of the trip. Rose was ordered to report to the Kaiser at his forest retreat in Wildpark near Potsdam and received the special honour of a personal interview with 'the great war lord'.[501] While Rose's meeting with the Kaiser was a personal honour, he was disappointed by the latter's refusal to seize the strategic opportunity launching unrestricted U-boat warfare offered:

> The *Kaiser* showed himself to be an expert in all things nautical, and he had obviously followed our voyage in detail. He told me U-boats could now conduct war according to prize rules; that is, we could sink vessels carrying contraband after searching them. I felt very strongly that we should be released from all restrictions. That was the view of all the officers of the line, and I knew I would

have only this one chance to express our attitude to the *Kaiser* himself. In addition I had not forgotten Commodore Bauer's promise when he gave me the American assignment two months earlier.

'Your Majesty,' I said, 'we will get nowhere conducting the war in this fashion.'

He looked at me and worked his lips in agitation. I don't suppose a junior officer had ever spoken to him like that. Then without another word he led me through the tea-time crowd to the Empress, introduced me, and walked off.[502]

Rose's brazen willingness to ignore the chain of command and seize the opportunity to castigate the *Kaiser* about strategic policy is the most dramatic example of Rose's readiness to contest those in authority when he felt strongly that they were not acting in the best interest of his navy and country.

Reflecting on the successes of the voyage, Rose wrote:

> I cannot but feel grateful to the commanders of the American destroyers for having preserved their neutrality so thoroughly. It was especially considerate of one of them who was obstructing my action to move out of my way when I signalled to him in Morse code.[503]

The danger had been driven home to Britain and her allies. His well-publicized mission to the American east coast in September and October 1916 and the five ships sunk in a single day were more than enough to underscore the U-boat menace. Nonetheless Rose noted that the trip failed of its chief purpose. A series of unusually severe autumn and early winter storms had reduced commercial traffic, decreasing the opportunity to inflict heavy losses on east coast shipping. And with the absence of *Bremen* to act as bait,

> ...we could not sink any British warships, because we could not find any. And, what was the worst of all, less use was made of U-boats, although as a direct result of our appearance over there they should have been employed more than ever – a state of affairs that lasted for several months. Looking back, I realized the mission was a failure. The worst thing that could have happened did happen: the restrictions on the use of submarines that were to have been removed the moment our submarine appeared in America were maintained for many more months.[504]
>
> The only result of our trip was that we had made our enemies understand what they could expect from German U-boats – though this warning unquestionably turned out to be a false one.[505] We warned them, and this warning was a mistake.[506]
>
> In the minds of us U-boat people, the trip intensified our confidence and brought home to us what German material was capable of when well managed.[507]

Rose concluded, 'We had the will to do our duty, but fate had decreed against it.'[508]

It is possible that the sheer technical and material success of Rose's mission to America contributed to the German leadership underestimating the impact that drawing the United States into the war could have as a result of launching an unrestricted campaign against merchant shipping. On 9 January 1917, ten weeks after Rose returned from America, the *Kaiser* ordered that as of 1 February unrestricted U-boat warfare against commerce would commence.

Chapter 13

Unshackled at Last (Missions 6–8)

SINKING THE BELGIAN STEAMER *HAINAUT* on 12 March 1917.
[Rose Family Archive]

'Now you have your cruiser war.'[509] Such was the comment the 'All Highest' made to Hans Rose when in November 1916 he granted Rose an audience congratulating him on the success of his fifth mission, the voyage to America. But much to the dismay of Rose and the men of the U-boat fleet in general, the *Kaiser* was not yet prepared to initiate an unrestricted campaign against merchant shipping. Rose described U-boat Chief Hermann Bauer's reaction:

> The BdU [*Befehlshaber der U-Boote*, Commander of Submarines] was not satisfied with the solution, because it merely led to a shift of [enemy commercial] ship traffic, with the waters around Britain used by neutral ships, while the British freighters found and made great profits across the ocean. Moreover, disguised vessels [Q-ships] endangered German U-boats... It was clear that the sea war could not be won in this manner.[510]

By 9 January 1917 economic and military pressures finally compelled the *Kaiser* to order the launch of the unrestricted U-boat campaign. Rose recalled the occasion he and other U-boat captains received the news:

> On 16 January all U-boat commanders were requested to come to Wilhelmshaven to meet with [Bauer] the Leader of the submarines. Approximately forty U-boat commanders assembled in the mess hall of the light cruiser *Hamburg*... Some belonged to the group which had been with the submarines since the beginning of the war. They had inscribed their names in the 'book of history'... But, the majority had volunteered at the beginning of hostilities to get a chance to engage with the enemy. They loved life and had no respect for death. They were a band of brothers.[511]

At the outset of the unlimited campaign, roughly a third of the sixty-nine U-boat commanders Bauer had at his disposition for the campaign around the British Isles were at sea when he convoked his commanders aboard *Hamburg*.

> There was deathly silence when commander Bauer entered and announced that the shackles would finally be loosened and unconditional U-boat war would be approved as of 1 February 1917... Everyone was impressed by the gravity of the situation and while champagne was served one of the older commanders offered three 'hurrahs' for the decision. The same evening the commander of *U 53* returned to Helgoland with his friend Werner of the sister-boat *U 55*. While on the destroyer they wondered whether the decision had not come too late.[512]

Although the campaign ultimately failed, those sixty-nine U-boat commanders would come within six weeks of bringing the British Empire to its knees.

Mission 6 – Account by *Kriegstagebuch* (20 January–10 February 1917)

In 1920, Admiral Reinhard Scheer sought to demonstrate the challenges posed by waging a U-boat campaign according to Prize Rules. To make his point, he analysed *Kriegstagebuch* entries for Rose's sixth wartime mission. At the conclusion of his recitation, Scheer comments:

> These extracts should suffice to show under what difficulties the boats worked so long as they had to consider the neutrality of steamers, and it also shows how many opportunities for sinking ships in the blockaded areas were lost.[513]

In fact the difficulties of a mission began well before Rose could sight his prey. On this mission, Rose had to first dare the British defences of the Dover Strait. Rose recalled the start of the mission begun in tandem with *U 55*:

> On 20 January 1917 the two boats left Helgoland harbour together taking a westerly course...
> Looking into the distance the watch officer said 'I hope it will warm up soon.'

'Why?' asked Stein, 'this bone chilling air gives us an infinite view of this damned country.'

'I'm just worried about the rapid venting. If [the valves] freeze tight, we won't be able to submerge.'

There was no remedy for this at the time, but luckily the U-boat did not need to dive.[514]

To the sea bed before the Dover Strait; Rose continues:

As dusk fell [the two U-boats] separated and passed the two light-vessels *Terschelling* and *Nordhindern* and next noon found a buoy ... located approximately eighty nautical miles east of Dover...

Near the buoy it was close to 38 metres deep and the U-boat headed for the sea bottom like a flounder. Moving forward slowly, and with a slight forward list, the U-boat rose to 36 metres. Then the engines were stopped. The boat sank slowly until it hit bottom with a slight jolt, at which point the vent regulators were opened and about 5,000 litres of water filled the tanks, grounding the U-boat with perhaps five tons of negative buoyancy.

At this point the current pushed the U-boat slowly tangential to its course, catching its side so that it started to tilt, rocking back and forth on one of its auxiliary keels. That was an unpleasant feeling because one had no idea whether the boat would right itself... But when the crew had gotten used to the rolling they viewed it as a mild, wonderful swaying and a time for relaxation. Cocoa and crumble cake were served and the gramophone played beautiful music. Only one crewman per station had watch responsibilities, everyone else was off duty.

The commander asked the radio engineer to come to him. 'Try to contact *U 55*. I have arranged with its commander to wait with his boat, as we are doing, until darkness falls.'

The radio was activated ... and *U 55* responded immediately. In code the two boats exchanged their location and agreed to start their surface voyage through the Channel separated by a half hour interval.[515]

Combining criticism of the politicians (or perhaps for Rose, the bureaucrats) who had delayed the launch of the unrestricted campaign, Rose described the passage below the anti-submarine nets:

The German War Office had given the British ample time to design intricate ways for catching German U-boats... Only by diving in high tide could the submarines avoid the nets and pass the big rafts of wood floating in the current... However, if the course was incorrect, another disaster could occur, the submarine would run aground on the Goodwin sands.

The boat moved at top speed, with frequent stops for depth soundings. They, reassuringly, indicated forty metres. However, the next sounding was only twenty metres and then it fell to ten metres. Thank goodness the one after that once again showed a depth of fifty metres. The exit channel had finally been reached.

'Course south, engines ahead full,' the commander instructed, as the boat shot past a dark object on the port side … it was one of the huge wooden floats. A light indicated Gris-Nez on the French coast.[516]

On 21 January Rose sank the French sailing ship *Anna* with gun-fire. Later he picked up enemy radio warnings that his U-boat was known to be operating in the area. On the 23rd he sank a steamer he believed to be British. But she was a Dutch neutral, the SS *Zeta*, and subsequently compensation would be paid. Later in the morning he verified and dismissed a Dutch merchantman and then, during the afternoon, dodged a British U-boat chaser and a picket vessel.

Over the next four days Rose encountered nothing but neutral vessels and bad weather. Then on the 28th he encountered the Spanish steamer *Nuevo Montana* carrying iron ore for Newcastle. Having evacuated the crew to their lifeboats he detonated three explosive charges in the vessel's engine-room. Then he towed the merchantman's crew near Ushant where he left them to row ashore.

On the 29th, after investigating and dismissing another neutral merchantman, Rose sank the steamer *Algorta* carrying iron ore for Stockton. Once again he took the merchant crewmen in tow until he sighted another steamer. Having cast his tow loose he signalled their presence to the steamer with star shells.

Rose only encountered enemy picket boats on the 30th. Then on the 31st, after dismissing two neutral vessels, he encountered the Norwegian steamer *Hekla* carrying pit props for Cardiff. He set the steamer on fire as the crew sailed for the Scilly Isles. Later that day he engaged a small steamer with artillery fire, but its return fire was accurate and he broke off the attack. At dusk the steamer slipped away. Just before midnight another neutral vessel was inspected and released.

Following a fruitless search for targets on 1 February Rose attacked the Norwegian steamer *Odin*:

In a night dark as pitch, everything was quiet as a tomb when the radio engineer remarked: 'I hear motor noises'…

They come from the port rear side. The enemy was steering directly toward us with all lights extinguished. The commander let the ship pass and followed in its wake…

It was scary; the submarine followed the ship so closely that one could have thrown a stone and hit it. Consequently the course and speed of the enemy could be exactly determined. He steered south (180 degrees) at nine knots. In this situation only a mathematically calculated attack would lead to success. Because the sine of thirty degrees is one half, if I moved out by thirty degrees and followed this course for five minutes at a speed of twelve knots, then I would be exactly one half nautical mile distant from the ship.

…At midnight sharp the U-boat, travelling at twelve knots, turned to starboard. The steamer disappeared from sight and the submarine passed it in the dark. At 0:05 a.m. the U-boat returned to its previous course of 180°, and at 0:25 a.m. it reduced its speed and turned to 90°.

At 0:30 a.m. all engines were stopped and the U-boat was ready to fire. The tension was unbelievable. Would the steamer really appear on the port side? Had it possibly changed its course or possibly been mis-steered and ram us? Or had it passed the U-boat? Seconds of great expectations passed. After a minute the steamer was sighted again. The engines started slowly. And then at 0:33 the torpedo left the tube. An unbelievable detonation followed, accompanied by huge flames that crackle through the night. Masts splintered, boilers exploded. The steamer sank quickly and a deathly silence once again dominated the sea. The ice-cold trigonometry had led to complete success.

It was a shattering experience. The watch returned to his berth and the new watch mounted his post silently. But no one could sleep. The Commander remained awake in his berth. His calculation had been totally correct. The success was demonstrable, but it gave him no satisfaction.[517] Finally, he too was overcome by exhaustion and fell asleep.

Later in the day, the *U 53*'s *Kriegstagebuch* describes a new encounter.

2.2 4 p.m. Near Bishop Rock stopped an old French square-rigged schooner, Anna Maria, *from St. Malo, about 150 gr.t., by using signal 'Abandon ship'. After a time the mate came on board in a little, keelless rowboat… In consideration of the impossibility of rescuing the crew in this boat, the ship was allowed to continue her journey. The mate gave a written promise in the name of the crew not to go to sea any more during the war. The cargo of the ship consisted of salt and wine.*

Rose would not hesitate to attack a merchant vessel without warning. But where it was possible he took care to wage merchant warfare with as little loss of life as possible. Still, there is more to the *Anna Maria* incident than meets the eye. He devotes six pages of *Auftauchen!* to the encounter:

In the late afternoon a small sailing ship appeared south of the Scilly Islands. It was signalled to stop and bring its papers. It took a long time before there was any action on the vessel. At the command to 'Provide papers,' a flag was hoisted. Suddenly the helmsman called: 'It is unfurling the tricolor.'

This indicated that it was not a neutral, but an enemy vessel….

A flag signal ordered the crew to abandon ship. The commander realized that this was a drastic order on an early February day, thirty nautical miles away from the nearest land… Suddenly, another signal was raised by the sailing vessel: 'Do not intend to abandon ship.' What did that mean? After a while a boat with three men was lowered… The pitiful vessel without a keel arrived full of water which the men tried to keep buoyant by bailing with sea boots, southwesters and tin cans… An old man with a sixteen-year-old-boy came aboard. The old man was unshaven and wore wooden shoes filled with straw, the young boy cried and begged for mercy with outstretched arms…

The commander asked the old man whether he was the captain.

'No,' answers the old man. 'He is sick.'

'What's the matter with him?'

The elderly gentleman indicated that he had drunk too much.

'What is your cargo?'

'Wine.'

The crew on the tower laugh… They were embarrassed to have to sink this small ship.

'Where do you come from and where are you going?'

'We come from Spain and are heading to St. Malo.'

'If you spare our lives, Captain, Sir, I promise that we will not again put out to sea.'

The commander asked 'Can I count on it?' and received the reply

'I will put it in writing.'...

'Your ship's name?'

'*Anna Maria.*'...

'I undersigned A Villemartin, boatswain make pledge to Monsieur the German commander of U 53 to abstain during the present war to navigate myself and my comrades in recognition of the good will to generously give us our liberty.'

(signed) A Villemartin

The boy's terror turned to joy as they returned to their little life-boat. When the sailing vessel disappeared into the dusk, the commander commented to Stein: 'I could not have sunk the ship, because it carries my wife's name!... I know that you approve, because this pitiful vessel will have played no role in the outcome of the war.'[518]

There is no record in *U 53*'s log book that any of her crew went aboard *Anna Maria* to verify the condition of any of the other life boats, nor did Rose choose to shepherd the sailing vessel to a safer location to sink it. It bore his wife's name, and that was enough.

The next day there was an epilogue to the encounter:

Shortly afterwards, the commander sighted a sailing vessel and suggested to Werner [of *U 55*] that they mount a joint attack. Werner has not sunk anything on his voyage and requested that he take this prize. Rose agreed replying, 'I will cover your attack.' He let the other boat forge ahead, stowed the gun and fell back...

[Werner] ultimately gained a lead of about 2000 metres and lobbed a few shells ahead of the sail vessel's bow. It lowers a boat and one saw three men row across [to *U 55*] pulling mightily. Two men appeared on the tower where a lengthy discussion occurred and then the three men returned to their sailing vessel. The U-boat departed without paying the slightest regard to *U 53*. It turned out that the sailing vessel was *Anna Maria*. The helmsman, Villemartin, had shown the note [to Werner] that the commander had had him sign the day before.[519]

The morning of 3 February 1917 proved to be unforgettable aboard *U 53*. Surfacing in the wake of a ship flying the neutral flag of the United States Rose ordered a warning shot that brought *Housatonic* to a halt and its captain across by lifeboat. 'The Captain, a slim, carefully groomed man came aboard. He made an excellent impression, which however did him no good because his ship was carrying 3862 tons of wheat for London.'[520]

In exchange for rowing Rose's demolition crew back to *Housatonic* Rose granted the captain permission to return to his ship to collect some warm clothing and belongings. Rose admitted a momentary anxiety for his demolition crew when, across the water, he watched a developing commotion on board.

His anxiety increased when the sound of a big brouhaha from the freighter reached him. But his men waved their hands from time to time across the span of water. The cause for the disturbance was the crew of the freighter. Joyously the men participated in the destruction of all the portholes and locks, so that the freighter would sink faster. The commander gave the Americans time to destroy their own property.[521]

With the demolition complete, the Americans and Germans returned to *U 53*.

In recognition of their excellent treatment, the Americans returned with a crate of 200 pieces of soap and a number of boxes of tobacco. The American captain complained about his untrained crew, calling them 'jumping jacks', useless as seafarers. This resulted in the commander's offer to pull their life-boats closer to the Scilly Isles.[522]

First *Housatonic* had to be sunk.

The submarine prepared for a torpedo shot. – 'Fire!' – A trembling in the boat but no track. It was a complete failure. The captain immediately ran into the bow compartment, put his ears to the torpedo tube and heard the torpedo still in the tube, its propeller slowly rotating. The torpedo had started, slipped and then jammed.

What should be done? One could not lock the muzzle-cover or the torpedo would have detonated instantly making the loss of the boat inevitable. Simply shooting the torpedo out was dangerous, since there was always the possibility that it would travel in a circular path and return to hit the U-boat itself. In spite of the danger the captain decided on the latter option. In the event the worst case came to pass the crew was ordered to muster on deck to give them a better chance to save their lives.

This was one of the most precarious situations in which the boat had ever found herself. Moment by moment one had the feeling of waiting to be killed. The tension dissolved when the boat was shaken by a sudden detonation. But it was not an explosion, nor was there a smoke or water column.

The torpedo had worked itself out of the tube and had travelled head first down to the ocean bottom where it detonated.[523]

The crew thanked the gods that this depth was 110 metres, and not as in the North Sea only fifty metres. A shallower depth would have meant the end of the boat.[524]

An older bronze torpedo was used to destroy *Housatonic*.

The second torpedo hit the freighter dead-centre. The U-boat took the Americans in tow. Progress towards the Scillies was slow. In the meantime *Housatonic* sank deeper and deeper until finally her bow submerged completely. The Captain of *Housatonic* and Captain Rose motioned a last 'Farewell' to the departing ship with their caps.[525]

While sinking *Housatonic* Rose kept the vessel between *U 53* and several English trawlers. Once *Housatonic* was sunk Rose fired several shots to attract the latter's attention and then retired on a course that caused the trawlers to encounter *Housatonic*'s lifeboats.

On 4 February Rose first sank the French barque *Aimée Marie* and then the schooner *Bangpuhtis* plying between St. Nazaire and Cardiff. Both crews rowed for the Scilly Isles.

The Taming of the Shrew

Various events during Rose's naval career demonstrate that he considered himself a warrior acting according to chivalrous rules of conduct. He routinely exhibited solicitous behaviour towards the merchant crews of vessels he sank. Frequently Rose would take life boats in tow bringing them close to shore. In the *Bravella* case, where that was impractical because weather conditions were too extreme, before sinking her, he shepherded the doomed vessel to a sheltered location from which the crew would have a better chance of survival. In a section of *Auftauchen!* entitled *The Taming of the Shrew* Rose laments the use of the incident as British propaganda.

It was way past midnight when the helmsman called out 'A boat at 80 degrees.'...

The commander climbed into the tower and the U-boat crept towards the adversary. It seemed very small and totally unaware of what was happening... As they came closer, we saw that the steamer was from a neutral country which could be attacked without warning during the restricted period... Thomas morsed him and shot a white flare at the bridge. The boat stopped but did not respond... He didn't seem to have any usable life-boats... The commander waited patiently assuming that the captain would be awakened...

A half-an-hour passed. Suddenly the boat roared away at top speed. Uncle Ernst lobbed another few shells before the bow creating towering water geysers and the U-boat pulled up while signalling that the steamer must follow in an easterly direction. But to no avail... The commander was aware that sinking the boat would constitute a death sentence for the crew... Throughout the night the U-boat circled like a sheep dog around its flock... Using flag signals they inquired about the ship's destination:

'Liverpool.'

'What is your cargo?'

'Nuts.'

Hurray, that is contraband... The commander signalled: 'follow me.'

The ship turned out to be the Swedish *Bravella*. The commander intended to communicate that he would scuttle the ship closer to shore... Using the English language to clarify his intentions, he signalled: 'I sink you!'

When the word 'you' was received the *Bravella*, in a seeming theatrical huff trying to intimidate the U-boat, lowered its signal and refused any further communication... The trip to the Scilly Isles commenced and the *Bravella* followed meekly.

Shortly before noon [05.02.17], the two ships were about 12 nautical miles south of the islands and the death sentence was about to be enforced... Suddenly the *Bravella* hoisted a number of flags... While the U-boat tried to decipher their meaning an escort vessel appeared on the horizon. It was evident that the *Bravella* wanted to draw attention to itself. The flag signals were meaningless. Now there was no time to lose. Uncle Ernst aimed his gun at the *Bravella* and fired a shell across its bow to speed up the action. After no more than two minutes the crew had abandoned ship leaving the engines running... When the boats were clear of the stern the commander gave Uncle Ernst permission to fire. He first shot some holes into the front cargo hold. A yellow mass flowed out. They were nuts. Luckily a rain-squall swept in obscuring the U-boat from the escort ship.

There was tremendous joy while crisscrossing the nut-filled wake because it left a large bounty on deck... Later it turned out that the captain of the *Bravella* was British. In spite of all of his consideration, the *Bravella* case was used [as propaganda] against the German 'submarine barbarians'.[526]

Towards the end of the voyage mechanical difficulties, as they had at the mission's start, compromised the boat's capacity to dive. Nonetheless Rose encountered an enemy fishing cutter. Hoping to impound the vessel Rose took the crew on board and began towing the cutter. But bad weather forced him to cut it loose and sink it with explosive charges. He then off-loaded the cutter's crew to the Terschelling bank lightship before returning to base.

Mission 7 – Six Shells Saved 'For Eventualities' (28 February–18 March 1917)

U 53's seventh mission is typical of Rose's aggressive style. To get to his hunting ground west of the English Channel Rose again traversed the dangerous Dover Strait. On 2 March he stopped, shelled and sank the British sailing vessels *Gazelle* and *Utopia*. On the 3rd, he torpedoed and sank the Greek steamer *Theodoros Pangalos*. On the 4th, off Wolf Rock, the seas were heavy with Force 8 winds and bridge personnel of the morning watch were swept overboard. Offensive actions were impossible so Rose changed course. But the next day Rose returned to the attack and torpedoed and sank the Italian steamer *Federico Bonfalonieri*. On the 9th he torpedoed and sank both the armed Italian steamer *Cavour* and the Norwegian steamer *Lars Fortenes*. On 10 March Rose shelled and damaged the Russian sailing vessel *Sviatoi Theodor*. Then on the 11th, with his last torpedo, Rose torpedoed and sank the armed English steamer *Folia* and then shelled and sank the Spanish steamer *Gracia*. Survivors of the *Folia* confirm Rose's concern for their well-being.

In ten days Rose had attacked nine vessels and sunk 21,456 tons of merchant shipping. With his torpedoes expended and the mission a success Rose set a course for home north around the British Isles. But on 12 March, west of Ireland, Rose encountered the Belgian steamer *Hainaut* and sank her with artillery fire. Two days later, on the 14th, still four days from home base, northwest of the Orkney Islands, Rose encountered the Norwegian barque *Aquila* and sank her too with artillery fire. Following that attack only six of the original supply of four hundred shells for his 10.5 cm artillery piece remained. Rose left a wry comment in *U 53*'s war diary: 'The rest of the artillery shells... are saved for eventualities in the North Sea.[527]

Rose fought until he could fight no more.

Mission 8 – 'Hurray! We're Still Alive'
(10 April–1 May 1917)

A painting by Claus Bergen depicts *U 53* moving towards the upper left hand side of the frame. In the lower left hand corner, moving in the opposite direction, barely several metres from the U-boat's side, the tip of a periscope rises above the water throwing up a small bow-wave as it speeds by. Atop the conning tower no less than twelve crewmen smiling and laughing, one of them pointing, join the captain to observe a hapless British submarine as it passes harmlessly by.

Based upon accounts of the incident by *U 53*'s crewmen, Bergen painted the picture, no doubt in homage to the Germany's U-boat men as cheerful, death-defying warriors. It is far from accurate.

It was 30 April 1917, 8:30 p.m., and *U 53* was in the war zone at the northern tip of the North Sea. Two-and-a-half hours earlier *U 61* had radioed that it had been attacked by an enemy U-boat. Ever since *U 53* had been executing an evasive zigzag course at fourteen knots. Protecting the U-boat four pairs of watchful eyes ceaselessly scanned their appointed quadrant of the ocean. Suddenly, from a mere 25 metres away, a torpedo fired at *U 53* by the British *J6* passed harmlessly under their boat. If anything, the relief Hans Rose and *U 53*'s crew must have felt reflected the title of Claus Bergen's painting of the encounter; 'Hurray! We're Still Alive!' Once again *U 53* and her crew had been lucky. The legendary Max Horton was commander of *J6*. Only momentarily aware of *U 53*'s presence Horton had chosen the only attack possible; a quick shot at *U 53* before she disappeared in a crash dive.

There is no mention whatsoever of *J6*'s attack upon *U 53* in Hans Rose's personal papers. And with the exception of a bare summation of nautical miles logged and ships sunk at the end of *Auftauchen!*, *U 53*'s eighth mission is passed over. Whatever the reason, Hans Rose chose not to report on his eighth mission. It was his third most prolific of the war. His second most successful mission had occurred just the month before. We must rely upon *U 53*'s *Kriegstagebuch* for information about *U 53*'s eighth mission.

It takes him six days to reach the west coast of Ireland on 15 April 1917. Three days later, he sinks the 1010-ton armed English steamer *Scalpa*. Several hours later he torpedoes the 3,846-ton British steamer *Sculptor*. It takes *Sculptor* two hours to sink and one crewman is killed. The next day Rose sinks the 2,981-ton armed English steamer *Tempus*, shelling her with four 10.5 cm shells and then torpedoing her with a C/03 torpedo. One of her crew dies.

On 21 April, still hunting along the western approaches to the British Isles, Rose encounters the 1,698-ton armed English steamer *Pontiac* and fires a C 45/91 torpedo killing two: 'Sinks after four minutes, 21 crew save themselves in a boat.'

The next day Rose sights the 1,799-ton armed British steamer *Neepawah*. Unable to sink her with a torpedo because her zigzagging makes targeting impossible Rose surfaces and engages the steamer in a short artillery duel. When *Neepawah* breaks off the engagement Rose sends over a demolition crew who sink the ship with explosive charges. Later that day a torpedo attack on the much larger 6,127-ton armed British steamer *Karroo* is also thwarted by the latter's zigzagging. Rose again surfaces and engages the steamer in a four-hour artillery duel. But when two destroyers arrive to rescue the steamer Rose must break off the attack.

At noon on 23 April Rose attacks the 4,307-ton armed English steamer *Eptapyrgion* with a G.A. V torpedo and then surfaces to finish her off with four 10.5 cm shells. 4,640 tons of meat and other food destined for the troops of Rose's enemies go down with her.

The next day is long and demanding. At 5:30 a.m., 160 nautical miles west of Bishop Rock, Rose encounters the 4,533-ton armed English steamer *Anglesia*. He sinks her with a G.A. V torpedo, six 10.5 cm shells and two explosive charges. Then thirty minutes after noon *U 53* is attacked by a destroyer that fires two depth charges at her. Rose executes a crash dive, only surfacing two hours and forty-five minutes later when nothing can be seen as far as the horizon. Then at 5:30 p.m. Rose sights another destroyer with three funnels and dives for another two hours.

At 9:30 p.m. Rose encounters the 3,770-ton armed British steamer *Ferndene*. He sinks her with a C/03 torpedo. Half-an-hour later, with nothing but a single old C/45 bronze torpedo in one of the stern tubes, Rose decides to head home. But targets remain, as does Rose's eagerness to attack them. The next day, around 2:20 p.m., still southwest of Ireland, Rose sights the 5,106-ton armed British steamer *Martabau*, a large prize, and twice tries to torpedo her, though she effectively zigzags preventing Rose from lining up a good shot. He surfaces at 3:50 p.m. and engages the steamer in a brief ten-minute artillery duel, to which she responds with well-aimed fire of her own, at the same time as she radios her position to Crookhaven. A nearby escort vessel immediately responds to her call for help and Rose breaks off the attack. Rose must be satisfied with a much lesser prize; the 335-ton English three-masted schooner *Laura*. Rose sinks the vessel with six explosive charges set below her waterline and then by firing three 10.5 cm shells. Two-and-a half-hours later he executes a surface attack upon the 217-ton Danish sailing vessel *Elizabeth*, shelling her and leaving her afire. But the ship remains afloat, drifting for five days, until it is sunk by *U 81* on 30 April.

The next day, 26 April at 10 a.m., Rose stops and sinks the 169-ton Danish sailing vessel *Hekla* west of Ireland. The schooner's cargo of wood is set afire and burns for hours. The following morning at 8 a.m. Rose's radio operator picks up an SOS from the *Roselea* indicating that it has been attacked by a U-boat. Rose plots an intercept course and sights the steamer at 8:40. He dives for the attack but his last torpedo misses. Unable to contact the other U-boat Rose surfaces and continues home north of the Hebrides, passing north of the Orkney Islands on the 29th.

At 6 p.m. on the 30th Rose receives *U 61*'s warning about *J6*, which attacks *U 53* two-and-a-half hours later. *J6*'s attack fails and *U 53* arrives back in Helgoland safely on 1 May 1917 having voyaged 4270 nautical miles during the course of the mission, 205 nautical miles submerged.

Rose's accomplishments during this period are exceptional when compared to the average tonnage of merchant vessels sunk by U-boats during the same period. These months marked the start of the unlimited campaign against merchant shipping when on average 143 U-boats were active. During this period Rose substantially outperformed his fellow U-boat captains; and this in the most dangerous theatre of the war for U-boats. He sank 14,282 tons during his sixth mission, 26.7% more than the monthly average. During his second most prolific seventh mission, Rose sank 26,662 tons, 88.6% more than the monthly average. And finally, during his eighth mission in April 1917, Rose sank 24,449 tons, 37.2% more than the monthly average. This eighth mission took place during the most prolific month of the unlimited campaign in terms of average tonnage sunk. Yet these accomplishments paled in comparison with his tenth and most successful mission of the war, carried out in August 1917, when Rose sank 45,187 tons during a month when, hobbled by the introduction of the convoy system, on average each active U-boat sank only 8,558 tons. Rose's consistent outperformance of other U-boat commanders reflected his extraordinary aggressiveness, coupled with his obvious talents as a tactician and commander.

Chapter 14

The Painter Tags Along – Mission 9

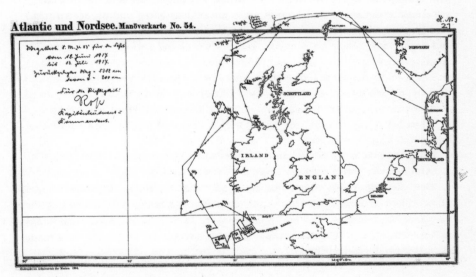

U 53 KTB MISSION 9 MAP Rose attacked 11 vessels. Locations of vessels sunk are marked. [Bundesarchiv – Militärarchiv (Freiburg)]

The boat lay alongside the pier, with its new light-grey coat of paint glistening in the sun, ready to put out to sea. Before they went below, the commander briefly explained the object and destination of the voyage to the crew. They were to lay a course north of the Shetlands to the entrance of the North Channel and the Irish Sea, and there carry on operations off the north-west coast of Ireland; thence cruise about the western entrance to the English Channel and the south coast of Ireland, where determined counter-measures on the part of the enemy were to be expected.

The gangway was pulled on shore, the ropes cast off; brief words of command rang out from the conning-tower, from which a flag was fluttering. The boat quivered as the engines began to revolve. Shouts of good-bye, waving of caps, silent farewells. Amid cries of 'Good-luck!' the vessel glided slowly towards the harbour mouth, and out between the two lofty moles, on which a few comrades stood and waved goodbye once more, into the green, gently heaving North Sea.[528]

With these words Claus Bergen began his account of the *U 53*'s ninth mission. The voyage would demonstrate the normal challenges and dangers of a U-boat mission anywhere in the heavily patrolled waters around the British Isles. Twice *U 53* would encounter and engage British Q-ships in battle. Rose reported thirteen encounters with destroyers, a number of which sighted and attacked *U 53*. She sustained minor damage the two times she was closely depth-charged. And there were days of bad weather that made military operations impossible. Despite these challenges, Rose sank eleven vessels, including seven during a single eight-and-a-half-hour running battle with a fishing fleet. What made *U 53*'s ninth mission unique was the participation of Claus Bergen.

Bergen recalled his first encounter with Hans Rose:

> One hot day in early summer a large submarine of the Fifty class, just returned from a long voyage, lay beside the U-boat pier. The huge conning tower (not unlike a Roman war-chariot) and the gun, were covered with red and orange rust; the sunburnt crew were full of their recent homecoming and in all the glow of youth and health. I sat down to paint the graceful vessel and I soon had a number of spectators in black, brown, salt-stained, oil-gleaming leather jackets.
>
> The commander came across the gangway on to the quay, walked up to me and cheerily introduced himself. He smilingly asked me about my work, and wondered if painters, too, got their hands dirty. Indeed, there was no doubt about that.
>
> 'Then I dare say you can make good use of a piece of real French soap that we have brought back with us.'
>
> I thanked him and took the precious gift.
>
> 'And I expect you get hungry, too?'
>
> That was not exactly true; however, I gladly accepted the apple preserve and a tin of American corned beef that he offered me. Both had come from a steamer he had sunk. Although our rations on *Sophie* were ample and excellent, such things meant a change that was unknown at that time. Moreover, his kindly spirit made me feel warmly grateful.[529]

Sometime later Bergen was invited to dine with Rose in the officer's club on the *Oberland*:

> Over a good glass of wine I asked the genial commander whether he would not sometime take me for one of the long trips on his U-boat. Without much hesitation he discussed the pros and cons of the matter with his three officers, sent a wireless message to the Admiral in command of the U-boat service at Wilhelmshaven, got the consent of his Navigating Officer and Warrant Officers as regards accommodation, and informed me next morning that there was no further obstacle to my accompanying him, on my own responsibility, if I still felt so disposed. Thus, sooner than I expected, I had the long-desired opportunity of a voyage on a U-boat. I quickly sent to say that I would come, got the necessary U-boat outfit, and was soon ready with my modest baggage.[530]

Rose's analysis of Bergen's request demonstrates his 'structured thinking'. He operates in real time and out loud, rather than in his own head. He considers the effects on his officers and presumably argues for Bergen's voyage with them. A positive outcome could have a salutary impact on his public image.

Bergen's account of the mission is particularly compelling because it is written by a landsman for whom everything about the voyage was novel. In addition to recounting the action and adventure of the mission, Bergen leaves us with anecdotes of life aboard *U 53*.

Claus Bergen was three days younger than Rose and, like him, was already a nationally recognized figure, having won accolades as a gifted painter of exotic scenes of Arabia, India and the Old West. Bergen was appointed Naval Painter to *Kaiser* Wilhelm II just prior to the outbreak of the Great War. After the Battle of Skagerrak, Admiral Scheer, the High Seas Fleet commander, took the armada into the Baltic to execute a replay of the battle, complete with the guns firing blanks, so that Bergen, among others aboard Scheer's flagship, could produce paintings of the engagement.

Throughout both World Wars Bergen would be commissioned to execute large-scale naval paintings. Some would hang in railway stations and other public buildings across Germany. Bergen would become Hans Rose's life-long friend. Following WWII, when the painter was destitute, Hans Rose would become a patron, purchasing a number of Bergen's paintings.[531]

Bergen's many paintings of WWI U-boats, and in particular his paintings of *U 53,* are considered among his finest artistic work.[532] In addition, Bergen published *My U-boat Voyage*, his account of *U 53*'s ninth mission, writing 'a new world seemed to have arisen before my eyes.'[533] That voyage would provide material for dozens of future paintings and his images and prose would establish Hans Rose and *U 53* in popular German consciousness.

Noting the Admiralty practice of according German submariners a bonus for each dive they participated in, Bergen wrote that the routine practice dive that Rose ordered on the first day of each mission was an occasion for good cheer among the crew. For Bergen, it was his first experience below the surface, and he described it in detail:

'Diving stations!' The order suddenly rang out from the conning-tower. In an instant the deck was empty. Everyone jumped, climbed, or swung himself on to the conning-tower; and thence down the open hatchway. The tall periscope is soon in its place. Quickly down the smooth greasy iron ladder; and don't let the great seaman's boots above you crush your fingers! And mind your head and your bones in this iron tube, plastered with iron plates, levers, screws, and wheels, and now crammed with scrambling men. In less time than it takes to describe, everyone from on deck has dashed to his appointed place, inside the conning-tower, in the control-room, or in one of the other compartments of the vessel. Last of all the commander climbs into the conning-tower and the heavy hatch is fastened above his head. The diesel engines are switched off and the electric motors started. Just as the commander stands at the periscope in the conning-tower, the eye of the U-boat, so in the control-room, the brain of the vessel, the Chief Engineer stands at the centre periscope. One's tense expectation of a unique experience, and all the impressions of one's first dive in a U-boat, are mastered by the amazing consciousness that here one is, in a huge heavy ship, shut up in it inescapably with a number of other men, sitting on a comfortable leather sofa in the little ward-room, or in the control-room, watching the sailors at the horizontal rudders and the depth-gauge, in a dry, brightly-lit compartment with pounding engines and a row of eel-smooth torpedoes, moving under the surface of the sea.

The alarm bell rings shrilly through the vessel after the report from the conning-tower: 'Conning-tower hatch closed.' The levers spin round: with a hiss and a roar the sea pours into the diving-tanks; it seems as though one ought to feel the weight of this invading water. Gently the floor sinks and the boat tips forward. The movement is quite gradual, barely perceptible. In the dim glow of the electric light, a mystic modulation of various shades of grey, stands a figure, enclosed in a narrow iron space surrounded by all manner of levers and wheels, on a sort of pedestal, connected with the periscope, that can be raised and lowered like a lift - the commander at the periscope, which is now fully raised; and in front of him the helmsman at the wheel. With the commander's permission I open the heavy iron safety-cover of one of the small side windows and press my face inquisitively against the thick glass. There in the light of day, as though in another world, I see the foaming masses of water crashing over our bows. The gun disappears in surging eddies. The waves rise and race towards us, break angrily against the conning-tower and sweep past my window. Then a confusion of bright foam and clear water, inaudible, fantastic, outside the glass: light grey, dark grey, the deep water grows ever darker and more calm. I can clearly discern the bow gun hovering in the magical green light. The sunshine pierces the clear water and glitters on the polished steel. A solemn stillness reigns. The only sounds audible to the vessel from the conning-tower are the adjustment of the periscope and the movement of the submarine steering-gear. The commander uses both hands to swing the greased and glittering periscope, now dripping with water. In his eye, the only eye in the vessel that is still in communication with the upper world, is the bright and shining reflection of the light of day. I swing back the iron cover to my window, leave the narrow tower and climb down to the control-room, where an officer stands in charge of the horizontal rudder.

The movement of the water again becomes perceptible; the stillness of our progress through the depths has vanished. The sea rustles past the hull. The diesel engines begin to hum once more. Thus our first dive came to an end.[534]

Upon surfacing off Hogstean, the watch would immediately resume quartering the horizon:

On the conning-tower everything was dripping with sea-water. Fragments of jelly-fish and strips of golden yellow sea-weed were hanging from the steel hawsers. Behind the conning-tower casing the look-out men, enveloped in yellow and black oilskins, stood like statues, immovable. The long, keen sight of these experienced seamen is almost beyond belief. Much depends on their alertness, and any weariness, carelessness or mistake might be fatal. The safety of the boat and the crew is in their charge. It is only their iron calm and experience that prevents them constantly seeing ghosts of periscope tracks in the little bright dancing eddies, or behind the sweeping lines of foam. And seagulls, too, balanced on the moving water, are very apt to lend themselves to such deceptions. With the naked eye, the look-out men can recognize the smoke of a completely invisible steamer by the merest suspicions of a shadow on the horizon as quickly as they can spy the needle-like line of a mast in the far distance. Before I could detect the smoke or the masthead with a pair of strong binoculars, the alarm was given.[535]

Later that day, still relatively safe within German patrolled waters, Bergen had the opportunity to familiarize himself with *U 53*'s deck and participate in a light-hearted camaraderie not yet curtailed by the demands of operating in the war zone:

It was refreshing and pleasant on deck and in the conning-tower, in the light sea-breeze of this glorious, clear, sunny weather. The almost level dark wooden deck, nearly fifty metres long, provided ample opportunity for movement, though on the smaller mine-laying submarines there was little possibility of stretching one's legs. After a great deal of stumbling about and clinging to the rails one soon became accustomed to the various square holes in the deck that catch one's boot-heels, and to various other pitfalls; indeed, one quickly finds one's sea legs on a U-boat. There is time to spare to contemplate at leisure the details of the 10.5 centimetre gun that stands in front of the fore-hatchway, the tall conning-tower welded with myriad rivets, and all the other equipment of the U-boat. The ubiquitous and plentiful oil and grease make little impression on the admirable leather overalls worn by U-boat crews. Only linen, hands, drawing-paper, and suchlike more genteel objects soon lose their original purity. One smokes quantities of cigars and cigarettes and talks to the genial members of the crew about their earlier experiences.[536]

As the voyage took its psychological toll, Bergen noted the change:

The rhythmical beat of the motors hammered on without a pause. Some of the crew who were off duty lingered on deck to enjoy the strong sea air and to smoke. Yes, if there were nothing to smoke, the voyage would have been wearisome indeed. All were silent, deep in their own thoughts. Our wake disappeared in zigzag lines into the twilight behind us. From time to time the officer on the watch shouts orders for a change of course through the open hatchway to the helmsman in the conning-tower. On each side of our bows the clear blue-green sea surged past us in white racing eddies. The sea grew rougher; waves began to break over the deck, and swept foaming across the oil-glistening iron-black curved and barrel-like outer tanks. From bow to stern, over the two masts fixed to either side of the conning-tower parapet, run two stout steel hawsers which serve as protection against nets and as antennae for short-distance wireless, when circumstances do not allow the erection of the tall wireless mast affixed to the diving-tank outside. The flag has long since been taken in, and every object that might cause inconvenience when moving under water has been removed. Several periscopes, heavily encased in grease, respond to the lightest touch, for at any moment an alarm may force us to dive.[537]

Still in the German Bight, *U 53* was protected by torpedo boats guiding her through German mine fields, and by sea-planes on watch for enemy submarines. Surrounded by local fishermen, the crew added to their larder:

> A German fishing-trawler came into sight and hove-to at once: U-boat and steamer were soon lying side by side. The steamer Captain, an old friend of our commander, passed several baskets of freshly caught fish over on to our boat; indeed, his generosity seemed endless. The deck looked like a fish market. Above and around screamed and hovered countless seagulls in expectation of a copious feast. The men were soon busy over the fish; the best ones were sorted out, washed, cut into pieces, and handed down in buckets through the fore-hatch into the tiny U-boat kitchen. We offered our warmest thanks to our kindly friends, and after much waving of caps the two vessels parted. Whole flocks of seagulls swept the sea clean behind us from the remains of the fish that we had thrown overboard. Above our heads circled two escorting aeroplanes. Their presence had a very comforting effect, for, in spite of the reassuringly peaceful fish transactions, dangers threatened us on every side. Enemy submarines might be on the watch even here...
>
> In front of us, two patrol boats, formerly steam-trawlers, fitted with mine-sweeping apparatus guided us through the mine-strewn zones of the German Gulf. When we had turned our course to starboard, and passed the long gleaming dunes of Sylt, the North Frisian Island that rises still and dreamlike on the far horizon from its grey-blue background, the two fishing-boats turned back and their place was taken by two torpedo-boats. The aeroplanes, too, were relieved later on by two seaplanes, until further north, on the edge of the German sea-zone, signals and flares indicated the departure of our brave guides and companions. With a message of 'Good-luck!' torpedo boats and seaplanes turned back in the light of the evening sun. We are left to ourselves. In the distant haze, beyond our wake, the torpedo-boats disappear, and the planes quickly vanish from our sight in the direction of List, on the island of Sylt. The engines are at full speed. Sharp and noiseless our bow ploughs the heaving sea.[538]

Travelling northward around the British Isles, the sea is empty of targets:

> For days we did not see a ship. Only driftwood, bulks and planks, intended originally for the construction of enemy trenches, and now, in contradiction of the proverb, that water is not planked over, swinging on the North Sea tides; perches for contemplative seagulls. From time to time a bale of cork, a small piece of wreckage thickly encrusted with mussels, came into view; and occasionally a rust-covered mine adrift from its moorings. For the rest, nothing was visible but indifferent sea-birds, and the almighty majestic sea.[539]

Bergen described the amenities below deck.

> Below, in the small but cosy wardroom, with its homelike wooden panelling, in such refreshing contrast to the iron world about us, the officers ate their excellent and varied meals prepared in the electric kitchen. We were very comfortable on the soft black leather sofas, which, when hung at night with dark green curtains to

help to keep out light and movement, served the officers as beds. In this excellent abode we soon got used, as our voyage progressed, to the most gracefully acrobatic methods of consuming our food and of drink: here we sat and passed from hand to hand some ancient novel, or an illustrated paper so old that it had lost all verisimilitude; and we found it easy to transport ourselves in spirit out of that iron vessel, the war, and the sticky sea-water, to peaceful shores and homely familiar towns and cities. The small library in the commander's room, the accumulation of many kindly gifts, was assiduously used.

Immediately adjoining the ward-room, and communicating with it by a door that was always left open when we were proceeding under water, was the smaller living-room and bedroom of the commander. He ate alone. A small writing-table, covered with photographs and all sorts of maps and sailing directions, served also as a dining table...

Between the commander's cabin and the control-room there is a small wireless cabinet, equipped with all its mysterious apparatus. Nearby is one of those strong rounded bulkhead doors, armoured and covered with levers, leading through a tubular passage to the somewhat less cramped control-room; but before passing through it one should bend down and be careful to remember that iron is always harder than one's head. A similar alleyway joins the control-room to the diesel engine room behind it. When the intruder opens the great riveted armoured door into this complicated domain of marvellous technology, he is assailed by a deafening din from the precious diesel engines. The noise of the pounding machinery is so terrific that only shouts have any chance of reaching the engineers, wedged among their levers, wheels, and a hundred technical devices... It is a little hell of rattling, whirring tumult. Every screw is watched, and not the slightest irregularity in the rhythm of the engines can escape those experts whose ears are attuned to noise. Everything is dripping with thick grease. In this place no cold air can penetrate.

In the next compartment, which is the home of the massive electric motors that drive the boat when it is under water, in contrast to the domain of the diesel engines, there reigns an almost solemn stillness, as also in the other compartments, except for the now somewhat hoarse but treasured gramophone rasping out ditties of home, of the sound of the compressed air whistling into the diving-tanks when the boat rises to the surface.

A smooth greasy iron ladder, about 2½ metres long, leads from the electric motor-room through a hatch, just large enough for one man, on to the after-deck, to the daylight and the fresh sea-air. Right astern, and also forward in the fo'c's'le, lie the torpedoes, the gleaming, red-tipped, death-dealing, precious 'eels,' the dreaded weapons of the U-boats... They cramp the quarters of the cheerful leather-clad ratings, who crouch in their bunks and hammocks above, below, and beside the firmly packed carcasses of the torpedoes.[540]

Bergen also describes more personal elements of the regime aboard, now well established.

I carefully push aside my green curtain and assure myself by a glance over the edge of my bunk, so near to the curved steel roof, whether the Navigating Officer below me, one of the most important persons on the boat, is still asleep. This officer's repose is sacred. However, this morning he is sitting on his bed, in his leather clothes, with his legs in his sea-boots, eating his breakfast... Then, with an agility to which I am now accustomed, I swing myself on to the floor. There are only sea-boots to put on, for the rest of one's clothing is worn, day and night, during a voyage that may last weeks. Thus, one's toilet is extremely simple, if not particularly thorough. Indeed, washing and shaving are seldom practised of a morning. It becomes easy to study the luxuriance or otherwise of our respective hair and beards. Probably the real pirates of old days looked much as we do; but the inner kernel behind this rough exterior does not justify any further comparison with that dreaded rabble of the seas. Water and soap are very precious on board a U-boat. Morning cocoa and bread and marmalade taste delicious under such conditions.[541]

This normalcy can be shattered at any moment. On this mission the only evidence of the British North Sea naval blockade *U 53* chances upon are a lone destroyer and a sub chaser encountered on 20 June, the third day of their voyage north:

The alarm bell shatters the morning repose, and brings with it the order: 'Diving stations!' The ship is suddenly full of hurrying men. The look-out men come crashing down from the conning-tower and report an English destroyer to port, whose masts, high bridge, and several funnels were already visible. When so much of one of those nimble sea-hounds can be seen above the dip of the horizon; it is high time to dive. She is bearing down on us with the speed of wind. But either our first enemy did not detect us, or she lost track of us when we dove. We were soon on the surface again. Nothing could be seen of our lively morning visitor... Very soon after, a second suspicious vessel approaches us from the port quarter and then quickly vanished. These northern waters seemed to be growing gradually more animated, and we could already feel the presence of the enemy.[542]

That evening, as *U 53* passes into the Atlantic, Bergen notes the change in the sea:

The steel-blue sea seemed to be heaving deep breaths. The Atlantic began to make itself felt. The great, powerful and majestic movement of that ocean replaced the lighter and more agitated currents of the enclosed North Sea...

A rising wind made the sea rougher. Waves began to break across the deck. The weather became cloudy and visibility was very limited. We reached the northernmost point of the Shetlands, and therewith the Scotland-Norway convoy-route. Now we might expect to see steamers, sailing-ships, and vessels of all kinds. In the ward-room that day there was a small glass of brandy and a cigar for every man, in celebration of the fact that we had reached the northernmost point of our trip. The conning-tower soon looked like a pleasant open-air club as the smoke of those excellent cigars rose upon the air. Late in the evening we talked to *U 54*, which came pretty close to us on her way home from the Bay of Biscay, after sinking 19,000 tons. Hereabouts, in fact, there were more U-boats than enemy ships.

When the watch was relieved, the setting sun conjured up the most magnificent colour effects on the clouds and the heaving sea. The fiery ball of the midnight sun hung, as it were, against a bright red wall. Dark violet tufts of cloud, rimmed with gold, drifted across the red blinding disc. It seemed hardly to approach the horizon, and when an hour had passed, it was almost at the same level. Just as I was carrying below a sketch of this marvellous spectacle that I had made under some difficulties on the conning-tower, the sun at last sank below the waters. But the rosy glow remained on the horizon all night, and another day soon dawned.[543]

The morning of the fifth day of their mission, 22 June 1917, *U 53* passed around the northern tip of the British Isles and heading south in company with *U 55*. Bergen describes the involved and meticulous five-hour preparations that led to an ultimately unsuccessful attack on a convoy of two merchant steamers, each protected by a pair of escort vessels:

Shortly after breakfast, about nine o'clock, several smoke-clouds appeared to starboard. At first, only two masts of a steamer were visible, continually shifting as a result of the vessel's zigzag course. Half an hour later the larger of the three vessels was clearly recognized through the periscope as a merchantman, accompanied by two escorts, steaming at top speed on a zigzag course and under cover of thick smoke-clouds, through the blockade zone to its port of destination. The commander decided to follow her. The conning-tower then became crowded. On a large sheet of paper, with the help of two T-squares, a pair of compasses and a pencil, the Navigating Officer traced the enemy's observed course, which the commander then checked on his bearings apparatus. Every movement of the vessel was watched through strong binoculars.

After some time and calculation the Navigating Officer was at last able to estimate the steamer's direction and speed. It was now our task to get ahead of the enemy vessel as fast as possible, or, in other words, to cut her off, and ourselves to remain unobserved. Fortunately a black cloud of smoke is always visible at a greater distance than the relatively inconspicuous conning-tower of a grey U-boat. At last everything was ready for the attack. At this point, another U-boat, to which we had sent a call, appeared upon the scene. After a mutual understanding as to the possibility of a combined action, both boats dove to attack the enemy now fast approaching.

Then began the nerve-racking hours of under-water navigation. The commander kept unceasing watch on his victim through his skilfully handled periscope; the oily water, that trickles in through the crevices round the periscope, dripping down over his cap and face. The reflection of the daylight shone brightly in his keen blue eyes.

Below was the silence of the grave; only the sound of the horizontal rudders broke the uneasy stillness. Every man was at his post, waiting for any orders that might come. I was sitting in the commander's room at his writing-table and listening through the speaking-tube to the reports from the conning-tower:

'Now she's turned again.'

'One of the escorts is coming straight at us.'

'The steamer's got a gun on deck.'

No one moved. The bulkhead doors and the heavy iron hatches were closed. The gun crew waited in the ward-room and discussed the position as the moments passed. The most important question was the supposed size and tonnage of the steamer that was approaching our torpedo-tube. Then once more we heard the sound of the periscope chain as it shifted up and down. We seemed to have been waiting an eternity: biding time we stare into vacancy. Everything depends on the commander's judgment and ability. Would the enemy sight our periscope? Would the patrol-boat manage to head us off just before we fired? However, after manoeuvres that lasted several hours, on this occasion some mishap defeated us and made any further attempt hopeless. The steamer had somehow become aware of our presence and turned away at the last moment; but the U-boat that we had met had then fired at her. We stayed for some considerable time at a depth of twenty metres with our periscope lowered. When we rose, our conning-tower had hardly appeared above the surface when the patrol-boats and their charge, now far off but still visible, opened rapid fire on us, but without success. Where we could see the jerking flashes of several guns to one side of us, a new cloud of smoke appeared ahead. This time it was a large tanker. 'Diving-stations!' Once more we plunged into the shelter of the blue-green depths.

An attack offered no prospect of success, so that after an hour we came up to the daylight once more. A destroyer which appeared on the scene later did not observe us. As a result of these failures we were all in rather low spirits, but hope of better luck soon restored us to our usual good humour.[544]

Commenting that 'Sailors are always superstitious' and 'this sort of prophecy is not always wrong,' Bergen noted that 'In the ward-room one of the officers was shuffling a pack of cards to predict the outcome of our next attack.'[545] Regardless of what the cards predicted, it ended with disappointment, followed by a two-day battle against the elements:

U 53 fought her way bravely through the raging waves; for two days and nights she pitched and rolled in the tumult of the waters. More than once the vessel seemed to be plunging into an abyss; then followed a crash and a quiver of the whole hull, when a watery mass stormed down upon the boat and flung her plunging bow upwards once again. All night long without ceasing, the furious waves could be heard smashing on to the decks and racing off the outer tanks. One had to wedge one's arms and legs most uncomfortably against the iron walls and partitions so as not to be flung out of one's bunk. Washing and eating were indeed a test of skill. In this fury of the elements we had nothing to fear from the enemy; he had enough to do to look after himself in such weather.[546]

When a huge in-bound 24,000-ton Cunard Liner hove into view, escorted by two destroyers, it too had to be ignored. The combination of its relative position and its speed, far too great to match, made it impossible to attack. Instead, U 53 became the hunted when, on June 27th, a tanker she was stalking turned out to be the English Q-ship *Viola*:

...the merciless alarm-bell put an abrupt end to nature study, and recalled us to the deadly seriousness of U-boat activity in the blockade zone. The closing hatchway shut the lovely sunshine out of the iron chambers. We lay at periscope-depth awaiting a steamer that was approaching on a rapid zigzag course. The torpedoes were ready in the outer tubes. Then suddenly, having detected our periscope, the Englishman altered course and bore straight down upon us. He was trying to surprise and ram us. Only about fifty metres separated his sharp and menacing bow from our periscope. Calm and resolute, our commander grasped the danger, which in a few nerve-racking seconds he averted by diving hastily to a considerable depth. The thudding of the steamer's propellers was clearly audible above us. There followed a deafening explosion, and a crashing blow that made the whole boat quiver. The glass of the depth-gauge was smashed. The lights went out. The emergency lighting was soon turned on and, in unshaken calm and discipline, measures were at once taken to deal with the damage. The horizontal rudder mechanism was out of action and seemed to be jammed. The boat was moving at a considerable depth. A second and third less powerful explosions followed quickly. Depth charges! All of them above the boat. Thank heaven, none of them had hit us. The horizontal rudder apparatus was soon put in order and all was well. The oil-tanks were undamaged and thus all trace of us was lost to our cunning adversary… The conning-tower hatch was open once again. With joyful grateful hearts, with radiant happy eyes, each and all of us, now that the danger was past, saluted the glorious sun as though it had been a fresh gift of God. We had come very near to death, but – we were still alive.[547]

One Sinking Equal to Winning an Entire Battle

Finally Bergen was able to describe a successful attack later the same day, southwest of Fastnet Rock. It was initiated against the Cunard steamer *Ultonia*, en route from New York to London with what at the time appeared only to be general cargo. The attack killed one of the steamer's crewmen; some sixty survived in four lifeboats:

'Diving stations!' We were not to enjoy the daylight for long. After two further hours of anxious movement under water we were ready for an attack upon a large steamer, escorted by a small black armoured patrol-boat. Nervous tension had reached its limit when at last the longed-for order came down the speaking tube and brought us deliverance. 'Fire!' Our first shot with a torpedo. The deadly missile left its tube with a jerk and sped through the water. All eyes were glued on the slowly moving second-hand of the clock, intent and anxious. Fifteen… twenty… twenty-five seconds had passed. Now!… A dull far-off crash shook the boat. A hit! If one could only see or know something of the tragedy that was being played out on the water in those moments. They are, perhaps, the last seconds of life for many human beings. The commander hurriedly sent for me to join him at the periscope in the conning-tower. No sooner had the unsuspecting escort passed us, than the torpedo tore its way through the iron walls of the great steamer's stern. In my brief glimpse at the bright reflection in the lens, I saw the vessel already sinking, the bow pointing to the sky, a red hull, thick white steam bursting from the funnel, a few crowded lifeboats, the helpless escort standing by, waves glittering in the bright sunshine, an English White Ensign. Then I had to make room for the commander. Scarcely had I got down to the ward-room again than I heard: 'She's sunk.' The periscope was lowered, and we proceeded under water for a long time so as to keep out of the way of the destroyer, which the sinking vessel and her escort had summoned by wireless. Lloyd's Register was now consulted as to the probable size and name of the steamer we had just sunk.

It was not until about midnight that we came up again. Through driving clouds, the moon casts her cold silver radiance on the phosphorescent sea, which has grown rougher in the interval. The water pours across the deck in myriad flashing green and blue pearls of light, and behind us the greenish-white silver band of our wake shines like a gleaming pathway. Great glittering masses of iridescence surge up to the surface of the waters. The look-out men stand motionless on the conning-tower, like dark shadows. Their faces, wet with sea-water, shine eerily in the bright green reflections of the sea.

The boat was slowly making her way towards the place where the steamer was sunk the day before. In the grey light of morning we could see far off on the tossing waves an apparently endless deposit of oil on which were floating hundreds of variously coloured barrels, pieces of wreckage, balks of timber, and other debris of a holed and shattered steamer now lying 4,000 metres beneath the surface of the sea.

This expanse of oil, glittering with all manner of colours, lay like a great shroud over this ocean grave. In oilskins and sea-boots, with hatchets and axes, the crew was on deck and searching among the floating casks and timbers for any object that might give any indication of the name of the torpedoed ship. An oar was sighted and quickly fished out of the water; then a red lifebelt. The latter was inscribed in white lettering with the steamer's name and port of origin. It is entered in Lloyd's Register as 10,402 tons, from Liverpool. What was the cargo? What was in all those casks? After much labour a few were dragged on to the deck. Thick brown oil trickled from the blue barrels: the red ones were packed with completely solidified whitish-yellow stearine. Hundreds of such barrels of both kinds were floating singly or in masses on the oily waters. Many were broken open or smashed. Glorious oil and fat! The rough sea prevented us from salving any part of this precious cargo. The oil would, of course, have been most useful for our motors. The contents of a single barrel of stearine was broken up with hatchets and taken below; then we left this strangely fascinating place of ruin, and the oil-smoothed heaving waters, the scene of a tragedy of the war.[548]

After the war, Rose discovered the military significance of sinking *Ultonia* and proudly wrote:

One of the largest ships sunk had been *Ultonia*, which had carried huge amounts of war materiel. Among them: 6 tanks, 11 trucks, 150,000 hand grenades; 140 machine guns; 20,000 guns; 500,000 cartridges; thirty 12cm Howitzers and 22,000 projectiles, plus 175 7.5 cm shells. This one sinking was equal to winning an entire battle.[549]

With Iron Calm our Gun-crew Bore their Part

Hunting four days later, on 1 July, *U 53* again became the hunted. Bergen described this second encounter with Q-ship *Penshurst*, a coastal steamer configured to look like a deeper draft tanker:

Above: *U 53*'s MORNING WATCH 1917 by Claus Bergen. The painter went aboard *U 53* for Hans Rose's 9th mission, sketching scenes from the conning tower to be rendered in subsequent years into dozens of paintings, some huge, hung throughout Germany. All of Bergen's paintings included here are of Rose's U-boat. [Rose Family Archives]

Right: 'HANS ROSE, RECIPIENT OF THE *ORDRE POUR LE MÉRITE*, THE 'BLUE MAX' Photographed 20 December 1917, the day he was awarded Germany's highest military honour. [Wehrgeschichtliches Ausbildungszentrum Marineschule Mürwik]

S.M. Unterseeboote U 51-56

Längsschnitt Einrichtungsplan Deckplan

Länge über alles .... 65,20 m
Grösste Breite über Spanten .... 6,44 m

Déplacement ausgetaucht .... 740 t
Déplacement untergetaucht ...... 900 t

Längsschnitt

Einrichtungsplan

Deckplan

U 53 TRAILS A SAILING SHIP Claus Bergen. [Author's Archive]

U 53 SHELLING THE DANISH THREE-MASTED BARQUE *ATLANTIC* By Claus Bergen. [Author's lithograph]

Above: HURRAY! WE'RE STILL ALIVE' British submarine *J6* attacks *U 53*. Romanticized painting by Claus Bergen. To fit an undersized picture frame Chris Rose cropped the two sides of the painting. [Rose Family Archive]

Opposite: U 53's WATCH Very large canvas painted by Claus Bergen for display in a railway station. [Deutsches Schiffahrtsmuseum]

Above: 'WE OPENED FIRE' Claus Bergen. [Author's Archive]

Left: *U 53*'s SISTER BOAT *U 54* FIRES ON A STEAMER The almost identical perspective is striking. [Otto Knüppel Archive]

WORKING ON HYDRO-PLANE IN BAD WEATHER *U 53* sister-boat *U 52*.
[Author's Archive]

TURKISH ROWBOATS ALONGSIDE SMS *LORELEY*. [Rose Family Archives]

THE WHITE SWAN, SMS *LORELEY c.* 1913 restored to glory under Rose's watchful eye. [Rose Family Archives]

1913 CONSTANTINOPLE Galata Bridge and before it to the right, the 17th-century Yeni Cami New Mosque. A number of warships anchor in the Bosporus Strait. SMS *Loreley*, the 'White Swan', is possibly anchored in front of the Dolmabahçe Palace. [Rose Family Archives]

MOSQUE by Hans Rose. [Rose Family Archives]

COSPOLI STREET SCENE by Hans Rose. [Rose Family Archives]

Above: ROSE ATTENDING A STURMABTEILUNG (SA) GATHERING Rose's swastika armband indicates that he is a member of the Nazi Party. After his 50th birthday in 1935 Rose would never wear the *Marine SA* uniform again; see page 229. [Rose Family Archives]

Left: ANNE-MARIE ROSE in Essen, 1935. *Kristallnacht*, 9 November 1938, further transformed her husband's thinking about the Nazi Party. Following the attack on Jewish people and businesses, Anne-Marie Rose wordlessly drove her son Christian from one demolished business to the next, ending at the Jewish-owned bank, Burghardt, where the Rose family had conducted their business. [Rose Family Archives]

ROSE FAMILY PORTRAIT 1938 Photographed in the family home at Springloh 32 in Essen-Heisingen, the expressions speak volumes: Anne-Marie looks at her husband, Christian out the window, Helga and Gerd (in his Hitler Youth uniform) at the photographer, Rose far off in the distance, and Heinz looks preoccupied. [Rose Family Archives]

HANS AND ANNE-MARIE ROSE, 1938 In their Springloh 32 home. The Claus Bergen painting in the background still hangs there today. [Rose Family Archives]

Left: HANS ROSE IN HIS
MID-SEVENTIES Late 1950s.
[Rose Family Archives]

Below: ROSE CONTEMPLATIVE
by Claus Bergen. [National
Maritime Museum (Greenwich)]

A black tanker hove into view ahead. Quite slowly, with very little smoke, and no attempt at a zigzag course, the ungainly oil tanker lurched on her way. She seemed unarmed, for the closest inspection did not discover any signs of a gun. Was she really so completely defenceless against U-boat perils in the blockade zone, as to steam through it with almost suspicious innocence at the very point at which a large steamer had been sunk only a few days before? The torpedo hissed out of the tube. Straight as a taut cable sped its greenish-white wake towards the centre of the steamer. Now!... Twenty ... twenty-five ... thirty ... thirty-five seconds, and still no explosion. It must have hit! But the steamer was still calmly afloat. It was now clear that this was no harmless tank-steamer, but a U-boat decoy, fitted with a deceptively shallow draught and possibly ballasted with cork. The commander did not take his eye off the suspicious vessel for a second. Suddenly she stopped, blew off some white steam, and expeditiously lowered her lifeboats, which had been swung out before the attack, fully manned into the water. She had observed our well-aimed and well-intentioned torpedo, which had unfortunately missed and gone under her keel. Orders soon came down the speaking-tube to rise to the surface and man the gun.

The conning-tower hatch was opened. The greasy iron ladder quivered and clattered under the hasty tread of several pairs of sea-boots clambering upwards. Men with unshaven stubbly beards, sou'westers tied to their heads, yellow oilskins, and set faces with their usual confident expression, shouldered their way past the commander's little platform up to the light and the gun. In a few minutes our first shell was screaming its way across to the apparently abandoned tank-steamer. A tall grey-green pillar of water shot upwards quite near her bows. The two lifeboats still kept the same distance from their ship, which seemed not yet to have been entirely abandoned. Admirable innocence!

Our commander drew a little nearer to the enemy, so that better aim could be taken as the sea was rather rough. Suddenly the harmless steamer turned and got under way again, moving at right angles to us. At the same moment the mask fell. The decoy opened a well-prepared broadside from quick-firing guns. Nearer and nearer came the shots. Shells whistled over our heads and splashed into the water. If only our tanks were not hit! With iron calm our gun-crew bore their part in this artillery duel.

In the meantime the lifeboats, containing actors in this unwelcome surprise performance had rowed round to the lee of their ship and were being taken on board again. The actual gunners, revealed at last and firing savagely, had, in malicious expectation of the success of the trap, been lying on their bellies beside the hidden guns. Under continued fire from the pursuing decoy we managed to draw out of the enemy's range. Urgent SOS calls soon brought two English destroyers to the spot, which forced us to dive and made it impossible for us to defeat our adversary.[550]

Making her way homeward on 8 July, *U 53* encountered and sank the beautiful Norwegian four-masted bark *Asheim*. Bergen described the attack and the subsequent realization that the action could have come at a very high price:

We gradually arrived off the northern point of Ireland in the neighborhood of Lough Swilly, a fjord-like inlet running deep into the land. Beyond, in the hazy distance, the mountains of the Emerald Isle rose some 2,000 feet above the sea. Against this lovely background moved a fully-rigged ship under sail. Our first sailing-ship!

Allowing for the possibility that this might be a U-boat trap, the commander opened fire at a distance of 4,000 yards. Breakers were dashing over the entire fore part of our vessel, much embarrassing the gunners who were lashed with ropes and belts to the gun, and often up to their hips in surging water.

After the first few shots the crew of the sailing-ship took to the boats, and one of them laboriously made its way alongside the U-boat. Several men, wearing the most diverse garments and unseamanlike headgear, clung to the benches of their boat as it danced on the waves like a nut-shell, casting timorous and questioning looks at the German blockade-runner, and especially at the gun trained on the ship, which was now hove-to and which they still appeared to think might be spared. They answered in English the commander's question regarding the origin, cargo, and crew of the ship, which was sailing under neutral colours. It was Norwegian, on its way in ballast from Dublin to America with a crew of twenty-four men. A gesture from the commander conveyed to them that they were dismissed and had better join their comrades in the second boat, which was now some distance off, and make for the coast of Ireland off which we were lying.

One shell after another tore great holes in the Norwegian's hull below the water-line. At every hit the whole rigging quivered, and great clouds of dust and powder floated up through the sails and spars high above the masts. A quarter of an hour later the proud sailing-ship, now full of water, began to move, turned uncertainly, and once more ran before the wind. Her stern was now noticeably down in the water. Her sails flapped: still struggling against her end, she turned once more, and, swaying several times to port and starboard, quivered and sank by the stern, almost majestically, with all sails set. A light green eddy, strewn with barrels and woodwork, marked her place of disappearance, from which a few minutes later loose timbers shot up out of the water.

Nothing was now between us and the view of a long chain of mountains, though again an approaching destroyer prevented any more prolonged enjoyment of the lovely coast-landscape... For six long hours we lay under water, steadily patrolling between Fanad Head, Horn Head, Tory Island, and Bloody Foreland. Later on in Helgoland, we learned that a few days before, a German mine-laying submarine had deposited its entire cargo in these waters, in which, all unsuspecting, but thanks to our good luck, we had manoeuvred without damage. It would have been a bitter end to be sent to the bottom by German mines.[551]

Rose was not yet satisfied with the mission's tally:

All the torpedoes had been fired except one, and the tonnage figure of the sinkings did not yet satisfy the commander. For this reason he was not yet disposed to sail for home. After all, we had an excellent gun, and might well expect to make good use of it some time. Such was the tenor of our conversation at luncheon that day, when the look-out men reported that the high rocky outline of St. Kilda was coming into view on the horizon.[552]

A couple of hours later, Rose shelled the Danish three-masted barque *Atlantic*, sinking her on 9 July as two patrol vessels arrived shooting wildly:

> Ahead of us, to starboard, a white sailing-ship was trying to out-distance our pursuit. With full speed ahead we managed to overhaul her; and a few shells induced the fugitive, a fine-looking ship under a neutral flag, to heave to. This time, too, the crew hurriedly took to the lifeboat and made for St. Kilda under sail. Suddenly there appeared round one of the rocky headlands two thick clouds of smoke, and, shortly after, the shapes of two armed patrol-vessels, which must have been stationed at St. Kilda, and which the sound of our firing had just reminded of the object of their hitherto aimless existence. We could already see the distant flashes of small guns. However, it was now essential to sink the sailing-ship quickly before any of their shells should damage our tanks. A direct hit had already set the vessel on fire amidships, and from it came a burst of reddish flame and thick clouds of brown and sulphur-yellow smoke.
>
> The sea poured in through the side of the ship in such volume that, at a distance of about fifty yards, the magnificent creature sank with all sails set in a very few minutes. Only the imperious necessity of sinking every ship within the blockade zone could master the grief natural to every true seaman at the sight of the destruction of so splendid a vessel. But, in this matter, beauty and poetry were as nothing against our duty to the Fatherland. If we were to perish like rats in a trap, then surely it was our sacred right to cut off the enemy's supply lines. Moreover, the declaration of the blockade zone was not mere words, but a visible reality marked by the motto: those who court danger perish in it.
>
> The helm was put over hard a-port. Without alteration of course we soon outdistanced our pursuers, who were still energetically but vainly bombarding us, until we lost sight of the yapping pack behind a romantic group of islands. The setting sun was coloring the St. Kilda rocks a rosy pink against the pale nordic sky. Later the desolate Flannan islands appeared in a reddish glow to port. A notable day, rich in material for an artist, was drawing to a close. Northwards again![553]

The next day, Rose encountered a flotilla of eight British fishing vessels, two of which were armed and put up a stiff resistance. The engagement would last eight-and-a-half hours, only concluding at 7 p.m. Bergen described the running gun battle that sank them, and then propagandises the discovery of ample rations the British crews enjoyed at a time when the British embargo was leading to mass starvation in Germany:

> A new day revealed to us, far off on the horizon, and partly obscured by heavy clouds, the jagged dark outline of the strange clear light of the turquoise-blue transparent northern sky, severed from the sea by a hard straight horizon-line. The seemingly endless distance was suddenly punctuated by eight smoke-clouds, well defined and within range; they belonged to a little steamer flotilla steaming northward... The heavy fishing-vessels had no chance to escape to the protection of Danish coastal waters. Understanding their plight, they divided into two sections, steaming in line, an armed escort bringing up the rear of each.

In this way our boat, as it plunged forward in pursuit, was brought under concentrated fire, which however, fell short. Our gun, set at a high elevation, fired alternating shells and shrapnel at both vessels, which were clearly recognizable as armed trawlers by their white funnels and English ensigns. The others sought safety in flight. Bursts of yellow and black smoke showed that our fire was proving effective; but the patrols fought obstinately and bravely. We drew nearer. The enemy shells splashed into the water only a few yards from our bows, and began to scream over our crowded conning-tower. I smoked a cigar and sketched. The patrols then drew together and began a well-directed rapid fire. Shortly after, a burst of black smoke rose high over one of the steamers whom we had christened the 'Admiral.' A series of hits followed in quick succession. She now tried to escape under the sulphur-yellow clouds of her smoke-bombs, but her wild zigzag steering brought her outside the veil of smoke as it moved obliquely across the water, and with every turn she offered an excellent target of which we took full advantage. They had soon had enough. Steam was pouring from their funnels. They stopped, and hurriedly manned and dropped their lifeboats. On approaching these shabby-looking black vessels where they lay pitching on the rollers, we saw the guns with their armoured shields hanging over the port bulwarks, completely wrecked by direct hits. Hanging by ropes over one of the guns was a boat-shaped object painted black which had served as a range-finder. So these oily fishing-tubs had been ready, when opportunity offered, to assume the part of U-boat decoys; and on that day their destiny was sealed. The shells tore their way through the thin iron hulls with dull booming crashes. The 'Admiral' sank bow foremost in the usual way; her consort vanished silently by the stern. The pressure of the air and water flung a little black cloud of soot from the funnels of both, the so-called 'black soul', the final farewell of a steamer on its way to the bottom of the sea.

The other six trawlers, which were still in flight, were soon overtaken and stopped. Six more lifeboats left the abandoned ships that lay scattered about us, none of which was equipped with wireless. We could proceed to sink them without fear of disturbance. Two of them were destroyed by gun-fire and the four others by high explosive cartridges. Our 'prize crew' in the small dinghy, the only small boat we had, was fully occupied with collecting various items of cargo that seemed likely to be useful to us, and with fixing the explosives. Six times the same performance was repeated; between the time the explosive was placed in position and the sinking of the ship, I made, as we passed, sketches of six dirty-looking steamers, each of them with a high bridge close to the funnel, two short masts, and their ports of origin and rather pompous names painted in white upon their hulls.

We were alone on the broad sea, except for six small black points away to the north rowing to the isles of refuge. A strange and unforgettable scene was taking place on the foredeck. The crew in their leather kit, and among them the officers keeping strict order; on the deck a medley of boxes and chests of cocoa, coffee and expensive tea, sacks of wonderful American meal, fresh butter and globes of margarine, cordage, unused nets, oilskins, rubber boots that did not fit the crew, fine white English bread, English marmalade, ham and bully-beef, bacon and beans, two bars of good soap, tobacco and various oddments. All these things, which were now completely strange to us, we had removed from a few paltry enemy fishing-boats, while in Germany the women and children were starving and dying of inanition, or supporting life on vile, injurious, almost inedible food-substitutes. The poor in Germany thought of the old days as they sat over their watery turnips; while in the cabins of these trawlers, which we happened to have sunk just at dinner time, were plates piled with, what seemed to us, lavish helpings of good fresh roast meat and potatoes, such as we only saw in dreams. No one was allowed to touch these appetizing meals for fear of poison. The stores, which would be useful to us and much appreciated at home, were stowed away below.[554]

Heading back into the North Sea, Bergen described a shark encounter:

There was a strange light in the evening sky. The sun had long since set, but the whole circle of the horizon was glowing with a fairy-like red splendour – a natural phenomenon that we could not explain. Our contemplation was cut short by a seal's desperate fight for life taking place nearby. Again and again the poor creature leaped right out of the water to escape its pursuer, a large, clearly discernible shark. It was soon over: the greedy monster grasped its wretched victim between its sharp teeth and disappeared.[555]

As the mission wound down, Bergen's account returned to observations of a more mundane nature:

Our course was south-west in the direction of the island of Utsire, on the Norwegian coast. The tall long-distance wireless masts which had been resting peacefully on the diving-tanks were now erected, and soon provided us with important news from home and from enemy countries. We were very glad to be in contact with the world again.

Next day the lofty snow-covered Norwegian mountains and fjords, glowing in the delicious morning sunshine, came into view. Within the three-mile limit, beyond the risk of U-boats, several sailing-boats and steamers were moving along the coast; and, through our glasses, the clean painted houses, the white windows, gleaming roads, wireless masts, and ships lying in the harbours, were clearly to be seen. Under a distant cloud of mist lay Stavanger. All who were off duty went up on deck and watched the passing panorama. For a whole day we sailed along an ever-changing mountain landscape until, towards evening, it dipped into a broad coastal plain...

The boat was swung sharply round, as the breakers dashed over us once more. We had been notified that the great U-boat and mine area began at the Danish coast, which we were following at the three-mile limit. We were ordered to put on our life-jackets. The Captain humorously recommended the excellent Danish cooking and the good clean hotels in case I had to swim ashore that night. The closed bulkheads made the ship feel like a gigantic mousetrap. During the early hours of the night I listened for any suspicious sound outside the hull. One waited – though one did not hope – for the ominous iron grating sound of a mine. In point of fact, it would then have been far too late for any lengthy reflections on how to escape from so unpleasant a proximity.

However, a sound sleep was the best way to get rid of such futile speculations. Next morning, with the deep and joyous consciousness of being still alive, we hailed the daylight, the German North Sea, two German torpedo-boats, and German airmen.

Our comrades came to meet us, just as they had escorted us on our way. Morning coffee and a good cigar tasted delicious. Everyone was busy cleaning himself up – washing, shaving, and hair brushing – for we did not want to enter Helgoland harbour looking like pirates. A wonderful peaceful summer day greeted our glad clean faces, radiant at the thought of home. The commander of a torpedo-boat fitted with mine-sweeping apparatus that came to bring us in flung us a hawser, on the end of which was a watertight tin box attached to a red lifebelt, containing fresh tomatoes for the ward-room and a bundle of rather stale newspapers. However, it was hardly to be expected that torpedo-boats on such remote service that often lasted for days on end should be able to produce the latest journals. Besides, what did we want with newspapers? Signs were quite enough to answer our mutual questions and to exchange the latest news of war and home. A few German patrol-boats and an outgoing U-boat hailed us. The green North Sea stretched away in front of us as smooth as a mirror. Seagulls from our own land circled above us and followed our wake. To port we could see once more the long shining dunes of the North Frisian Islands. At last the shout: 'Helgoland in sight ahead!'[556]

In terms of enemy tonnage sunk, Rose's ninth mission between June 18 and 13 July 1917, was not one of his most successful. Repeated torpedo failures conspired to reduce the success of the mission. Rose would comment in *U 53*'s *Kriegstagebuch*:

The large number of torpedo misses is at present inexplicable. The enemy ship course and speed calculations were extremely carefully prepared. They all promised a success rate which was not achieved.[557]

Nonetheless he would sink 15,352 tons of merchant shipping, 2,644 tons more than the average sunk by U-boats between February and July 1917.

Chapter 15
Convoy Time (Missions 10–12)

CONVOY ZIGZAGGING The confusing tracks of eight vessels viewed from the air. Unless a freighter captain maintained a highly repetitive pattern, something that was discouraged, viewed from sea level it was much more difficult to predict the future positions of a U-boat's targets. [Imperial War Museum]

As March 1917 drew to a close Rear Admiral William Sowden Sims received an urgent order from the Navy Department summoning him incognito to Washington. As soon as he arrived Sims was informed that the United States would soon be at war with Germany, and that the Navy Department was ordering him to London immediately to liaise with the British Admiralty. Admiral Sims was instructed 'to study the naval situation and learn how we could best and most quickly co-operate in the naval war... On reaching the other side I was to get immediately in communication with the British Admiralty, and send to Washington detailed reports on prevailing conditions.'[558]

Several days later the American steamship *New York* sailed for Liverpool with the Rear Admiral and his aide, Commander J. V. Babcock, aboard, travelling incognito as V. J. Richardson and S. W. Davidson. Met at the dock on 9 April Sims and his aide were rushed aboard a special train for London.

Over the course of the next several days, Rear Admiral Sims, taking the pulse of the population, recalled:

> The fear of German submarines was not disturbing the London season, which had now reached its height; the theatres were packed every night; everywhere, indeed, the men and women of the upper classes were apparently giving little thought to any danger that might be hanging over their country.[559]

Sims found an 'atmosphere of cheerful ignorance ... everywhere in London society'[560] sustained by the press and official reports of the middling success of Germany's unlimited U-boat campaign, now entering its third month. The Admiralty was publishing tables indicating that between four and five thousand ships were sailing to and from the British Isles weekly. For the week of Sims' arrival the Admiralty reported that although 2,406 vessels had arrived at British ports and 2,367 had left, only eighteen ships along with seven fishing vessels had been sunk by Germany's U-boat marauders. Sims remarked:

> Newspapers all over the British Isles showed no signs of perturbation; on the contrary, they were drawing favorable conclusions from these statistics ... the generally prevailing feeling both in the press and in general discussions of the war seemed to be that the submarine campaign had already failed, that Germany's last desperate attempt to win the war had already broken down, and that peace would probably not be long delayed.[561]

Admiral Sims, however, had learned otherwise.

On 10 April, the morning after his arrival, Sims was rushed to a meeting with his old friend, the First Sea Lord, Admiral Jellicoe:

> After the usual greetings, Admiral Jellicoe took a paper out of his drawer and handed it to me. It was a record of tonnage losses for the last few months. This showed that the total sinkings, British and neutral, had reached 536,000 tons in February and 603,000 in March; it further disclosed that sinkings were taking place in April which indicated the destruction of nearly 900,000 tons. These figures indicated that the losses were three and four times as large as those which were then being published in the press.
>
> It is expressing it mildly to say that I was surprised by this disclosure. I was fairly astounded; for I had never imagined anything so terrible. I expressed my consternation to Admiral Jellicoe.
>
> 'Yes,' he said, as quietly as though he were discussing the weather and not the future of the British Empire. 'It is impossible for us to go on with the war if losses like this continue.'
>
> 'What are you doing about it?' I asked.
>
> 'Everything that we can. We are increasing our anti-submarine forces in every possible way. We are using every possible craft we can find with which to fight submarines. We are building destroyers, trawlers, and other like craft as fast as we can. But the situation is very serious and we shall need all the assistance we can get.'
>
> 'It looks as though the Germans are winning the war,' I remarked.
>
> 'They will win, unless we can stop these losses, and stop them soon,' the Admiral replied.
>
> 'Is there no solution for the problem?' I asked.
>
> 'Absolutely none that we can see now,' Jellicoe announced.[562]

The situation was dire. In the twenty-three months prior to unleashing the unlimited campaign against merchant shipping, the average tonnage sunk by each of the German U-boats was 8,909 tons a month. In the six months following the start of the unlimited campaign, and before the institution of the convoy system, its U-boats were averaging 12,708 tons sunk per boat per month, an increase of forty-three per cent.

The forty-three per cent per boat increase provides an incomplete picture of the damage being done to British shipping. Twenty-three months before launching the unlimited campaign Germany had only had 37 U-boats available for operations. At the start of the unlimited campaign, it had 142 U-boats available, almost four times as many. Over those prior twenty-three months Germany had sent 3,666,195 tons of merchant shipping to the bottom, most of it British. It represented almost twenty per cent of Britain's prewar merchant fleet capacity. But in the first six months of the unlimited campaign alone she sank even more; 3,813,798 tons of merchant shipping.

For Great Britain it was an unsustainable rate. By April, the third month of the unlimited campaign, losses were so high that one in four British ships leaving the British Isle would never return. The German Admiralty had calculated that by throttling Britain's imports it would take six months to starve Britain into offering terms. The British Admiralty and her Ministry of Shipping concurred:

> This was a scientific forecast, founded on an accurate knowledge of our ocean-going shipping and the demands we had to meet. Had no improvements been made in the Admiralty's systems of defence, it would certainly have been fulfilled, though probably the period would have been extended by two or three months.[563]

Despite frantic efforts to build new merchant ships and purchase anything that would float, by the end of April 1917, three months into the unlimited campaign, Germany had whittled down Britain's merchant fleet to 15,000,000 tons, an 18% reduction.

The Canary in the Coal Mine

How could the hemorrhage of the merchant fleet be staunched? When Admiral Jellicoe, the First Sea Lord, presented Great Britain's dire straits to American Rear Admiral Sims, he had no idea. His mindset, like that of the British Admiralty as a whole for over a hundred years, had been cast by its greatest hero. Horatio Nelson's career, culminating in the Battle of Trafalgar, had demonstrated his tactical opinion: 'No Captain can do very wrong if he places his Ship alongside that of an Enemy.'[564]

In the 16th and early 17th centuries the Spanish Navy, at that time the most powerful navy in the world, used naval escorts to protect their galleons. The British Navy had used the time-honoured merchant vessel convoy system effectively in its war against France at the start of the 18th century, and before that, in its battles with the thirteen American colonies. In 1914 the Royal Navy provided naval escorts for troopship convoys bringing Dominion troops to Europe. Why was the British Admiralty reticent to reintroduce the merchant vessel convoy? Did it believe playing nursemaid to merchant vessel convoys was less prestigious than laying 'alongside' the enemy?

The Admiralty presented other justifications:

> The protection of merchant shipping by some form of convoy was loosely discussed in January 1917, but did not develop owing to the objections raised... The main objections being that the convoy provided a larger target than the single ship and that delay in assembling the vessels would seriously impair their efficiency.[565]

And so, despite Jellicoe's 'every expectation that it would grow worse',[566] the Admiralty relied upon a program of building and otherwise acquiring new merchant ships. Reliance upon offensive actions against the U-boats could not be expected to yield results greater than those achieved prior to the introduction of Germany's unlimited campaign. Neither were attempts to mine German U-boat departure channels and the English Channel effective. And of course there was no way that ships could be built fast enough to replace the losses. The entire construction program for 1917 would only contribute 1,163,000 tons of merchant capacity, making up about a quarter of the 4,010,000 tons the British Empire lost during the same period.

Yet all the while the solution was staring them in the face, if only they chose to check the health of the canary in the coal mine.

To keep her armament industry in production France required a million and a half tons of British coal a month; a flow of coal guaranteed by the monthly cross-Channel passage of some 800 colliers. Unfortunately the Channel was now unsafe; having become the happy hunting ground of Germany's fleet of small UB and UC-class U-boats of the Belgian-based Flanders Flotilla. U-boat depredations, particularly in the last three months of 1916, had resulted in a thirty-nine per cent reduction in coal delivery. French naval authorities urgently demanded a solution be found. Royal Navy commander R. G. H. Henderson introduced a program of 'controlled sailings' comprised of convoys of up to 45 colliers escorted by three or four armed trawlers of the British Auxiliary Patrol. The system was initiated on 10 January 1917. By the end of April, 2,600 colliers had safely made the cross-Channel passage while only five (0.19%) were sunk by U-boats.

The canary was demonstrably alive. The extraordinary effectiveness of his 'controlled sailings' led Henderson to become an advocate of open ocean convoys:

> He rejected the theory of the larger target, holding that if the convoy were adequately guarded the enemy would as a rule only be able to have one shot, and that would be a browning shot, which might or might not hit. If it did hit there was only a certain percentage of the convoy lost as far as that submarine was concerned; whereas out of a similar number of steamers coming along the track independently, he would probably account for two or three or even more. Further, he argued that the convoy would be under control, and could be diverted from the presence of a known submarine in a way which was impossible with single ships, many of which at that time would not be fitted with wireless.[567]

Henderson presented his arguments up the chain of command. Unfortunately 'some considerable time elapsed before the Admiralty was satisfied that these figures were accurate.'[568] In April the War Cabinet urged the Admiralty to initiate a system of convoys forthwith. In May the Admiralty agreed to a series of trials, and on the 10th of that month, the first convoy departed Gibraltar:

> The convoy arrived without loss, making a voyage two days shorter than would have been the case had the vessels come home independently on the various devious routes which were then prescribed. Station keeping, the point on which the Admiralty were very dubious, and which was essential to the success of the system, was quite good, and the Captains who were interviewed stated that they had enjoyed more sleep than they had had for months. Being relieved of the unwonted responsibility of coping with an enemy, they accepted without demur the increased difficulties of their proper business of navigation.[569]

On 17 May the Admiralty appointed a committee to organize a general system of convoy. Its recommendations were submitted to the Board of the Admiralty on 6 June and approved by Admiral Jellicoe, the First Sea Lord, on the 14th. Admiral Duff, Assistant Chief of Naval Staff (ACNS), was given responsibility for convoys, but found it extremely difficult to find the requisite ships:

> Towards the end of June pressure of a very urgent nature was brought to bear through the Shipping Controller, and the Board of the Admiralty at last consented to give effect to its own approval. Forces were provided from patrol area commands, destroyers, sloops, 'P' boats, and trawlers; the United States of America were invited to help with ocean escorts as well as with destroyers.[570]

Finally on 2 July 1917 the first four-day convoy left Hampton Roads with twenty-four steamers. By the end of the month thirteen others had followed: 'The success of these convoys was phenomenal. Fourteen convoys comprising 242 steamers were brought in without the loss of a vessel, although the convoys were sometimes attacked.'[571]

The convoy system had been introduced, and the consequences were immediate. By the end of the war, 1,134 convoys, 527 outward bound from the British Isles, and 607 homeward bound, had safely shepherded 16,539 merchant vessels. A mere 0.92%, 154 of them, were lost. Of those 154, thirty-six had lost contact with their convoy and sixteen had been lost to miscellaneous marine perils. U-boats had only been able to sink 102 ships in convoy inbound or outbound from the British Isles. Remarkably, Hans Rose had sunk 18 of them.

Without a wholesale change of tactics, the introduction of the convoy system posed several ultimately insoluble problems for most German U-boat commanders. The first was an inability to locate targets. Heretofore the stream of individual merchant vessels travelling independently could be counted upon to pass any given point along shipping routes with considerable frequency. By the end of October 1917, 99 homeward convoys brought in 1,502 merchant vessels, totalling 10,656,300 tons with the loss, while in convoy, of only ten ships (0.66%). In an age where what you could see from the conning tower was essentially all you knew, the conglomeration of those targets into convoys had reduced the frequency at which U-boats encountered their targets fifteen fold. And if they did find them, attacking them was a lot harder:

> There seems to be no doubt that many of the enemy submarines were afraid to attack a convoy. Not only were they liable to instant counter-attack by the destroyers, but the very appearance of a convoy of merchant vessels was very unnerving when seen through a periscope. To take up from ahead a suitable position for attack, when some twenty-five steamers, each with a different turning circle were performing a zigzag, was more than any but the ablest and most daring German commander cared to tackle. The larger the convoy, the more unpleasant it looked.[572]

Admiral Scheer concurred, although he ascribed the difficulty to the effectiveness of escort countermeasures. Both of Commander Henderson's assertions were correct; 'one large target ran much less risk than several small ones,' and 'six escorting vessels afforded more protection to twenty merchantmen than three escorting vessels would to a convoy of ten ships.'[573] The veracity of the British Shipping Board conclusion was confirmed:

> Thus convoys of 1917/18, though considered a defensive scheme, possessed the same elements of bringing the enemy to action as their forerunners of the times of Drake and Nelson; the same causes operated with the same effects, but, with changed weapons, in an extended and more varied form.[574]

This was the dangerous tactical context Rose faced when he set out upon his tenth mission of the war.

Mission 10 – Fast and Successful (12–30 August 1917)

> As a young officer, the commander had experienced wonderful days on the green island of Ireland. His ship had been stationed in Queenstown ... he lost touch with his friends from the past. Yet, his penchant for Erin Island remained. This might have been part of the reason why he returned to the Irish coast during WWI, when, through his periscope in balmy weather, he searched for familiar spots.[575]

It is more likely that Rose's choice of hunting grounds was motivated by the lack of targets inbound for the British Isles on its western approaches. Two months before, the British had instituted homeward-bound convoys. During this mission Rose spent the entire time on station prowling the waters at the entrance of the Northern Channel to the Irish Sea. But his first attack was bitterly disappointing. The failure offers a window into both his personal character and how he ran his ship:

> On 16 August 1917 the submarine once again arrived off the north coast of Ireland... The commander turns the periscope in a circle musing out loud, 'Nothing to be seen.'

No picket vessels. In the south, the mountains of Ireland. In the east, Inishtrahull. In the west, the [target] ship seems to be all alone and quite large. About 8,000 BRTs. It is approaching quite rapidly. Will manoeuvre for a bow shot. Wonderful weather with a nearly cloudless sky. Ideal for an attack. Everyone in the submarine is listening in.

'The U-boat is on course,' Stein reports, 'I can hold the depth exactly.'

The enemy is ready to be felled. When the first of the four masts passes the [periscope] sight line, the first torpedo is fired and when the fourth mast passes the sight line, the commander sends a second torpedo after it. The distance from the enemy is eight hundred metres. The terrifying torpedoes are racing towards him. The speed of the enemy is estimated at ten knots. But both torpedoes pass behind the ship. The ship must be larger than the commander estimated, is therefore further away, and must be cruising at no less than fourteen knots. Probably an erroneous estimate. No one on the ship seems to have noticed the attack. It proceeds without changing its course. The U-boat dives to thirty metres and two new torpedoes are loaded.

The atmosphere on board is depressed. The commander is embarrassed to appear before his men in the *Zentrale*. How could he explain, excuse, and justify the miss? His crew is willing to follow him into the most dangerous situations... Might the two misses have had something to do with the torpedoes themselves?

'Was the depth properly set Schnackelfranz?'

'Yes.'

'Did you follow all regulations?'

'Yes, all – along with Katzera.'

'And what does he say?'

'The torpedoes were in perfect order.'

'Two misses,' the commander sighs, 'we have only eleven torpedoes left. If matters continue like this...'

Schnackelfranz salutes and says:

'Mr. Captain Lieutenant, a soldier has to also be able to bear failure.'

The commander stares at him. Should he put him in his place?

'You are right Schnackelfranz. Dive to 20 metres.'[576]

Schnackelfranz has apprised his commander that an effective warrior must embrace self-acceptance and self-forgiveness. Daring to take such a liberty could only have occurred because Rose fostered a collegial environment. Commenting on the crew in general, Rose explained:

The submarine was well known for its quick trips and its short and well written entries in the War Diaries... Every crew member was aware of his co-responsibility. A band of reciprocal trust and respect connected everyone on board. No service was counted as less important than any other. Everyone had his sphere of activity, which he fulfilled conscientiously and with justifiable pride. The crew changed constantly. After every mission, three to four were posted elsewhere, either to apply their knowledge on a newly commissioned U-boat, or to take courses and then return with new expertise. The men were not pleased to be rotated, yet they were filled with pride at what they had learned and carried their confidence and reliability to other boats… After every mission the commander would call the crew together to announce that the boat had been granted a certain number of Iron Crosses… and that these were meant for all of the crew. In spite of that only a chosen few received them at any given time. Rose noted that these assignments were unfair, since Gerd Noorman had steered *U 53* into battle more than a hundred times, but had never received the Iron Cross first class.[577]

Almost immediately Rose was offered another target, the 8,668-ton armed English steamer *Athenia*. He sank her with a single torpedo killing fifteen. Rose writes in the *Kriegstagebuch*: 'Crew disembarks in 8 full and 2 lightly filled boats, 3 more drift empty. About 250 people.'

On 21 August, executing an extraordinary display of seamanship, Rose was the principal author of what the British Ministry of Shipping would term a 'disastrous initial venture'.[578] The first outbound convoy to be organized from the British Isles set out from Buncrana in the Irish Sea and formed up in Lough Swilly. Adequate defences were not in place. In a daring attack while the convoy was forming up, Ernst Killmann commanding *U 102* would torpedo and severely damage the 10,757-ton armed merchant cruiser *Virginian*, while Rose, with simultaneous bow and stern torpedo shots, would sink both the 8,238-ton *Roscommon* and the 10,435-ton *Devonian*. Two men aboard *Devonian* died. In an age without radar or sonar, the only way Rose could navigate unseen among the crowded ships of the convoy was with brief glimpses through his periscope and dead-reckoning. Rose described the attack:

A large, extended formation of ships, a very strong convoy was coming from Innisthrahull. It contained at least twenty-six ships and other large and small vessels, not counting the escorts. The formation was led by a 5000 BRT auxiliary cruiser with heavy hull armour. The ships moved in four columns, with the smallest vessels in the two outside columns. The larger ships were located at the front of the columns. The formation was surrounded by destroyers and other escort vessels, some of which were also located between the columns.

Slowly the U-boat established a course opposite that of the destroyers. The commander only used his periscope for a few seconds. Yet, a glance was sufficient to determine that one destroyer crew was busy cleaning its artillery. The next panoramic view showed a destroyer passing close in front of the U-boat's bow. Once more the commander repeated his observations in a low murmur. He felt his heart beat in his throat. 'Calm down,' he thought, 'Calm down,' while tightening his grip on the periscope. Slowly he raised it. Stop! Another quick look forward.

'We will take an opposite course between the two middle columns. The distance to the leading ships is 800 metres. Need a report every ten seconds!'

Another quick look behind to starboard and to port.

'We have passed the vanguard, the auxiliary cruisers and destroyers are already behind us.'

'They haven't seen us.'

'Lower the periscope!'

'Please ready all four torpedoes.'

'Ready tube 4 at 270 degrees!'

The commander calculated: passing speed about fifteen knots. Every second we are advancing seven and a half metres. That means we will arrive between the ships in one hundred seconds.

The Chief Navigator counted serenely 'thirty seconds, forty seconds.'

The commander ordered 'raise the periscope once more.'

'Lower the periscope.'

'Correct!'

'Watch the depth rudder carefully!'

'We will initially attempt a stern shot angled to the port side and then a clean stern shot – and then we'll see what next!'

'70 seconds, 80 seconds!'

'Both engines half speed ahead.'

'Raise the periscope.'

'There they are.'

'We are between them.'

'Fourth torpedo ready.'

'Fire!'

'Port 20!'

'Third tube, ready!'

Boom, the first torpedo hit its mark.

'Twenty-five seconds running time,' the Chief Navigator announced.

'Third torpedo – fire!'

The commander turned the periscope forward. There was no purpose in looking towards the rear, since the torpedo tubes were empty. Boom, the second torpedo detonated.

'It also took twenty-five seconds to its destination,' the Chief Navigator observed laconically.

The convoy ships were in total disarray. The periscope was being shot at from somewhere. Soon it would hail depth charges! The passenger ship turned sharp to starboard and seemed to be moving backward, in order not to collide with the vessels in the neighbouring column.

'First tube. Attention... Fire!'

But it was an illusion; the vessel was careening full speed ahead. The torpedo missed. There is nothing more to do now, the commander thought, but to rise to fifty metres.

'Full speed ahead.'

He threw a last glance at the two stricken ships, one of which had sunk up to its railings, while the other had such a heavy list that the periscope revealed its entire deck.

While the submarine disappeared into the cool depths, one heard the quick buzzing sounds of destroyer propellers and shortly afterward the horrendous cracking and breaking of a sinking ship. The commander came down to the command centre. Everyone shook hands.

'Excellent steering, Stein. The torpedoes moved superbly, Schnackelfranz. Fabulous timing Chief Engineer. Our reputation has been saved, Jung. Monsieur

Guilleaume, please let everyone know that the commander congratulates the crew
on their achievements.'

These sentiments were accompanied by the fast moving electric motors that
seemed to be whistling a victory song. The joyous spirit was interrupted by the
Senior Petty Officer of Engineering, who was concerned about conserving sufficient
electricity... The U-boat slowed down. A half hour later however, when the
commander wanted to take a look at what was going on above, strong destroyer
propeller sounds forced the U-boat into a deeper dive.[579]

The next day, still in pursuit of the previous day's convoy, Rose encountered the
armed British mixed-cargo steamer *Verdi*. He damaged her with a submerged
torpedo shot, and then sank her with shells after about 150 crew and passengers
rowed away in five lifeboats. Six died.

The following day, the 23rd, in Donegal Bight, the scene repeated itself
almost exactly when Rose sank the 3,799-ton armed British steamer *Boniface*
after the crew rowed away in three lifeboats. One man died.

Three days later, 26 August 1917, would be his last on station. At 4 a.m. in
the morning Rose torpedoed the armed 3,919-ton British mixed-cargo steamer
Kenmore. With the ship slow to sink, three hours later, in order to attack his
next target, the 3,008-ton steamer *Durango*, he was obliged to use his last
torpedoes to finish *Kenmore* off. Having expended the U-boat's weapon of
choice, Rose had to depend upon his artillery. With destroyers about to join
the fray, and *Kenmore* proving a tenacious target, Rose relied on subterfuge to
win the day:

At dawn on 26 August 1917 the last torpedo was used to deliver a *coup de
grace* to a coal ship departing the North Channel. Ordinarily it was considered
wasteful to use two torpedoes on one ship, but in this case, in order not to lose
the opportunity with another departing ship, speed was of the essence... When
Kenmore sank after having been hit twice, the U-boat followed the other vessel.
They no longer had any torpedoes and because the swell was heavy, an artillery
battle was impossible. So it was decided to wait... The crew ate a substantial
lunch. After that there was a call for the gunners to prepare themselves. Petty
Deck Officer Gläschick saw to it that his men donned rubber suits and put
cotton into their ears. In a deep basso voice, he announced 'Artillery is clear
for action.'

Stein passed the message on to the commander, who was in a bad mood since he
detested gun battles. There were frequent misses and he hated the noise.

Stein turned to the commander and raised his hand. He responded in the same
way and called 'Open fire!'

Uncle Ernst's big moment had arrived.

'Fifty-five left, 210,' Stein commanded. 'Ready to fire.'

Shot after shot left the barrel... Uncle Ernst aimed 'true' ... not 'into the
air', firing while the last shot was still en route... The enemy was not, however,
intimidated. He responded with the same calibre shots... The return shots were
uncomfortably close... The Signal Mate Zummack called for Schnackelfranz. He

came down and returned with the message: 'The ship's name is *Durango* and it is urgently calling for help.'

It was an uneven battle, the U-boat fired into the wind and sun, from a lurching platform, at a relatively large target, whereas the ship shot from a stable platform at a small, moving target. On the whole, *Durango* had the advantage, its impacts occasionally detonated only five metres away from the submarine... Schnackelfranz reported the message, 'The land station informed *Durango* that help is on the way, please give your position, steer to the north.' Consequently the commander immediately set a north-west course forcing *Durango* from a westerly to a southerly course. *Durango* then informed CGZ: 'Am being pushed on a south-westerly course by the submarine. We urgently need help.' Bang, bang the shells fly. Huiii, splash, come the impacts.

'Hurray, a hit!' screams Thomas.

There was heavy smoke near the enemy, who as a result disappeared very skilfully using this new cover... The situation was very unpleasant. Signal from DGZ to *Durango*: 'Persevere, destroyer on the way. Steer south-east.' The submarine roared full speed ahead in a southerly direction, pushing the ship north-west again, a course which offered greater visibility. Firing commenced once more on the part of the submarine. The contest had already consumed two and a half hours...

Though the enemy continued to respond, his calls for help became more desperate. At the same time, ever louder, came the answers from the approaching destroyers... The commander asked the Wireless Mate 'Can you imitate the British sender?'

'Yes, pretty much. I'll have to let the converter run more slowly.'

'Give me a paper.'

The commander scribbled a message.

'When I call you, please send this signal as loud as you can.'

The Wireless Mate disappeared below deck. Stein called the commander down to the front deck [who ordered] 'As soon as this small rain shower is over, steer at *Durango* at top speed and increase the rate of firing to twelve shells with scatter shrapnel interspersed after each second shot.'

When the third shrapnel shell burst, the ship's calls for help were desperate. That was the [commander's] intention... Bang, bang, shrapnel shot. The [commander's] signal is sent and received. *Durango* ceased firing, stopped and lowered her lifeboats. The ship lay abandoned on the waves. The signal that Zummack had sent was: 'OGZ to *Durango*: Leave the ship before the lifeboats are damaged.' Whether *Durango*'s signal mate had recognized the deception or not was of no consequence. What is important is that the captain responded to it... The weather had meanwhile turned dusky and quiet. The U-boat steered close up to *Durango*. At close range, Senior Petty Officer Gläschick shot a few shells below the waterline... The commander ordered: 'Stop batteries, stop – belay artillery.'

Gläschick took his eyes off the gun sight and called to the tower: 'Mr Captain, please let me take one more shot at the cannon of that ass.'

The commander raised his hand in acquiescence. Bang, the enemy's cannon flew out of the gun carriage and the detonating munitions whizzed around the U-boat men's ears. When the U-boat made its exit, the billowing smoke of the arriving enemy destroyers was already visible over the wake. The U-boat's remaining stock of munitions consisted of five shells.

Repeatedly, a destroyer's message floated across the ether: '*Durango* we are coming. Where are you? Give your position.' The U-boat answered 'Too late. *Durango* awaits you at the bottom of the sea. Signed UUU.' Rarely has a ship been destroyed by a wireless message. Signal Mate Zummack was awarded the Iron Cross First Class.[580]

Rose leaves us with a vignette about life in the tiny wireless-telegraphy compartment.

The wireless-telegraphers were this trip's trump. In addition to the chief of this weapon, Lieutenant Schnackelfranz, there was the lanky *FT-gast*, Wireless Telegraphy mate, Hubig, an intellectually alert, single-minded young man, motivated by holy aspirations. He helped the shorter Lieutenant Schnackelfranz with his written work, reducing it to a minimum, and with the ordering of his personal affairs. Hubig called him 'Bubi'. All the crew found it hilarious when in bad weather Schnackelfranz used the loudspeaker, and in a high woman's voice called: 'Bubi – Bubi come to Papa!'

Bubi elegantly lurched through the bulkhead: 'Come Bubi dear, give Daddy your hand....'

The fantastic atmosphere that reigned was unchanging, even when the wireless, that had worked so well, broke down in the North Sea.[581]

Rose returned to Helgoland from his brief eighteen-day mission believing he had sunk seven vessels totalling an astounding 45,187 tons.

Upon return, the unexpectedly short mission lead to a comic misunderstanding. The Fleet commander hurried down to the pier.

'Welcome, there you are.'

'Yes, I report the boat's return from our voyage.'

'Well, well the most important thing is that you are back. What's broken?'

'Nothing, Captain, Sir, everything is O.K.'

'But why are you back so soon?'

'We don't have any more torpedoes and there are only five shells left.'

[After a pause] 'How many ships have you sunk?'

'Seven ships and 44,000 BRTs.'

The Flotilla Chief took a deep breath and looked around for others to inspire with the news. Then he ripped his hat from his head and bellowed

'Three hurrahs for the victorious U-boat.'[582]

The next day, 31 August, while *U 53* cruised back to the mainland from Helgoland, the German Navy issued an official communiqué lauding Rose's accomplishment. Rose continues:

When *U 53* cruised up the Jade the next morning, the crews of all the ships they passed were arrayed aft with flags conveying congratulatory messages. A while later the commander was called to the BdU, who said: 'The Admiralty has informed the *Kaiser* about your trip. The *Kaiser* is giving you a signed picture of himself.'

Deeply touched the commander received the picture in its iron frame. Its dedication read: 'To the valiant commander of *U 53*', signed Wilhelm J. R.

When he reported to Berlin a few weeks later, in September 1917, the commander was told that the Chief of Cabinet, Admiral von Müller, wished to see him. The Admiral received him cordially:

As a particular token of gratitude, I am presenting you with the Admiralty Report that contains the *Kaiser*'s personal comments in the margins. May it be a special remembrance for your family. I myself wish you all the best for your future voyages.[583]

Mission ten was Rose's most prolific of the war.

Mission 11 – Nothing but Convoys (5–20 October 1917)

When, between 5 and 20 October 1917, Rose returned to sea for his eleventh mission of the war, he found that almost all ships now travelled in convoy. He first sank the 1,031-ton English steamer *Gowrie* with a surface torpedo attack, and then, out of the same inbound convoy, sank the 5,735-ton armed English steamer *Bostonian* with a submerged torpedo shot. The next day, 11 October, he sank the 3,967-ton American steamer *Lewis Ludenbach* in an outbound convoy, pursuing her even though she sighted his periscope, turned towards the U-boat to ram him, and began firing her guns. Rose was forced to dive to fifty metres, completing his attack two-and-a-half hours later. Four days later he attacked an outbound convoy of twenty large steamers travelling in several lines protected by a destroyer. Rose attacked the convoy three times, twice missing his targets, and once missing his target but hitting a steamer in the next line. It was the 10,064-ton armed English steamer *San Nazario*, but she managed to limp to harbour.

On 17 October, Rose encountered a convoy of seventeen ships travelling in a four-line formation spaced about a thousand metres apart. They were protected by a destroyer, a trawler and an escort cruiser. In the mid-afternoon he torpedoed the 4,750-ton armed English steamer *Polvena*. Rose continued to pursue the convoy, catching up with it again as dusk fell, when he sank the 2,997-ton, armed English steamer *Manchuria*, by surface torpedo attack. Headed back to base on the 19th, he encountered the 2,655-ton Dutch steamer *Parkhaven* and sank her with artillery fire. While engaged in the artillery attack, *U 53*'s lookouts sighted a distant submarine that dove in response to an E.S. star signal. It was the English submarine *E45* which attacked *U 53* with a triple torpedo attack. *U 53*'s lookouts spotted two of the three torpedoes, one of which broke the surface. They missed the U-boat by 150 metres. Again Rose was lucky. *E45* was a dangerous adversary. The same day, October 19, she attacked and sank *UC 79*.

On this mission, Rose sank more than twice the October 1917 monthly average. The mission was lauded with another official navy communiqué.

Mission 12 – Happy Prisoners
(17 November–12 December 1917)

For his twelfth mission, Rose again used the English Channel to reach the Western Approaches. Four days later, in bad weather off South Falls, Rose attacked a Dutch convoy under destroyer escort. When his submerged torpedo attack failed Rose surfaced and taking advantage of poor visibility, successively stopped the Dutch cargo steamers *Nederland* (1,832 tons) and *Megrez* (2,695 tons) when they were out of sight of the destroyer screen. He signalled them by flag to abandon ship, and then sank both by 10.5 cm shell artillery fire.

Two days later, on the 23rd, in a two hour and forty-five minute operation, Rose sank the 3,112-ton armed British coal-carrier *Westlands* travelling in convoy from England to France. He stopped the steamer with a surface torpedo shot that struck it in one of the two forward cargo holds, and then sank her with artillery fire 'just as the crew were ready to climb out of the lifeboats again'.[584] The next day Rose attacked yet another inbound convoy of eight ships travelling in two lines under strong destroyer escort. At 1:10 a.m., despite close cover of a destroyer using search lights to scan the waters around the convoy, Rose fired a surfaced bow shot at the 3,617-ton armed British steamer *Dunrobin*, sinking her in only four minutes. Thirty-one men including the master were killed.

On 1 December, off Lizard Head, Rose noted the assembly of a number of destroyers and trawlers and suspected that an ocean-going convoy was in the offing. It arrived from the English Channel in the afternoon and in heavy seas Rose launched a submerged torpedo attack that required superb depth-keeping by *Oberleutnant zur See* Klein. The torpedo struck the 7,555-ton armed English steamer *Helenus* travelling in the convoy's middle line. Rose dove to forty metres after launching his torpedo, but within four minutes the first depth charge, followed by eight others, was launched against him. When he surfaced fifty minutes later, destroyers kept him from re-approaching the convoy and it disappeared. The damaged *Helenus* was towed safely to harbour.

Four days later, cruising within the three-mile limit off Start Point, Rose torpedoed the 2,353-ton armed British steamer *Earlswood* in sight of land. The torpedo's detonation in the engine room enveloped the ship in a cloud of smoke as the crew fled to the lifeboats. But sea conditions were calm, patrol vessels rushed up, and the ship was salvaged.

That night, at midnight, the events that would lead Rose to sink the American destroyer *Jacob Jones* began. Rose plucked two drowning American sailors out of the sea and he radioed his famous message to the enemy: 'Destroyer *JACOB JONES* sunk 49°20′ N., 6°18′ W. Go Rescue survivors. UUU.'

Three days later, on 9 December, with the two American sailors aboard, Rose would attack yet another convoy, sinking the 2,045-ton armed English steamer

War Tune and damaging the 4,053-ton armed English steamer *Nyanza*. The next day Rose would sink his final ship of the voyage; the 450-ton Norwegian coastal vessel *Oiekast* travelling from England to France. He destroyed her with thirty artillery shells: 'The American sporting blood in our two involuntary guests showed itself strongly on these occasions. They were greatly interested and apparently quite as eager as we were that there should be no clumsy misses.'[585]

Rose remembered:

Our prisoners accommodated themselves rapidly to their new manner of life, and they and the crew became fast friends. One was a middle-aged man named Murphy, a cook; the other, a youth around eighteen, a signalman named Albert DeMello, of Portuguese descent.

I fitted them out with pipes and the crew gave them some tobacco. When the weather was good the crew used to come up on deck and sing old German songs. Then Murphy contributed American airs, 'Oh the moon is all agleam on the stream' and so on – 'Hiawatha,' I think, was the name of it – and 'Yankee Doodle' and other songs.

The time hung a bit heavily on the hands of Murphy, the quiet Yankee. He came to me one day and begged to be allowed to peel potatoes. 'Sure,' I said; 'peel for the whole crew if you want to.'

He went away happy and started to work.[586]

Happy prisoners can be talkative prisoners, and *U 53*'s *Kriegstagebuch* records the intelligence that Rose extracted from the two men about American destroyer strength, depth charge capability, convoy organization, inter-ally bickering, damage to a mine sweeper and the destroyer *Cassin*, and the hitherto unexplained loss of *U 58*.

After sinking *Oiekast*, Rose returned to base braving the dangers of the Dover Strait anti-U-boat defences; a route that concerned Murphy and DeMello:

Only one thing worried them. That was the matter of getting through the English Channel, with its mines, nets and patrols. They were astonished and frankly incredulous when, two or three days later, I said to them: 'Well, boys, we're in the North Sea.' I showed them our location on the chart and also our course.

'That's impossible,' said Albert, 'No U-boat can get through the Channel.' From the beginning, young DeMello was 'Albert' to everybody.

He was mistaken. He did not know that I had taken *U 53* through the Channel seven times, six times over the Channel net and once under it. It was dangerous and unpleasant, but it could be done.

The prisoners were very surprised when they were told one quiet hour on 11 December: 'We are on the floor of the North Sea not far from a Dutch light-vessel; we intend to wait for darkness.'

With particular satisfaction, they drank the chocolate which had been served for this festive occasion marking completion of the successful trip.[587]

The next day the twenty-five-day mission came to an end. After a night spent aboard *Sophie*, Rose took *U 53* to Wilhelmshaven for a refit, and to hand the prisoners over for incarceration.

Over the course of his last two missions, Rose took out of commission 56,898 tons of enemy merchant shipping; 30,231 tons sunk, and 26,667 tons heavily damaged. His accomplishment was the subject of German propaganda in the English-language radio broadcast on 18 December. But far more significant for Hans Rose was his award, on 20 December 1917, of Germany's highest military medal, the *Ordre Pour le Mérite*, the Blue Max. He was the fourteenth U-boat commander to receive the honour.

More significant for DeMello's mother was Rose's final empathetic gesture. A knight was not only a warrior, but just, noble, considerate, the champion of the weak. Completing his account of the sinking of *Jacob Jones* in the 13 May 1923 edition of Washington D.C.'s *Sunday Star*, Rose wrote:

We reached Helgoland on 12 December, in the evening. Early the next morning I was awakened by lusty singing. The crew had lined up before the cabin of Lieutenant Stein on the submarine tender and was singing a self-composed poem in honour of his birthday. And in the midst of the troop stood my two Americans, singing the German song as best they could, and entering fully into the spirit of the occasion.

They beamed when the Lieutenant gave them the same hearty handclasp with which he thanked the members of the crew. The former enemies had become good comrades.

I think it is worthwhile to say that the first song which the men sang that morning was the old Lutheran choral, 'Praise God, the Mighty King of Heaven.' they were patriotic men of simple, unmoved faith, which the revolution did not destroy.

When Murphy and DeMello, or Albert, as I always think of him, came to say goodbye before being taken to a prison camp, they were so deeply moved that they could hardly stammer out: 'We don't know how to thank you Captain.'

I was as deeply moved myself. I liked these Americans, the earnest, honest Murphy and the grateful, sprightly Albert, and hated to see them led away to the terrible monotony of their prison. I was glad, as a last service, to be able to send a letter to DeMello's mother.[588]

Chapter 16

Stuck, Upended, Nearly Sunk, but Still Deadly (Missions 13–15)

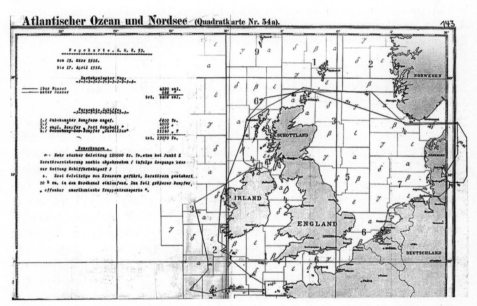

MISSION 14 'QUADRANT' MAP When sending coded information about a U-boat's location, the first component of the location was its quadrant location specified by a Latin letter. Rose included this map showing those quadrants in *U 53*'s *Kriegstagebuch*. The halcyon days of early 1917 are over and anti-U-boat measures have become increasingly effective. In order to safely leave and return to Helgoland, Rose is forced to take a long, circuitous route from Helgoland up the Elbe River, through the Kiel Canal to the Baltic, thence around Denmark via Skagerrak and then skirt along the Norwegian coast before transiting the North Sea and rounding Scotland to the north above the Orkneys. It is a voyage of some 4,220 nautical miles using up precious days simply to get to and return from his hunting grounds in the western approaches to the English Channel. [Bundesarchiv – Militärarchiv (Freiburg)]

Despite the horrific losses that the great land battles of 1915, 1916 and 1917 had wrought upon both sides, there was stalemate in the trenches of the Western Front at the end of 1917. On 6 April 1917 the United States declared war on Germany. By the end of the year fresh American troops and supplies were beginning to pour into France. At home the German people had suffered through the disastrous 'Turnip Winter' of 1916-1917. The British naval blockade of all food and materials destined for Germany had increasingly bit into the bone of the German Everyman's willingness to continue the war.

At the same time the November 1917 Bolshevik revolution led to the creation of the Soviet Union. On 2 December hostilities between the Russian and German armies were suspended and on 3 March 1918 the Treaty of Brest-Litovsk was formally signed. It offered Germany the opportunity to extract itself from a two-front war and transfer critical military reserves to the western front, increasing available troops there by thirty per cent. In March, April, May and July 1918, Germany would be in a position to launch her last great offensives on the western front.

Capturing that critical moment, Hans Rose's account of the period begins: 'On the Western Front, guns roared, tanks sped forward, machine guns spewed fire, and propellers whined. The decisive battle was in full swing.'[589]

Mission 13 – Ninety-Three Lives and 16,397 Tons (19 January–20 February 1918)

Rose leaves no explanation why he did not recount his eighth and thirteenth missions in *Auftauchen!*. His thirteenth mission, marked by 'Busy traffic in the English Channel, lone steamers near land, convoys in open sea',[590] accounted for seven ships grossing 16,397 tons. It was his sixth most prolific mission. But it was also his most deadly, killing at least ninety-three sailors; 35% of all the mercantile casualties his attacks produced. In the course of the war Rose would be responsible for the deaths of 64 navy personnel killed when he sank the destroyer USS *Jacob Jones*, and at least 264 sailors killed when he sank merchant and fishing vessels. Perhaps Rose was sanitizing his account for posterity. Or perhaps he, who had always tried to save lives, bore the shades of those souls and simply didn't want to highlight his role in the war's human agony.

For his thirteenth mission, Rose reached the Western Approaches via circumnavigation of the British Isles. On 4 February he sank the English steamer *Treveal* out of a convoy just outside Liverpool Bay. The heavily loaded ship sank in three minutes killing thirty-three men. Two days later he sank two fishing vessels off the Cornwall Light; shelling the French *Marsouin* in heavy seas and rain, and the British fishing trawler *Holkar*. The following day, 7 February, near Land's End, Rose torpedoed the armed English steamer *Beaumaris*. Her master was able to beach her in Whitesand Bay, but she was a total loss. On the 8th, Rose torpedoed the armed English steamer *Basuta* out of another convoy, sinking her with one death. On the 9th, Rose sank another collier, the armed English steamer *Lydie* headed for Brest from Cardiff. Two crewmen were lost when the ship sank in ten minutes. Two days later Rose would sink his final ship of the mission; the 4,327-ton armed English steamer *Merton Hall*.[591] Fifty-seven members of her crew including the master were lost.

Making an ultimate effort to win the war on the western front between March and July 1918, Germany committed every resource it could bring to bear.

The day after their return from their twenty-three-day thirteenth mission, *U 53* was sent for a ten-day refit in Wilhelmshaven. By the middle of March, less than two weeks later, they set out again. Time, Rose explained, was of the essence:

> There is no time to be lost! Let's get going; to support our brothers heavily engaged in the trenches, to participate in the universal and bloody struggle of nations, and to take part in shaping the future world.[592]

At this point in the war many of the large ocean-going U-boats based in Helgoland were choosing the safer northern-circumnavigation around the British Isles. But it too was becoming more dangerous as threats from enemy minefields and submarines multiplied. To mitigate these hazards in the North Sea, many of the U-boats based at Helgoland were routed via the Kiel Canal, to the Baltic, and up around the Jutland Peninsula, only re-entering the North Sea at its northern end.

Several days into Rose's fourteenth mission, having reached Danish waters at the northern tip of Flensburg Fjord, *U 53* literally ran into a problem. Rose takes up the account as *U 53* left Kiel Fjord at the northwestern exit of the Kiel Canal:

> Kiel was shrouded in fog. The submarine crept toward the buoy to wait. As soon as the weather cleared the commander set a bearing for the mouth of the harbour and left. He moved carefully from buoy to buoy. Passing the last one, he set course for the Baltic Sea at high speed. He was completely sure of his navigation, since he and the Chief Navigator had mastered more difficult things than a foggy trip in the Baltic. His reasoning was that the higher the speed, the smaller the uncertainty about the Baltic Sea's current displacement. He issued the required fog signals and raced ahead. He expected to encounter no one in the darkness!
>
> The trip continued for a number of hours. The commander had just finished his dinner, when two violent jolts pitched his soup plate into his lap at the same time he was smashed against the wall. There was a loud bang.
>
> 'Both engines stop' he bellowed and raced upstairs. The water boiled around the boat: It was stuck. It had hit Pöhls Reef at 12 knots.
>
> 'Everyone on deck, except two people to remain with the diesel engines.'
>
> The commander announced: 'To free the boat, I will run the engines in reverse at top speed. The crew will line up side-by-side at the starboard railing and run over to the port side on Esch's command and back again. Let's see, if we cannot free the boat.'
>
> However, nothing helped. The boat was badly stuck.
>
> 'Check the controls and blow out the diving tanks!'
>
> Another attempt, but the boat did not budge. The Chief Navigator took soundings around the boat's circumference and entered the depths onto a chart. Indeed, the boat was stuck both at the front and in the middle. In order to free it, it would have to be lightened by 200,000 kg. This was impossible to achieve without outside help. A telegraph message for help went out for lighters and tugboats, which were promised. In the meantime one was stuck in the deepest fog. Where an hour ago, one was proud of one's knowledge, one was now a laughing stock and unable to participate in the showdown. All preparations for the unloading were made; a hideous, annoying job.
>
> Towards evening, fog signals were heard, two torpedo boats appeared. One passed over a tow line and slowly started pulling, while the other roared past to

create waves. The tow line twice snapped and the boat did not budge. A mass of ships appeared, among them tugs and barges. The unloading began. Everyone worked at a fever pitch, including the officers. The tow line snapped for the third time. The failure was radioed to headquarters. The commander declared, 'We've got to get away from here, even if we turn into a wreck. We will not leave our boat in the hands of the Danes.'

Renewed soundings determined that the water level had fallen, which meant that the boat was stuck even more tightly than it had been originally. The commander requested additional help. Next morning, in a deep glow, the spring sun rose out of the sea. Close by Danish islands sparkled in their greenness. The lighthouse signal was extinguished. Around noon [SMS *Kolberg*] appeared and attached its strongest lines to the U-boat's tower and gun bases. Except for the commander, who remained in the tower, the whole crew was ordered off the vessel. The U-boat's bulkheads were closed. The cruiser and tug pulled together, while the torpedo boats created high waves and the U-boat's diesel engines were revved in reverse at top speed. Suddenly, a scraping and banging, as though a thousand ships were sinking.

'Hurray – it's moving!'

More scraping, rocking and banging. Now the scraping was further forward. The water rushed past the tower. Both engines stopped. The boat was clear! But in what condition?

The Chief Engineer ran forward and reported 'All compartments are watertight, while all diving tanks are emptied. A few battery cells are unusable, but the diving tanks seem to be O.K.'

The crew returned aboard, heartily exchanged thanks with their rescuers, especially the torpedo boat crews. It was decided that all their equipment would be taken on board again in Kiel. A message was radioed to the BdU: 'Am free, intend to have the U-boat inspected and repaired in the Kiel wharf.' In the dark of night the U-boat raced toward home.

'Heavens, how the hull had struck! Is it possible for a U-boat to withstand such a treatment?'

Once again the workmanship of *Germaniawerft* had turned out to be unbelievably resilient.[593]

In a section of *Auftauchen!* entitled *Strafgericht*, Criminal Court, Rose describes the denouement:

A summons from the BdU ordered *U 53* to come to Wilhelmshaven immediately. The commander was very uncomfortable, expecting to be carpeted for his negligence. Meisner informed the commander that the BdU was on *Hamburg* and wanted to inspect the boat in dry dock. Prepared for the worst, the commander was freshly dressed in his uniform festooned with the *Ordre Pour le Mérite*. The Commodore alighted with his staff, looked at the commander with twinkling blue eyes, and commented 'Well, well there you are.'

Nothing in his war experience surprised the commander as much as this reception. Wordlessly he looked from one to the other, still touching his cap. Everyone was grinning. The BdU asked 'How did that happen, you old Viking?'

'I had not realized that a strong easterly wind had funnelled the water into the Kiel Bay for days on end. When the wind finally abated, the water quickly ebbed away at about 1.5 knots, which pushed us north.'

'What's with the boat?'

'The specialists who had inspected the boat in dry dock report that only a few metal plates have been damaged and need repair. Otherwise everything is in good shape.'

'How long will that take?'

Summoning his renewed energy, the commander replied:

'I will be ready to leave at noon, the day after tomorrow.'

Unconvinced, the Commodore smiled:

'Not so fast.'

But the repair people were on the commander's side; he had brought the shipyard workers corned beef from his last trip a year ago... The crew were happy about the unexpected night in the home harbour and enjoyed a thorough bath.[594]

The Premier Convoy Ace of WWI

Many years after the war a fellow U-boat ace, probably *Kapitänleutnant* Hans von Mellenthin, wrote to Rose, 'I have to give you particular credit for your successes in 1918... You deserve the top position among all submarine commanders 1914/1918.'[595]

In 1920, commenting upon Rose's accomplishments against convoys, American Vice Admiral William Sowden Sims, supreme commander of all United States naval forces operating in Europe, wrote:

'Old Hans is out again,' the officers in the convoy room would remark.

They were speaking of Hans Rose, the commander of *U 53*; this was that submarine officer who, in the fall of 1916, brought that boat to Newport, Rhode Island, and torpedoed five or six ships off Nantucket. Our men never saw Hans Rose face to face; they had not the faintest idea whether he was fat or lean, whether he was fair or dark; yet they knew his military characteristics intimately. He became such a familiar personality in the convoy room and his methods of operation were so individual that we came to have almost a certain liking for the old chap. Other U-boat commanders would appear off the hunting grounds and attack ships in more or less easy-going fashion. Then another boat would suddenly appear, and – bang! bang! bang! Torpedo after torpedo would fly, four or five ships would sink, and then this disturbing person would vanish as unexpectedly as he had arrived. Such an experience informed the convoy officers that Hans Rose was once more at large. We acquired a certain respect for Hans, because he was a brave man who would take chances that most of his compatriots would avoid.[36]

On 20 April 1918 the German Admiralty published a communiqué under the title 'Once Again 28,000 BRTs Have Been Sunk' that stated:

After almost two days of stalking the convoy, and under adverse weather conditions, one of our submarines, under the knowledgeable leadership of Lieutenant-Captain Rose, shot eight steamers totalling 21,000 BRTs out of a convoy.[596]

That propaganda communiqué exaggerated Rose's accomplishment. But it accurately reflected how extraordinary Rose's successes against convoys were. Hans Rose sank 18 (17.6%) of the 102 convoyed ships lost to U-boats inbound or outbound from the British Isles and damaged 7 more, totalling 128,326 tons. No other U-boat commander in WWI would come close to his success against convoys.

Mission 14 – A 37-Hour Pursuit (25 March–17 April 1918)

On 25 March 1918, her iron sheathing made whole again, Hans Rose took *U 53* out once again for his penultimate mission of the war. Departing Wilhelmshaven, by way of Helgoland, Rose chose once again to minimize the dangers in the North Sea by selecting a route northward via the Baltic Sea. Trainee Lieutenant-commander Krapohl, 'the newcomer', was aboard.

On 2 April, the ninth day of the voyage, Rose arrived at his hunting grounds off the southernmost tip of Ireland. There, near Skellig Lighthouse, he reported sinking a 'small unidentified ship about 1,800 tons',[597] subsequently never identified.

Four days later, Rose initiated the dogged pursuit of a rich prize; an outgoing convoy of fifteen ships protected by several destroyers, reported in the German Admiralty communiqué. It would become an extended ordeal that kept Rose actively in command the entire time.

Rose chose to 'reprise the attack on the convoy in such detail [as]… to convey the monstrous effort expended and the extent of the danger involved.'

On 6 April 1918 the weather was cloudy and overcast. Visibility was only three nautical miles and the wind blew from the south west at a strength 4. Esch shared the morning watch with petty officer Kuck. It was 10:09 am.

'I see something, a destroyer course 240 degrees.'

'Hard to starboard to 135 degrees, both engines full speed ahead!'

'Let's move away for the time being,' the commander said, 'so that they don't see us. But then follow them immediately!'

He turned to Esch. 'Please turn the rudder hard to 220 degrees, let's see what's going on.'

The U-boat had barely turned on to the south-westerly course, when a second destroyer appeared that followed the same course. 'Hard to port, go to 160 degrees.'

Everything disappeared in the fog. 'Well, that worked. No one has seen us. This seems to be a busy place.'…

The commander explained to the newcomer: 'When I see destroyers in hazy weather, I first turn the stern of the U-boat toward them for protection, because the enemy is only about two nautical miles distant and could be on top of us in minutes. Caution is necessary, but immediately afterwards it is important to go on the attack again, because the destroyers are not here on a pleasure cruise'.

Kuck reported 'A merchantman at 90 degrees, course west.'

'I see nothing, Kuck, you are day-dreaming!'

'No, I see it clearly.'

'What does it look like?'

'A two-master, with a funnel, approximately 4,000 BRT.'

'Surprising, I see nothing.'

'Nor do I at this point,' the newcomer announces.

'Let's go to 280 degrees and get closer.'

'You're right, there is one, as well as the destroyers. Let's disappear. Hard to port at 180 degrees'...

Then a protective destroyer forced us to turn away and everything disappeared. The commander followed a north-westerly course at high speed, occasionally going to 200 degrees, assuming that it was an existing convoy he was following... By 12:30 p.m. visibility had been reduced to 1.5 nautical miles. They had turned away to the east from a convoy of steamers and destroyers.

Since 10:09, the Navigator had entered the U-boat's course and course changes on his charting board. He knew the distance the boat had travelled exactly. [Navigator] Schroeter commented in a neutral tone, 'The enemy is following a course of 270 degrees at 9 knots.'

The rain stopped and visibility grew to 3-4 nautical miles... The wind increased to strength 6 and blew away the mist.

'What about a wireless message to other U-boats?' It was the commander's pre-occupation at the moment. He turned to Esch [who replied] 'No use, we [the U-boat and the convoy] are so far away that nobody can get close enough and furthermore we don't want to alert the enemy.'

'What a shame.' the commander noted, 'I count at least fifteen ships protected by the destroyers.'

'If we could only increase our speed, the sea swell slows us down dramatically. But it would also damage the engines, without our making any progress.'

'We have been pursuing the convoy for nine hours and what have we achieved? We are at a 90 degree angle, but 12 nautical miles away. We cannot get any closer, because the waves crashing against the tower would give us away... Let's wait for night fall to push ourselves closer.'

By 23:30 p.m., as planned, the U-boat was near the forward ship of the right column. It steered beside them, while the destroyer was about 1,500 metres behind, providing starboard protection. Everybody on board was ready to dive. The commander, the Chief Navigator, the newcomer and Kuck were on the tower. The excitement was palpable, all torpedo tubes were clear. Gerd Noormann, as Rudder Mate and Meisner, as Torpedo Officer, were in the *Zentrale*.

'Fifteen degrees to port,' the commander called... 'Please transmit to everyone that we will attack by squeezing through the starboard defences.'

The submarine crept to within 500 metres of the first ship and the front ships were aligned from the U-boat's point of view. The commander turned hard to starboard and let go the 4th torpedo in the rear [23:50 p.m.]. It took a long time to detonate. The ship was in the middle row... The torpedoed ship sent a code message. The destroyer did nothing... According to the British White Book, it was the *Knight Templar* 7,175 BRT.

'The fact that the destroyer has noticed nothing needs to be taken advantage of. So at it again.'

The U-boat crept up to the enemy convoy once more and waited until various ships were aligned, yet this time the destroyer was in the way. The shot had to be fired earlier... and missed [0:06 am]... The U-boat found itself so close to the destroyer that it would no longer remain unseen...

'Alarm,' the commander shouted.

The diving manoeuvre was performed flawlessly, there were no depth charges. Everything remained quiet. The commander steered north-west and after twenty-four minutes the boat had resurfaced and was again making its way toward the enemy.

'Aha, there is another heavily loaded tanker.'

However it was on the alert. As soon as the torpedo left its tube [1:22 am] the tanker made a sharp turn to starboard, thus avoiding disaster. It signalled SOS and returned to the protection of the convoy... The U-boat could not, however, be shaken off. It raced ahead and shot a K torpedo toward the ship ahead in the line, hitting it in its middle [1:58 am]. *Port Campbell* a 6,230 BRT tanker sank. It had been two hours full of activity. Now the commander had time for the newcomer.

'Well, little one, that is two ships that we have destroyed. What shall we do now that we are at the tail of the convoy?'

'We have to gain at least one nautical mile lead. To attain that, will require at least one to two hours with these strong sea swells. If we are seen by a destroyer, everything will have been for naught and we will have to begin again from scratch. If we don't get rid of more torpedoes in this weather, we will not be able to attack another ship all day.'

Every few seconds the tower was inundated with spray and breakers, and the soaked crew had to hang on for dear life. The commander decided to re-think his plans and to abandon the night attacks in order to get ahead of the convoy once more.

'Set the watch,' the commander called into the tower, 'the night attacks will be abandoned'...For an hour and twenty minutes the U-boat held a course of thirty degrees and then reverted to its original course. It should be about eight nautical miles away from the convoy [2:20 a.m. to 3:40 am]. In the remaining two and a half hours before sunrise, the commander hoped to gain about a five nautical mile lead... He lay down to rest in his berth. But his thoughts were racing. Weren't his deliberations of many hours, weeks and months coming to fruition? He was finally chasing an enemy convoy far away in the Atlantic Ocean. He would follow it until every single weapon had been used up. He wanted to force the enemy captains into a mental collapse...

In the east the darkness lifted and the stars lost some of their glow. The horizon became visible, its colors turning reddish. The sun rose silently out of the waves. The commander, thinking of Wacker, raised his arms

'Hail to the daylight gods!'

Meisner and Thomas joined in:

'As fighters, give us our victory!'

All eyes turned to starboard.

'There they are, a ship with one mast, probably a tanker and far to stern a number of others. What a disappointment, the tanker seems to be faster than the others, he has gained three nautical miles... We will have to attack him first, because if we turn on the others, he will see us.'...

Throughout many hours, the U-boat moved ahead and the enemy fell back behind the stern. We will dive at 13:30 and attack at 14:00 (to lighten the boat's weight). Meanwhile the commander walked through the U-boat and found everything ship-shape... The men rested in bunks and slept dreamlessly... In the lieutenant's quarters, two men were playing chess... The commander joined the deck officers in their mess, where the Chief Navigator had activated the chronometer and determined the position of the morning sun.

'How large is the permutation?'

'Two and a half minutes to the east.'...

The stern room too was ship-shape. The men were playing cards.

'Are you winning Hannemann?'

'We have a few thousand, and are about even.'

'When do you do the final accounting?'

'In harbour.'

'Time for lunch,' Göthling announced.

It tasted delicious. Promptly at 13:30 the commander announced

'Everyone ready at their diving stations.'

The torpedo left its tube at 13:58 for a 480 metre shot. The torpedo hit close to the engine room. The ship listed badly and targeted its stern gun shots toward the periscope. Depth charges, whose detonations were clearly heard on board, were also directed at the sub.

'I think he's had it,' the newcomer noted after a look through the periscope.

'We can skip the *coup de grâce*,' the commander answered, 'there are many more enemies around.'

In the meantime an attack occurred against a four-master sighted to the north. Then more than twenty large ships, following a zigzag course, were sighted on the horizon. They seemed to be a sure prey requiring no course change on the part of the submarine. The ship turned out to be empty, approximately 4,000 BRT, and was straining against the sea swells. The torpedo, the last bow torpedo available, past underneath the vessel (14:59). And the tanker? It had righted itself, changed direction slowly, and set a course for Europe. It took equanimity to accept the disappointment, though the search for another ship in the convoy began immediately. By 15:10 an attack was given up as impossible. As soon as the distance from the four-master permitted, the submarine surfaced. The pursuit of the large crowd, which was no longer visible, was taken up once more at 15:52. Shortly afterward, a wireless message was received: 'SOS 4813N 1129W *Cadillac* torpedoed, requires immediate assistance.'...

The Lead Engineer called from the *Zentrale*, '*Cadillac* registers 11,140 BRTs.'

The newcomer murmured 'I doubt that it will be able to get home, and even if it does, it will be out of commission for months.'

'If we had only used one of our old stern torpedoes for the *coup de grâce*.'

The Chief Engineer appeared with his hand to his cap: 'An exhaust valve on the port engine has broken. Our top speed is thirteen knots. Duration of the disruption is still undetermined.'

Everybody looked at the commander.

'That is faster than the enemy is cruising. We'll continue the pursuit.'

Since the large group of vessels had not been found, even though the visibility was excellent, the pursuit was ended at 19:00 hours and the earlier pursuit of the four-master, now about eight nautical miles away, re-established. Yet, when dusk fell, it too was abandoned and a three-master that was closer was followed instead. The seas calmed, the white combs disappeared. Still, the frothy bow sprays that rained down on the foredeck and the eddies of the keel waters could not be covered up. From now on, only stern shots were available which could not be used in the heavy seas, and yet the seas were too wild for an artillery duel. The forward manoeuvres had to be undertaken very close to the enemy, but as soon as the U-boat had managed to get ahead, the enemy veered off. It was a wearing, laborious, hours-long chase. Finally, the time was ripe. The U-boat managed to pass the bow of the enemy line. The U-boat made a 90-degree turn, reduced its speed and everyone disappeared into the U-boat.

'Tube 4 attention!'

In the last minute it seemed to the commander as though the enemy was moving very slowly. But wasn't it more reasonable to believe in the hours-long observations, rather than in that of the moment?...

'4th tube fire!' [23:21]

Luminously, the torpedo followed its course. But the enemy, it was the steamer *Kunara*, 6,063 BRT, did not intersect with that course. It had seen the U-boat, and had reversed its engines a minute earlier. It turned, opened fire with its stern gun, and disappeared into the dark.[598]

Rose is mistaken, he has hit *Kunara* and she will sink.

The commander gave instructions for the night run and returned below deck. He was at the end of his strength. He lay down in his bunk, closed the curtain and sobbed uncontrollably. Don't feel beaten down, his inner voice retorted. The stress of the chase had been so great that it had to be discharged somehow. The psychological struggle lasted for about an hour, and then sleep erased everything. The next day was spent discussing the events of April 6 and 7 with the officers. While he was rendering an account of all of his decisions, hasty notes of events were combined with the more detailed descriptions in the Chief Navigator's and Engineer's diaries, which were summarized into a short account in the *Kriegstagebuch*. In spite of the dry matter-of-factness of this account, he felt compelled to include a small hint of the psychological stress he had encountered... the commander had not yet regained his composure when he wrote 'And thus this thirty-seven hour long pursuit, that had been begun with high expectations and was sustained by high hopes, found a depressing end with the firing of the seventh torpedo.'[599]

Uncharacteristically, Rose acknowledges the emotional toll that the pursuit has taken. Being a perfectionist, he is disappointed that it has not been crowned with greater success. At the same time it has demonstrated how Rose's ability to maintain tight control over his emotions while in crisis made him such a tenacious and dangerous adversary. He only allowed his emotions expression after the action was over.

Rose had pursued the convoy more than 400 nautical miles due-west out into the Atlantic, from *Ille de Ouessant* off the Brest on the northwest coast of France. With only two older, short-range bronze torpedoes remaining, Rose chose to break off the pursuit and continue his campaign in the Irish Sea where those torpedoes could be used more effectively. He turned back east northeast. But the successes of the mission were over.

U 53 'Stood on Her Head'

On 11 April 1918, four days after Rose broke off his dogged pursuit of the convoy, and six days before the end of their fourteenth mission, Rose faced a near fatal accident. It is the subject of an 11 July 1933 radio 'conversation' between Captain Rose and Torpedo Officer Esch entitled 'Our Most Difficult Day'. This is not of course a verbatim conversation; sentences such as 'My dear Esch you are to be thanked for your immaculate radio telegraphy' were not uttered during this dramatic and potentially fatal episode. Rose uses the 'conversation' as a literary framework to explain events.

> Rose – It still gives me the shivers when I think back to the time that we were stood on our head. You will remember that we had used up all of our torpedoes except for two old bronze beasts in the Atlantic Ocean. Because they have limited range, they were the reason we headed into the North Channel where it would be easier to close with the enemy, than it would have been in the Atlantic.
>
> Esch – Our expectations were completely fulfilled. We had arrived in the North Channel during the night and at the break of dawn immediately saw a large convoy which consisted of enormous passenger steamers led by an American cruiser. The latter was recognizable by its superstructure. A large number of destroyers were circling around. We had a target before our eyes that every U-boat dreams of; namely a large American troop transport carrying troops for the Western Front.
>
> Rose – This target was worth the sweat of the honourable. I immediately increased speed and had the two rear torpedoes pulled out of their tubes in order to have them pumped up to their requisite pressure. As you know, unfortunately these old bronze animals had to be re-pressurized just before an attack.
>
> Esch – While you were atop the conning tower as usual, we were awaiting the command to submerge. I was in the *Zentrale* in order to oversee the depth gauges. The Chief Engineer stood beside me responsible for the engineering aspects of the dive. Meanwhile in the aft compartment, Lieutenant Meisner prepared the two bronze torpedoes. You frequently called from the tower that the re-pressurizing had to be sped up, because we would soon have to dive.
>
> Rose – Yes on the bridge, with the Irish Coast already in view, I was rocking from foot to foot with impatience. From a previous visit to the Green Island, I knew it well, and was aware of the fact that there was a chain of observation posts around it. When I finally received the notification from the rear that the

torpedoes were pumped up, I immediately sounded the diving alarm. BANG! The conning tower hatch was closed and we were cut off from the outside world. I ordered the tanks be flooded and a few seconds later Chief Engineer Burkhardt laconically informed me that the compressed air valves were open. The air whistled out of the tanks and the boat headed into the depths. Under normal circumstances we would have been at twelve metres depth and clear for an attack.

Esch – But these were not normal circumstances. Immediately the boat canted forward with its list growing quickly from six to more than eight degrees. There must be a problem somewhere. I can still hear your warning voicing calling 'Woe, Woe, Woe!' and responded 'It's impossible to hold the boat.'

Rose – I noticed that too and in order to bring the boat back into balance ordered maximum engine speed to counteract the hydroplanes lack of grip. But this measure was insufficient.

Esch – We were in a position which we never experienced again, thank goodness. The bow of the boat fell into the depths like a block of ice, while the stern remained on the surface. Our diving gauge indicated a forward list of ten, twenty, then thirty degrees, at which point it flooded and stopped registering. Tables, chairs, china, sailors, books, instruments, sub-officers, cooking pots, repair tools, *Tauchretter*, everything flew toward the bow. We continued to hang in the ocean like a herring caught by its tail. Instinctively I looked back, where a veritable hail of everything that was not tied down came towards us. High above I saw the huge 1,200 horsepower diesels and behind them the electric motors. I was certain that momentarily these installations would break loose and crash down on our heads. The crew in the forward portion of the boat was clumped below me. Their terrified eyes bulged out of their heads. Be happy that you couldn't see that from your position in the conning tower.

Rose – Well for me, I'm certain this experience will also remain unforgettable. I was looking at Lieutenant-Commander Krapohl, whom we had on board as a trainee. His eyes were as large as teacups. It all happened in the blink of an eye. I thought I was going crazy when my feet got caught behind the diving fin controls and in front of me the floor looked like a steep wall. I screamed 'Stop Engines' so that we would not careen into the abyss at top speed. Then I gave the command that is only permitted in a moment of utmost danger: 'Blow all tanks!'

Esch – Up! Up! was the thought that preoccupied everyone in the *Zentrale*, but your command was difficult to fulfil, because we had no purchase anywhere and a heavy tool box had crashed into the Air Pressure control valve. Damaged, bit by tiny bit, it could only be opened with the greatest effort.

Rose – It took a long time before the compressed air took effect. Seconds turned into the usual eternity, but finally we did notice that the bow began to lift. However we had no time to breathe a sigh of relief, because the boat popped to the surface like a beach ball. The tower hatch was opened and we jumped out into the open air and immediately noticed that air was bubbling from the compressed air equipment in the rear.

Esch – I ran aft and found everything in huge disarray. In the compartment one of the two bronze torpedoes lay bent and unusable outside its tube.

This is how the disaster happened. When the command to dive was given one of the torpedoes was not yet fully pressurized and its compressed air hose, pressurized to 15O atmospheric pressures, burst whipping around the crewmen's heads like a snake held by its tail. As a result it was impossible to open the compressed air valves. Then with the boat's bow plunged into the depths, while its stern remained above surface, the 1,000kg torpedo dislodged and flew through the compartment.

Rose – At this point Meisner performed his famous act. As it was rushing past him, Meisner grabbed the monster with both hands between the firing pin and its head containing 150kg of high explosives. By doing so he prevented the inevitable detonation which would, of course, have destroyed our boat... While you and the LI were fighting against the internal enemy, I was watching the enemy outside and continued my attack at top speed. The Americans had come over but had not yet seen us. When you and the LI reported the internal situation of the ship twenty minutes later, I immediately gave the command to dive in order to reinforce the crew's belief in their boat. This practice dive lasted not more than two minutes and then we continued to attack.

Esch – I can vividly remember how the LI and I were very worried about that dive, but I must admit that you were completely right to test the diving capacity of the boat.

Rose – It worked thank god, otherwise the continuation of the attack would have made no sense. We had to risk everything in order to launch our last torpedo against the valuable target ahead of us.

Esch – In the meantime we discovered that the accumulator batteries, which were the power source for underwater propulsion, had been badly damaged by our headstand. They had almost burst into flames in the short diving practice. We had about a hundred cells on board, each of which was half a metre high and weighed approximately 500kg. Twenty-six of these were broken and partly spilt. The acid was mixing with the salt water in the bilge, creating ghastly chlorine fumes, which made it almost impossible to proceed underwater. We could only work with gas masks and were worrying that any minute there might be a conflagration.

Rose – I certainly knew that you were working diligently, because I noticed that buckets full of chlorine mixed water and cotton waste were being thrown overboard. But I did not let that bother me, because the game that we were tracking was both too valuable and too rare.

Esch – In spite of all that the LI had to report to you that the technical installations of the boat no longer permitted an attack.

Rose – Yes that was a bit of a disappointment and it almost seems like a fairy-tale that while he was making that report a second German U-boat appeared on the scene. Having received our telegraphic signals, it was *UB 73*. My dear Esch you are to be thanked for your immaculate radio telegraphy.

Esch – The coordination was absolutely masterful and when *UB 73* indicated that it had understood and prepared for the attack, it filled us all with joy.

Rose –The enemy destroyers having now discovered us, *UB 73*'s arrival occurred at the very last moment. They contacted us by Morse code and we answered with our small handheld signal lamp. At the same time we shot signal flares into the sky, in order to confuse the enemy into thinking that we were friends who had nothing to hide.

Esch – The subterfuge was successful. The destroyers delayed opening fire and in this way we and *UB 73* gained valuable time.

Rose – My heart still smiles when I remember how much good luck we had in spite of all of the bad luck. We drew the enemy destroyers behind us and thereby facilitated the attack of *UB 73*.

Esch – It did however get quite unpleasant when enemy shells finally began to fly around forcing us, after all, to dive with the badly damaged boat.

Rose – But this too worked out OK, because we spread a smoke screen between the charging destroyers and our boat. However, shortly afterwards the destroyers launched depth charges that slammed us against the walls, extinguished our lights, blew out our fuses, and smashed our gauges. We had little hope that we would be alive an hour later. Nonetheless, suddenly a chorus of hurrahs bursts through the gas masks at the typical sound of the detonation of a torpedo. It was the shot that *UB 73* had launched.

Esch – *UB 73*'s successful shot provided us both redemption and salvation, because our batteries were nearly exhausted. If the destroyers had continued to follow us we would have been lost. We had neither air nor power for further underwater travel.

Rose – As I looked through the periscope, thanks to *UB 73*'s deed, I saw the destroyers racing towards a sinking troop transport. After a fairly short time we could surface, discard our gas masks, and flee out of sight. Never has Schiller's utterance been as real for me as on that day: 'And he breathed deep, and he breathed long, and he greeted the heavenly delight of the day.'

Rose – It is certainly true that the crew was wonderful. But the officers served as a glowing example. Without the determination of Meisner the wild torpedo would have sunk us all. Without the LI and Ober-Ingenieur Burghardt, the diving capacity of the boat would not have been restored and we would surely have become victims of the enemy shells. And without you my dear Esch, we would not have had *UB 73* at our side, the depth charges would have ultimately destroyed us, and *UB 73* would not have known anything of the convoy. As long as I live I will continue to have the warmest appreciation for my officers and crew. As long as they have confidence in their leaders, I am sure that our German men will continue to perform to the utmost.[600]

The accident occurred between Inishtrahull and Dubh Artach in the Irish Sea. With his boat seriously damaged and its diving capacity significantly reduced, Rose sets sail for home, having sunk 12,293 tons.

Rose entitled *Auftauchen!*'s eighth chapter 'Growing Difficulties 1918'. With *U 53* undergoing repairs, Rose cast around for ways to contribute to the war effort while ashore:

Though he had never given a lecture before in his life, he reasoned that if one was determined to serve the fatherland, even such activities had to be contemplated. The lectures brought him in contact with leading men in the economy, politics and science and enlarged his perspectives. But his belief in the wisdom of the German government had suffered substantial shocks.[601]

In the course of those lectures Rose was invited to the home of the German composer Richard Wagner:

He had felt as though he were in a holy site… The famous man was already seriously ill. He could not raise himself from his chair and spoke only haltingly. But what he said indicated his deep spiritual understanding of all questions concerning war. Magical powers brightened his wide open eyes and his words clearly expressed that he was aware of his compelling personality, through which the wisdom of the old Druids spoke. When the commander rose to take his leave the wise old man held out his hand and mumbled: 'Please go to my study across the hall. There you will see a picture of yourself on my desk. I cut it out of a magazine many years ago. I am very happy to have had the opportunity to meet you personally. I wish you success and victory.'

The commander was deeply touched and he felt as though he was walking on air when he stepped out into the sunny May day.[602]

Here was the external validation of his life well lived, so important to Rose, delivered not by politically motivated superiors or the Admiralty propaganda machine, but by a personal idol who existentially represented Rose's romantic ideal of the German *Volk*.

Mission 15 – A Depth Charge for Every Man (16 June–10 July 1918)

Hans Rose set out for what would become his last mission of the war on 16 June 1918. This time Rose chose not to avoid the multiplying dangers in the North Sea. It was a decision that almost proved fatal. At 5:30 a.m., less than twenty-four hours into the mission, half way up the North Sea, a British submarine fired two torpedoes at *U 53*.

'Torpedo trail on port' the watch called out. 'Both engines full speed ahead,' Esch commanded and the torpedo passed close behind the boat. Then another one was sighted and only a hard turn to starboard saved the U-boat. 'A ghastly feeling when these objects head towards one,' the commander observed.[603]

By the end of the war, the forces arrayed against Germany were becoming overwhelming. Had excessive aggressiveness, so long nuanced by caution, contributed to the risks Rose now took?

Later that day Rose sighted five large English steamers protected by twenty destroyers. 'Their speed was too fast to be intercepted,'[604] and attempts to lure the enemy back by 'imitating the Marconi-tone and doing radio transmissions in the English language' failed, 'the British refused to bite.'[605]

On the 20th, Rose engaged in an inconclusive three-and-a-half hour gun battle with six British fishing boats. *U 53*, which at this point in the war has been fitted with a second 8.8 cm gun aft, fired one hundred and forty 10.5 cm shells and thirty 8.8 cm shells. But the fishing boats, breaking out the white ensign, formed a line, and responded in kind with 5 and 7 cm. shell fire. Though 'Gläschick, Senior Petty Officer in charge of artillery, achieved a number of hits'[606] Rose was obliged to break off the encounter as having little chance of success. He concluded that 'if we had had a larger, faster boat with larger oil reserves, we could have prevailed.'[607]

Seven days later on 27 June Rose encountered another convoy. He pursued the convoy for more than twenty hours and succeeded in sinking *Keelung*, despite near fatal counter measures.

> Slowly it emerged that it was a convoy of nine big ships, among them a four-master, a tanker etc., obviously valuable targets. They are proceeding in keel lines consisting of three ships. Row spacing approximately 1,000 metres apart. They are protected by six or seven destroyers, one of which moves back and forth in front of the ships, dragging an observation balloon, while the others provide tight side and rear protection. We shorten the convoy's approach by increasing our speed... The destroyers protecting the side of the line, possibly alerted by the balloon, steer toward U 52 at top speed. One torpedo hits. The U-boat quickly dives to fifty metres and receives thirty-nine tremendously heavy depth charges that make the boat rock from side to side and the crew lurch against the walls. It is a heavy penance for the successful attack.
>
> Time 13:55: Rise to periscope depth and see two destroyers cross and re-cross behind the heavily damaged ship, whose stern lies deep in the water. One of them drops another three depth charges that make an enormous roar, in spite of the fact that we are about six nautical miles distant from the location of the drop. Then the destroyer hurriedly chases after the convoy. The crew is shaken by the plethora of depth charges, especially the new men, who have only recently joined the boat. Senior Petty Officer Gläschick restores everyone's spirits by reporting in a deep basso voice: 'Forty-two depth charges. One for every man, only the commander gets two.'

At 3 a.m. a greater prize presents itself and Rose switches targets. Though he will once again draw blood, sinking SS *Queen*, engine failure will bring a premature termination to the mission and his hopes for another long convoy pursuit.

> Quadrant 0 19 epsilon V. A much larger and stronger out-going convoy is sighted. We attach ourselves, but because of inflexible theoretical considerations, almost lose it. Forward manoeuvre to south-east, the enemy is steering a course of 190 degrees, approximately toward Cape Finistère in north-west Spain. As the light increases we have to sidestep the convoy, which prevents us from getting into a promising attack position. Time 7:50 am. The boat gives a sudden jolt. The Chief Engineer climbs up the tower and reports that the starboard engine has ceased functioning. Repairs will require at least a few hours. Have to dive for the attack immediately, without making further inquiries. There are twenty-four ships that are arranged in seven keel lines, travelling extremely closely together. Our plan to enter between rows three and four, making two stern shots and then using the two bow torpedoes fails, because the vanguard escort that is travelling close to the line of ships is heading straight at the U-boat. For safety's sake, we therefore dive to forty metres and turn toward the line of ships...
>
> At 8:45 a.m. the U-boat rises to periscope height and immediately fires two bow shots toward the first ships in lines five and six. In the tower we hear only faint cracking sounds and one slightly stronger bang, like that of a grenade... When I turn my periscope toward the stricken ships, I see an explosive cloud behind

the main mast... 8:50 am. Dive to forty metres, because of the danger of being rammed. 9:10 am. Look around with periscope and see that all ships except one, which crisscrosses and throws depth charges, are following the convoy.[608]

At 10:35 a.m., June 28, Rose surfaced and identified the 4,956-ton English steamer by 'a lifeboat half full of water with the name *Queen* and a field of debris. Beyond this a huge oil patch'.[609] Twenty men including *Queen*'s Master had perished. At 11:40 Rose attacked another ship in the convoy, the 2,459-ton American ship *Ruby*, but missed. But by this time his Chief Engineer reported to him that the breakdown in the port engine had reduced the U-boat's top speed below the ten knots required to catch back up to the convoy.

> The commander sat on the tower, letting his legs dangle.
> 'What a shame, chief engineer, my most well-laid plans have been derailed. It was my greatest dream to follow a convoy going south. This is where it would have commenced. I wanted to follow it to Gibraltar and from there to the Mediterranean and to Pola or Cattaro. Such a destination would have given the crew a relaxing vacation... However, to travel to the Mediterranean with a faulty diesel engine is quite unrealistic. Even the best MAN engines do fail sometimes. Thus far they have taken us the equivalent of three times around the equator.'...
> In the evening the Chief Engineer reported that the engine could not be repaired at sea, because of its cylinder damage, resulting in the fact that *U 53* missed a chance to sink the American destroyer *DD-52*, an old acquaintance from Newport.[610]

Rose set sail for home, attacking small game along the way. On the 30th he shelled and sank the 144-ton English three-masted schooner *W.M.L.* bringing copper goods from Spain to Liverpool. On 2 July he sank the 116-ton English motor schooner *Erme* west of Ireland. And on the 6th, he sank the 45-ton Icelandic fishing sailboat *Gullfaxi*.

In *Auftauchen!*'s table 'List of Ships Sunk by U 53' Rose asserts that he sank ninety merchant vessels. The identity and sinking of eighty of those ships (totalling 220,051 tons) can be definitively corroborated by Allied records on the basis of the times and locations of attacks, and the absence of other U-boats at those locations at the times of attack. It can be positively ascertained that the seven vessels (126T *Saint Theodor* 3/10/17, 300T *Elizabeth* 4/25/17, 4,750T *Polvena* 10/17/17, 7,555T *Helenus* 12/1/17, 2,353T *Earlswood* 12/5/17, 6,695T *Nyanza* 12/19/17, and 11,140T *Cadillac* 4/7/18) that Rose believed he had sunk, though damaged by Rose, either succeeded in reaching harbour safely, or were sunk by other U-boats at a later date. Apparently after the war, Rose identified one ship, the 4,313T *Rhodesia* as being sunk on 10/11/17 and specified the cargo as oil, but it has not been possible to corroborate that claim. Arno Spindler believed it possible that the ship attacked at that time and location was *Voronezh*, damaged but not sunk. In the fog of war, in those situations where Rose attacked a number of vessels without first definitively ascertaining their identities, it has been impossible to establish the identities of two others claimed sunk on 2/8/18 and 4/2/18 respectively. It is possible therefore that Hans Rose sank as many as eighty-three vessels totalling approximately 227,733 tons.

Rescuing *U 86*

At 5 a.m. on 8 July 1918, two-days out from Helgoland and cruising twenty-five miles off the Norwegian coast, Rose's Wireless Operator picked up a distress signal from *U 86* forty-five nautical miles north of *U 53*: 'Quad 130 beta II. Hit mine. Need help urgently. Last possible signal.'[611]

U 86 had strayed into a mine field fifteen miles inside the British restricted zone. Two hours earlier the U-boat's Lieutenant Commander Patzig had reported hearing 'a weak detonation far away'.[612] But then thirty-five minutes later a heavy detonation rocked *U 86* forward between the conning tower and the forward gun. A cloud of water, debris and smoke shot eighty metres into the air. The boat shuddered, the engines stopped, the lights failed, and smoke and fire spread in the bow. Within five minutes the captain was able to determine that the diesel engines were still functional, the rudder operative, and that, with difficulty, the boat could be steered by hand. But the batteries were smoking and could not be used, there was a leak in the control room and forward bunker III has been cracked open and emptied. His LI told him that he had barely sufficient diesel fuel to creep to Norwegian territorial waters. At 5 a.m., with just enough battery power remaining, he sent his emergency message. Miraculously *U 53* responded immediately, sending rendezvous coordinates: 'Heading toward location of accident. Help in offing Quad. 100 alpha.'[613]

At sunrise of 8 July 1918 the boat travelled through the mined areas between the Shetland Islands and Norway... The commander believed that it was best not to acknowledge the mines, but though he himself survived well with this attitude, others were not so fortunate... It was a beautiful summer morning when the commander was awakened from a short rest by the radio officer who brought the message '*U 86* here, have run into a mine at 130 beta 11.' 'Good heavens, they are only thirty nautical miles behind us,' the commander thought... *U 53* turned around and returned to the mined area, catching up with *U 86* about an hour and a half later...

The mine had not detonated on impact with the boat, but approximately ten metres below it and as a result it had lost all of its diesel fuel... Only enough for a one-hour-long voyage remained. The radio system was also out of commission and the accumulator batteries were no longer working... However, the two boats were protected from enemy attack by the mines. *U 53* transferred enough oil to its comrade so that it could reach Danish waters... It also sent over hot coffee for the stricken crew and helped with some minor repairs, while keeping a watchful eye on the surroundings... Then the commander decided that the two boats would move south together as close to the Norwegian three mile zone as possible, with *U 53* providing protection from behind. It was not pleasant for the boats to be shadowed by a Norwegian torpedo craft sent out to protect the country's sovereignty. But they managed because *U 53* had devised an ingenious contraption consisting of a white canvas attached to the back of the bridge that camouflaged the usually unmistakable outlines of the U-boat tower... *U 53*'s crew was very proud of this war stratagem… In the Kattegat, the cripple was welcomed by a German torpedo flotilla, which refuelled it and led it to its home harbour.[614]

Rose ends his account of *U 86* with a denunciation of the conviction for war crimes of two of Patzig's subordinate officers, Lieutenants Dithmar and Boldt. They were found guilty of complicity in firing upon and sinking the lifeboats of the British Hospital Ship *Llandovery Castle* on 27 June 1918, earlier in *U 86*'s mission. Patzig fled from justice but his subordinates, arguing that they had only been following orders, went to trial. Both officers were sentenced to four years in prison.

> The rescue of *U 86* had been successful. Years later, in the gruesome time when our country had no standing and was impotent, the officers of this boat were called before the Supreme Court in Leipzig, because the commander, who lived abroad by that time, had sunk a hospital-ship on this voyage.
>
> Not influenced by current prejudices the goddess Justitia is blind. But in this instance, she was not deaf. So the officers were convicted and imprisoned, because the voices of vengeful foreigners screeched for a victim.
>
> No upright person approved of this shameful judicial error.[615]

Throughout his life Rose demonstrated a willingness to contest higher authority when he felt the situation called for it. Yet here Rose argues that 'following orders' absolved the two men of responsibility. *Auftauchen!* was published in 1939 at a time when the Nazis were trumpeting German exceptionalism. Had Rose's narrow nationalism trumped his ethics?

On 10 July 1918, having sunk an additional 11,934 tons of enemy merchant shipping, Hans Rose completed his fifteenth mission and stepped ashore at Helgoland for the last time.

Perhaps more than all the others, these last three missions highlight the deadliness of the avocation to which Hans Rose had pledged himself; to kill or be killed. Rose's extraordinary successes reflect his mastery of the art of submarine warfare, a psychological makeup that allowed him to practise it with calm, determined aggression – and his birth under a lucky star.

Chapter 17

Defeat and Dislocation

As 1918 ground on, Germany's capacity to wage war began to disintegrate. By favouring supply of its armed forces over the civilian population Germany was able to keep its fighting men relatively physically fit. But the civilian population's health declined under the effects of the blockade.

In the final month of the war mutinies broke out on many of the surface vessels of the High Seas Fleet, though none ever broke out on a U-boat. There, morale remained high. The crews and officers had shared tight quarters and developed a camaraderie and singleness of purpose born of effectively attacking the enemy.

Rose alluded to the catastrophic situation confronting Germany in 1918 when, during his lecture tour ashore, he acknowledged that his 'belief in the wisdom of the German government had suffered substantial shocks'.[601] But though the situation was disintegrating around him, as a successful U-boat commander he had remained somewhat insulated from the realities that would soon overwhelm the nation.

U 52 APPROACHING HELGOLAND Sister-boat to *U 53*. [Author's Archive]

At the end of *U 53*'s fifteenth mission Rose was granted a month-long furlough. He recalled:

The commander went on leave to one of the most beautiful places in the world, Berchtesgaden. Since he had been there as a student it was a place that his heart was drawn to.

He lived on the Obersalzberg. This wonderful place appeared to him in 1918 to be the German mountain of the Holy Grail...

He took long hikes in glorious sunshine. From the Purschteller House one could see allied Austria. From the peak of Jenner Mountain he looked down on the motionless surface of the Königsee on which tiny, nearly invisible boats were tracing delicate patterns. Mountain goats were grazing on the steep cliffs at the foot of the Gröll. Small bugs danced in the sunny sky.

Through the narrow valley of the Scharitzkehl-Alpe, the sounds of cow-bells wafted, as well as the smell of the meadows. The softwoods radiated energizing heat. And over all activity, the rocky, jagged, icy and yet glowing giants of the mountain world towered, immutable and unchanging for thousands of years.

They made the Commander urgently conscious of the insignificance of a single individual's life. They encouraged him to feel that a human being acquires worth, direction and goals, as a small link in a long chain. He may himself show the way, or follow those with a visionary talent for intuiting the immortal human community.

It was indeed a spot to gain distance from the stifling everyday concerns that reduce the vision and understanding of larger concerns.[616]

Rose, ever the lead actor, neglects to mention that his wife Anne-Marie spent the leave with him.[617]

But pressing 'everyday concerns' did impinge upon Rose's idyllic leave. Few U-boat captains had the courage, skill, and tenacity Rose did to latch on to a convoy and attack multiple times. The institution of the convoy system had blunted the German U-boat attack. Struggling to adjust the tactics of his U-boats to fit the new reality, Hermann Bauer enlisted Rose and Otto Schultze of *U 63*: 'While there he received the order from the BdU to write up his experiences about how to carry on the U-boat war in the Atlantic.'[618]

By early 1918 Ludendorff had abandoned his hope that the Allies would sue for peace as a result of the unlimited U-boat campaign and tried instead to end the war on land. By July the last German offensive had been stopped at the Marne and the troops were pinned down near Reims. The German army lacked the personnel, food and war materiel to continue. On 8 August, two days before Rose returned from his last leave, the Allies, with strong American support, broke through the Siegfried Line. Once it was overrun the Allied invasion of German territory was unstoppable. Mobile warfare ensued and the German army began to be beaten back. It was, Ludendorff said, 'The Black Day of the German Army.'

With his leave over, Rose reported back for duty.

On 10 August 1918 the commander returned to Wilhelmshaven where Meisner picked him up at the station. 'Hi there old friend, How's the boat?'

Meisner looked straight ahead and replied: 'It's OK.'

'When are we going to leave port?'

'*U 53* will leave for Helgoland day after tomorrow.'

'What do you mean by that? Who is making this decision?'

After a short pause Meisner gasped, 'We have a new commander.'

'What? Have I been replaced without being informed?'

'The BdU requests you report immediately to the *Hamburg.*'...

On arrival he is told that he will join the BdU and become a staff officer. Not for ever, he is assured. At the beginning of December 1918 a brand new submarine cruiser, built by *Germaniawerft*, is going to be commissioned.

It has two 3,000 horsepower diesel engines, built by MAN. It will be armed with two 15cm and two 8.8cm cannons, have an armoured deck, twenty torpedoes and cruise at a speed of at least eighteen knots [with provisions] for at least three months. For reconnaissance there will be a plane on board.

'You are chosen to be the commander of this monster. You will also have two fast U-boats with superior fighting strength and speed at your disposal. This means you will be the first German Submarine Staff Commander in the Atlantic.'

'And my crew?'

'You can decide whom you wish to take from your old crew; two of your non-commissioned officers have already been requisitioned to the cruiser for design purposes. Others will be made available as you need them. Agreed old Viking?'

The commander jumped up, 'Your wish is my command.'

The commodore patted him on the shoulder.[619]

Of course it was not to be. With the war going badly the German Admiralty, seeking to protect a core of knowledgeable leaders for the future rebuilding of the German navy, relieved many of its most important and successful U-boat *Kommandanten* of their front-line commands. It re-assigned Hans Rose to Hermann Bauer's staff ashore and his career as an active U-boat *Kommandant* came to an end.

With the rapid evolution of submarine technology, most of the best U-boat commanders successively commanded several U-boats. But Hans Rose remained in command of *U 53* throughout his career as a front-line submarine commander. By the time he stepped off *U 53* at the end of his fifteenth mission, Hans Rose had spent 290 days at sea in her; about 36% of the 810 days that had elapsed since he took command of the brand new U-boat on 22 April 1916. Although *U 53* returned to sea for two final missions under Otto von Schrader, the vast majority of her successes are those of Hans Rose and the crew he forged. He had sunk the US destroyer *Jacob Jones* and at least eighty merchant vessels totalling 220,051 tons. It was an achievement acknowledged by Rose's enemies. Vice Admiral William Sims, commander of American Naval Forces in European waters, asserted: 'There was no U-boat in the German navy which the Allied forces were so ambitious to "get" as *U 53*.'[620] Nonetheless he continued: 'Rose is one of the few German U-boat commanders with whom Allied naval officers would be willing today to shake hands. I have heard naval officers say that they would like to meet him after the war.'[36]

Believing his authority only came through the respect accord him by the men under his command, Rose counseled *U 53*'s new commander Otto von Schrader:

One of the most important issues is, naturally, the proper handling of the crew. It is composed of exceptional individuals who are hugely responsible and willing to make sacrifices. They pay attention like watchdogs and are always willing to follow you into the most difficult and dangerous circumstances.[621] ... I consider strict and militaristic form of utmost importance, minor negligence I censure. A faith and trust in each other has drawn us together. The crew understood that I depended upon them and they in turn depend upon me. But authority does not grow of itself, authority is not synonymous with gold braid, authority has to be re-established daily.[622]

Then he departed:

The commander made the farewell from his old crew as short as possible since it is imprudent to show emotions or condone ovations in these occasions... The old commander shook every man's hand and turned away.[623]

On 9 November the Kaiser abdicated, and two days later Germany signed the Armistice. For Rose, still a staunch royalist, the abdication of the *Kaiser* was a bitter pill to swallow. He blamed Prince Max von Baden, the last Chancellor of the Second Reich, for having orchestrated the abdication. Rose considered it a betrayal.[624] Reflecting upon the reasons for defeat, Rose wrote:

The German people collapsed. All hopes for victory disintegrated into a terrible defeat. If we had started earlier with the massive production of submarines, and permitted them to attack the enemy, everything could have worked out differently.[625]

Here and in subsequent private conversations with fellow officers, Rose embraced the theory that Germany's military forces were not beaten in WWI, but that her people had given up the will to wage war. Better weapons, more aggressively employed would, in his view, have guaranteed victory.

A Sacred Memento of *U 53*

Rose must have felt uncomfortably 'at sea'. His country had been defeated; seemingly betrayed by political bureaucrats and an insufficiently determined populace. Shorn of his command, and effectively though not formally out of a job, all norms had been swept away by the ensuing collapse.

The commander worried about what to do next... Where to start? Wherever he inquired he was rejected... The future lay clouded and grey before him, as it did for most of the fighters for freedom and justice. The door-bell rang, a delegation from *U 53* came in.[626]

It was a few days after they had surrendered *U 53* to the British at Harwich on 1 December 1918. Now standing to attention before Hans Rose they 'looked their best in their leather uniforms.'[627] Acting as spokesman, Engineering-Mate Crome presents Rose with the centre portion of the *U 53* war ensign:

'Lieutenant Commander, I raised the flag on *U 53* in April 1916. I hauled it down a few days ago in Harwich and hid it under my coat so it would not fall into British hands. We have cut up the flag and everyone has a piece of it. The centre piece I herewith give to our old commander as a remembrance of proud days and the trust of his old crew'...

He continued with a breaking voice: 'For me the boat's surrender was the most difficult because I was on board the longest. We sank ninety-nine ships. I would have wished that we could have destroyed *U 53* itself as our hundredth.'

Silently the men shook each other's hands. The commander kept the centre piece as a sacred memento, and as a proof of his belief in the German people.[628]

Rose rejected Admiral Adolf von Trotha's invitation to remain in the navy. On 24 January 1919 Hans Rose retired from active service with the rank of *Korvettenkapitän*, Lieutenant Commander.[629] His decision to leave the German navy astonishes. The Admiralty kept only the essential sliver of its officer corps at the end of WWI. Von Trotha had wanted Rose to be a part of that cadre. Yet Rose refused. Why? Rose's papers do not offer us any insight. We can only speculate. Perhaps the Admiralty's October 1918 plan to sacrifice the bulk of the surface fleet in a final hopeless battle for glory contributed to Rose's disenchantment, and for a time he lost confidence in its leadership. Perhaps he felt that everything that he who considered himself a knight had fought for, king, country, *Volk*, had proven unworthy. Perhaps Rose felt that his knight's quest had ended in failure and he wanted nothing more to do with it.

These *Auftauchen!* vignettes, written in 1939, share none of the immediacy of the letters he wrote to Anne-Marie from the Levant. Here an older Rose seems to be looking back, perhaps sanitizing. Maybe at the time it was just all too horrible and he has blocked it from memory – or doesn't want to remember. Throughout these pieces Rose shares no sense of community. Rose refers to no-one else. He is not relying on anyone, perhaps not even his wife, or on his crew who come to him in an act full of communal grace. He goes through the psychological turmoil alone – apparently by choice. He is a loner. Perhaps that was one reason he was such a good U-boat commander – the lone wolf descending on the fold.

Chapter 18

Le Comte de Varennes Sends His Regards: The Weimar Years 1919–1929

Heretofore in charge of his own destiny as a naval officer and U-boat commander, Rose's situation would change in the turbulent decades of the twenties and thirties. His life would be buffeted by forces vying for power in a Germany groaning under the effects of the Treaty of Versailles imposed in 1919, exacerbated by the world-wide economic slump begun in 1929, and framed by the political shortcomings of the Weimar Republic and the rise of Hitler's Third Reich.

Through its War Guilt Clause the Treaty of Versailles forced Germany to accept total responsibility for the hostilities. It included a series of onerous territorial clauses: Germany lost her overseas colonies in Africa and elsewhere,[630] ten per cent of her population, and one-eighth of her territory.[631] Heavy reparations in both money and materials amounting to 132 billion gold marks were decreed, including 26% of all exported goods. This almost immediately led to the first inflation of 1923, which ruined the middle class.[632] The hyper-inflation of 1923 would leave Rose and Anne-Marie virtually penniless.

Rose was thirty-three years old when the war ended. Unsure what direction his new life would take, he first joined the *Marine Offiziers Hilfe* (MOH), Navy Officers Aid, whose aim was to place naval members into industrial and

CIVILIAN HANS ROSE Shortly after WWI. [Rose Family Archives]

administrative positions or into organizations where they might contribute to rebuilding society. He considered becoming an architect, but his inferiority complex got in the way:

> Building – Creating – Planning. A wonderful idea, always taken up again, always discarded. I knew from personal experience the magnificent creations of timeless human genius: the Hagia Sofia, the pyramids, the Acropolis and the Gothic, Roman and Greek cathedrals, as well as the Nordic proofs of old Germanic culture... I drew layouts, facades, development plans and interiors of all kinds. However, over and over again I had to lay down my pencil full of disappointment... The more I understood my own inadequacy, the higher my admiration for those who are able to pass down outstanding designs for towering edifices. I wondered whether there wasn't a middle ground between mathematics, physics and architecture... I consulted experts in harbour, bridge and canal design and was assured that I would thrive, which encouraged me to enroll in the *Technische Hochschule* in Berlin-Charlottenburg and attend lectures.[633]

A small educational fund, held in trust by his mother, was adequate to pay for these studies. Rose became a student once again:

> One evening Anne and I were having dinner when the door-bell rang. She announced: 'Three young men wish to invite Mr. Rose.' I went to the living room where one of them announced: 'We would like to take your son to a pub and induct him into our fraternity'... I ran my hand through my greying hair and announced smiling: 'There is no son here; he is at present only a heart's desire in our dreams. I am my son.' Three heads bowed in embarrassment. When I told Anne the story she became thoughtful and looked up at me saying: 'The wish we have had for years must finally come to fruition.' Anne decided to undergo an operation by a well-known doctor, which laid her up for quite a while, but ultimately turned her into a healthy and optimistic personality.[634]

Anne-Marie found a secretarial position, and her salary plus occasional income from student projects permitted a sparse existence for the young couple. However by November 1919 the rapidly deteriorating monetary situation persuaded Hans Rose to accept a business apprenticeship in the petrochemical firm *Theodor Goldschmidt A.G.* in Essen, where his crew comrade Beno Goldschmidt, son of the founder and owner, was employed. Rose's decision would soon place him at the centre of the civil strife that was tearing the country apart.

Throughout the next year, while Anne-Marie remained in Berlin, Rose, an unpaid apprentice in Essen, moved from department to department getting to know the business. He recalled:

> I started in the archives where I and my colleague Fess looked through newspapers and magazines to determine whether their content might interest someone in the firm... This comfortable existence did not last long; I was soon transferred to another department and thus acquired insights into the whole administrative set-up. It was most interesting.[635]

Outside the company's walls the situation was 'interesting' as well. Political chaos reigned and bullets would soon fly. Between 1919 and 1924 the new Weimar republican government and the Reichstag were still trying to establish themselves. On the left the Communists (KPD) demanded a Bolshevik-Russian solution. The three rightist parties all wanted a return of the *Kaiser* and central control imposed from the top down. These right-wing conservative nationalists were the *Deutschnationale Volkspartei* (DNVP), which Hans Rose supported, the *Deutsche Volkspartei* (DVP) and the *Deutsche Zentrumspartei (Zentrum)*. They began 1919 with a combined vote of 76.2%, but their representation steadily declined, becoming a permanent minority throughout the inflationary twenties.[636] At the same time the Weimar Republic was weakened by its failure to win the whole-hearted support of the army, the navy and the civil service, all of which found it difficult to adjust to the transition from the authoritarian Reich to the democratic Republic in 1919.

In the street, armed struggle had already broken out in the shadow of the mutinies begun in the Navy in October/November 1918. From the right the Kapp-Lüttwitz Putsch, a coup attempt launched against the Weimar government, occupied the capital on 13 March 1920. It failed when a general strike launched by the government was widely respected. Nonetheless on the day of the coup, in response, four left-wing parties founded the Red Ruhr Army, composed primarily of workers and between 50,000 and 80,000 strong. They launched an insurgency in Berlin, Thüringen, and the Ruhr valley, Germany's richest industrial region, with Essen at its heart. It would become the largest insurrection in post-WWI Germany, and was actively supported by 300,000 striking mine workers. The insurrection was put down, and large-scale summary executions followed.

As the winter of 1919/1920 progressed Rose recalled his disgust at both the victors and the German government:

> The winter was cold; I lugged coal for the household in my rucksack. Food was scarce. The victorious enemy, who had promised the German people a peace with justice, shamefully exploited the trust of the defeated. Thousands of Germans died of hunger after laying down their arms and the devaluation of our currency progressed by leaps and bounds. [Yet] the spiritual, moral and physical strengths of the German people as a whole seemed to be unstoppable.
>
> During the World War we believed that the fatherland was to be valued higher than the family. We were willing to make sacrifices at any time and place. Now however, when everything was tottering and the men whose views and actions we did not respect were in leadership positions, we placed the family at the centre. It provided a healthy, vigorous germ cell for the future when everything else was sick and rotten.[637]

On 4 April 1920, prior to the revolt's suppression, Essen was surrounded by three rings of *Rote Ruhrarmee* barricades. Opposing them further out were the *Reichswehr* and *Freikorps* forces. Rose recalled that suddenly an unexpected visitor arrived:

> The political situation was very uncomfortable on Easter Monday when I was having lunch with Theo Goldschmidt, Begos' older brother. In spite of this we

were in a good mood. Suddenly the doorbell rang and my darling and fearless wife entered beaming with red cheeks, apparently rejoicing at the success of her surprise. Theo Goldschmidt was open-mouthed at her appearance. Anne had left Berlin in spite of her pregnancy, had taken a train as far as Dortmund, and then, by foot and other means of transportation, made her way through three battle lines to Bredeney.[638]

Rose was delighted to see her, particularly as he had just rented a spacious apartment on Tirpitz street, a relief after his existence in the Goldschmidt's attic. The apartment consisted of a kitchen, maid's room, four living rooms/bedrooms, and a large veranda. The only things missing were a bathroom and central heating. The couple was young and enterprising however, and looked forward to having their own quarters:

> In making the new apartment more habitable it was my job to hang the curtains. I fell off the wobbly ladder that had seen better days and sprained both hands. A few days later I tried to jump on a moving tram, forgetting about my hands, and fell to the ground. Now my feet were sprained as well. That was really bad because the *Theodor Goldschmidt A.G.* did not pay its apprentices and my officer's pension had been cancelled, which meant that we lacked the money for a doctor... Knoespel, who worked as a locksmith in the accounting office, saved the day. He grabbed (both) my hands, gave them a quick yank back and prescribed two days of cold compresses. The operation, though very painful, was a success and cost only two cigars.[639]

On Sunday, 18 July 1920, while Anne-Marie was playing the piano and animatedly singing a *risqué* song, she turned around and announced: 'It's coming.'

> We immediately left for the clinic where I had to leave my dear wife to her destiny. Shortly before midnight a policeman came and announced 'Dr. Veit sends his congratulations on the arrival of a darling little boy.'[640] The infant was baptized Heinz Viktor – both of his Grandfathers lent their names. He was a pretty child.[641]

Shortly after, at the instigation of Theo Goldschmidt's wife Emma, the Roses were among six young couples who met for a weekly dance class, which, Rose recalled, 'provided a wonderful opportunity for relaxation'.[642]

The apartment on Tirpitz Street became too small.[643] Anticipating the arrival of a second child, Rose began seeking larger accommodation. He found an empty parcel of land near the *Gymnasium* in Bredeney that *Theodor Goldschmidt A.G.* purchased in order to build two buildings. He was delighted when the firm allowed him to move into the first completed building. The Roses occupied the entire second floor, knocking out the wall separating the two apartments but leaving the two kitchens.

> We moved in during the fall of 1922. At the time the road was hardly navigable and there were no other houses around. There was only one house opposite the high school that my navy comrade Meyer and his wife Trautelchen had recently built and moved into.[644]

Helga was born on 18 October 1922:

> We had gone to bed early. Outside there was a storm in full swing and the so-called road was impassable. Shortly after midnight Anne woke up with labour pains... I rushed to the phone to call an ambulance... Early in the morning Heinz's little sister Helga was born. The happy mother of course found the little mite 'cute'. I was quite appalled. Her nose was flat, her hair dark, and her mouth looked like that of a flounder... The little one was christened under the Christmas tree. In remembrance of the proud island of Helgoland which had been my base, and to give the child a Germanic touch, she was given the name of Helga.[645]

Still, 'lean days'[646] stalked Hans and Anne-Marie Rose, and he held a variety of jobs including work in the lead-paint department. Nonetheless, Rose eventually worked himself up to the position of clerk and with it more pay. Things improved.[647]

Unfortunately, the joy of these hard-fought steps towards familial bliss was spoiled when, because Dr. Karl Goldschmidt wanted to withdraw from daily business involvement, Rose was asked to become his assets manager on the management board. For the next year-and-a-half Rose struggled with the impossible task of trying to persuade the nine commercial directors to include him in their deliberations; something they refused to do. As the Goldschmidt family trustee, he was furthermore involved with tax wrangles, where his advice was frequently set aside, though his stock trades substantially increased the family's wealth. Having not been able to manage the conflict in a way which retained the support of his benefactor, all of these failures led to a visible and painful cooling of Rose's personal relationship with his patron.

By the end of 1922 French and Belgian troops invaded the Ruhr. The German Republic's response was to order the workers to strike and encourage the population to engage in passive resistance against the invading armies. Disaster ensued: 132 people were killed and over 150,000 Ruhr Germans were expelled from their homes. These had to be resettled elsewhere at public expense.[648] The government's response to the invasion also marked the start of the hyperinflation of 1923. It subsidized the general strike in the Ruhr by printing money to pay the striking workers and resettlement costs.

In 1918 a loaf of bread cost a quarter of a Reichsmark. In 1919 it cost one mark and three marks in 1922. But then the wheels fell off. In January 1923 that loaf cost 700 Reichsmarks, 1,200 in May, 100,000 in July, 2 million in September, 670 million in October and by November 1923, 80 billion Reichsmarks.[649]

The catastrophe swept away income, financial security, economic order as well as the predictability of life that lay at the heart of bourgeois existence. Even though people were paid by the hour and rushed out to spend the money before it became worthless, pensioners on fixed incomes and middle class people like Hans Rose lost the most:

> The inflation continued. To pick a date, on 18 September 1923 one million paper money was worth ten Pfennigs in the past. A tram ride from our house to the company cost

three million marks. The general economic situation was wretched. Many companies dismissed employees and thus increased the misery. Every city printed its own money which, though pretty to look at, had only collector's value. The lowest point was hit in November, when one billion paper marks were worth one gold mark.[650]

In contrast, the great German industrial empires like *Krupp*, *Thyssen*, *IG Farben* and *Stinnes* as well as *Theodor Goldschmidt A.G.* survived the first inflation well. For them the new mark made German goods cheaper and thus increased exports. They could use the export earnings to buy raw materials abroad. The paradoxical result was full employment in which, because prices continued to increase, workers and small business establishments could not save for future security. Hans Rose recalled:

> After I had worked in the Administrative Department of the firm, I was assigned to the Tin Division. Our tin came packed in small sacks from Bolivian mines and was refined into different kinds of ingots in Essen. Inflation was in full swing in Germany while prices were quoted in London; we had to adapt our prices daily to the falling mark. Deals were made by telephone with one ear glued to the customer and the other to the bank's exchange rate. As a result one had to calculate carefully and make deals in split seconds. Those calculations were easy for my boss, the executive secretary, to make. But he was incapable of completing a sale. Frequently the client would hang up before he responded. It was, therefore, best to act independently. But that led to quarrels... The division director, let's call him 'Lion', was the greatest commercial tyrant that I ever met in my entire life... Yet in spite of this my work in the Tin Division was so mesmerizing that I sometimes forgot about lunch. Considering that everyone was starving at the time, this is saying something.[651]

Le Comte Sends His Regards

With the German population engaged in passive resistance to the French and Belgian occupation of the Ruhr valley, arrests and harassment became daily events. To punish the population the French intercepted the delivery of food from the surrounding countryside, causing great hardship for the Ruhr population, including the Rose family. In addition, the occupying authorities restricted rail travel, requiring travellers to obtain an occupation travel pass.

In June 1923 Rose planned to visit his family in Beselin, near Rostock, and set out to obtain the required pass in Essen. The process meant 'one had to spend at least half a day in waiting rooms.'[652] On 22 June, seeking to bypass the delay, Rose called upon the French Chief of Staff, *Le Comte de Varennes*:

> Please, tell the Count of Varennes that I was an officer in active service, and that now I have had to adapt myself to the life of a businessman. I beg to have the pass validated without the normal waiting period.

Shortly thereafter the officer on duty returned, and with a slight bow handed Rose the visa, saying: '*Le Comte de Varennes* sends his regards.'[653]

'I received the passport within minutes. "What a surprise," I thought, "decent enemies do exist."'[654]

Pass in hand Rose took the local tram to the Hervest-Dorsten station on the northern border of the occupied territory, there to await the express to Hamburg. Rose described the scene on the platform:

> At the station a terribly excited Belgian guard made a constant nuisance of himself by ordering: '*Circulez! circulez!*' Thus he caused all the waiting passengers to trek up and down the platform.[655] There were about sixty people, mostly market women, with me on the platform. I definitely stood out in the crowd... Suddenly [the guard] shouted in German: 'Everyone circulates except the guard!' The market women with their baskets slowly started to move. '*Circulez, circulez plus vite, plus vite!*' Slowly, everyone quickened. Meanwhile, the guard ran around like a circus trainer, thereby contradicting his own recent command.[656]

Several weeks later, an American reporter would interview Rose about sinking *Jacob Jones*. The reporter described him:

> But thirty-seven years old, Captain Rose's hair is gray on the temples and silvered on top. His carriage, the bronzed face, the clear blue eyes and the tiny suggestion of an imperial on a face otherwise clean shaven except for a small mustache, betray the naval officer and will always betray him.[657]

Something in Rose's actions or demeanour 'betrayed' him on the platform, drawing the guard's attention. The guard yelled at him and marched him to a sentry.[658] Not comprehending what was required Rose asked to be taken to the commander for clarification. Confronted by a very young, inexperienced French-speaking junior officer, who barked that he was in command, Rose was searched for weapons. Three heavily armed soldiers escorted him to the gymnasium of a school in Hervest-Dorsten, where they ordered him to stand with his face against the wall. Rose's request to see the commanding officer was ignored.[659] Things then spun out of control and Rose, recounting in the third person as he often did, demonstrated just how angry he was about the occupation:

> '*Prenez la position!*' Stand at attention! cried the soldiers. The captain complied in order to win time. They threw his pass on the ground and struck his legs with horse-whips. He did not resist, 'to win time' was most important.[660] Suddenly a helmeted soldier, 'apparently just relieved of duty',[661] struck Rose in the back of the neck:
>
> This affront was too much; the Captain spun around and hit the soldier in the face with all his might. The cracking of teeth was heard. The captain observed the teeth-marks on his knuckles with great satisfaction. He found relish in looking at the scars there for many a year to come.
>
> He intended to fight his way to the door, but like hounds they fell upon him and gouged him with their rifle butts. A bayonet thrust into his back went unnoticed by the captain until the next day.

Opportunely a calm man of authority appeared. The nearly unconscious Captain held fast to him. 'Kill the damn pig,' yelled the others. They dragged him to the infirmary, where, with thirty-one stitches, a Belgian doctor closed the cuts his patient had received from the rifle butts to his hands and head. The Captain had managed to fend off all the attackers from the front but could not protect himself from the others. Apparently a rifle butt was broken during the fray.[662]

Subsequently Rose and a number of local mayors were incarcerated overnight in a cellar in Sterkerade. The next morning Rose discovered the bayonet wound in the back[663] and he was running a temperature. Hoping to gain time before incarceration, Rose massaged the thermometer to increase his temperature.

Handcuffed and under maximum security the captain was brought to a hospital in Sterkerade by boxcar. The door to his room had to remain open day and night, and a sentry with drawn rifle stood at the threshold. The prisoner's clothes had been taken away...

When the Captain had to fulfil his natural needs he had to leave the bed with great pains and simply turn his shining behind towards the sentry. The guard replied to the greeting by directing his rifle towards the point of the Captain's body which had already been punctured by another Belgian the day before.

All meals brought by friendly Belgian nuns were checked by the guard. He opened every potato with unwashed fingers; they could contain some message. Untouched by the Captain, the potatoes were carried out the way they came in.[664]

From the military hospital, Rose, whose headache and back pains precluded much thought, requested his family be notified. The situation was grave. A Dutch lawyer, Mr. Curtius, confirmed a day later that the occupying Belgian authorities intended to charge Rose with *résistance*, 'resisting a military command', punishable by twenty years forced labour. Rose, following diplomatic practice, demanded complete '*réparations et satisfaction*'[665] for his treatment, and the punishment of the Belgian commander.

Cut off from his family as well as the firm, Rose wondered who might be able to help. Luckily, Wassili Rabinowitsch, an agronomist employed by *Theodor Goldschmidt A.G.*, came to intervene with the French occupation forces. There was one silver lining; German newspapers had gotten wind of his inhumane treatment and chronicled his plight, saying that 'he had been beaten within an inch of his life.'[666] News of Rose's arrest quickly spread and American Vice Admiral Sims cabled his belief in Rose's innocence. *Le Comte de Varennes* also intervened in his favour. A week later, perhaps through fear of the bad publicity of a trial, the charges were dropped. Curtius, the Dutch lawyer, visited him at the hospital and stated simply: 'You are free.'[667]

Shortly thereafter the interview in Berlin with an American reporter for the Washington *Sunday Star* netted the munificent sum of $50 with which, in this period of hyper-inflation, Rose financed a four-week stay of recuperation in the Navy hospital of Obersalzberg near Berchtesgaden.

Upon his return to Essen, now fully recovered, the Roses used an allowance from the Goldschmidts to buy land for a future garden, and to stabilize their existence during the period of hyperinflation:

> That Dr. Karl Goldschmidt gave me some stock as a compensation for my personal suffering, was for me a great honour and a great pleasure. This noble gift provided the foundation for a modest fortune and eased our existence. I have many good reasons for thanking my patron and to be grateful for the rest of my life.[668]

Back in Essen Rose was informed that the *Comte de Varennes* wished to see him.

> The *Comte de Varennes* repeatedly begged the Captain for a visit. Only reluctantly did the Captain yield to the request. The Count received him graciously. When the Captain expressed his gratitude for the Count's intervention, the Count replied, 'If all Germans would behave as you did, our troops would not take so much for granted.' A formal bow and shaking of hands ended the short meeting.[669]

Rose's encounter with the Belgian occupation authorities had an unexpected denouement twenty years later, when as Sea Commander in Trondheim during WWII Rose received a letter from a Franconian countess. She wrote that a French officer, *le Comte de Varennes*, was imprisoned in a prisoner-of-war camp near her estate. *Le Comte* was in poor health and his estates were being neglected. He had indicated to her that the only person that might be able to help him obtain his release would be *Korvettenkapitän* Rose. Writing 'at once to all possible officials with any responsibility for prisoners of war'[670] including Admiral Reader, Rose was gratified a short time later to receive a letter from *le Comte* himself at La Rochelle thanking Rose for his help in obtaining his release. Rose replied: 'Dear Count; I am pleased to hear that you are free. I wish you health and luck. Now we're even.'[671]

The section of Rose's autobiography *A Life Portrait* that recounts his fight with the Belgian soldiers, is titled 'The Knight'. This choice is illuminating because on the surface it involves an event where Hans Rose, now a businessman, appears to have become only accidentally involved in 'martial' action. There can be little doubt about Rose's frame of mind: 'Most of the crowd [on the station platform] were fat market women loaded with heavy baskets – truly an excellent example of bravery – an armed soldier against defenceless old women.'[672]

Disappointments in the Land of the Cheruskers (1925–1928)

By declaring a State of Emergency and governing by decree from September 1923 through February 1924, the Weimar government was finally able to end the hyperinflation and stabilize the exchange rate of one billion paper Reichsmarks for one gold mark. By the fall of 1923 Great Britain and the United States realized that the Weimar Republic was close to collapse and agreed to a fixed German border in the west, precluding further French incursions. Despite the Weimar government's efforts the fledgling Nazi Party was able to win thirty-two Reichstag seats in the 8 November 1923 election. Railing against 'the Berlin Jew government and the November criminals of 1918'[673] Hitler led the Nazi Party's November Beer Hall Putsch in Munich.

During the middle period of the Weimar Republic, in the three years between 1925 and 1928, Germany's socio-political situation improved. Field Marshal Hindenburg's *Deutschnationale Volkspartei* (DNVP), the Center (*Zentrum*) party and the German Nationalists (DNP) cooperated and finally achieved a solid majority in the Reichstag. The coalition stabilized the Weimar Republic, while the devaluation package broke the inflationary spiral. The Republic's middle period thus provided not only economic survival, but also modest income growth for professionals and workers who had gained unionization rights. Industrialists began to rebuild their trade relations with the outside world and were more willing to cooperate, though they remained sceptical of foreign policy.

Hans Rose spent the beginning of the Weimar Republic's 'golden years', 1924 and 1925, away from Essen where his position had become increasingly untenable:

Easter Monday, 20 April 1924
A quarter of a year passed swiftly when there were no more than ordinary experiences. We drifted with the tide, bobbing on the surface of the ocean of existence. I was frequently in Essen over the past months preparing myself for the new responsibilities that await me at the Kondorworks in Lemgo and Nordhausen. While in Essen, I was depressed with my activities at Theo Goldschmidt, and therefore did not have the energy to write in my diary.

Now I am quitting my positions as the private secretary for Dr Karl and the family's assets manager. This means that I have completed my present responsibilities and can concentrate exclusively on the Kondorworks. Whether this work will be of benefit to me and my family is not at present knowable. I hope it will because I will invest myself in the endeavour.[674]

Rose had agreed to run Kondorworks, a small business consisting of two woodworking shops that had originally been part of the Goldschmidt interests in the newly emerging aircraft industry. The two workshops were located near Lemgo, in the *Teutoburger Wald*, in the state of Lippe, 'the land of the Cheruskers'.[675] Lemgo was not far from the picturesque Hanseatic town of Hameln on the Weser river, the birthplace of both his parents, where Rose had spent many happy childhood summers.

Anxious about the deteriorating health of his wife, Rose moved the family to Lemgo:

One could fault me for bringing Anne and the children to Lemgo. I did it, because in the summer I did not foresee the wretchedness of the business prospects and because Anne's health deteriorated precipitously as a result of our separation. She, who during the war was able to bear her solitude for weeks on end when I was at sea, is no longer as strong and requires the presence of her husband.[676]

Anne moved to Lemgo in the summer of 1924 and was expecting their third child, Gerd, who was born on 13 February 1925. He was named in honour of Rose's crew mate Gerd Noormann, an Able Seaman who had served as rudder mate and battle helmsman in *U 53*'s conning tower.[677]

The business prospects for the small company were much less rosy than anticipated: 'I understood perfectly that what I was getting into was a quagmire in more ways than one... My hair turned white as a result of all of the nagging worries.'[678]

It began with the cancellation of an order for a few thousand radio-casings for the *Krupp* factory, which the sawmills were to produce from high quality wood. Unfortunately, the Lemgo firm's usual production of doors and window frames was not sufficient to cover operational costs. Rose cast around for new ideas and found that staircases and window production for social housing also did not live up to expectations. Not only did the local forestry office deliver rotten wood, which Rose refused to accept, but they also miscalculated their needs. This led to a temporary closure of one of the sawmills, and a lowering of everyone's wages.

At Christmas 1924, Rose confided to his diary:

> In the summer we moved to Lemgo, the attractive little Hanseatic town. We lived very simply in surroundings with lovely gabled houses ... everything so quaint that one was seized with a sense of inner well-being.[679]
>
> ...Unfortunately the Kondorworks are not making any progress so that we will probably not be here for long. That is too bad; the isolation of this old town is only endurable if the business prospers.[680]

Throughout 1925 business went from bad to worse. Rose had to lay off workers, reduce pay once more, and also take capital losses. In addition to these financial concerns Rose was worried about his wife's health, which, week by week, was deteriorating.

Though Rose suggested closure of the business, the Goldschmidt family demurred, calling on him to stay the course in light of plans to open a wood factory in Ankara, Turkey's thriving capital. Rose summed up his experiences: 'With deep regret I had to bury the hope of finding an independent future in the wood-production business.'[681]

In early 1926 fate intervened with the death of Rose's fatherly friend and patron, Dr. Karl Goldschmidt. His sons requested Rose return to the central office in Essen; a move that made him once again master of his own destiny. He and his family moved into a company-renovated apartment on *Steubenstraße* near the water tower in 1926. While their cook, Paula, 'ruled the dark kitchen',[682] Rose set up another garden: 'I leased an eight-metre strip of unused land next to the building so that the children had a place to play. We felt very comfortable.'[683]

The Rose family spent the next thirteen years, until the outbreak of WWII, in Essen, working in various departments of *Goldschmidt A.G.*'s newly created Lead Division. As a consequence, the second half of the 'golden years' was more prosperous for Rose than the first. Under his leadership the division grew steadily between 1926 and 1928 and the company's production facilities were modernized. Moreover, Rose found new customers for the division's new products. 'Finally I had the opportunity to experience how satisfying it is to build up a business.'[684]

Hand in hand with his growing business experience came a return of self-confidence which had been sorely tested in Lemgo. Open to new opportunities, Rose mentioned Lindberg's flight across the Atlantic in the summer of 1927 as the beginning of a new business era, which would deeply affect both commerce and travel. He began to take Russian language lessons preparatory to exploring private investment opportunities in Russia and also travelled to England to renew pre-war acquaintances. While the plans for Russian investments turned out to be premature, those with England expanded the Lead Division's customer base.

Between accounts of business successes, Rose interspersed comments that Anne's health remained broken and did not improve. In the fall of 1929 there was more trouble with the children. Heinz was run over by a car and Gerd needed a tonsillectomy. Anne contracted an infection in the hospital requiring months of recuperation. Rose, never much of a hands-on father to his birth children, remarked: 'Unfortunately, all of these misfortunes were combined with our inability to find a responsible nanny.'[685]

Nonetheless Hans Rose had finally achieved a degree of middle class success, and in so doing had achieved one of the goals of being a good father; providing for the future of his family.

Chapter 19

The Titan of the Will

Rose met Adolf Hitler for the first time in the summer of 1923. It was during his convalescence in Berchtesgaden following his beating at the hands of the Belgian occupiers of the Ruhr. No doubt Rose was still deeply affected by his recent misfortune. Hitler was, Rose recalled, 'a man possessed by his own ideas'.[686] Rose's *von Tampen* description sets this event in a pristine, sunlight-drenched mountain meadow:

> One morning walking alone, I encountered a young man wearing an impeccable Bavarian outfit with a spotless white shirt, colourful tie and a brand new set of *Lederhosen*, surrounded by a group of less well-dressed young men … who listened spell-bound to his monologue.[687]

Passing the group, Rose wondered who they were. On returning for lunch with his head still bandaged, some naval friends told him they were going to a speech by Adolf Hitler, the leader of the National Socialist party. Rose decided to accompany them:

> His party's political slogans had appealed to my nationalist sentiments, but at the time I had not yet seen a picture of Hitler... who avoided being photographed... My jaw dropped when the Tyrolean of the morning turned out to be Adolf Hitler.[688]

HITLER'S ADDRESS AT HINDENBURG'S TANNENBERG FUNERAL 7 August 1934. Rose remembered 'With teary eyes and lips pressed together we stood motionless until the casket disappeared into the Field-Marshal's mausoleum, and the solemn Führer returned into the sun-drenched memorial field.' [Bundesarchiv, Bild 183-2006-0429-502 / CC-BY-SA 3.0]

After the speech Rose's colleagues urged him, as a badly wounded Ruhr resister, to make Hitler's acquaintance. Hitler, however, was so preoccupied with his own thoughts that he failed to pay any attention to Rose:

> I ... was dragged by them to the podium. Now, standing before the speaker with my heavily bandaged white turban, I expected him to inquire about conditions in the Ruhr, as well as my personal experiences there. Hitler, was however so preoccupied with his own thoughts, one can almost call it 'possessed', that he did not respond to anything that I tried to convey to him. He lectured on, and in order not to appear impolite, I listened to him *nolens volens* (willing or not).[689]
>
> ...Anne and I agreed that the speakers' arguments were similar to our own opinions, but that the speech had contained platitudes ... that were only convincing because of Hitler's personality and inspiring populist rhetoric.[690]

Nevertheless, Rose found the meeting pivotal and later recalled:

> Anne and I looked back at this first encounter frequently, trying to retain its immediacy.[691] Two more times after 1933, I had the opportunity to meet this titan of the will. Both times I looked deep into Hitler's eyes. If he had had a single wise and principled friend, world history might have turned out differently.[692]

Here is evidence both of Hans Rose's well-established nationalist ideology, his philosophy regarding the role of the individual, and an example of his tendency to romanticism, which his wife and children describe as a tendency to believe in unrealistic ideals.

During WWI Hans Rose was nicknamed the 'Pink Commander' and 'Pink Rose' by his naval colleagues.[693] The monikers reflected his comparatively liberal politics and association with social democratic ideals. By the middle of the 1920s however, when the centre-right established a solid coalition government that would last for four years, it was a political perspective increasingly on the defensive. Despite his nicknames, the coalition had won Rose's vote.

In 1928 the centre-right coalition lost its Reichstag majority.[694] Reflecting increasing polarization within German society, on the extreme left the communist *Kommunistische Partei Deutschlands* (KPD) and on the extreme right Hitler's National Socialists, the *Nationalsozialistische Deutsche Arbeiterpartei* (NSDAP) together controlled 13.5% of all Reichstag seats. The results guaranteed a new period of political instability and precipitated the dissolution of the Weimar Republic. Between 1928 and 1930, all kinds of splinter groups, both right and left, had to be included into the ruling coalition.

The global stock market crash of 1929 also precipitated the end of the Weimar Republic. It dried up the US dollar subvention and precipitated a huge 40% drop in German industrial production.[695] Brüning prorogued the Reichstag in July 1930 and proposed new elections for September 1930. These elections had an unanticipated outcome; to everyone's surprise Hitler's fringe party, the NSDAP, suddenly became the second strongest party in the Reichstag.[694] The two primary reasons for the rise of the Nazis were first the impoverishment of both labour and business, and second a return to nationalistic feelings. In the coming two years, as the parties splintered and battled, the Reichstag sat for only a paltry fifty days, while the economic storm clouds darkened.

In Rose's opinion the Nazi Party's success was primarily caused by the worldwide economic crisis. He argued that the depression disproportionately affected the working population, as well as small businesses. In his view these 2.8 million unemployed Germans viewed Hitler as their last chance for survival. In addition, Rose believed that the inequities of the Versailles treaty and Germany's treatment by the Allies were propelling German voters into the arms of the radical parties. Germans of all stripes had become more nationalistic throughout the Weimar years.[696] Rose believed that National Socialism provided a revitalization of the country's atrophied and outdated party system and that the economy would be transformed by their new ideas. For Rose, the third and most important reason for the NSDAP success was Hitler's personality. He posited that Hitler stood out from the other party leaders because of his leadership qualities and his inspiring populist rhetoric.

Historian Sebastian Haffner agrees with Rose's assessment that Hitler's personality played an important role in his rise to power. Haffner explains that Hitler, at one and the same time, projected determination and stealth, as well as the vision to ask his countrymen to rise and make sacrifices for the common good, so that Germany would once again take its rightful place on the European stage. It was this vision that turned National Socialism into a mass movement.[697]

Convenient to a demagogue such as Hitler, historian Richard Evans asserts that the Nazi Party's success was precisely its *lack* of a platform – its social protest transcended social boundaries and united disparate social groups. Among the crossovers were

> ...farmers, various kinds of workers, civil servants, first-time voters (including many women) and voters from older age groups in a powerful expression of their dissatisfaction with the Weimar years, resentment fostered by the Versailles treaty and fear of the future... The vagueness of the Nazi program, its symbolic mixture of old and new, its eclectic, often inconsistent character, allowed people to read into it what they wanted and to edit out anything they might find disturbing. Many middle-class voters coped with Nazi violence on the streets by writing it off as the product of excessive youthful ardour and energy.[698]

In the September 1930 general election Rose once again voted for the conservative DNVP, which declined from 73 to 41 seats, while the Nazis (NSDAP) grew from a mere 12 seats in 1928 to 107 two years later. Rose household loyalties split in that election:

> The female part of my household went over to the Nazis, impressed by their attitude and optimism. I too sympathize with these manly and open fellows. There is only one reason why I have not yet voted for them, and that is that even though I am in agreement with most of their points, I am afraid that their program will have severe negative economic repercussions.[699]

Nonetheless, Rose argued:

> Though their program may be interpreted as an 'ideal form of communism', I am happy that they received such strong support in yesterday's vote. If their party had not existed the Communists would have received an extra few million ballots and that would have been a disaster for Germany.[700]

While political turmoil increasingly gripped the nation, 1930 brought success, happiness and hope in the Rose family. Early in the year Anne-Marie and Hans Rose's fourth and last child was born:

> The storm clouds cleared and the sun shone in the souls of all family members, when our son Christian Sorgenfrei opened his eyes to the world at 5:30 on Sunday afternoon 2 February 1930... The happiness of the other children at the news of the birth of their little brother was lovely to behold. Helga in particular was delightful to observe. She was jumping into the air like a little cannibal overcome by rapture.[701]

In September Rose articulated his hopes for his son's destiny:

> It might seem presumptuous in this politically and economically difficult time to give a child a generations-old family name 'Christian' and the middle name 'Sorgenfrei' (carefree). But we believe in this period of sadness it is precisely the future that will justify the name. We hope that the little man will from the beginning enter the fight for existence with a sense of victory and success. Moreover, [we hope] that he will find his way through the countless daily adversities without losing his enjoyment of life and the belief in himself and his destiny. We wish him to be a 'bringer of light'.[702]

At the same time Rose would find his youngest child a considerable challenge, and unlike his other children, Rose felt compelled at times to enforce discipline with a switch. Christian would find it a heavy burden, commenting in his mid-eighties:

> 'Bringer of Light' is a burden a little heavy to carry, and I have no intention of hanging from a cross. Although I feel that I have carried in my mind my own cross, and this since a very early age.[703]

Rose enthused:

> The year 1930 turned out to be a business success. [The *Theodor Goldschmidt A.G.'s* Lead Division] is doing well and has a sales turnover of 1.5 million Reichsmark, with excellent returns. I suggested to Mutti that she take a winter vacation in Seefeld/Tirol. We took Heinz, who continued to be frail, out of school and I accompanied him to Winterberg, where he blossomed during a week of skiing. But then Gerd caused anxiety. His glandular lumps refused to heal... We sent him to Königsfeld for a change of air, while Anne and I limited ourselves to

a hiking tour in the Sauerland because my salary and pension had been reduced in April… In November it was Helga's turn to fall ill. She had a pain in her stomach, which turned out to be appendicitis, but she recovered quickly after an operation… Heinz seems finally to have reached a good physical and mental state. His membership in the *Deutsche Freischar*, the German Youth Organization, led by a senior student, seems to have contributed to this situation.[704]

Two years later, at the beginning of 1932, Hans Rose also became a crossover and joined the NSDAP, the Nazi Party: 'The times are portentous. We enter the year 1932 with serious presentiments. I have joined the National Socialists because they have the healthiest plans for the future and I believe that they will prevail.'[705]

Gerd and Helga become members of the Hitler Youth. In 1934, his youngest son, four-year old Christian, greets visitors to the house with a hearty '*Heil Hitler.*'[706] Rose himself opens and closes his diary entries the same way.[707]

As 1932 dawned the venerable Paul von Hindenburg's seven-year term of office as President came to an end. In view of his eighty-four years he was reluctant to stand again, but was willing to extend his service if no election was involved. This proposal received astonishing support because party leaders thought he would keep Brüning in office and thus guarantee a return to democratic norms. However, in the run-off between Hitler, Hindenburg and Thälmann, the Nazis pulled out all the stops and Brüning, failing to persuade the right wing nationalist parties to support Hindenburg's reinstatement, had to resign.

Goebbels fought the 31 July 1932 election based not on the performance of the von Papen cabinet, but on the performance of the Weimar Republic. In apocalyptic terms the Nazi films and vast open air speeches and assemblies purveyed an image of 'red civil war over Germany' in which voters were confronted with a stark choice: either the old forces of betrayal and corruption, or a national rebirth to a glorious future. The propaganda was successful. The Nazis doubled their votes from 6.4 to 13.1 million, making them the largest party in the Reichstag with 230 seats. Hermann Göring, presiding over the autumn session of the Reichstag as the representative of the largest party, allowed the Communist motion of no-confidence in the government to go ahead. This *coup de grâce* led to the latter's resignation.

General Schleicher's inability to win over the nationalist parties obliged him to resign, and so on the morning of 30 January 1933 Hitler was sworn in as Reich Chancellor. The government he headed was dominated numerically by von Papen and his fellow Conservatives, while Hitler got only two major offices: the Ministry of the Interior occupied by Wilhelm Frick and the Chancellery. Göring was appointed Reich Minister without portfolio and Acting Prussian Minister of the Interior, which gave him direct control over the police in most of Germany. The Nazis could now manipulate the domestic law-and-order situation to their advantage.[708]

Rose's change in political affiliation had to do with a number of factors. First, he argued that hyperinflation and the depression hit Germany harder than other countries because of the unreasonable reparation demands contained in the

Versailles treaty. To remedy this situation, Rose opined that Germany needed to reclaim its military sovereignty and to double the size of its army and navy. He felt the country should reclaim some of the lost colonies to assure the trade associated with them. Rose noted that each German soldier was confronted by forty-seven well-armed French troops, and that Germany's existing 125,000-ton shipping fleet constituted not more than 3½% of the world's tonnage, a huge decline from its once dominant position, second only to Great Britain, prior to WWI.

This context of renewed economic turmoil, rising nationalism, and the fear of anarchy or a communist takeover led Hans Rose, authoritarian, romantic, idealist, and nationalist, to turn towards the Nazis.[709]

The Swift Consolidation of the Nazi Dictatorship: January–July 1933

Hitler's appointment as Reich Chancellor was no ordinary change of government. This became immediately clear as Goebbels organized a torchlight parade of brownshirts, *Der Stahlhelm*, and SS men through Berlin. Hermann Göring believed that the public mood of the moment 'could only be compared with that of August 1914, when a nation also rose up to defend everything it possessed. The shame and disgrace of the last fourteen years have been wiped out.'[710]

The swift and radical consolidation of the Nazi dictatorship was accomplished in a short six months and began with Göring's statement that from 30 January 1933 onwards German society would be put, as quickly as possible, on a permanent war footing and that the legitimate Weimar parties would be abolished. Leading Social Democrats and trade unionists were eliminated by having their party's newspapers closed, their meetings disrupted and their speakers beaten up.[711] Pitched battles broke out across the country. In Essen, Christian Rose recalled the turmoil at the intersection of Von-der-Tann Strasse and Steeler Strasse leading up to the *Wasserturm*, the main water supply for the city:[712]

> Inside our apartment my mother did her utmost to keep peace and harmony while on the streets below the social turmoil was evident – gun battles were raging between the communists and the NSDAP-Storm Troopers. The city water tower just up the street was a strategic centre for control over Essen, desired by both factions.[713]

The Reichstag fire of 27 February 1933 gave the Nazis an excuse for further crackdowns. More than 4,000 deputies, representatives in other legislatures, officials, bureaucrats, organizers and activists were arrested. On 28 February 1933, Hitler, accompanied by von Papen, called on the President to sign the Decree to protect the German people and the state. It annulled all the important fundamental rights of citizens, including *habeas corpus*, and extended the list of crimes subject to the death penalty. It also suspended several sections of the Weimar constitution, particularly those governing freedom of expression, freedom of the press and freedom of assembly and association. It allowed the police to detain people in protective custody indefinitely and without a court order. Beyond that, Paragraph 2 allowed the government to take over the

Right: KAPITÄNLEUTNANT
HANS ROSE Propaganda postcard
annotated 'Commander of the
German Undersea-boat *U 53* from
Wilhelmshaven to New York'.
[Author's Archive]

Below: GERMAN EMBASSY IN
PERA The European quarter of
Constantinople. [Author's Archive]

SMS *HESSEN*, A PRE-DREADNOUGHT SHIP-OF-THE-LINE VISITING VENICE In 1905 Rose served aboard as a sea-cadet in training. [Das Bundesarchiv Koblenz]

ARMOURED CRUISER SMS *FREYA* was modernized in 1905–7 and served as a school-ship for cadets. Rose taught aboard as a midshipman. [Author's Archive]

Above: HEINZ ROSE in the family's living room, 1936. [Rose Family Archives]

Right: WWII *U 53* CHRISTENING CEREMONY 24 June 1939; Hans Rose centre. [U-Boot-Archiv in Cuxhaven-Altenbruch]

Below right: SEA COMMANDER HANS ROSE IN HIS TRONDHEIM OFFICE Rose served in Norway between 1 July 1940 and 31 July 1943. [Rose Family Archives]

ANTON PRYTZ
GREETING GERMAN
OFFICERS May 27,
1941: Anton Frederik
Prytz, soon to be
Minister of Finance in
the puppet Quisling
government, inspects
the marine shipyard in
Trondheim with Hans
Rose and other German
officers. [Schroeder –
Sverresborg Trøndelag
Folkemuseum]

HANS ROSE SHAKES
HANDS WITH
BIRGER GRØNN,
Director of the marine
shipyard in Trondheim
600 metres from
Rose's office in Folkets
Hus. Unbeknownst
to Rose, Grønn was
working with the
Resistance. [Schroeder
– Sverresborg Trøndelag
Folkemuseum]

THE WRECK OF *U 51*
Raised in 1968 because
she had become a
danger to shipping, the
forward portion of *U
51* lies ashore separated
from the rear that had
to be cut off during
the salvage operation.
[U-Boot-Archiv,
Cuxhaven-Altenbruch]

federated states, if public order was endangered. The Nazi seizure of power could now begin in earnest.[714]

The Nazis campaign in the last 'free' election on 5 March 1933 was carried out under widespread intimidation. The coalition parties, Nazis and Nationalists (the *Zentrum* party) had won 288 and 74 seats respectively, winning 51.9% of the popular vote. Seventeen million people voted Nazi and another 3 million *Zentrum*. For worried conservatives and traditionalists who still possessed formal power, Hitler and his allies staged a reassuring ceremony on 21 March 1933 in the garrison church at Potsdam, above the tomb of Frederick the Great. Hindenburg stood next to the *Kaiser*'s vacant throne, dressed in the uniform of a Prussian Field Marshal symbolically restoring the old Germany. The ceremony had an extraordinary effect on all participants, including deputies, soldiers, diplomats and foreign observers. It has been characterized as one of the turning points in modern history.[715]

Two days later Hitler emerged in a brown-shirt paramilitary uniform and spoke beneath a huge swastika banner introducing the long-planned Enabling Act. It would authorize the Reich Chancellor to prepare laws that deviated from the constitution without the approval of the Reichstag and without reference to the President. From May 1933 onwards Nazi terror led to mass resignations and the incarceration of *Zentrum* party members as well as leading Catholic politicians, lawyers and others.

The ongoing crackdown not only affected the politically suspect and the marginal after Hitler's accession to power, but also every other aspect of German society. Between February and July 1933 almost every facet of social and group life was 'coordinated'. Attacks on the Jewish population were considered crucial in this coordination effort, because they were described as repositories of un-German spirit, and provided an internal 'enemy' against which the population could be mobilized. Hitler and Goebbels ordered the first boycott of small Jewish shops on 1 April 1933, but it caused relatively little physical damage and spared the large companies because of their importance to the national economy. The unexpected outcry in the foreign press, however, caused the Nazis to adopt a 'quasi legal route' against the Jews until *Kristallnacht*.

Between 30 January and 1 May 1933 1.6 million people joined the Nazi Party, many simply to save their jobs.[716] Industry represented a final power centre the Nazis needed to bring into line. In the business sector the Reich Association of German Industry incorporated Nazis into their boards and declared their loyalty to the regime by supporting it financially in the March 1933 election. With the trade unions smashed, socialism off the agenda, and new arms and munitions contracts already looming, big business felt satisfied that the concessions made to the new regime were worth it. Rose commented:

> For our firm [*Theodor Goldschmidt A.G.*'s Lead Division], the government's measures have resulted in the utilization of 100% of our manufacturing capacity and the sale of all of our stock. For this too we raise our arms in appreciation and our voices in the common chorus of '*Heil* Hitler.'[717]

For the Nazis and their supporters, the very term 'Third Reich' constituted a powerful symbolic link to the imagined greatness of the past, embodied in the

First Reich of Charlemagne and the Second Reich of Bismarck. Yet despite their egalitarian rhetoric, what mattered most to the Nazis were race, culture and ideology. The speed and enthusiasm with which so many people came to identify with the new regime strongly suggests that a large majority of the educated elites in German society, whatever their political allegiance might have been, were already predisposed to embrace many of the principles upon which Nazism rested. In the wake of WWI these principles and beliefs were held by the major social and political institutions.[718] In this sense, Rose was no different from the herd.

By mid-1933, Rose's hopes for a renewed Germany were beginning to be realized:

Much has happened and we are witnessing great times for which future generations will envy us. We endeavour to live up to these expectations at a time when enthusiasm for change provides the spark in the daily struggle for existence. Events have however, also highlighted the wretchedness and lack of character of many others. May it encourage us to look forward to the future, rather than the past. In this future the family plays an important role.[719]

To demonstrate the prevailing spirit of optimism Rose included an article in his diary about the Führer's 27 August 1934 speech on the Ehrenbreitstein ruin, which 'was greeted with thunderous applause'. Then Rose, the romantic idealist, again shifts from 'family' back to '*Volk*'. His diary entry for 21 July 1934 articulates his support for the populist Nazi doctrine. Stating that his diary's purpose is to convey the 'spirit of the times' Rose writes:

As I return to my diary, which was begun in a period of drastic change, I can no longer place the individual and the family at the centre of my concerns, but must focus on the 'we' and proudly acknowledge my membership in the German *Volk*. I closed my last entry with '*Heil* Hitler' and shall begin the current one with the same salutation. A year and a half ago, this man with his unyielding will took over the leadership of our people's destiny and understood how to revive the long-buried noble and idealistic feelings [in our hearts]. Who else in the last fifteen years spoke of each individual's responsibility to make sacrifices for the common good? Who else had the courage to demand that industry serve state interests? Who else raised the workers' self-respect by referring to their honour? Coming generations will envy us for having lived in these times, when a people once again awakens to its manly destiny. His call 'Germany awake' proclaims a life-giving rush to action.[720]

Rose goes on to articulate his understanding of 'national socialism' and its strengths and weaknesses. In this tripartite definition he mentions the 'nationalistic' component first, since from the beginning it has dominated his own thinking. For Rose, the 'Pink Commander',

National socialist ideology, as far as I am concerned, is nothing new. It refers to the convictions of every nationalistic, socially responsible and decent person... To my mind therefore every nationalistically inclined worker is thus a natural member of the movement.[721]

A second component of Rose's understanding of national socialism involves the need for expert knowledge:

> That is however not the case with other strata in our society, among them the so-called capitalists and the industrial elite. They have yet to be persuaded to collaborate. Their participation is important because our country's leadership needs not only the talents of long-time party members, but also those with penetrating intelligence, initiative and rich economic experience. This requires continued vigilance over our government appointment process.[722]

In another entry dated July 1934 Rose gives another reason why he supports the Hitler state: its measures for economic survival and the elimination of unemployment.

> I believe that our government's interpretation of the economic prerequisites for Germany's *Volk* prosperity are correct and that every week of peaceful coexistence leads the European economy one step further away from the abyss, and on to a course of recovery for all of us. Though the 'world economy' is an inspiring concept, the self-contained economy of a single people is more important.[723]

The government's plan to reduce unemployment, even though it implies material sacrifices, is good:

> [In this process] everyone seems to overestimate the importance of money... This is wrong. More important than money is the availability of work. I therefore support [the government's] attempts to eliminate unemployment, even if the material costs are high. A year and a half ago we suffered from a huge 7.5 million unemployment figure, today this number has been reduced to 2.5 million. This success trumps all other initiatives. Should it become possible to eliminate unemployment all together, trade and commerce will automatically revive. If, in addition, people's inborn idealism is reconstituted, and it is shown that the dignity of work is more important than all material goods, then the gospel of National Socialism will surely triumph.[724]

Initially, the Nazis devised a voluntary Labour Service model that acted as a magnet for unemployed youth. A year later, in 1936, full employment was achieved.[725] As the economic upswing took hold, new social policies were instituted for the working class to camouflage state control of their unions and their inability to strike. Among these were organizations like *Kraft durch Freude*, Strength through Joy, which provided members with vacation travel, sports festivals, shows, dances and training classes. Giving work to the unemployed led to the construction of the famous German Autobahn network, expanded rail traffic, urbanized the country and ultimately provided the infrastructure for the war economy.

At the same time, Rose, the nationalist, offered a modest humanist critique:

> The motto 'Germany Awake!' has without doubt a strong and invigorating effect. Yet why in this time of sloganeering could the movement not find a better name

for itself than 'National Socialist'. This is a terrible misnomer to my mind. I also disapprove of singing the narrow-minded Horst Wessel song with its questionable formulations alongside the beautiful *Deutschland* song. Even stranger are the two flags [the German black/red/gold and the Swastika] which decorate our streets. Why is this necessary? Moreover there is talk about the need for national socialist 'training' and a national-socialist 'ideology'. To my mind these [two concepts] refer to a belief system shared by every nationally oriented, socially concerned decent human being.[726]

Choosing to ignore its substance (in so far as he was prepared to confide to his diary), Rose believed that anti-Semitic Nazi doctrine was nothing more than a tactical excess:

And finally there is the threat posed by foreign countries. Unfortunately anti-Semitism, which is part of the fundamental conviction of the party, was short-sightedly *over-emphasized* [authors' italics] in the transition period a year and a half ago. I explained this to a Jew who was emigrating to Palestine as 'giving a poor account' of ourselves ... he is joining an international Jewish movement, which is vocally opposing us. Bitterness inflames hate, and it is unforgivable to fuel hate. In the process a two-thousand-year-old motto has been forgotten: *fortiter in re, suaviter in modo* [resolute in execution, gentle in manner]. Germany's encirclement, which began at the turn of the century, continues and worsens. It is our hope that a people, even without defensive weapons, remain unconquerable as long as they stand united behind their government, and the world is convinced that their unity will remain firm in spite of tribulations.[727]

Though couched in an economic analysis of its benefits, the language of Rose's account of his enthusiasm for the Nazi Party displays a level of naive optimism, not unlike his optimism at the start of WWI. His romanticism, recurrent bouts of depression, and unrealistically high personal standards seemed to provoke cycles of optimism and pessimism.

Though Rose restricts himself to relatively modest criticisms of the Nazi regime, one must balance the impression left by the materials Rose committed to paper in a period when the Nazis were imposing their police state, and actions that Rose took during that period. As we will see, there is evidence that Rose, at considerable risk, took a personal stand against a number of the Nazi measures.

Chapter 20

Amending the Catastrophic Want of Good Leaders

There is a single photograph of Hans Rose wearing the Nazi *Marine SA* uniform (below). Having become a member of the naval Sturmabteilung, the three pips on his collars indicate that Rose was an *SA Sturmführer*, the lowest SA commissioned officer rank, and more or less the military equivalent of a second lieutenant. The swastika armband, worn on his left arm, designates him as a member of the Nazi Party. Daughter Helga recalled that her father was fully committed: 'Father organized demonstrations, gave lessons in seamanship and was busy from morning to night.'[728]

On 25 August 1934 Rose addressed the gathered *Marine SA* in the Essen-Borbeck market square in front of the newly constructed *Sturmheim*. The consecration of the building had been postponed from 1 July because of the 'Night of the Long Knives', Hitler's bloody purge of top SA officers and other anti-Nazi leaders, of 30 June 1934. Speaking of the purge, Rose began:

There were men in the SA who swore allegiance to the Führer. They broke that allegiance. Faithfulness, my dear comrades, is one of the cardinal virtues of the German male... The Führer personally proceeded against the traitors with unbelievable energy... Adolf Hitler is a human being like the rest of us; a human, however, with a holy mission, as I found out eleven years ago when I first talked to him. Since then, he has grown to the mythic proportions which he embodies today. He achieved this status through unwavering energy, through iron application, through unflagging volition. Every one of you, my comrades, who works on himself with similar devotion will achieve inner greatness and completion and find the peace of God which is higher than all our earthly understanding.

HANS ROSE WEARING THE NAZI *MARINE SA* UNIFORM After his birthday in 1935, Rose would never wear the *Marine SA* uniform again; wearing only the German navy uniform. [Rose Family Archives]

229

To achieve this state does not require you to become ministers or directors, but rather to fulfil your daily duties punctually, since it is character, rather than social position, which determines the quality of one's life.

Rose's speech did not mention – though perhaps he was unaware of – Hitler's assassination of political leaders who were not members of the Nazi Party and owed no allegiance to the Führer. Rose described how Hitler moved him at the culmination of Field Marshal Hindenburg's funeral at Tannenberg:

The Führer concluded his speech saying 'Field Marshal, enter the gates of Valhalla.' Soldiers, who had fearlessly fought and won many battles, felt a shiver go up their spines. With teary eyes and lips pressed together we stood motionless until the casket disappeared into the Field-Marshal's mausoleum, and the solemn Führer returned into the sun-drenched memorial field.

Rose concluded his short speech with a return to the consecration of the *Sturmheim*: 'May the eternal Gods permit us to work in it diligently and happily for the good of our *Volk. Sieg Heil!*'[729]

Rose's speech represents the public high-water mark of his enthusiasm for the *Marine SA*. Less than a year later he had taken off the uniform, never to wear it again.

Politics Becomes Taboo: 1934–1939

Over the last six years of the 1930s Germany would descend into a totalitarian police state, compelling Rose to adopt a guarded attitude with respect to politics. Christian Rose recalled that as the fascist regime became ever harsher it was understood by all of Rose's children that under no circumstances, *ever*, was there to be any discussion or criticism of German politics. Christian:

Politics was never discussed at the table. It was taboo. If [his] older brother Gerd would make some off-the-cuff, sometimes cynical remark, the knife, tack, tack, tack. It was a question of survival.[730]

...Everyone knew of them [the Gestapo and the SS] and were afraid of these people and what they might do to you... It was a time of fear of the '*horrible unknown*'.[731]

In December 1934, Rose's eldest son Heinz was put on a ship and then spent half a year with relatives in Niagara Falls, New York. He returned in the summer of 1935. Rose recalled:

The boy was delicate when he left home, but he returned from his trip across the ocean a young man with a broadened horizon. He was successful in the American school and developed a good command of the English language in all its particulars. Later on he also finished the States' examination as interpreter of French and also managed to gain a reasonable knowledge of the Italian language.[732]

Heinz was following in his father's linguistic footsteps. Upon his return both the SA and the SS attempted to recruit him, but Hans Rose refuses to permit it.[733]

For Hans Rose, the 1936 Olympics were a 'glorious time'.[734] And up until then, Rose was very active in the *Marine SA*.[735] But in 1935, on the occasion of his fiftieth birthday, the SA held a celebratory march for Rose. According to Christian it profoundly disturbed him. Rose's autobiography does not go into detail. After his birthday Rose stopped wearing the Nazi SA uniform[736] and henceforth would only wear the traditional German naval uniform. At the end of 1937 he would quit the *Marine SA*. A year later *Kristallnacht* represented another transformational moment in Rose's attitude about the Nazi Party.

Rose's wife Anne-Marie was like-minded. She remained a courageous woman during the period when most Germans embraced the hysteria of the xenophobic, anti-Semitic Nazi message. She continued to play Mendelsohn and Mahler on the piano at a time when the Nazis were condemning anything Jewish. 'It was' Christian recalls, 'indicative of how she silently exhibited her position about things.'[737] The morning of 10 November 1938, the day after *Kristallnacht*, the horrific night of Nazi-coordinated attacks upon Jews and their property, Christian Rose was seated in his schoolroom:

> I was called out by the principal and escorted to my waiting mother. She asked me to get into the car and without another word she drove past a radio store where the windows had been smashed, expensive broken Telefunken, Siemens radios, all mixed with broken glass lay on the sidewalk. Who would do such a stupid thing? Next we drove past the burning massive stone structure of the Synagogue; in an alcove an old man was hovering, crying, obviously in deep despair. From the synagogue we drove to the Old Market, an area of a multitude of expensive [Jewish] stores – a disaster zone – silk dresses, porcelain, mink coats, furniture, bolts of linen, shoes, crystal glass all smashed on the street. Not one store remained intact. Finally we drove past the *Kaiserhof* where my father had taken us for the occasional lunch or dinner when he combined his visit to the [Jewish] *Bankhaus Burkhardt* with a meal. The bank [where the family had always conducted their business][738] was located on the opposite side of the street. It seemed like a hurricane had hit the building. The car ride lasted an hour or more.[739]

The wordless lesson complete, Anne-Marie Rose, *Mutti*, brought her eight-year-old son home. There was no need to pull her other children out of school to deliver the same tutorial; unlike Christian, his brothers attended the public *Humboldt Schule* located right next to a synagogue, which Christian recalled was 'a burning mess'.[740] Christian asserts it was inconceivable that Anne-Marie would have taught him this lesson without the acquiescence of her husband.

Making the distinction between supporting Nazi ideology and being a member of the party, both son Christian and stepson Peter Brickenstein emphatically state that Hans Rose was not a Nazi.[741] Nonetheless, daughter Helga disputes her brother's assertion that *Kristallnacht* represented a key transformational moment for their father, asserting that her father did not definitively turn against the Nazis until the second assassination attempt on Hitler in July 1944. She comments: 'Yes he took off the *Marine SA* uniform and wore the old navy blue, but he remained a nationalist doing his duty almost to the end.'[742]

Christian agrees with that essential point:

> He remained a nationalist all his life. As far as he was concerned, I am born a German, I live in Germany and I die in and for Germany. There is no mistake about that. I think my father would have said: 'The Fatherland is what you have to defend, not a party or a Führer' – my father would have supported whoever supported that concept; This Land, our country is where we live, our country is what nourishes us, we have to protect our country.[743]

Hans Rose's speeches and diary entries during the war corroborate that time-line. Rose's public declarations supporting Germany's Nazi leaders and articulating the leadership role that the German race was destined to exercise in world affairs were unflagging up until his retirement from the navy in 1943.

Being a military man, Rose's support for the Nazi leadership cannot be divorced from the fact that not only was Hitler a political leader, but also Germany's military leader, to whom every soldier in the Wehrmacht swore a *personal* oath of fealty. Peter Brickenstein recalled a discussion in the early 1950s between Hans Rose and his old naval colleagues General Admiral Hermann Boehm, Goldschmidt, and Lindower. In that conversation the admirals remarked: 'It was unthinkable to go against the man [Hitler] we swore to help. It was unthinkable to kill him.'[744]

As it was for Rose: 'You can't kill your leader.'[745] For Hans Rose, a career naval officer, the chain of command remained inviolate. At the same time, Rose's stepson Hans-Joachim (Achim) Brickenstein commented that Rose always encouraged his stepchildren to stand up and do the right thing.

What is clear is that beginning in 1937, Rose, while continuing to rally to the Nazis' call 'to protect our country', carefully and surreptitiously began disassociating himself from them. Two years later, when duty called with the outbreak of WWII, Rose once again became a warrior. He would continue to follow that calling almost until the end of the war; while at the same time, through his conduct, he disassociated himself from the worst of the Nazis' human rights violations.

Through the Looking Glass of Post-War Denazification

Ten per cent of the German population, some 8.5 million persons, ended up becoming members of the Nazi Party. Many more, perhaps an additional 36.5 million persons, were members of organizations like the Hitler Youth, National Socialist People's Welfare, German Labour Front, the *Marine SA* and other organizations created by the Nazis.

In December 1946, because of his membership in the Nazi Party, the *Marine SA*, and probably his role as a senior naval officer during the occupation of Norway, Hans Rose was required to appear before a denazification panel.

In preparation for this hearing he amassed a set of eight sworn testimonials, seven German[746] and one Norwegian. These testimonials allow us a glimpse into the evolution of Rose's attitudes not found elsewhere among Rose's papers; papers that were kept necessarily circumspect during the period of the totalitarian police state.

Those offering testimonials to Hans Rose's good character ranged across the social spectrum. A retired miner, Hermann Habermann, was Rose's gardener before the war. He testified that '*Herr Rose* is very popular among the miners living in this district' and that Rose always endeavoured 'to promote public welfare'. Until the hearing, Habermann had not known that Rose had been a member of the Nazi Party.

Retired Police Inspector Johannes Siebke, previously an attorney, had become Rose's friend in the early 1930s. Siebke also testified that '*Herr* Rose is well known in Heisingen as a real gentleman' who had 'at all times been endeavouring to act in the common interest.' Siebke continued that Rose had 'made many friends by his outgoing and candid character'. It was only much later that Siebke learned that Rose had been a party member or had been in the *Marine SA*. Even then, 'I do not remember that we discussed *Parteipolitik* at any time.'[747]

Ludger Langensiepen, a deeply religious man and a friend of twelve years testified:

> I had many occasions to observe [Rose's] manners and conduct. If he had not worn the *Marine SA*-uniform occasionally, when preparing for his service, I would not know of his membership at all.
>
> He has been very kind and social at all times and has never shown any forms of arrogance. Whenever he could, he was helpful and did not hesitate to lend a hand whenever there was a case of emergency, regardless of the other man's sins. It is well-known to me that he made his children attend church service and that he valued communication with the Church and its ministers. He is generally known in Heisingen and greatly esteemed by the Heisingen-population.[747]

Rudolf Stöcker was a Freemason, a twenty-year business colleague, and a good friend of Rose. Stöcker spent a lot of time sailing with Rose. He testified that Rose was a 'liberal and tolerant man of noble character' who had 'never displayed any national-socialistic exaggerations, but at all times maintained a conservative position of old traditions'.[747]

These four testimonials all corroborate the fact that Rose, far from being a Nazi ideologue, was a well-respected member of the community, who rarely discussed politics, embraced traditional values, and worked actively for the common good. All were friends of Hans Rose, but probably not intimate friends. The three remaining German testimonials come from men who were more intimate confidants; Rose having confided in them during the increasingly dangerous period of the thirties.

In his testimonial, Dr. Hans Germscheid described himself as a colleague of twenty years at *Theodor Goldschmidt A.G.*, and as someone known in the office to be 'an outspoken opponent of National Socialism'. His testimonial suggests motivation for Rose's participation in the *Marine SA* and insight into Rose's attitude towards Nazi oppression of Germany's Jewish population:

> Up to the start of the war [Rose and I] interacted professionally on an almost daily basis... *Herr Rose* was never one-sided, he acknowledged counterarguments and he preferred adopting a middle-of-the road perspective. He joined the *Marine SA*, because he, as a successful former submarine commander, and as a member of the *Stahlhelm* organization could scarcely avoid the task of educating the simple man. He often pointed out that the educated people of the nation must not stand around and sulk, but had better co-operate in order to amend the catastrophic want of good leaders of the [Nazi] Party and SA. In his view, if things went wrong, the outsiders were more to blame than the collaborators. Rose believed it essential to exert every effort to get as much influence as possible to avoid foolishness. Later [Rose] repeatedly stressed the point that he had the impression there was a deliberate intention to suppress old Imperial officers [like himself], who were known for their fairness and sense of responsibility...
>
> In spite of that, he remained true to the course, so that one could not accuse him of wounded vanity.
>
> As to the actions against the Jews, he was deeply upset by the destruction of their synagogues and other cruelties. He was absolutely tolerant in matters concerning religious life and hated the word 'fanaticism'. In my opinion, *Herr* Rose took up the tasks in the *Marine SA* solely out of a sense of duty... As soon as he discovered that the *Marine SA* had other objectives, he quit. From the start of hostilities, he had nothing to do with the [Nazi] movement.[747]

Dr. Germscheid's testimonial rings true. His assertion that Rose felt obliged to take a local leadership role in the *Marine SA* 'in order to amend the catastrophic want of good leaders' is consistent with Rose's somewhat airy comment that if Hitler 'had had a single intelligent and highly principled friend, world history would have developed differently'. It is also consistent with Christian Rose's assertion that Rose's view of the *Marine SA* changed in 1936.

At a time when the Nazis captured the national narrative they put Germany's professional military officers in a difficult position. Rose's experience reflects the ambivalence many German military officers felt towards Nazism. That the Nazi's did not manage to penetrate the officer corps completely is attested to by their creation of parallel military organizations controlled by the SS.

Paul Mahler, an Essen merchant, who had known Hans Rose since 1933, provides the context for Rose's departure from the *Marine SA*. Mahler and Rose had been sporting partners on the *Baldeney-See*. Rose had been a founding member of the Essen Gymnastics and Fencing Club *ETUF* sailing squadron:

> I knew that *Herr* Rose was in charge of the *Marine SA* at the same time. My impression was that *Herr* Rose, as retired naval officer, took a mere sportsman's interest in that form of service because he was a passionate mariner and was very fond of any display of a seaman's activity and water-sports... At the end of 1937

Herr Rose resigned from his post as the leader of the *Marine SA* which he disliked, this being the only chance to retire from this service.

It never struck me that *Herr* Rose took a special interest in the NSDAP or sympathized with its aims... I kept a keen eye on things like this. In November 1938, when the NSDAP took its criminal [*Kristallnacht*] measures against the Jews, I observed that they were rejected and strongly criticized by *Herr* Rose. During one of our sailing excursions on the *Baldeney-See* we were talking about the struggle that the Church was having with the [Nazi] Party. I discovered that *Herr Rose* unmistakably defended the position of the Church which he stressed by telling me that he had given strict orders to his [*Marine SA*] naval troopers not to leave the Church or to entertain intentions directed to that purpose. This can only be interpreted as clear evidence that *Herr* Rose was a supporter of the Church, by which attitude he stood in an evident opposition to the Party.[747]

Professor Doctor Alois M. Memmesheimer was known to his colleagues in the German military as the 'Navy Professor'.[748] A German patriot who served with distinction in both World Wars, and who also actively participated in the resistance to the French/Belgian occupation of the Ruhr, Memmesheimer was a brilliant medical scholar and a tireless doctor. His wide-ranging areas of expertise included dermatology, internal medicine, gynaecology, therapeutic radiology, and the spread of venereal diseases. By 1933, Memmesheimer, only thirty-nine years old, had already published over a hundred articles and scientific papers.[749]

Rose and Memmesheimer were naval contemporaries, had known each other since 1920, and Memmesheimer had been Rose's doctor. They became good friends. In many respects Rose and Memmesheimer were cut from the same cloth. Professor Doctor Götz, eventually his successor as chief of the dermatological clinic of the Essen city hospital, recalled:

> [Memmesheimer's] continuing commitment to truthfulness, his sense of duty which he followed even if it was detrimental to his person, must have also involved great disappointments. He remained an upright and courageous friend. His sense of duty determined the people and things he would remain true to, because they corresponded to his own values.[750]

Memmesheimer was a Catholic who courageously criticized Nazi state doctrine on race. He valued Jewish colleagues among his patients and friends. Publicly demonstrating his disapproval he insisted that none of the medical staff at his Essen clinic greet patients with the Nazi address '*Heil* Hitler'.[751] Inevitably, as Nazi attacks on its critics increased, Dr. Memmesheimer was targeted. In 1933-34 during the ultra-nationalist, anti-Semitic *Kreisleiter Freytag* demonstrations, Dr. Memmesheimer was imprisoned. His stature as a patriotic war hero obliged the Nazis to tread lightly. Under pressure from American medical colleagues and outspoken German supporters like Hans Rose, Memmesheimer was released after six weeks.[752] He was demoted in his hospital practice, refused permission to lecture or attend foreign conferences, and forbidden to publish or republish any of his scientific papers.

Twelve years later Dr. Memmesheimer returned the favour. His testimonial, coming from a man of impeccable international credentials, provides the clearest evidence of Rose's willingness to oppose the excesses of the Nazi Party when he could. It states:

Certificate 13.12. 1946

I've known Captain Hans Rose since 1920. I had frequent opportunities to talk to him about political matters. Mr. Rose became a member of the Nazi Party for idealist reasons. However he strongly opposed the excesses of those in power. When I was imprisoned in 1933/34, he energetically defended me, in spite of the fact that this created great difficulties for him. [Rose] courageously rejected all encroachments of *Kreisleiter Freytag*. In 1938 he openly called the Jewish pogroms a disgrace for Germany. At the end of 1944 he was put in charge of the Heisingen *Volksturm* unit. After a short time he resigned this post, because he considered the deployment of the *Volksturm* wrong and criminal.[747]

These testimonials describe Hans Rose much as our other sources do. They reinforce the perspective that Hans Rose joined the Nazi Party for naive, idealistic reasons that ultimately were completely at odds with the party's practice.

Rose agreed to lead the *Marine SA* to provide it responsible leadership. When he discovered that would not be possible and that it was being used to attack such revered German institutions as the Catholic and Protestant churches, he quit. Both Hans and Anne-Marie Rose came to abhor the Nazi attacks on Jews. Each, according to their positions, did what they could to oppose the abominations of the Nazi regime. As demonstrated by his defence of Dr. Memmesheimer, Hans Rose did so even when it brought dangerous attention to himself. When WWII broke out Rose continued making this distinction between fighting for his country and supporting the Nazi regime's atrocities.

'Daily Bread', Illness and Deaths in the Family

The tumultuous political events of the 1930s, coupled with the national slide into fascism, overshadow the 'daily bread' of Rose family events. Christian remembered the garden as a different kind of classroom in the decade that brought the long climb out of economic catastrophe:

Next to our [Essen Steubenstraße] apartment building was an empty lot which my parents leased for our garden. Thus we had the opportunity to have chickens, ducks, geese, rabbits and pigeons as well as vegetables and some flowers. 'Chickens' was Heinz, my oldest brother's business – he supplied most of the eggs and the meat for Sunday dinners. Similarly my sister Helga attended to the ducks and the Christmas goose while my second oldest brother Gerd provided occasionally pigeons or a rabbit for the family table. For all these productive activities my mother paid market prices. The money earned by my siblings was used to pay for feed, housing and other expenses required raising the animals. Any money left over was their personal profit. Thus we learned early the concept of free enterprise as well as the fact that animals have emotions, fears, likes and dislikes as we do. Maxi the rabbit was certainly a good example of these emotions as he liked to snuggle up in the comfort of my brother's bed. But my mother taught us early that attachments have their limits when it comes to food.[753]

In 1936 the family moved again, this time to a home Rose had built just outside of Essen on an acre of land he had bought from a farmer who was subdividing his land. It would become Springloh 32 in Essen-Heisingen. Rose notes:

On 2 May 1936 we moved into our house. It was a memorable day in our lives. Anne was so happy that in future years she often mentioned 'I will never leave this house while I am alive.' And that is what happened.[754]

Christian recalled:

In a gully across the centre of the lot we discovered a seam of brown coal surfacing below a rock ledge. This seam was a blessing just after the war as it helped us cook our meals and keep one room warm during the winters of the British occupation in 1945-46.[755]

Located on the outskirts of the expanding metropolis, the children had longer commutes to school. Chris had a two-kilometre walk, but his older siblings would have to ride their bikes nine kilometres each way. Exercise was important to his parents and Chris recalled: 'Only on really miserable days and during the winter were [we] allowed to use the public transportation system.'[756]

Mealtime in Hans Rose's first family was a formal affair, taken in the dining room. It was Rose's view that children at the table should be 'silent as fish'.[757] To demand his children's attention at mealtime Rose would tap his glass with his knife.

Years later, during his visit to Canada, daughter-in-law Margaret remembered handing Rose his little six-month-old grandson Nick to hold. 'It was apparent that he had never held a baby in his lap.'[758] Rose's discomfort is emblematic of strains in his relationships with the two of his birth children the authors interviewed. Christian was headstrong and contested his father's authority. Rose's approach can be summed up as 'Spare the rod and spoil the child.' Christian recalled his father as having 'a very short fuse, very forceful, irritable at the slightest cause [such as] my inability to understand simple math equations or a Latin conjugation, [which] caused major outbursts when his body would shake with physical irritations.'[217]

Christian was sent off to boarding schools for almost his entire education and felt abandoned by his father. He felt his father believed that having a young child underfoot was incompatible with his role as a national hero. Christian felt his father had been 'thrown into a life situation that required him to play a public role that suited him very well as an actor and good speaker. He survived very well while doing it.'[218]

Yet, commenting in 2003 on his relationship with his father, Christian remarked to the authors that 'apples don't fall far from the tree.'[759] Nine years later, Christian, then 82, concluded some remarks about his father with 'I did my homage to the throne.' According to stepbrother Peter, Christian 'was his mother's son'.[760]

Rose brought his conduct in the especially tight naval 'family' on board ship home into his personal life with poor effect; at least for Chris, who essentially mutinied. It was not the first time that a military upbringing spoiled the man for his private family. And Rose had not yet realized that what worked in his navy family didn't work with his children. Anne-Marie acted as a counterbalance, and appeared to be the only person Rose seemed not to apply his naval model to, because she fulfilled Rose's revered position of mother.

As the 1930s advanced Hans Rose was able to renew his enthusiasm for sailing; racing his sailboat *Loreley*, named in memory of his posting aboard its namesake in Constantinople.[761] Rose was the president of the *ETUF*'s sailing squadron from its founding on 7 November 1932 until he asked to be replaced for health reasons in 1945.[762]

In the 1930s, as Hans Rose's attitude towards the Nazi regime became increasingly guarded, it is not surprising that the final ten pages of the *von Tampen* autobiography, which ends with the outbreak of WWII, chronicles nothing but family events, both sad and happy. Among them are the death of Rose's mother and Anne's parents. Rose's mother died on 19 November 1933. He recalled: 'She spent the last weeks of her life in (a home for the aged) in Lüttringhausen. Her spirit no longer rested on earth... It was shocking to experience the passing of this spirit, previously so lively and agile.'[763]

In the autumn of 1935 Rose described the orderly death of Anne-Marie's father, who 'put his accounts in order and sat down at his desk. In the evening he left his desk with the words: "Now everything is in order." The next morning he died of a heart attack.'[764]

Towards the end of 1934 and in early 1935 illness stalked the family. Anne-Marie contracted measles from her son Gerd, and the two spent weeks in hospital isolation wards. Christian recalled: 'Immediately, my father went into defensive mode, stress reduction for my mother was the order of the day! I was sent by my father for a year to Haus Bodo, a children's home in Sorge in the Hartz Mountains.'[765]

Hans Rose's fiftieth birthday on 15 April 1935 was celebrated in Hattingen. Fifty family friends and guests partied into the night. A year later, on 2 May 1936, came the move into the new house with its beautiful garden. Anne, whose health was slowly deteriorating, found it more practical than anything she had ever lived in and loved it for its garden. The Roses celebrated their silver wedding anniversary there on 20 September 1938; an event presaged by an example both of Rose's self-critical nature and rare emotional agitation. Eight-year-old Christian had arrived by train from his boarding school an hour early, having accidentally taken the express. No one was there to greet him at the station but he remembered how to get to the family's old house, from there to the cemetery and from there to the family's new home in the suburbs, some nine kilometres. Hans Rose was both apprehensive and furious when he arrived at the station and there was no sign of his son. But it was a fury directed at himself; he had nothing but admiration for his son.[766]

Anne-Marie's delicate health and long physical decline had to be a constant concern for Rose. Sadly, Christian appears to have experienced Rose's concern for his wife as a rejection of the son.

In October 1938 Rose began to write up his WWI experiences. He mentions that a publisher agreed to take on the project after reading the first chapter of what would become Rose memoir, *Auftauchen!*:

> Now I began to write from morning to night inhaling chamomile fumes to combat a bad cold. These were wonderful weeks of creative work. But in the end the project has to be postponed because of Anne's cancer operation.[767]

An advance from the publishing house of the Nazi Party financed a trip to Italy in the spring of 1939 to celebrate her recovery. On the way down they travel to Amalfi via Naples and Pompei, returning by way of Rome. In the beginning of June, shortly before the outbreak of WWII, there was a trip to Kiel for the commissioning of the new *U 53*. Though retired and surrounded by his old crewmates, the emotional restraint that had always characterized Rose's command style remained firm. He commented 'One had to be careful not to become sentimental.'[768]

On 30 June 1939 Rose resigned from *Theodor Goldschmidt A.G.*:

> I became an independent Ruhr representative for the Lead Division [its departments of Lead and Structural Steel] that I had founded. I had wanted to leave for years (because of the incompetent authorized officer with whom I had to work) but could not afford the risk. But now, because the firm facilitated my departure by offering some compensation, and I had teamed up with several other representatives to minimize the risk, I could risk the change.[769]

A month later, when the war broke out, he was remobilized: 'And thus one of the most important parts of my life, the fight for our "daily bread", came to an end.'[770]

Chapter 21

WWII – Once More unto the Breach

'I swear by God this sacred oath, that to the Leader of the German empire and people, Adolf Hitler, supreme commander of the armed forces, I shall render unconditional obedience, and that, as a brave soldier, I shall at all times be prepared to give my life for this oath.'

Every member of the German army, air force and navy swore this oath, the *Führereid*, the 'Hitler Oath', not to the German constitution, but personal loyalty to Adolf Hitler himself. Describing the taking of this oath as 'the greatest moment in the life of the German male', Hans Rose would later admonish new recruits in occupied Norway: 'May you never forget the honour, nor the pride, nor the deep seriousness and the commitment, as well as the joy of this holy hour.'[771]

Hans Rose considered this an unalterable personal commitment. Whatever misgivings he might have or develop about Hitler, or where the Nazi leadership was taking Germany, he would, once again, do his best to do his duty, and be a good soldier.

For Hans Rose, the start of WWII was not of German making. His October 1943 diary described the road to war:

The Führer offered the Poles a decade-long alliance in return for a corridor which would connect East Prussia with the 'Reich'. His proposals were met with scorn,

CORPORAL HEINZ ROSE AT THE FRONT France 1940. Rose (right) would be killed in Crimea in 1944. [Rose Family Archives]

240

mockery and accusations of cowardice. Over and over again the Führer had also sought contacts with the British and the French, yet his efforts were to no avail.

I am convinced that Hitler was serious in his attempts to avoid a war. There was a 1938 meeting in Munich [with Chamberlain] at which the storm was once more averted. However, the world's antipathy against National Socialism fanned by Jewish influences had become so strong that a peaceful détente proved impossible.

The incorporation of Danzig into the German 'Reich' started the avalanche, and Great Britain and France declared war when we marched into Poland. Poland was conquered in eighteen days. We negotiated a demarcation line with the Russians, which followed the San [river] and then turned north. The Russians supplied us with huge quantities of raw materials, mostly grain, while our troops protected the 'West Wall' to foil any Allied invasion of Germany. The French in contrast were dug in, behind their supposedly invincible Maginot Line. The fronts became static.

On 9 April 1940 the German navy transported about 42,000 men to Norway and shortly afterwards the whole country was in our hands. The British, French, and other enemy troops were routed... One month later, on 9 May 1940, our troops suddenly broke through the 'West Wall' and overran all of northern France in a triumphant and unbroken victory push. The British that had landed fled over the Channel from Dunkirk, leaving behind almost all of their equipment. *That we gave the British force time to avoid capture or annihilation was perhaps the worst mistake made by our High Command. They continued to believe that they could come to an understanding with the enemy and consequently recoiled from inflicting a fatal blow. Such thinking is counterproductive in war* [authors' italics]. The French government moved to Vichy.[772]

This portrayal of the events leading to the outbreak of the war is starkly at odds with the reality of how Hitler, the fascist aggressor, manipulated German popular opinion and the national and international political landscape to achieve his goals. In the March 1960 draft of his autobiography Rose would write of this diary entry:

I have transcribed it here in the spirit of the original... [But] because it was life-threatening at the time to even harbour such critical thought, only the short sentences criticizing the high command were added later.[773]

Its inclusion is an example of Rose's life-long practice of speaking the truth even when it was personally unflattering. Both his stepsons, Hans-Joachim and Rudolf, remembered that he was utterly honest. Rose's comments about Hitler demonstrate that his disillusionment with the Nazis only reached fruition in 1944 when Rose would hold Hitler responsible for destroying Germany.[774] At the same time, nowhere in his autobiographical writing do we find any indication that he ever renounced this 1943 perspective. Rose's narrow nationalism coupled with some combination of his embrace of hierarchy, his idealism, naiveté and his general romanticism, clouded his capacity to see Nazi politics for what they were. While Rose's activities as a soldier during WWII are without reproach, up until his final retirement from a soldier's life in June 1943, he placed his own narrow-nationalist pan-Germanic theories in the service of the of Nazi regime's politics of conquest and racial superiority.

Return to Active Service

With German preparations for the invasion of Poland actively underway, Hans Rose went back to war. In August and September 1939, as *Fregattenkapitän zur See*[775] he was posted to the *Wehrwirtschaftsinspektion* (Army Economic Inspection) *VI*, subordinate to the *Oberkommando der Wehrmacht* (OKW), the Supreme Command of the armed forces.[776] Rose reported to a section responsible for armament and military economy. In October, for less than a month, he reported to the *Wehrwirtschaftsinspektion Ober-Ost,* Section for Military Economy to the Supreme Military Command East responsible for Krakow in Poland.[777]

Christian Rose remembered that the September 1939 invasion of Poland 'broke the family tranquility forever':[778]

> The first few months of the war brought the introduction of ration cards... The threat of heavy fines and public condemnation descended on us if we did not adhere to a full blackout after sun down. Times were changing. The old hobbies, family, play in the garden, school, everything became coloured by Radio *Deutschland*'s daily news as other radio stations were prohibited [as] sources of information.[779]

His father and oldest brother had departed; Heinz having been drafted into the army as an interpreter of English and French. Brother Gerd was still at home. Christian recalled that Gerd would listen to prohibited radio stations, using a set of earphones and a small radio receiver he built from fine wire and a pyrite.[780]

In November Rose reported to the *Befehlshaber der U-Boote*, Commander of Submarines. He was detached to the infantry, probably for liaison purposes, and posted to newly conquered Krakow. Helga Rose described her father's role in Krakow as 'army occupation commander'.[781] He was garrisoned in the city for three months, through January 1940. While Rose was horrified by the physical condition of the city, particularly the fleas and cockroaches, it was an increasing disquiet about the role that the Gestapo and SS were playing that concerned him most.[782]

The invasion and conquest of Poland divided the country between Hitler and Stalin. The Nazis absorbed about half of that area directly into Germany as the new *Reichsgau* of Danzig-West Prussia. The conquered remainder became the rump Polish state called the 'General Government' territory, with Krakow as its capital. On 26 October 1939, only days before Rose's arrival in Krakow, Hans Frank was appointed its governor general.

Objectives in the earliest months of the occupation were the elimination of the threat of insurgency, preparations for the launch of the Nazi solution to the 'Jewish problem', and the mobilization of Polish resources in the service of the German war effort. Two years later Frank explained how he merged the two latter objectives:

> A problem that occupies us in particular is the Jews. This *Völklein*, which wallows in dirt and filth, has been gathered together by us in ghettos and [special] quarters and will probably not remain in the General Government for very long.
>
> We will get these Jews marching and cause them – as they have already covered the distance from Jerusalem to Poland – to move eastward a few thousand

kilometres. But these Jews are not that parasite gang alone, from our point of view, but strangely enough – we only realized it over there [in Poland] – there is another category of Jews, something one would never have thought possible.

There are labouring Jews ... who work in transport, in building, in factories, and others are skilled workers such as tailors, shoemakers, etc. We have put together Jewish workshops with the help of these skilled Jewish workers, in which goods will be made. These will greatly ease the position of German production; in exchange for the supply of foodstuffs and whatever else the Jews urgently need for their existence.

That these Jews may well be left to work in this way, in the way in which we are now using them, is something of an achievement for the work-Jews themselves; but for the other Jews we must provide suitable arrangements... Since the Jews moved away from Jerusalem there has been nothing for them, except an existence as parasites: that has now come to an end.[783]

Addressing his senior officials in the General Government, Hans Frank spelled out exactly what those 'suitable arrangements' were:

But what should we do with the Jews? Do you think they will be settled in Ostland, in villages? We were told in Berlin, 'Why all this bother? We can do nothing with them either in Ostland or in the *Reichskommissariat*. So liquidate them yourselves.' Gentlemen, I must ask you to rid yourself of all feelings of pity. We must annihilate the Jews wherever we find them and whenever it is possible.[784]

While annihilation of the Jewish population of Poland only started in 1941, the preparations for the ultimate solution (registration, relocation, dehumanization) began immediately. Krakow's Jewish population was constrained to perform forced labour by the end of September 1939. As of November all the city's Jews over the age of twelve were forced to wear a ten-centimetre-wide white arm band with an eight-centimetre blue Star of David on it. Holocaust survivor Dr. Moshe Bejski working in Krakow at the time recalled:

When the initial upheaval passed and the fighting ceased, the first edicts against Jews began. One decree followed another, and each day brought new restrictions against Jews. Some were national decrees that involved all the Jews in the country, and some were local decrees that applied only to local Jews... Our money, gold, and jewelry were stolen. It was forbidden for Jews to leave their homes when it was dark, it was forbidden to go beyond the outskirts of the town, and it was mandatory to wear an armband identifying one as a Jew. It was forbidden for Jews to travel on trains or deal in business, their properties were confiscated, etc., etc. Already, during the first months of the war, dozens of different and varied decrees were enacted and passed that limited the living conditions of Jews.[785]

Wide-scale Nazi persecution and abuse was not limited to Poland's Jewish population. The larger Polish population required merciless, iron-handed control as well. Contemporaneous with Hans Rose's posting in the city, immediately following the invasion, *SS-Obersturmbannführer* Bruno Müller became head of the Gestapo in Krakow.

On 6 November, at about the time of Rose's arrival in Krakow, Müller was personally responsible for the execution of *Sonderaktion Krakau*; the arrest of the President of Krakow, Stanislaw Klimecki, a rector and 184 professors, doctors, and lecturers from five universities. The international outcry against the arrests included protests from academics, the Vatican, and even Hitler's ally Benito Mussolini. It was widely reported, and led to their release several months later. But not before a dozen had died.

It was one of the earliest operations in the larger *Intelligenzaktion*, a nation-wide plan orchestrated by Hans Frank, to wipe out the Polish intelligentsia and so pre-empt organized resistance. It would result in the murder of some 60,000 'Polish nobles, teachers, entrepreneurs, social workers, priests, judges and political activists'.[786] From the autumn of 1939 through early 1940, the entire period Rose was in Krakow, the Gestapo systematically registered members of almost all of these groups by temporarily arresting and then releasing them.

Rose's deployment to Krakow was concurrent with condemnation of SS activities in the world press, so it is hard to imagine that he would not have been witness to this process from his earliest days there. After his own previous experience with the *Marine SA*, and now exposed to the terrible activities of the SS and the Gestapo during his posting to Krakow, Rose would keep them at arm's-length in Norway.[787]

Peacocks in Plön

In February 1940 Rose departed Krakow. But he did not return home to Essen. He had been personally selected by Grand Admiral of the Fleet, Karl Dönitz, to be the first *Kommandeur der Unterseebootsausbildungsabteilung* (UAA), Commanding Officer of the Submarine Training Division, the UAA, based at Plön in Schleswig-Holstein. For four months, through to May 1940, Rose oversaw the development and commissioning of this *Endstation*, the final stage of a submarine crew's training prior to being posted to its U-boat.[788] It would be his last direct responsibility within the U-boat arm of the German Navy. Harking back to the halcyon days of duty at the court of the Turkish Sultan, Rose had peacocks brought to the grounds of the submarine school.[789] It was a bizarre touch, but the war was going well. Invited to visit his father at the UAA, son Christian recalled a visit without much in the way of paternal warmth: 'I saw him only on the day I arrived and a week later when he put me on the train to travel back home.'[790]

Returning home to the smokestacks of Essen, Christian was diagnosed with incipient tuberculosis. His mother sent him to a sanatorium in Seefeld in the Black Forest, followed by a stay at his aunt's estate in Beselin near Rostock. But even in the country, early in the war, its signs were obvious to the eleven-year-old:

I remember it was the time for harvesting white asparagus. Each day early in the morning and again in the evening we went out to long rows of metre-high earth berms to cut the fresh shoots just breaking through the sandy crust. It took some experience cutting the stocks deep down in the earth, the longer the white stem the higher the price on the market. The short pieces landed on our dining table in a variety of menus. After three weeks of two daily servings of asparagus even turnips became acceptable. The visit to Beselin was my real introduction to farm life as well as the consequences of the war. About thirty prisoners lived under the watchful eye of an old German soldier in one of the larger sheds. I was forbidden to go near them and we were not allowed to speak to them. They worked in the field. Only one prisoner worked without a guard to milk the thirty sheep in the barn twice a day. Without exchanging words – with eye contact we became friends – I wondered, was he married? Did he have a family? Was he from Russia, Poland, or Ukraine? Where was his home? It must have been awful to have to do jobs he did not want to do for people he hated. Were they always under the threat of a gun? What kind of food did they get? These were questions I could not ask at the table.[791]

There were other signs of the war:

I noticed marked changes after half a year away from home. The depletion of oil supplies forces the government to increase its efforts to reduce benzene consumption on all transit buses. Big gas balloons appeared on top of transport vehicles... Recycling of all metals, glass, wood and other materials became a responsibility for all citizens – nothing was wasted. The food lines were longer. Textiles became more difficult to buy and those we could buy had French or other labels inside. Fish, especially sardines, appeared for rationed distribution from Norway. Was it the might of the conqueror that made these things available?[792]

At the outbreak of World War II, having learned the lesson of World War One, the Allies immediately organized their merchant fleets into protected convoys. Germany, having learned her lessons, organized her U-boats into Wolf Packs and launched them against those convoys with superb initial results. It was what her U-boat commanders called 'The Happy time'.

Hans Rose had been Germany's most successful WWI ace following the Allied institution of the convoy system. As WWI drew to a close the BdU, Commodore Hermann Bauer, had asked Rose to articulate convoy tactics and hand-picked him to become the first German Submarine Staff Commander in the Atlantic, leading the first Wolf Pack. Then Rose was personally selected by Grand Admiral of the Fleet, Karl Dönitz, to be the first Commanding Officer of the Submarine Training Division, the UAA, based at Plön. It all seems to make perfect sense. Rose has a demonstrated successful record using the form of submarine warfare that will define WWII. To focus their new campaign against convoys, the German navy, as it did with the other top WWI U-boat aces, will take advantage of Rose's anti-convoy expertise.

Only it doesn't.

To Norway

Four months later Rose's short tenure as Commanding Officer of the Submarine Training Division is over and he spends the last three years of his military career in Trondheim, Norway. Trondheim will become the ninth most important

U-boat base the Germans possessed in WWII, and their largest U-boat base outside of Germany. And yet Hans Rose does not devote a single word of his copious memoirs related to Trondheim to U-boat activities of any sort. He is apparently not assigned any formal role at the U-boat base. Rather, he would become Sea Commander at Trondheim, responsible for protecting it and the related Norwegian coast line from Allied attack. Rose was certainly up to the task. But by assigning this strategically secondary role to him, the German Admiralty chose to forgo the leadership that its most successful WWI U-boat convoy ace had to offer. Similarly, three of the other top five WWI U-boat aces held naval commands in WWII, though only one of them, Max Valentiner, had a role directly related to U-boats. Nonetheless, this is the single greatest enigma of the last portion of Hans Rose's military career.

In 1942, with the war still going fairly well for Germany, Hans Rose hoped that his 175-page manuscript *The Sea Commander: Nordic Sketches*, would demonstrate the hope and heroism that the invasion and occupation of Norway represented for his Germanic *Volk*. It was never published.

According to the table of contents the book was to have twenty-one chapters. The first eleven, slightly more than half the manuscript, are devoted to the invasion and the period before Rose became Sea Commander of occupied Norway on 1 July 1940.

During the initial weeks of the invasion in April, Rose was still the commanding officer at the U-boat training school at Plön. Then, in May and June 1940, Rose became Chief of Staff to the Office of the Commanding Officer for the Coastal Defence of Trondheim. Its commanding officer, August Thiele, whose responsibilities included being Sea Commander, was Rose's direct superior. Rose's posting was staff officer overseeing the forces assigned to his *Dienststelle*, or shore office. Rose relieved Thiele there in May 1940, after the latter was promoted to Rear Admiral of the Northern Coast of Norway.

The German invasion of Norway under von Falkenhorst is Hitler's first land victory against the Western Allies. The main components of this initial invasion group numbered no more than 8,850 men. It succeeded in large measure because it maintained the element of surprise and because it used naval warships as troop transports, which allowed it simultaneously to land the invading forces at all of the invasion points. According to Chris Mann, it was

> ...a brilliantly executed campaign, in which the Germans showed a remarkable grasp of operations in 'three dimensions', land, sea and air, constituting the first proper 'combined arms' operation used in any theatre of war anywhere.[793]

Just how audaciously the German invasion proceeded is recorded in Hans Rose's Chapter 2, *Destination Trondheim*, which describes the battleship *Hipper* racing through the searchlight screen at the mouth of the Trondheim Fjord followed by four destroyers. Three of these remained behind to disgorge a company of navy artillery, a navy shock detachment and two companies of infantry to conquer the battery at Hysnes. Rose provides a description of these events in which racial affinity plays an important role in the resolution of the conflict.

On the same day that the cruiser *Blücher* was sunk, other naval forces were entering Tröndelang in Norway, a country with the oldest Germanic culture in the world... The Commander looked out at the batteries and the farms near Trondheim, immortalized by Ibsen... But at that moment these are useless thoughts, since it is important to look to the present, or even better to the future, and the reconstruction of the great Northern Reich... Fire lights up the ghostly sky, but the *Hipper* stares it down and ploughs ahead into the fjord, ghostlike in its fearlessness... Three of the destroyers pull to starboard and lower their boats to disgorge the landing parties, with the blue-eyed Lieutenant Vogler in the lead. He jumps on to the pier and breathes in deeply, feeling the rush of conquest.[794]

As the Norwegians discover them, the Germans disembark their Mountain troops further inland and target their grenade throwers at the site, sparing the batteries and troop billets, which they intend to utilize themselves. Shortly afterwards the Norwegian commander capitulates on the erroneous assumption that his 150 men are confronted by 2,000 invaders, instead of the 200 actually present. An hour's march brings the Germans to Brettingen, where another 120 Norwegians surrender without a fight.

Meanwhile, the *Hipper* and its single remaining destroyer land six officers and 416 navy and Alpine troops in the shadow of Trondheim. A Norwegian car is confiscated and used to transport German gear toward town. A messenger arrives from the reconnaissance detachment saying that the Norwegians are training their two sets of batteries on them. In the afternoon the Germans counter-attack and after two hours the Norwegians surrender.[795]

In the *Hipper*'s wake, the fourth destroyer *Eckolt* continues north and heads for the Trondheim harbour. The troops disembark and head for the bridges, signal station and railroad. The small number of troops has such a large area to police that they are unable to prevent the disappearance of young Norwegian students at the Technical Schools, who elsewhere join in the fight for their country's independence.[796] The *Hipper* continues past the inner island and disappears into the inner fjord where it secures the airfield at Vernaes an hour later. Six officers and 208 navy men, as well as about the same number of Alpine troops, have accomplished the impossible: they have conquered Trondheim. Rose concludes: 'This proves that it is not the numbers, but careful planning and execution that leads to success.'[797]

Now the conquered lands have to be protected. Since the fjord's east side is not yet in German hands, they begin to negotiate using the argument that they are not the enemy. In Rose's interpretation:

We come as tribal friends, of the same blood as yours, which we do not wish to shed. Please save us from the violence we ourselves reject and give us your hand in brotherhood. We know that the British want to carry their war into your peaceful country. Let us together resist this disaster.[798]

Below the windows the sound of marching and German songs are heard. They transform the Norwegian reticence into liberating action. The doors to the fortress are opened: 'Daring, speed and skill worked like an "open sesame". They not only open the doors of Hysnes, but stand as glowing symbols for the road to a New Europe.'[799]

Rose describes how the major

> ...wonders why these keen seafarers had given up without a fight. A tall blond Germanic looking Norwegian officer at the Hysnes battery, whose Aryan purity was evident to all, provided the answer. He was a member of the Quisling organization that believed that Norway's future lay in a coalition with another Germanic nation, and he was therefore merely participating in the defensive action out of a sense of duty. It was the conflict between duty and idealism that resulted in the half-heartedness of the Norwegian defensive measures and his people's actions. The major responded that the Germans were not the enemy, but of the same Nordic stock and thus 'blood-brothers' and mentioned that he did not wish to use force, but rather to reach out his hand in friendship.[800]

This idealized, racial and pan-Germanic interpretation of events is corrected by Derry. First, the fifty-year-old Norwegian *Norge* and *Eidsvold* that guarded Trondheim did not immediately open fire because of bad visibility and their expectation of British aid. Instead they asked for identification papers from the *Hipper* and when these are returned the German destroyer that had already reached the quay opened fire sinking the *Eidsvold*. This unprovoked aggression costs nearly 300 Norwegian lives. Moreover, the garrison of 450 defenders Rose indicates gave up without a fight, who were located on higher ground, in fact gave up after a two-hour battle because they were commanded by a follower of the Quisling movement who betrayed his countrymen.

In fact, Quisling's *Nasjonal Samling*, the National Gathering party, never garnered more than 2.5% of the popular vote in Norway. Tor Dagre reports:

> About 6,000 Norwegians served the German war cause, and 709 of them had fallen in battle. After the war, legal proceedings were initiated against those who had betrayed their country. About 46,000 persons [approximately 1.5% of the population] were punished for treason. Among these, 18,000 were sentenced to prison terms, 28,000 were fined and deprived of their rights as citizens. A total of 45 Norwegians and Germans received death sentences, 37 of the executions were carried out.[801]

The legitimate government-in-exile opposed the Nazis and the small percentage of the Norwegian population that collaborated with the German occupation. It refused to sign a peace treaty with Germany and by the end of the war developed an armed underground resistance movement of 44,000 partisans. They were supported by a widespread passive resistance movement that encompassed the Lutheran church, schools, and the country's roughly fifty professional organizations. Forty-three of the latter, numbering more than 750,000 members, organized their members to send letters of protest to *Reichskommissar* Josef Terboven's occupation regime.

Terboven, the Nazi commissioner of Norway, eliminated freedom of the press, abolished all political parties except the *Nasjonal Samling*, and decreed that only his regime could hire and fire court officials. When judges protested, he told them that they should not 'presume to question'[802] his decrees. In response they resigned *en masse*. Similarly, decrees that priests disclose confessions by their parishioners and desist from criticizing the occupation regime or face imprisonment resulted in protests. It also led to the resignation of seven of the country's Lutheran bishops and the imprisonment of another. In the face of Terboven's decree abolishing the nation's sports organizations, and their replacement by a single national organization, Norwegians simply resigned. A 1942 cup final, organized by the puppet regime, drew an audience of twenty-seven.

Chapter 4, 'Men of Action', recounts the attempts of the Trondheim Division commander and his staff, including Rose, to reach their post from a North German harbour. It describes the disastrous week-long weather. After deciding to reduce the staff that would travel with him, the general convinced two planes to depart, one of them piloted by Oberleutnant Viebahn. Rose:

> Finally, he won, two planes started into the infernal clouds. The flight was bumpy, had zero visibility, with snow squalls buffeting the craft. When visibility cleared a bit, they were notified that the second plane was turning back... They however, persisted. Suddenly the sky cleared, the General saw fjords and small islands below and blue patches appeared on the horizon. Lieutenant Viebahn pointed to the defences of Dröbak and Oscarsborg topped by the Hakenkreuz flag... A warm hand-shake thanked the pilot for his courageous navigation. United by their experience, the group worked their way through the airport's knee-deep snow to the road, where an old truck picked them up. Mission accomplished.[803]

In August Thiele was finally ready to activate the most important sea command of central Norway.

Two Men, One Post

Rose's sixth chapter sketch, 'Looking out to Sea', recounts the steps taken to secure the fjords leading to Trondheim and pre-empt the anticipated British counter attack. It includes an inspiring speech made by the Sea Commander to the German soldiers that have secured Brettingen about twenty kilometres northwest of Trondheim:

> The Sea Commander rubbed his hands, showing a row of strong pearly teeth, as his radiant smile fell on his circle of officers: 'That worked, but our realm is the sea, our job is to secure the fjord.'
>
> To do that he had to inspect the coastal batteries and the old-fashioned barracks, taken over from the Norwegians, where they were housed. Addressing the German personnel at Brettingen, the Sea Commander said:
>
> 'When you arrived here unexpectedly fourteen days ago [25 April 1940] your advance must have seemed like a bold undertaking. It was certainly that, and I congratulate you and our *Volk* on this success. However, it was more than this, as many realize today. It was a deed of world-changing significance. The front-lines had ground to a halt. It seemed as though the British would be able to use the war between the Finns and the Russians to invade Scandinavia and thus attack us in the

Baltic Sea. Through our inspired leadership, this plan was thwarted... Now we are in control of everything from here at the Brettig to the Ems River. You, my young comrades, comprise the forward position. The fatherland looks to you to defend it under all circumstances... You are the cornerstone for the creation of the Nordic empire of the future... That the British with their mighty fighting forces have not yet arrived to force open the narrows is surprising... On your dependability and combat readiness depend the relief not only of Narvik, but also the expansion of our supremacy over Norway, up to the Northern Cape and the Russian border. I depend on you, my young comrades of the Brettingen, when I send German ships further north. Be aware of the greatness of your assignment.'

The address was effective, because all of the participants recognized the solemn intentions and the unbending and fearless will behind the words.[804]

It is early May 1940 and the Sea Commander making the speech is August Thiele, though Rose's sketch does not say so explicitly. It is possible that Rose was present for the speech since he was Thiele's Chief of Staff in May and June before taking over as Sea Commander at the beginning of July. Then in a manner that sounds remarkably akin to his own, Rose expands upon the Sea Commander's private reflections:

The Sea Commander's heart expanded thinking about the Vikings. These dreams of the past were interwoven with the present. Now he himself stood here as a fearless conqueror. He was the first naval commander-in-chief who had conquered the Oslo fjord as well as the capital city. From now on it would be his mission to protect the second capital, the carrier of the Nordic traditions of seamanship. Gazing left to the island of Leksen ... he thanked the almighty for his quarter hour of solitary concentration and clear recognition of the peculiar beauty of this northern region. He vowed that no enemy force would touch this land – and that his forces would have to safeguard it more effectively.[805]

By 8 June 1940 the war for Norway was over. In less than two months Germany consolidated its control of the entire country. Following the invasion of Norway Hitler had hoped that he could reach an accommodation with the Norwegian government, thereby lending some shred of legitimacy to the ongoing occupation. The Norwegian parliament refused to surrender. Shortly after the invasion, the *Storting*, the Norwegian national assembly, gave King Haakon the mandate to continue governing. Some days later, transported by the British cruiser HMS *Devonshire*, he and the Nygaardsvold government were forced to flee to Britain, where they maintained a government-in-exile for the duration of the war.[806] The resistance of Norway's freely elected government and her King substantially bolstered popular resistance to the occupation.

In a radio broadcast on the first day of the invasion, Vidkun Quisling announced that he was the new Prime Minister. When talks between the Reich Commissariat of Norway and the Norwegian Parliament failed, *Reichskommissar* Josef Terboven had no alternative but to recognize Quisling's regime. Terboven appointed Quisling the titular head of state on 20 February 1942, while retaining complete control over the oppressive apparatus of the occupation.

CHAPTER 22

In the Land of the Vikings: Norway 1940–1943

Hans Rose was Sea Commander for Trondheim from 1 July 1940 to 31 July 1943. It was a posting that 'lasted three short summers and three long winters'.[807] Having always had great admiration for the Vikings and their descendants, and being an active naval command, the posting suited Rose.

Trondheim was also the departure point for at least 214 U-boat missions. During the period that Rose was Sea Commander at least 53 U-boats put in to Trondheim. In June 1943, before his departure, the 13th U-boat Flotilla was created there. And yet only a single anecdote, passed down orally by Rose to his stepson Rudolph Brickenstein, makes any reference to U-boats in Trondheim. A famous U-boat captain returned to Trondheim from a mission. Rose went down to greet him at the harbour where he was told that the Captain was asleep. Rose told the orderly 'Let him sleep, I'll see him later.'[808] We find all the love and respect Rose held for the submarine service in that simple statement.

Why, after devoting the first eleven chapters of his *Nordic Sketches* to the role of the Navy in the invasion, did Rose choose to pass in silence the presence of U-boats and U-boat men at Trondheim? Rose was, after all, first and foremost, a submariner. Maybe wartime censors would not have permitted its publication. Or possibly the offensive role of U-boats based in Norway was inconsistent with Rose's narrative justifying Germany's invasion. Possibly he felt a focus on the new generation of submariners would have stolen the thunder from his own role

HITLER BIRTHDAY INSPECTION OF TRONDHEIM Rose (second from left) with Admiral-General Hermann Bohm, 20 April 1941. [Rose Family Archives]

in WWII, and his other Nordic accounts. Or perhaps, Rose was simply terribly disappointed that he was not given a role in the WWII U-boat campaign. It was to be a convoy war, a war he knew how to fight, and yet he was not called upon to play any significant role in it.

Full Of Vitality

Describing Rose's role and responsibilities, the commander-in-Chief of the German Navy in Norway, General-Admiral Hermann Boehm (CINC), wrote:

> It became the duty of the German Navy to protect the endless coastal region from any Allied attacks, and to keep it open to German sea traffic...
>
> For the CINC it was naturally of great interest to know that strategic points along the coast were in the hands of experienced, knowledgeable men... Trondheim, because of its geographic position, the deep sea lanes, and its harbour capable of servicing the largest vessels was strategically the most important point along the coast.
>
> The CINC was both highly satisfied and relieved to find that *Korvettenkapitän* Hans Rose was appointed Sea Commander of Trondheim. *Korvettenkapitän* Rose reported for duty soon after the occupation... [H]is hair ... had turned white, but he was still as flexible, full of vitality and as upright in carriage as in his youth. The CINC and Rose were members of the same crew, and therefore had known each other for decades. The CINC not only remembered Rose's glorious deeds during WWI, but he also knew that he had been able to inspire his crew of *U 53* to the highest discipline... One could expect that these qualities of the Sea Commander would have their effect on the men stationed in various spots, scattered over the many fjords and lonely cliffs, and on the many war vessels under his command. He fulfilled those expectations: the discipline of the Trondheim region was exceptional. During his posting, the region became sufficiently fortified, despite adverse conditions, that any enemy attack could only have brought them great losses.[809]

Rose 'loved the water, cliffs, fjords, the mountains and the glaciers, but most of all he loved the people'[810] and so upon arrival in Trondheim he urged his subordinates 'not to consider themselves as the victor in enemy territory, but rather to think of themselves as assistants in a land of friends'.[811]

The Viking King Tryggvason founded Trondheim in 997. By 1940, the city's population had grown to roughly 55,000. It lies some fifty kilometres (thirty-one miles) from the North Atlantic in Trondheimsfjorden, a vast, deep, protected, ice-free fjord. Some 390 kilometres (242 miles) due north of Norway's capital Oslo, Trondheim is situated roughly at the same latitude as the southern coast of Iceland. At summer solstice, three hours and twenty minutes separate sunset from sunrise and there is no complete darkness. 'Summer' is the period between 23 May and 19 July. 'Winters' lasted most of the remaining ten months, with, at winter solstice, the sun rising at 10 a.m., and setting at 14:30. Three very short summers and three very long winters indeed, as Rose described his time there.[812]

The city's excellent sheltered harbour, the vast fjord in which it is positioned, and its location with direct access to the North Atlantic and the Arctic Ocean, well above the North Sea, made Trondheim the most important strategic port in Norway, and a vital strategic asset for the occupying Germans.

The Germans built Dora-1, their largest naval and U-boat base in Northern Europe, at Trondheim. Completed just two months before Rose would leave Trondheim and retire from the German Navy, it became home to the 13th U-boat Flotilla. Dora-2, a smaller German bunker and U-boat base to the west of it was half-finished at the end of the war.[813] But the two Dora projects are nothing in comparison to Hitler's intention to erect *Projekt Nordstern* at Trondheim. Project North Star, officially commissioned in 1941, was to be a huge 55,000-home German metropolis for 250,000 to 300,000 persons to be built in conjunction with a massively expanded naval base. This 'German Singapore'[814], as Hitler described the project he personally named, was slated to become the most important foreign base of the German *Kriegsmarine*.

The strategic relevance of the Dora and Nordstern projects, and of Trondheim itself, reflected by its importance over the course of the war as the ninth most active German U-boat base, required that Rose assume a multiplicity of tasks. Among them was responsibility for protection from Allied attacks of the Trondheim coastal region, and keeping it open to German sea traffic. This required that he train and motivate the men under his command and oversee the creation and operation of a naval flotilla to perform the necessary patrols, as well as establish the necessary land-based defences. Under his direct superior August Thiele, Admiral of the Norwegian North Coast, Rose had to execute these responsibilities in coordination with the two other non-naval German occupation forces; the army, and *Reichskommissar* Josef Terboven's occupation administration with its SS and Gestapo men.

Between 6 and 12 October 1942, at roughly the midpoint of Rose's posting as Sea Commander, an extreme manifestation of Terboven's 'iron fist' policy was enacted. Terboven's intent to terrorize the Trondheim population was barbarically demonstrated by his decision to carry out *soneofre*, atonement sacrifices, by executing ten leading citizens of Trondheim on the first night of martial law. Railing against 'inferior racial elements ... [conspiring with the] emigrant,' Terboven declared that 'this evening the public will become familiar with how this principle is put into action.' Then, within earshot of eight of the men confined in Gestapo cells nearby who would subsequently be shot,[815] he announced, by naming them, the immediate execution of two attorneys, a theatre director, an editor, a merchant, an engineer, a bank president, a labour leader, a captain and a ship owner.[816] One of the men was explicitly noted to be a Jew. The martial law was enforced by 13,000 police officers, military officials and Hirden collaborationists. Over its course, 1,434 residences were raided, ninety-three Norwegians were arrested including a number of Jews, and twenty-four other Norwegians would also be summarily executed.[817]

All branches of the German occupation forces would certainly have been informed of Terboven's imposition of martial law in Trondheim. Thus Hans Rose would have known in advance and have been kept informed of what was intended as a very public campaign designed to intimidate the Norwegian population.

Rose had known *Reichskommissar* Josef Terboven from his time in Essen. Terboven, born there, had helped establish the local Nazi Party in 1923, participated in Hitler's unsuccessful Beer Hall Putsch the same year, and had become the *Gauleiter*, the district leader, in 1927. In 1925 Terboven joined the Essen branch of the *Sturmabteilung*, the SA. In 1935, Hermann Göring appointed Terboven President of the Upper Rhine Province, where he 'earned a reputation as a petty and ruthless ruler'.[818] Rose, in his capacity as leader of the local *Marine SA*, interacted with Terboven in the mid-1930s. Daughter Helga recalled that her father 'could not suffer Terboven.'[819] Rose's stepson Rudolf recalled that Rose considered him an 'asshole'.[820]

Rose's romantic attitude towards the Norwegians would hardly have sat well with Terboven, nor the fact that the Sea Commander had major disagreements with him.[821] Rose's son, Christian, remarked:

> I suspect that my father would not hesitate to express his disagreements with the political directions of the Nazis. It would have been done in a very *höflichen Stiel* [polite style], but leaving no doubt where he stood.[822]

Christian considered that his father 'didn't suffer fools'[823] yet 'was a man who could cut someone's head off without that person ever knowing that his head had been cut off.'[824]

Apparently Rose's relationship with his direct superior, Admiral Thiele, was not entirely comfortable either. Rose assumed substantial responsibilities as Sea Commander for Trondheim including for a flotilla of modest patrol vessels in the most strategic theatre of the Norwegian coast. Yet Rose never received the promotion to the rank of rear admiral that he coveted. It must have been a disappointment for Rose when Thiele, who was eight years younger and had not yet received his Knight's Cross with Oak Leaves, was promoted Admiral, while Rose, himself a more prestigious *Ordre Pour le Mérite* holder, remained *Kapitän zur See z.V*, Captain in the Navy for disposition.

Ostensibly the promotion was denied because Rose had been recalled out of retirement to serve in WWII. But another explanation suggests itself. In an environment where Rose would have been politically suspect as far as Terboven's Nazi regime was concerned, and where Rose did not enjoy the unconditional support of his superior, his propensity to contest the decisions of his superiors or the occupation regime perhaps contributed to his being denied promotion. Any disagreements with his direct superior, Admiral Thiele, or other officers up the chain of command in Norway, could have blocked it.

Sea Commander of Trondheim: July 1940–July 1943

Rose's experiences as Sea Commander of Trondheim are recounted in the last ten chapters of his largely unpublished manuscript *Sea Commander: Nordic Sketches*. They provide a vivid picture of the daily challenges that the commander of the coastal defence of Trondheim encountered and have a more personal feel, despite Rose's insistence upon writing in the third person. Unlike the initial chapters which portray the heroic and 'history-changing' invasion of

Norway, the remaining chapters are more anecdotal in both form and content. There is no mention of Dora-1, nor of Project North Star, yet it is inconceivable that Rose as Sea Commander would not have been involved in activities associated with their execution. These chapters lack the heroic and death-defying excitement of his experiences as captain of *U 53*. Another difference between *Auftauchen!* and *Nordic Sketches*, is that the latter, having been written in 1940-1942, might be considered war-time propaganda, in particular with its not-infrequent repetition of Nazi justifications for the war and invasion of Norway and in its postulation of the racial arguments of the Third Reich.

Rose's sea-borne responsibilities included minesweeping, helping ships in distress, escorting vessels to protect them from enemy attacks, supplying occupation troops on isolated islands with weapons, food and clothing, as well as protecting the Trondheim fjord.[825] Rose understood that 'even though the British had been driven out of Norway, there was no guarantee that they would not want to return.'[826]

It was a task made more difficult, Rose explained, because the invasions of Denmark, Belgium and France starting in April and May 1940 required the transfer of Germany's most advanced weaponry to those theatres. As a result, less important areas like Norway had to make do with 'otherwise inadequate means',[827] to wit, local resources. In his chapter, 'Dwarfs of the Atlantic', Rose explained: 'This meant using for mine sweeping duties twenty- to forty-year-old restored wooden fishing boats, whose top speed was seven knots.'

Rose acknowledged the Norwegian's passive resistance:

Of course the Norwegian fishermen tried to hide their newer boats in the many bays and harbours, negotiating hard for delivery of the least desirable boats. Then these were repaired with many delays and at inflated costs to their German customers. Twenty of these boats divided into two groups were finally commissioned by the German navy, and went to sea for week-long explorations under their enterprising young flotilla chiefs. Initially these ships had endless mishaps and breakdowns until the seven-man crews got used to the old-fashioned oil motors and their tiny quarters, which the officers shared with the petty officers.[828]

It is doubtful, however, that Rose had any inkling of his close proximity to the Norwegian resistance. The Trondheim shipyard was only 600 metres from Rose's office in Folkets Hus. Birger Grønn, its director, who worked with Rose, was secretly a resistance member. After the war he would be decorated with the British King's Medal for Courage in the Cause of Freedom.

Rose described the physical challenges:

...the continual darkness, the bitter cold, and the seething ocean with its roaring wind and whipping snow; all of which made it virtually impossible to determine a boat's position... Initially the chief of the flotilla and the Sea Commander were overwhelmed with alarming accounts of near disasters though slowly all turned into seasoned hands and disasters were few.[829]

The men Rose could draw upon to form the crews of his flotilla were initially unprepared for the new tasks that awaited them:

> Each of these boats received a German crew made up of highly qualified men who knew how to run the sophisticated machinery of their sunken destroyers, but nothing about the primitive motors of the preceding century.[830]

But the delays by the largely uncooperative Norwegian population provided plenty of time to train them:

> What to do in a situation where nothing seemed to fit together?... the crews were all bored with life in the shipyard and wanted to get to sea as soon as possible... Moreover, their future chiefs were not only ill-equipped to deal with shipyard problems, but also unprepared for the leadership positions they were required to fill... The group leaders, in particular Lieutenant Wachtel, tried to prepare them for leadership by teaching them navigation, but what is the use of theory when there had been no practical nautical experience to build on? To relieve the boredom the Sea Commander instituted 9 a.m. meetings for the group leaders and commanders of the various ships. Based on Asto's sarcastic suggestion, these came to be known as 'Happy Morning Hour'. When the Sea Commander entered these meetings, everyone jumped up and greeted him with a raised arm and a loud chorus of '*Heil* Hitler'. Even though this show of unity was overdone, the greeting raised everyone's spirits.
>
> Eventually by the end of 1940 those crewmen who knew nothing about their craft were weeded out and the energy of all participants finally brought about change... The challenging times had melded the men as well as the officers into a group.[831]

Ever aware that the physical, spiritual and intellectual needs of his men affected their morale, cohesion and efficiency, Rose made sure that

> ...the group leaders became concerned not only with the food, but also the intellectual needs of their men on board. Better food preparation was guaranteed by having a master-chef prepare the menus and that a bakery on shore supplied the ships with tasty breads. A laundry kept clothes and bedding clean. Furthermore there were film presentations and other recreational entertainments available, so that the flotilla, as small as it was, transformed itself into a substantial guardian of the city. Its motto became: 'ships sail; crews fight and fighters win.'[832]

At the same time, in the interest of discipline, Rose was not above taking advantage of a traditional naval superstition. Well aware of the challenge of maintaining discipline aboard the many small, lightly-crewed picket vessels under his command, and the difficulty of eliminating fraternization with the local female population, Rose resorted to an old saw: 'Women on board ship will bring bad luck sooner or later. They must be kept away under all circumstances, particularly from the decks of warships.[833]

When the winter with its seemingly endless night began to wane, Rose decided to review his flotilla. Wearing his Knight's Cross, he arrived at the dock on an icy day with the sun peeking low over the snow-clad hills while

Force 10 winds whipped across the fjord. He climbed on board the nearest vessel of Group I, which at the signal '[form a] Keel Line' lurched into the lead, causing Rose to lose his footing on the icy deck. He staggered up and acted as though nothing had happened, responding to the Flotilla chief's comment that conditions were icy, with 'Yes, I noticed.'[834] Subsequently various manoeuvres were performed with varying degrees of success. On returning to port the Sea Commander nonetheless signalled 'Greatly impressed by your performance.'[835]

Safely ashore following review of Group II, Rose relates a conversation with its commander who, Rose was pleased to note, properly regurgitated the official justification for Germany's invasion of Norway:

Group II was led by a tall, knowledgeable, widely travelled *Oberleutnant* full of idealism. His troops demonstrated their knowledge of weaponry, equipment and signalling, as well as politics. In passing the Sea Commander asked:

'Why did we invade Norway?'

'Because the British were about to misuse the country's neutrality for their own purposes.'

'Why is Norway of particular interest to the British?'

'They want to use Norway to reach the Baltic Sea and to strangle Germany.'

'Do the British have any economic interests in Norway?'

'Yes indeed, they import iron ore, foodstuffs and wood from here.'

The Sea Commander thanked the officers and men for what they had shown him and then took the opportunity to present the Iron Cross to various men, as well as the highly valued Minesweeper Medal to those who had earned it.[836]

To help ensure Trondheim's protection, Sea Commander Rose was responsible for the installation of a heavy battery on an island at the mouth of Trondheim Fjord. The island 'consisted of high cliffs capped with heather and berries, where every step oozed ground water'. All of the island's Norwegian inhabitants had been removed and consequently, 'there was nothing but whirling birds overhead.'[837]

Remarking upon the dislocation of the Norwegian islanders, Rose noted:

Only one of the little houses was in the future battery area and would be needed for the artillery personnel. It was inhabited by a seventy-year-old couple, who were dismayed at being displaced, even though they had a most meagre existence. There were no requests for monetary indemnification, no requests for a new home, just hopelessness in their eyes, indicating how deeply the northerner is attached to his land.'[838]

The location for this defensive battery was chosen almost immediately following Germany's invasion. The transfer of the battery from the Baltic, begun on 14 May 1940 would require more than two months to complete. But preparation of the battery site itself would take far longer. Several hundred men had been transported to Norway to carry out the construction of the battery. Framing his account as if in another age, Rose recalled they were

...serious, weathered, middle-aged men from Pomerania and Meklenburg, [many of whom] had owned their own businesses and were master artisans.[839]...

A seasoned captain was made the 'island commander' and was soon recognized as the 'king of the rock'.[840]

Progress lagged and Rose set out to investigate, making the seven-hour journey by boat down the fjord. He met the captain and discovered that his master artisans

> ...were divided into three groups: the drillers, the blasters and the transporters, who lived in a tent city where it was almost impossible to dry one's clothes. The Norwegian assistants, who lived on their cutters, were better housed and fed, and disappeared home for the week-ends. This 'Viking fleet' which anchored in Hornack harbour, was well paid and they were to build the road from the harbour to the battery. The 'Island King' reported that the atmosphere in his realm was bad because of the constant rain and lack of boots and gear needed for the outdoor work.[841]

While Rose found the 'Island King' to be competent and energetic, the same was not the case with his sub-lieutenants:

> Three months had passed, yet much remained to be done... After talking to the 'Island King' and informing him that he would help, the Sea Commander asked to speak to the three working groups, as well as its officers and men. He asked the blasters how many explosions they set daily, and was told about a hundred, while they worked around the clock. He watched the drillers sink deep holes that filled with brown water for the harbour pier and observed the transport group move machinery and materiel. Meanwhile two sub-lieutenants were standing by doing nothing. The Sea Commander turned to them and said: 'It is your job to show the men how to do their job, not just stand around.'[842]

Demonstrating his signature appreciation of the dignity of work and importance of motivated personnel, Rose asked to meet the 'Ordnance' group in their barracks. He shared lunch with the men. The food was simple and there was no beer to drink because the 'Island King' had forbidden the use of alcohol until the evening. Turning to the 'Island King', the Sea Commander commented that the absenteeism of workers could possibly be avoided by promising them more frequent Trondheim leave to assuage the boredom. 'In facing the men,' during the general inspection, 'the Sea Commander sees sullen expressions.' He praised the men for their contribution to building the axis of the new Germanic Reich from Klagenfurt in the south to Trondheim, the city of light, in the north. For this enterprise to succeed he explained: 'Everyone must not only think of his own well-being, but that of the German nation as a whole, which is presently making advances in western Europe.'[843]

Though the work was difficult and monotonous, Rose proposed that their daily life might be enriched by lectures about Norway's history, botany, zoology and the star-studded firmament, as well as instruction in the German language. To the interjection that the men would fall asleep, he retorted: 'Then the lecturers will have to improve the quality of their presentation, because there is a yearning in everyone for immortality, for knowledge about one's surroundings.'[844]

Furthermore, as a reward, he promised that henceforth groups of sixteen men would always be on three-day furloughs in Trondheim: 'I hope this will raise the productivity and spirits of those who remain, because they too have something to look forward to.'[845]

Then Rose delivered a final admonition to their military overseers:

'Your men, many of whom were owners of their own small businesses, do not require supervision. Instead, it is your responsibility to get to know each of them personally, so you can ameliorate their problems. Second, you must therefore play a liaison role between them and your superior officers, so that they can understand their needs. Finally, the alcohol ban does not only apply to your men, as you know, but also to yourselves, who should be setting an example for your group. Thank you for your attention, gentlemen.'

It was this last sentence that made the deepest impression, because it indicated the Sea Commander's understanding of 'the dignity of work'.[846]

In March 1941, almost a year after the decision to build the battery had been made, most of the work had been completed:

The heavy machinery finally arrived on the Huascaran, and the men braved storms, snow, fierce frost as well as blinding snow squalls in the weeks-long rush to set it up on the island.

Their hard work was further motivated by the appearance of British aeroplanes that flew over the island without dropping any bombs.[847]

CINC General-Admiral Boehm and Admiral Thiele promised their attendance at the festivities marking the battery's completion. But in the end they 'had other duties to fulfil' and it fell to Sea Commander Rose to honour the men:

After the shooting demonstration the Sea Commander inspected the competent men of the building brigade, the soldiers, the workers and other employees, as well as the cannoneers. A three-fold '*Heil*' to the Führer concluded the ceremony acknowledging the back-breaking work that had been accomplished.[848]

Rose demonstrates his preoccupation with the conditions his men faced in these remote postings by recounting an unexpected visit to a remote lighthouse:

The lighthouse Kya was situated on one of the small nearly circular islands. It was fifty metres in diameter and three metres high. The tower was occupied by an NCO and three or four men. They were supposed to report the approach of any enemies... In foggy weather they were cut off from the rest of the world. In case of stormy seas they could not be reached for days. From the Sea Commander's perspective the occupation of the tower was senseless, but his superiors insisted on maintaining the tower.

During the summer in Norway it remains light at night. One morning at 3 a.m. Kya came in sight on one of the trips the Sea Commander undertook... The Sea Commander had a signal made to the tower. There was no answer. He slowly moved to a hundred metres distance – still no answer. He had a small boat launched and he and an NCO rowed to land. Carefully, like Indians, the two moved to the tower. The iron door was wide open... Rose climbed up to the lighthouse catwalk. Not a soul in sight! He climbed down into the men's quarter, there he found the whole gang completely naked and tanned like Negroes... They slept the sleep of the innocent. The Sea Commander stepped towards the bed of the sergeant in charge: 'Freeze! Or you are dead!' For the others the same procedure was employed. Two floors further down he found the man who should have been on guard. He was in the kitchen sound asleep like his other comrades. The Sea Commander returned to the men's quarters and ordered:

'I insist that from now on a guard is to be on duty at all times. You shall be relieved immediately. The consequences will be considered later.'

Guard negligence in the face of the enemy required court-martial. The guard on duty was a man of thirty-five years with a happy family life and two children. Should one condone that he be punished severely? Was not the real reason for this neglect a silly order? The doctor found that the man had taken a tablet the night before because of stomach pains. This tablet made the man sleepy. The Sea Commander had the man arrested and put into jail for two weeks, because he had not reported to the sergeant that he was unwell. After serving two weeks the man reported to the Sea Commander, tears in his eyes. He could hardly express his indebtedness. One has to have understanding for the people of the simple walks of life.[849]

Making a similar point in his *Life Story*, Rose recounts a conversation with a Chief Mechanic experiencing difficulties with his commanding officer. As the man began complaining, Rose interrupted him: 'If you intend to launch a complaint against your superior you will have to do it through official channels.'

The man began again and Rose interrupted him again: 'Remember the official procedures.'

When the man tried yet again to discuss his grievance, Rose said: 'Well Chief Mechanic, let's forget the formalities and talk man to man.'

The man poured out his distress. Later, summing up the event, Rose commented the man's commander 'seemed to have been very unfair'. Having received a sympathetic audience the Chief Mechanic got up saying: 'Sir, I feel much better already.'

Rose concluded, 'No actions were undertaken; at such times one has to let the men pour out their woes.'[850]

Rose is also purported to have commuted the death sentence of a deserter while in Trondheim although there are no details.[851]

These concessions to the needs of men of the 'simple walks of life' were, nonetheless, made by a strict naval authoritarian. Recalling a staff meeting at Trondheim, Rose remarked:

One always had to keep an eye on the frame of mind of the men, particularly during the monotony and the endless darkness of the long winter nights. Flattering the Sea Commander could not be tolerated. At one of the staff meetings with 180 officers present this had happened again. Greatly annoyed, the Sea Commander got up and bluntly told the entire assembly:

'Gentlemen, people who attempt to creep up my pants will find themselves chewing on granite!'

From that day forward the Sea Commander was known in Trondheim as the 'Anatomical Curiosity.'[852]

Rose's seventeenth chapter of the *Nordic Sketches* is titled 'Damned George'. It describes a large North German Lloyd tanker running aground on a reef in Norway's skerries. The ship was captained by 'Damned George', a heroic German mariner. Following navigational hand-off to a local pilot, disaster ensued and the tanker found its centre hard aground, balanced on a reef, oil gushing from ruptured tanks forward. The Sea Commander received the emergency message and mobilized a small flotilla of mine sweepers, tugs, an auxiliary tanker and a repair ship. For three days the crew and the rescue flotilla rushed to pump out as much oil while unloading as much materiel as possible.

> Damned George and the Head Engineer were everywhere. They calculated, made drawings, planned, gave a helping hand where needed; encouraged and were themselves in a desperate mood... 'Ships don't wage war, men do!' In dogged rage, [Damned George] repeated the sentence to himself over and over again, while fighting day and night. There was no sleep for him while the crew continued its activities.
>
> The repair ship pumped heated air through the oil tanks and out through the leaks. The officers crawled around in the oily rain, while all the ships drifted in a sea of oil upon which dead animals floated. Damned George's ship had caused a great and woeful dying. When on the third day a strong westerly storm blew up, and the decks became slippery with oil, the Commander requested that all seven ships return to Trondheim.[853]

Two more days of feverish activity were required before the damaged ship could be towed free of the reef and slowly motored back to Trondheim. With great rents in her hull and cracks to her keel below the water line, emergency repairs were essential before the tanker could limp back to Germany. With the tanker hidden in a narrow fjord protected with antiaircraft guns, 3,200 tons of additional temporary buoyancy were created by filling the leaking forecastle and ruptured oil tanks with seventeen thousand empty barrels delivered from Germany. These were secured with 300 truckloads of brushwood 'driven down to the fjord on the icy, breakneck mountain paths'. On the last night Rose made a final visit:

> The Sea Commander came aboard at the completion of the task and shook hands with all involved, especially the carpenters, thanking them for their meticulous work. He then retired for a private conversation with his friend George, the tanker's Commander. He took his leave with a friendly pat on the shoulder:
>
> 'I hope you will never again be in a position to mess up this beautiful coast for miles and miles with your damned oil, Damned George. May you at least have one centimetre of water under your keel. Have a good trip... May luck be with you, Damned George, in your future trips in silent self-sacrificing service for the fatherland.'[854]

Rose's Notions of the 'North Country'

The final chapter of *Nordic Sketches*, Chapter 21, *In Elk Country*, embodies Rose's love for the 'North Country'. It describes an elk hunt north of Trondheim:

> The period of mushroom hunting and the rich berry harvest in Norway is over. The birch ladies are taking leave of summer and changing into their golden robes, when the Sea Commander's car reaches Nomseneln. He crosses the broad stream with the elk guide Sigurd Schilliaas and the porter Norman. Thick snow flakes shroud the views. Meat, milk, potatoes and bread are loaded into a wagon and the ascent begins.
>
> The path leads steeply upward and out of the snow flurries. The trees are suddenly festooned with small diamonds of melting snow. Every minute the air becomes purer.[855]

A long mountain lake appears with a Viking boat where the group takes leave of the porter. The boat comes to rest on a rocky shore with a log cabin where Frau Margarete throws birch logs into the fireplace and makes sandwiches. Then Sigurd and the Sea Commander set off for a reconnaissance walk, joined by the enthusiastic dog Hallah. They find fresh elk tracks which look like those of a huge male.[856] At the top of the hill there is a panoramic view of heather, moors and fallen trees two hundred metres below.

> In the stillness the Sea Commander hears the pounding of his own heart and the solitude sings in his ears... That night the Sea Commander dreams of gods and Niebelungen and Nordic battles, with the dog moaning at the foot of his bed. In this half waking dream, yesterday and tomorrow are connected and a consciousness of Germanic prehistory and the German future come together.[857]
>
> ...On the fourth day they see a mother cow with her two calves crossing the moors not more than 150 metres away. The hunters freeze, overwhelmed by the peacefulness of the scene and the beauty of nature... On their silent descent to Namsos valley the next day the hunters agree that only those who have experienced these animals in their natural habitat have an idea of the essence of the North Country.[858]

Rose's nationalism rests upon three foundations; romantic nationalism, pan-Germanic nationalism, and narrow nationalism. Two of the three legs of that tripod are on display here.

The Romantic Nationalism of the earliest German adherents, Johann Gottfried Herder and Immanuel Kant, drew its inspiration from French philosophers Jean Jacques Rousseau and Emmanuel-Joseph Sieyès. They had previously developed the concept of naturalism, and asserted that to be legitimate a nation 'must have been conceived in the state of nature'.[859] Herder asserted that Providence 'wonderfully separated nationalities not only by woods and mountains, seas and deserts, rivers and climates, but more particularly by languages, inclinations and characters.'[860]

In this natural state, Herder argued:

The savage who loves himself, his wife and child with quiet joy and glows with limited activity of his tribe, as for his own life, is, in my opinion, a more real being than that cultivated shadow who is enraptured with the shadow of the whole species.[861]

Herder's is a succinct description both of Rose's romantic view of Germanic prehistory, the place gardens and country life occupy in Rose's life, and his rapture for the 'North Country'. Anthony Smith notes:

This emphasis on the naturalness of ethno-linguistic nations continued to be upheld by the early 19th-century Romantic German nationalists Johann Gottlieb Fichte, Ernst Moritz Arndt, and Friedrich Ludwig Jahn, who all were proponents of Pan-Germanism.[862]

In 1871 Pan-Germanism played a significant role in the 19th-century unification of the disparate states of the German Empire into a nation-state, and subsequently, the creation of the Pan-German League in 1891, whose purpose was 'to nurture and protect the ideology of German nationality as a unifying force'.[863] Between 1100 and the start of the 20th century that linguistic diaspora was variously considered to include Low Saxon speakers, the Middle Saxon of the Hanseatic League, which influenced the Scandinavian languages, as well as the Frisian and Dutch-speaking populations originally organized into the Holy Roman Empire. Given Hans Rose's romantic nature, his erudition, and his classical education, it is not surprising that his nationalism mirrors the Romantic Nationalism and Pan-Germanism of these earliest German adherents.

General-Admiral Hermann Boehm's confidence had not been misplaced. Rose accomplished his mission. By example Rose would inspire his troops to the highest discipline. He would motivate them and the civilian workers engaged with them by acknowledging their contributions and looking after their well-being. How could he do anything else? He had been called to duty in the land of the Vikings. He could not have asked for a more heroic and for him pan-Germanic setting. And yet Rose remained a loner at a distance. Anyone who tried to get too close would find themselves 'chewing on granite'.

Chapter 23

An Officer Who Could Think in Political Terms

Commander-in-Chief (CINC) of the German Navy in Norway, General-Admiral Boehm, concluded his remarks about Sea Commander Rose thus:

> Rose was also an officer who could think in political terms. He understood the political task and its meaning in relationship to his men; and also the problem of the occupation force, in relationship to the present war efforts and the future after the war. He had great understanding for the natural bitterness of the Norwegian people towards the occupation. He tried to be just to them and to recognize their national feelings. He made every effort to improve conditions and thus tried to build a basis for better understandings in the future.

During the Nürnberg trial the State Secretary Weizsäcker, a former Ambassador to Norway was asked: 'Can you say anything about the behaviour of the German Navy and the popular opinion about the German Navy during the occupation in Norway?' Mr. von Weizsäcker answered, 'The navy enjoyed a good name or possibly even an exceptionally good name, as far as I know.'

The Sea Commander of Trondheim, *Korvettenkapitän* Hans Rose, deserves partial credit for the above statement.[864]

EUROPE REBORN Line drawing by Hans Rose, 4 April 1943. [Rose Family Archives]

It is impossible to divorce Rose's political nationalism from his idealism and romantic world view, and his self-assumed code of knightly chivalry. This is strikingly demonstrated by the thirteenth chapter of his *Nordic Sketches*, 'Of "Morning Star" and "Dewdrop"', which recounts his Easter 1941 visit to a Norwegian Quisling's island abode.

Rose begins his account with a quote from the tenth book of Homer's *Odyssey*: 'We brought the ship noiselessly to shore, and with some divinity as our guide we put in at the sheltering Harbour.'[865]

Rose describes the visit's mundane origin:

> The telephone rang. When the Sea Commander lifted the receiver a smile played in his eyes, and he responded 'Many thanks, I would love to come and promise that Dewdrop will be delighted as well.'... It was the wife of a high-level Norwegian official, who was inviting us to their island property for Easter.[866]

Dewdrop was an unidentified fellow officer, a German Admiral stationed at Trondheim. The high-level Norwegian official was Anton Frederik Winter Jakhelln Prytz, soon to be the Minister of Finance in the Quisling puppet government. Prytz was a close friend of Vidkun Quisling, and co-founder of the *Nasjonal Samling*. But he was a moderate within the Quisling party who publicly opposed the anti-Semitism both of the Germans and the NS.

The two men were transported to Prytz's island abode by the nineteenth-century sailing schooner *Falcon*, which had been 'transformed from a graceful floating swan into a dull delivery vehicle'.[867]

> The gentlemen greatly enjoyed the clear views of the snow-covered mountains at the end of the fjord. Dewdrop enjoyed the afternoon coffee with its cheese canapés, while the Sea Commander found the liquor and the Brazilian cigar to his taste.

There was a brief period of anxiety when the *Falcon*'s engine died and the schooner drifted towards a German minefield. But when Rose radioed nearby picket vessels they towed the schooner to safety: 'The *Falcon* was, after all, an ancient bird, whose wings were lame and whose digestion was bad'.

With the engine restarted the voyage was completed without incident. Arriving at their destination, Rose found himself transported into the age of Viking lore:

> At dusk the *Falcon* entered the island's strange harbour located between high rocky cliffs. One will remember that in the grey past this had been the anchoring place for the sea-faring population. Here the Viking princes collected their fleets, in which they undertook their world-wide trips. Here the dragon ships anchored to take on water and other necessary provisions. Here the 'Thing' took place. Here the princes and leaders made their plans. Here the look-outs and keepers of the fire sat in the hollows of the mountain, signalling the first greetings to the returning seafarers. Here everything breathed ancient immemorial lore of the beginnings of Nordic seafaring. The hearts of Dewdrop and of the Sea Commander opened wide at the realization of how ancient this spot was.

Travelling across the island, past houses devoid of man or beast, they pass a pine-covered hillock to descend into a valley where a long stable was painted the traditional Norwegian red, and the gable of a two-story home could be glimpsed. Greetings were exchanged with their host and tulips brought from Trondheim were offered to his wife Caroline:

> The Squire walked toward the visitors with long slow strides.
> 'Welcome on my property.'

His big blue eyes greeted them while a smile played around his lips. He was a head taller than Dewdrop and also taller than the Sea Commander. He was over sixty years of age and had a strong Nordic appearance.

Rose, ever gallant and enthused when it came to the fairer sex, continues his account with effusive descriptions of the squire's three daughters, one of whom works at the German headquarters in Trondheim:

When the gentlemen returned downstairs they were greeted by the daughters dressed in Norwegian costumes.

'Good afternoon Morningstar,' they greeted the oldest of the three daughters.

She had received this name because she had, during the long winter months, often breakfasted in the same room as the German officers. They had smiled at each other even before they had been introduced. The officers had been happy to see the shapely figure in the dark winter mornings and decided to name her 'Morningstar', which she had been quickly informed of, and which of course affected her demeanour.

'Siehe da, Sunshine,' they said turning toward the second, who was perhaps an even better representative of the blond North Germanic race. 'How are you, young Viking princess?'

'We are happy to see you here and will show you the island,' she replied smiling gracefully.

'And here is the "Fawn"' the guests replied and hugged the tall young girl with the large grey eyes.

Over the course of the visit, the three daughters will dominate Rose's descriptions of meals shared, their tour of the farm, games played and explorations of the island:

Next morning at ten o'clock there were knocks on the doors of the guest-rooms. A Nordic girl curtsied and wished them a 'good morning', while depositing glowing peat blocks into their ovens. After a while she reappeared with a tray full of white bread sandwiches, a cup of hot tea and a cognac glass full of cod liver oil. Everything was ingested in reverse order. One enjoyed one's warm bed a bit longer, before arising after the room had pleasantly warmed. There was a wonderful breakfast waiting in the dining hall, including smoked ham; goat cheese; young radishes; honey from local hives; rye crisp and Easter eggs. The table was beautifully decorated by the dew-fresh daughters.

Exploring:

The group wandered across the wide moors up to the northern point of the island; jumping from one heather bush to the other, the moor squished and the rubber boots were close to getting stuck. Morningstar and Sunshine were always a few steps ahead. They helped Dewdrop if the distance between the heather pads seemed too far apart. There were snow showers. The girls laughed and did not worry about the climate or the wet ground. Sunshine climbed up a big peat heap and threw snow down on the guests. In no time a snow fight was launched with the Valkyries battling the Rocks until the girls were vanquished:

'Goodbye you keen wonderful child – with your gleaming eyes?'
The song carried over the island and the fjord. Peace returned.

The following day there was another excursion:

The next morning, to cross the bay, everyone got on to a small boat resembling those of Viking ancestors. Pathless, everyone scrambled up and across the heather moors to a mysterious cave. Run-off waters dripped endlessly from the ceiling to the narrow floor. The sun shone brightly. One could see far across the island and the peat moors in the north, up to the far-away skerry and over the glistening blue sea of the north. Cumulus clouds sailed above. One passed high rocky cliffs in front of which there seemed to be remains of walls from cave dwellings from the ancient past. Finally, the wanderers had reached the crest. Up to now they had only been able to look north, now they could view the high mountains of the mainland. Now range upon range of the snow-covered mountains lay at their feet in the sunlight and the blue fjord with its bays was visible. In the sky high above, a pair of eagles floated on the wind.

At the highest point of the mountain, where a stone wall indicated an ancient fire place of the ancestors, the blond Morningstar stood waving a white handkerchief.

'Who are you hailing?' the Admiral inquired smiling.

Without looking back the girl responded:

'No one really, but someone will surely be pleased.'

She was right, the Sea Commander thought, if one could only paint this moment in time.

Later, descending, they took a break:

Silently, the girls crept up to the guests: 'Shut your eyes and open your mouth.'

They bent down to the men and gave each of them a hand-full of berries commenting: 'If a person looks for berries under the snow, to feed another, it means good health and long friendship.'

The Sea Commander responded: 'And those who eat them must love this land and its people forever.'

Deciding not to wait several hours to return across the bay, the group chose to walk around the shore, daring the tide. For Rose there is a hint of the noble savage in his hosts:

Dewdrop went first. His feet were completely wet. The Sea Commander, though he walked carefully and slowly, had streams of water flowing into his rubber boots. He stood as though he were in a champagne cooler. Sunshine took no precautions whatever. She stomped through the flood with a happy laugh and returned home and changed into dry clothes. Morningstar turned around once more to fetch the Admiral. In the meantime the tide had fallen so that Dewdrop remained more or less dry, while Morningstar, who was supporting him, sacrificed herself. All of this did not, as in Germany, take place in an atmosphere of exultation, but in the deep silence of the children of nature...

The girls almost danced with happiness and lust for life. 'There is nothing more beautiful than our island.'

Rose found a game of *Skotthill*, played with the girls, to be 'a competition almost like that among the Nibelungen' of old Germanic and Norse mythology.

Within this romantic description, Rose relates the political conversation between himself, Admiral 'Dewdrop', and their host Anton Prytz, who begins:

I became a Norwegian officer and was sent to Russia as our attaché. There I got to know Vidkun Quisling and worked with him to develop the foundations and aims for the *Nasjonal Samling*. Its program mirrored many of the NSDAP's principles, though it preceded these by a number of years. It is therefore complete nonsense to view the Quisling enterprise as Hitler's doing, and as a traitorous movement against Norway.

Having spent years in the Soviet Union, Prytz believes its ultimate objective is to reach the Atlantic:

I know they are aiming at conquering North Finland and Norway, with its ice-free harbours from Murmansk up to and including Narvik and Trondheim. Then the piece of land on which we are living today will become the Bolshevik portal to the world. The peak on which the fires of the Vikings, our ancestors, used to blaze, will be threatened by the Soviet Star with its hammer and sickle. And with it the culture of the West... I see the huge danger and have been agitating for years for the consolidation of all Germanic nations, in order to counteract this huge danger... I am therefore deeply troubled by the war between Great Britain and Germany. Your Führer has frequently reached out to them offering peace. That there was no response is a sign that Great Britain no longer views itself as a European, but merely as an Atlantic superpower. Perhaps this is a good development, if the bloody wrestling results in a united Europe without Russia and Great Britain. If this does not come to pass, then the inescapable consequence will be the decline of the West.

The moment in which Europe will take up arms against Bolshevism will be the greatest in my life. I do hope to be around to experience when the huge Russian areas that I headed for many years, and which are as large as Holland and Belgium together, are securely in Germanic hands and the Slavs are pushed back behind the Ural Mountains.

Rose responds:

We came to your country not as plundering conquerors, but because the enemy forced us to occupy your coast. The British threatened us with destruction by occupying Trondheim, which would have put Sweden under their influence and closed down their essential trade routes. They would have thus attacked us from behind and we would have had to fight a hopeless fight for existence, like the Trojans. Then the Russians, with their huge population, would have invaded the Germanic East and the independence of Scandinavia would have disappeared. The Führer's skillful political moves avoided a war on two fronts. Strong German armies are at the ready from the North Cape to the Black Sea, to contain our eastern neighbours. The Russians won't dare to attack Norway, because they know that they will encounter our Alpine troops. I am sure that when peace in Europe is proclaimed, your country will once again attain its independence, as soon as all

Norwegians share your ideas for the future and realize that our racial, political and economic solidarity are a pre-condition for this future. Paracelsus' wisdom will become reality: 'That gold will flow to the north, not the metal, but the golden sunrise of a new Germanic Day.'

Admiral Dewdrop declares:

The racial closeness of our people is obvious. But spiritually as well, the people's nature is so similar that within the bounds of normal development, that which split them apart will soon be bridged. The same goals, the same concerns, the same enemies also force us together politically and economically.

Rose's Easter weekend represented the perfect ancestral Germanic myth for him; the Viking ideal that he wished he could have lived and grafted his fantastical pan-Germanic model onto. It was his gestalt. But it is reality turned on its head; Germany's invasions of her neighbours, the active resistance of Norway's legitimate government and Quisling's traitorous seizure of power give it the lie. Yet for Rose, the romantic warrior fighting in the land of 'the noble descendants of the old *"GERMANEN"* and the Germanic gods of Thor, Wotan, Odin and Valhalla',[868] these arguments for a racially pure 'Europe reborn' must have seemed to him to have had an almost mythological inevitability.

Among Hans Rose's papers one finds a photocopy from an unidentified publication. The unsigned text, entitled 'Europe Reborn', is folded about a line drawing Rose created. Framed by Doric columns, the vista of a winding road receding into the distance opens below an arch. In the foreground, holding aloft a small pot with what appears to be a young plant with a single half-moon leaf, a partially-dressed young woman, not unlike Eugène Delacroix's *Liberty Leading the People*, strides determinedly down the road towards us. In the arch above, Nordic looking block letters spell out: '*Es Bluteten Völker verbrannte das Land, bis endlich Europa zur Einigkeit fand*'; which unpoetically translates as 'The blood of peoples seared the continent, until European unity was finally achieved.' (See page 264.)

Above the arch, on the left, a ravenous wolf stalks, fangs bared and tongue drooling. On the right, three log houses of Nordic appearance are being devoured by flames. At the four corners of the arch's keystone the numbers 3 4 4 3 encircle a five-petal rose and date the drawing, 3 April 1943.

'Europe Reborn' begins: 'War is not a deed of single individuals, it descends upon us like an act of God.'[869]

Drawing upon his classical education, Rose's treatise reprises the argument of Greek Philosopher Heraclitus of Ephesus who famously posited, *Polemos Pater Panton*, war is the father of all things. War, Rose argues, is 'responsible not only for the ruination of whole cultures and countless individual beings, war is also the great creator of developments typically taking decades or centuries to bring to fruition.'

After demonstrating that war had been relied upon to resolve issues between European powers in the course of the last century, Rose marshals the old (and erroneous) argument by Germany's WWI military leadership, reprised by the Nazis, that Germany didn't lose that war, 'though it was not fought through to a conclusion, the peoples of Europe were the prime cause of the World War 1914-1918.'

Thus, war had returned:

Today whole continents are fighting for supremacy, for existence or extinction. New means of ground and air transport and of telegraphy have reduced distances. Those who previously barely encountered each other are now indivisibly intertwined. Large companies, industrial combines, weapons producers, whole cities sink into rubble. Thousands of people previously unaffected by war are now destroyed. If the cohabitating peoples of Europe persist with these sorts of wars in the future, the decline of the western world will be inevitable.

So this time the war must be won. And by the right people: 'Those who are destined to fulfil this leadership role in the Europe of the future are of the Germanic race.'

Here is evidence of the third facet of Rose's nationalism; narrow nationalism. Patriotism is devotion to one's country or nation devoid of any project for political action. Nationalism turns devotion to the nation into principles or programs. 'It thus contains a different dimension from mere patriotism.'[870] Where Rose's view and that of Herder diverge, is in their respective views about the political benefit of nationalism. Herder warned:

National glory is a deceiving seducer. When it reaches a certain height it clasps the head with an iron band. The enclosed sees nothing in the mist but his own picture; he is susceptible to no foreign impressions.[871]

But while in *Das Junge Europa* Rose reprised Herder's warning that European rejection of Christianity coupled with Slavic retention of their religions would inevitably result in the latter's domination of Europe,[872] he did not embrace Herder's warning about narrow nationalism.

Narrow nationalism is the claim of nationalist superiority of one's own nation over all others. This was the narrow nationalism of the Nazis. Rose's embrace of romantic pan-Germanic narrow nationalism allowed him to justify the occupation of Norway and the leading role of the German nation in crafting a new Europe.

'Europe Reborn' was delivered around 3 April 1943, five months before Rose's departure from Norway and three months after Rose's wife Anne-Marie died at the beginning of the year. Almost exactly two months earlier, on 2 February, the Soviet Union had won the decisive victory at the Battle of Stalingrad. Within that context Rose declared:

The more successfully we pursue the U-boat war, the more ruthlessly we strike our enemies, the stronger we resist, when the war demands defensive tactics... the more completely and quickly we will overcome.

And if one was to die in that struggle, it was the heroic thing to do: 'To fight for that unceasingly and if fate requires, to die for it, is the fulfilment of a manly life.'

The text is as significant for what it doesn't say as for what it says. There is no '*Heil* Hitler' at the end of the treatise. Bernd Molter notes:

> He could also have expanded on the unique role and personality of Hitler, his ideology, and his party in this struggle, which was often done in those days and which had proven very helpful for publication and success. He didn't. Maybe the addressees he had in mind were not primarily the Germans.[873]

While 'Europe Reborn' highlights Rose's narrow nationalism, inevitably overlapping with arguments of racial superiority, Molter's thesis mirrors that of General Boehm, where it speaks of Rose's sensitivity to the population of occupied Norway. But it goes further by remarking upon the text's refusal to reference Hitler at all; a daring thing to do in 1943. It links to the decision Rose took in 1937 to leave the *Marine SA*, and earlier to avoid wearing the Nazi uniform. It is possible that this is evidence that Rose's enthusiasm for Hitler was already waning.

Rose leaves us with two other speeches, 'Heroes' Remembrance', and 'Oath Taking', both apparently addressed uniquely to German soldiers. The first was presented on Remembrance Day. The second was delivered to a group of young soldiers being inducted.

German Volk (Hundreds of Years Ahead of the British)

'Heroes' Remembrance' is a long, bombastic review of the history of German greatness from earliest times, down to 'today, dear comrades, when the destiny of Germany and Europe is designated by a single individual'.[874]

Hitler, according to Rose, is simply following in the footsteps of previous great German leaders like the King of Stauffen, one of the Holy Roman Emperors in the High Middle Ages. Rose's speech enlists many of the arguments of Pan-Germanism, starting with its reference to Roman efforts to conquer the tribes in Germania. Rose's reference to the King of Stauffen, one of three members of the Swabian dynasty who were crowned Holy Roman Emperors in the High Middle Ages, mirrors that of Herder, who, musing that he would have preferred to have lived during the Middle Ages, questioned whether 'the times of the Swabian emperors [did not] deserve to be set forth in their true light in accordance with the German mode of thought'.[875]

Opposing 'the Germany of Schiller, Kant, and Mozart' is an England that has never 'create[d] anything of cultural value', only lately come to the table of civilization. Rose continues:

> While the thought of the German kingdom's glory, of its persistence and demise, preoccupied the best German thinkers, while thousands of the gallant sacrificed their blood and life, we hear, for the first time, about the formation of an English language, an English law, and English culture... Even in 1600, the English philosopher Bacon wondered whether he should write his works in the English language, because then they would [only] be read by a small island population and no one else in the world.

Make no mistake; the British Empire is the enemy: 'There are many enemies surrounding us, but fundamentally we are only fighting this war against one country, Great Britain, that will not permit us to rise.'

It is, in Rose's view, an insidious enemy, whose conquests have been carried out

> ...with a brutality hardly known anywhere else and alien to the Germans. They were the result of a steely will and a politics of subjugation and force... In cold calculation and ruthless savagery, Great Britain has always exploited European crises in order to fish in troubled waters to enlarge its empire. The unbelievable advantage of its geographical location, not their superior talent, gave them this opportunity.

Propaganda, designed to belittle and dehumanize the enemy, is an art as accepted during war-time as fighting itself. Yet the speech makes for uncomfortable reading, particularly coming from a widely read man with a classical education, a man who as a boy remembered the family's cosmopolitan meals, who himself had observed the role of the SS and the Gestapo in Krakow and in Trondheim, and who ended his autobiography with a reflection on 'what the sea taught us' including this:

> Our understanding broadened in the interaction with foreigners and foreign cultures. We learned to appreciate them; we learned that all events can be interpreted from different points of view. We learned to include foreign reactions, viewpoints, to develop a fuller understanding of the world around us. The sea taught us JUDGEMENT.[876]

Rose's history lesson in 'Heroes' Remembrance' mirrors that of the early Pan-Germanists. By word and action Rose demonstrated that his pan-Germanic narrow nationalism had nothing to do with the anti-Semitic narrow nationalism of the Nazis. Unfortunately, with political power in the hands of the Nazis, it nonetheless contributed to allowing him, for a time, to place his considerable reputation and leadership abilities in the service of their plan for racial domination and world conquest.

Rose's short speech, 'Oath Taking', was made to a group of recruits, each 'no more than a leaf on the forest floor',[771] who have completed their first training in Norway. It is an inspirational call to duty in which he articulates his view of the importance of each soldier:

> You stand before me, men from different backgrounds, different professions, as well as different districts of the fatherland. You are mostly young people who have not yet been imprinted by the stamp of life. But one thing we all have in common: you are German men. Now you will be formed into German soldiers. That does not mean giving up your own personality, but on the contrary, becoming part of a common mission in the service of the fatherland...
>
> You have lined up here today in order to promise the Führer loyalty, and to dedicate your body and soul to the fatherland. That is the greatest moment in the life of the German male. Be aware of the fullness and the sovereignty of this moment. The holy black, white and red colors of the German Reich flutter above your heads. In the ancient Germanic swastika, you see a Nordic symbol on the bright white

ground of the sun. The whole is surrounded by the flaming young red of the new day; of unbreakable German fellowship. May you never forget the honour, nor the pride, nor the deep seriousness and the commitment, as well as the joy of this holy hour.

Rose reminds the new recruits of his view that their conduct should not cause them to be viewed by the Norwegians as enemy occupiers, but rather 'people over whom we presently have command.'

We are here, standing on foreign soil, in a country whose people are racially close to us and whose ancestors were enterprising seafarers. Vikings are particularly close to us sailors. It is therefore all the more important that the German soldier never forgets to demonstrate his firmness of demeanour and purity of mind, so that the people over whom we presently have command, do not lose their respect for the German soldier.

The contrast between this last speech and the first two epitomises the striking difference between Rose's narrow nationalism on the one hand and his honourable practice as a soldier on the other. While some of Rose's political views during the Hitler period are regrettable, the old saying actions speak louder than words can legitimately be marshalled in his defence. There is an anecdote that Rose chose to include in his short biography, *A Life Portrait*.

From a peripheral island, the leader of the occupation troops complained about the conduct of the village teacher. The Sea Commander arrived at the island after a six-hour trip by speed boat. He asked the teacher for an interview and walked over the treeless island with him.
  'Sir,' said the Sea Commander, 'the sergeant has complained about you. If I were Norwegian I too would wish the Germans would leave the country.'
  'I understand, Captain.'
  'Sir, we are not here for our pleasure, we need your territory and your sea-routes.'
  'I understand, Captain.'
  'Our orders need to be followed.'
  'I understand, Captain.'
  'We try to make the occupation easy for you!'
  The teacher smiled; 'I understand, Captain.'
  'The sergeant is a fine man; I hope everything will be alright from now on.'
  A shaking of hands. When, after several weeks, the Sea Commander returned to the island for the second time, he found the sergeant's face beaming.
  'Everything is perfect, Sir. The teacher and I have been mutual guests over a cup of coffee at each other's residence.'[877]

How do we judge this interchange and Rose's choice to include it? (Sometimes history can be written by the defeated.) If we accept that it is essentially a true conversation, the sentence 'If I were Norwegian I too would wish the Germans would leave the country' is important, if only on the un-nuanced basis that the sentiment would never have occurred to, let alone been uttered by, the murderer Hans Frank. There is no doubt that Rose distanced himself from the worst excesses of the Nazi regime and demonstrated exemplary military behaviour.

There is, however, no evidence in his writings that he ever reflected critically upon those aspects of his personality (his romanticism and idealism) and his political perspective that allowed him for a time to become an instrument of the fascists who destroyed his country and attempted, by invasion, to impose the Third Reich on the world.

Departure

Rose's service as Sea Commander was cut short by the death of his beloved wife Anne-Marie in January 1943. Whenever leave permitted, Rose had returned to Germany to visit her. There is a photograph of a middle-aged Hans Rose, circa 1942, and Anne-Marie, eight years his junior, both standing knee-deep in water, and both dressed in period swimming gear. The annotation, in Rose's hand, below the photo reads: 'With the Westerland beach photographer prowling around Anne, I finally remarked: "Well then, why not take a picture of my daughter and me!" Everyone rejoiced.'[878]

Following Anne-Marie's death, with no one to take care of his children, Rose submitted a request to retire from the navy and return to Essen.[879] It was granted and Rose departed Trondheim at the end of June 1943. He was fifty-eight years old.

As news of his imminent departure spread the Bishop of Trondheim[880] hosted a goodbye party for Rose.[881] It was a reflection of the real friendships[882] that Rose had established with a number of Norwegian families. Rose is keen to demonstrate 'how well [he] got along with the Norwegian population'.[883] Along with several other families, the Lord Mayor of Trondheim, Olav Bergan, and his wife were guests at a luncheon:

> During the cocktails [he] gave a little speech in Norwegian. He was highly credited for that. As bacon wrapped asparagus was served, the lady to the right of the Sea Commander whispered into his ear: 'Captain please direct your attention to the young lady to the left for a little while, so that I can indulge in the asparagus.'[884]

At the end of his posting an honour guard awaited Rose at the Trondheim train station. Members of the army, navy and air force stood to attention. A number of Norwegian families also came to pay their respects. As Rose prepared to bid his adieu, the Bishop of Trondheim stepped forward and clasping Rose's hand between his own said: 'Captain, we wish all the very best for your future. Captain you've won the greatest victory, you've won the heart of the people.'

Rose replied: 'Most Reverent, this is the most gratifying thing you could have told me in farewell.'[885] Rose ends his short autobiographical *Life Story* with this anecdote about his departure from Norway:

> The express train rolled through the countryside. Silently the beautiful nature of this country passed before his eyes.
>
> 'All the time my real longing must have been to win the heart of my fellow-man. Have I really obtained this?'
>
> In devotion he bowed his head.[886]

Had Rose won the heart of his fellow-man? Rose's interactions with the Norwegians fall into two categories; with those Norwegians collaborating with the German occupation, and with those who were not collaborating. Not surprisingly, the Norwegians that Rose befriended fall into the former category. The two friends it is possible to identify were both high-ranking members of the Quisling *Nasjonal Samling*, whose views and affections reflected a very small percentage of the Norwegian population. The recalcitrant Norwegian teacher represents the vast majority of the Norwegian population.

On 24 February 1942, while Rose was Sea Commander in Trondheim, with great fanfare and in protest at the occupation, Trondheim's Bishop Johan Nicolai Støren resigned along with the six other Norwegian Lutheran Bishops. In response to their resignation as bishops of the state church, the Quisling government immediately suspended them from their positions as public officials and appointed new acting bishops. To replace Støren in the Diocese of Nidaros, they appointed Einar Lothe, the prior vicar of Vesterålen, and a member of *Nasjonal Samling*. This is the man Hans Rose identifies as the Bishop of Trondheim. Hans Rose must surely have known this.

Yet stepson Peter Brickenstein recalled that Hans Rose had good friends in Norway[887] and his brother Hans-Joachim Brickenstein recalled that in the early 1950s, 'at a time when it was very difficult to be a German',[888] Norwegians came to Winterberg to visit his stepfather bringing food for Rose and the rest of the family. Olav Bergan, the mayor of Trondheim, a city subject to the terror of the SS, was willing to put his opinion on record during the denazification hearings that Hans Rose was obliged to undergo after the war. It must be noted however, that Bergan was a member of the Quisling *Nasjonal Samling* installed by the Nazis, replacing the previous mayor who had been incarcerated in a concentration camp. Bergan's testimonial:

> During my time as Lord Mayor of the city of Trondheim I had the opportunity in 1940/43 to meet Captain-at-Sea Hans Rose on many occasions while he was Sea Commander. It gives me great pleasure to vouch for Mr. Rose, as a representative of the occupation forces, showed first-class decency at all times. The behaviour of Mr. Rose was correct, but at all times he tried to ease the position of the people of the city of Trondheim. Eventually he was respected and liked by all parties. I have never heard a person saying anything detrimental about Mr. Rose.[889]

By the time he departed in June 1943 Rose's explicit question of whether he had accomplished his personal objectives in Norway became an implicit reflection upon the meaning of the entire occupation and perhaps the war effort as a whole. It could only have posed an emotionally disquieting paradox. The Nordic way of life represented for Rose the ancestral Germanic ideal. So to repeat the question: had Rose won the heart of his fellow-man? Deep down he knew the answer. Hans Rose the warrior chose to lay down his weapons and go home. He had lost the will to fight, and perhaps belief in the goals of his country's leaders. He was no longer willing to participate in that effort. For the remainder of the war he would do what he could to save his homeland and his fellow citizens.

Chapter 24

The Abyss and
Beyond – Life after Hitler

Rose's posting to Trondheim ended in July 1943 and he returned to his home at
Springloh 32 in Essen-Heisingen. Between March and July that year the city had
been half destroyed by Allied bombing. One exploded bomb landed 200 metres
from the house.[890] The raid destroyed the private school Christian had attended,
and the old Krupp *Krankenhaus* where Anne-Marie had been hospitalized for
her mastectomy. Christian saw a dead mother and her baby 'burned to shrivels';
an image forever seared into his memory.[891]

The home Rose returned to was empty. War and illness had taken his family
from him. His country was in extremis. Anne-Marie was dead. And separated
from his second family, the navy, Rose was alone.

Writing in his diary on 20 October 1943 Rose described the overall military
situation and the conduct of the war up to that point:

> Churchill had been appointed Prime Minister, the grave digger of Europe! He returned
> to one of his WWI plans and decided to destroy Germany starting from the Balkans.
> Once more we forestalled him. In a lightning strike our troops conquered Serbia,
> Montenegro, Greece and Crete. We had arrived at the Aegean. On 21 June 1941
> the fateful fight against the 'Bolshevik Menace' commenced. *It constituted a disaster*

THE BRICKENSTEIN
FAMILY Bremen
1939. Left to right,
Rudolf, Peter,
Theodora Brügmann
Brickenstein, Karolina,
Wilhelm Rolf-Jürgen,
Hans-Joachim [Rose
Family Archive]

because we could not afford to fight a war on two fronts. This was beyond our capacities. [Italicized text here and subsequently added by Rose post-war.]

At the time my officers and I were guests of [Olav Bergan] the Norwegian Mayor of Trondheim at his summer home in Röros. At 4 a.m. our host stormed into my room announcing: 'The war against Russia has begun!'

We then settled down to discuss the implications of this declaration of war. I must admit this declaration was not totally unexpected because a few days earlier General Dietl had confided to me in strictest confidence: 'Captain – I am supposed to occupy Murmansk. Captain, this is impossible, even if I had two additional divisions.'

Initially everything seemed to go well. Our troops stormed forward almost to Moscow. However, our men were overextended and the supply lines impossible to maintain. Then we encountered unexpectedly strong resistance and our tanks stalled in an early frost. We had to retreat, leaving behind a few hundred tanks. The Russians followed us precipitously and the situation became extremely critical. However the enemy hordes were halted further west and in the summer of 1942 a new [German] attack began which brought us to the Caucasus and Stalingrad on the lower Volga River. It is said that large troop contingents were destroyed in Stalingrad because of our Allies' inaction. At the beginning of 1943 the city was once again in Russian hands. *I consider the decision not to retreat from Stalingrad the second great irreversible strategic mistake of this war. We should not have sacrificed more than a hundred thousand men in order to hold an untenable position.*

The summer of 1943 was marked by continued and strong Russian attacks. We retreated further and further. Today we are at the Dnieper River and hope to be able to maintain the front... The Russians have called on the Allies to open a 'second front' in Western Europe. The enemy landed successfully in North Africa. They forced us out of that continent. They conquered Sicily, Corsica, and Sardinia and have gotten as far as Naples in southern Italy. This 'second front' consists primarily of the [Allied] air force, which is destroying our cities, particularly their industrial centres. That is what the situation looks like at present, serious – very serious. We are aware that we cannot count on leniency if we give up. There is only one alternative: 'fight or be destroyed'.[892]

The situation had grown increasingly serious on the home front as well. In the fall of 1938 a lump had been discovered in Anne-Marie's breast and the doctors had performed a radical mastectomy along with removal of all of her lymph nodes. She appeared to make a fast recovery, and in the fall of 1939 Rose's concern for his wife's health was overtaken by the outbreak of WWII. Rose left home to take up his military responsibilities. Anne-Marie was left alone with the children.

As 1941 drew to a close Anne-Marie told her children she 'wanted to spend some money before it would be too late'.[893] With the exception of Heinz on active duty, her three remaining children joined her for a skiing vacation in Austria over the Christmas holiday. Upon their return to Essen-Heisingen at the beginning of 1942, Christian recalled:

We heard the air-raid sirens for the first time at night and watched the allied aeroplanes caught in a web of searchlights and being attacked by German anti-aircraft artillery and fighter planes. This experience was followed with ever increasing frequency during the summer and the first firebombs attacks started by year's end.[894]

In April, worried that he would be drafted into the army, Gerd volunteered for the navy. After basic training he was sent to Holland to be trained as skipper of a two-man submarine. He remained posted there until the end of the war.

In September 1942 a wasp sting triggered abnormal swelling in Anne-Marie's left arm. With no interest in food she lost weight and was hospitalized. Rose was granted leave to visit her in November but his request to extend his leave or be transferred to a posting in Germany was denied. Anne-Marie was sure that she would soon get well and they planned a spring trip to southern France or Italy. But she was diagnosed with cancer that had metastasized to her liver and stomach. Rose described the weeks in November spent by her bedside in the hospital:

> I immediately came from Trondheim and spent hours of supernatural exultation at my loving wife's bedside. They will remain unforgettable and sacred for me. We talked a lot about the past and when we first met each other, as well as the year-long separation in 1912/13... We also talked about the children, and exchanged ideas about their development and future, about our hopes and fears for them...
>
> On my arrival at the hospital I would usually whistle a few notes. One time I did not do it because I thought she might be asleep. Yet when I opened the door to her room her smiling face glowed as usual, but then her lovely eyes filled with tears and she said reproachfully: 'You didn't whistle.'
>
> I can only suggest the solemnity of these hours. My request for an extension of my leave was turned down. Brave, as always, Anne accepted the sacrifice. She acceded, as well, because she did not want to make it more difficult for me. It was frightful for me to leave for Norway in the middle of December. However, I had to do my duty, because every leave transgression had to be severely punished and I, as the Sea Commander, had to set an example for the thousands of soldiers that were under my command.[895]

In fact, with his relationship with his immediate superior Admiral Thiele strained, Rose feared court-martial if he disobeyed.[896] For the first time Hans Rose did not spend Christmas with his family.

After her husband's departure Anne-Marie returned home but remained confined to bed. All of her children spent the Christmas holidays with her. Christian, her youngest, was almost thirteen:

> My brothers Heinz and Gerd, and sister Helga were encouraged by my mother to have a party for New Year's Eve 1942 and they did... I got up in the morning about 8 a.m. Everyone was still asleep. I went into my parents' bedroom and found pills all over the place... My mother was in her bed and breathing very heavily. I opened the blinds and left her sleeping. Later the doctor was called and ... the decision was made to leave matters as they were... My mother died 3 January 1943 in the early morning. She never recovered consciousness.[897]

After Anne-Marie's death the mayor of Essen was notified and Hans Rose was flown back to Essen by special plane to participate in the funeral before returning to Trondheim for another five months.

With Anne-Marie's death Rose's request for a posting in Germany became a request to retire.[898] Ostensibly it was to care for his children, though in fact they were now away. Why then did he leave the navy? Had he become disenchanted with a role outside the U-boat campaign? Was he no longer willing to work in the shadow of lesser men without promotion to rear admiral? Had he recognized that victory was impossible? What we know is that without Anne-Marie, Rose had no desire to remain in the navy. She was the Guinevere to his Lancelot. 'A woman knows the face of the man she loves as a sailor knows the open sea.' (Honoré de Balzac.)

After the funeral for their mother, oldest son Heinz, age twenty-two, returned to his posting with the army on the Eastern Front, while second son Gerd, age eighteen, returned to his training as a naval cadet.[899] At the end of March 1943, three months after her mother's death, and four months before her father's return from Trondheim, Rose's twenty-year-old daughter Helga sent thirteen year-old Christian off to a children's evacuation home in Ledce near Prague. It was not a happy place. Helga herself, an enthusiastic and fairly senior member of the Hitler youth, became so traumatized by the incessant bombing that she was evacuated to Hameln on the Weser river to live in the ancestral home there with Rose's maternal aunt Olga Kroseberg.[900]

When Rose returned from Norway he immediately withdrew Christian from the Nazi Youth Home, arranging to send him 430 kilometres south to a prestigious boarding school that was part of the *Schloss Salem* school system.

Then for the remainder of the war Rose became a civilian official working for the government to expedite the production of armaments at firms like Siemens and Krupp. He was based with Siemens in Wuppertal about seventeen kilometres south, commuting by train daily from Essen-Heisingen. With all his children away after September 1943 Rose lived alone at Springloh 32, with an old caretaker couple he had hired in 1940 when he had been commander of the submarine school in Plön.

The 1943 marriage of Rose's daughter to Siegfried Schimanski was not a particularly joyous occasion for her father. Helga was several months pregnant at the time of the wedding, and Rose's comment upon learning that she wanted to marry Schimanski was 'Do you really want to marry such a subaltern personality?'[901] His criticism was rather unfair. Schimanski had wanted to become a naval officer but was instead pushed towards an engineering position below decks. Wanting nothing to do with such a posting Schimanski intentionally flunked the necessary examination, and as a result was classified as a mate. He would serve on a mine sweeper between St. Nazaire and Bordeaux from 1939 to 1944. After the war Schimanski would become a lawyer for the *Bergbau Berufsgenossenschaft*, a professional mining cooperative, having worked himself up from the bottom. In his sixties, Schimanski earned a Ph.D. based upon his work in the Coal Union movement. His work earned him the *Bundesverdienstkreuz*, the Federal Service Cross. Commenting upon her choice, Helga remarked:

It was difficult for father to digest the thought that his own daughter was crossing his wishes. The result was that I went through forty difficult years with my father, and that he refused to acknowledge Schimanski's presence in the 'barracks'. Only our strong marriage and Schimanski's generosity made it possible to survive these divided loyalties.[902]

With Essen wrecked and dangerous, the Roses planned to celebrate the 1944 Christmas holiday at their ancestral home in Hameln. In September 1944, after the summer holidays, Christian returned to school. Things had changed. In the fall of 1944 the Nazi government took over all private schools placing them under SS governance. Christian recalled 'the wonderful Dr. Blendinger was squeezed out and deported to the Upper Gate,'[903] replaced by Dr. Schmidt who the students called 'Alei', short for *Anstalt Leiter*, 'the warden'.

> Much had changed in a very few weeks. Every morning the students, room by room, had to line up in formation, the swastika flag was raised on a newly installed pole and the singing of '*Germany, Germany above all*' became the first order of the day... There was a change in the atmosphere and feeling of the school as though the soul had been ripped out of the school's body... However, we did not wear the Hitler Youth uniform, because the war meltdown prevented the government from supplying any to us... This was very much to the displeasure of the Alei.[904]

It didn't take long for Christian to run foul of the new leadership.

> I remember one day we had a debate in our room about the problem that German war planes were unable to defend the cities from Allied air attacks because there was not enough fuel to get them off the ground. I made the unwise comment that fermentation plants could convert our potatoes into alcohol for airplane fuel. A few weeks later I applied for a railway pass to meet my father and sister for Christmas. When Alei handed me the pass he said: 'Go, don't come back! We do not want boys like you in the New Salem.'[905]

At the end of the Christmas holiday, with his return train trip to school scheduled for the next morning, Christian, afraid how his father might react, had still not broached the warden's order with him. When he did, 'It wasn't five minutes before my father had a telephone discussion with the Alei. I was on the train to Salem the next morning and in my same old bed that evening.[906]

Rose maintained a judgmental, detached, and authoritarian position that alienated him from Helga and Christian. But he defended them.

Perhaps von Stauffenberg Had Been Right

Month after month 1944 brought further military disaster. The Russian juggernaut on the Eastern Front could not be held back, and Heinz became one of 31,700 Germans killed during the Russian Crimean Offensive between 8 April and 12 May 1944. There are few details about Heinz's death. He had joined the army on the ninth day of the war, spurning a safe desk job in Berlin that his linguistic skills and his father's connections could have ensured. But he was the oldest son of a war-hero father, and he volunteered for front-line service in France, Norway, Yugoslavia, Italy and then the Russian front.[907]

With the fortunes of war turned decisively against the Third Reich, dismay in the ranks of Germany's military hierarchy made it fertile ground for the various conspiracies and plots to assassinate Hitler. Four attempts preceded Claus von Stauffenberg's assassination attempt at the Wolf's Lair, in East Prussia. Hearing a radio report about that latest attempt, Christian told his father, who was working in the garden: 'I came rushing out to tell him. His face dropped, he was extremely upset. All he said was "This is the end!" without any further explanation.[908]

Field Marshal Erwin Rommel was implicated in the conspiracy. By far the most popular military leader in Germany, Rommel supported the conspiracy to kill Hitler believing that he must 'come to the rescue of Germany'. Fearing the negative publicity and effect upon morale that the arrest and certain conviction of Rommel would engender, Rommel was given the opportunity to commit suicide by cyanide. When Rose learned of Rommel's death 'his face just dropped.' He had known Rommel personally. The fact that a man held in such high regard had supported assassinating Hitler demonstrated that 'things must be in really terrible shape.'[909] In the last years of WWII, despite his unbending belief in the chain of command, Rose began to wonder whether perhaps von Stauffenberg had been right.[910]

Helga asserts that her father did not give up his idealism until one of the first attempts on Hitler's life in 1944. In the aftermath, he commented to his daughter:

It was a great disappointment for me when the *Kaiser* left Germany after WWI. And now that Hitler has destroyed Germany I feel a similar disappointment. I cannot and do not want to endure any more such disappointments.[774]

Rose never shared his feelings about the death of his brother in the early months of WWI, nor how the death of his eldest son affected him. His only comment relates to Anne-Marie's death the year before: 'Perhaps this was a blessing, since the death of her eldest son would have been too much for her to endure.'[911]

Had his pan-Germanic dreams been fulfilled perhaps he might have thought of these as glorious deaths. But that did not transpire and close to the end of his autobiography Rose observes:

Every one of us was ready to give his best. Destiny set us this task twice. Many of our comrades gave their lives to demonstrate their willingness to sacrifice. Twice we Germans had to lay down our arms after four years of warfare against almost the entire world. Such a destiny is perhaps too much for a single generation to bear.[876]

Rose had been a humanist for whom individuals matter in the evolution of human society and progress. Germany had suffered defeat not only on the battlefield. WWII had laid bare the disastrous consequences of policies of a leader Rose had idealized. Hitler had destroyed his beloved country. Perhaps he could not help but feel that it was all a huge waste, and all these sacrifices made no difference. How could one possibly extol the 'wonderful sacrifice' of lost comrades, children, wives, anything? So he said nothing.

At the end of 1944, with the Allies invading Germany from the east and the west, the local Nazi Party placed Rose in command of Essen-Heisingen's *Volksturm* unit; an armed militia established by the Nazi Party under orders from Adolf Hitler. It was a last-ditch effort to mobilize six million German civilians in the final defence of Germany. Because the *Volksturm* was neither organized, nor commanded by Germany's regular army, Rose considered it an unlawful undertaking, resigned his command, and refused to participate.[912]

As 1945 dawned, the collapse of the German war effort became inevitable. In January American troops broke through the static defences of the Siegfried Line, while on 14 January Russian troops invaded eastern Germany. On 8 February British and Canadian soldiers entered the Reichswald in Germany's North Rhine-Westphalia. A week later, on 15 February, Allied troops reached the Rhine, crossing it on 7 March. By 23 April Russian troops reached Berlin. Two days later, Russian and American troops linked up at the Elbe River and the country was cut in two. Berlin fell on 2 May, and by 8 May Germany was defeated and her war was over.

At the beginning of April, with the Russians closing in, the authorities at *Schloss Salem* closed the school and sent the children home by whatever means they could devise. The previous Christmas, Hans Rose, unsure what would happen to himself, had told his son that in the event of collapse they should all try to 'rendezvous in Hameln'[913] at the ancestral Krosberg family home. By the end of March Christian had had no news of his father for more than a month: '...what had happened in Essen? Was my father still alive? Was he in prison? Or had he been shot by the Allies as Hitler promised they would do to senior German officers?'[914]

Christian was a piece of flotsam in 'a sea of moving people of all ages' with but 'one aim – to get away from the Russians'.[915] His round-about voyage by train and foot via Munich, Dresden, and Brunswick took him about a week. In the final stage of the war, after the strategically meaningless firebombing of Dresden that killed more than 25,000 civilians, trains and train stations were being bombed and he was forced to walk 'for long distances beside the tracks in the hope of finding another shuttle train at the other end'.[916] He had a close shave in the Braunschweig Central Railway Station when a fellow refugee dragged him off the train just before the building was obliterated by Allied bombing.[917] Christian arrived just before the U.S. 117th Infantry Regiment reached the Weser River, where it found the Germans still defending Hameln on the opposite bank. The defenders had blown up the bridges. Christian experienced the city's shelling and the attack that seized the town on 7 April.[918]

On the first morning of the American occupation of Hameln there was a knock on the door. A huge black American soldier, 'over two metres tall, a multitude of watches and bracelets dangling from both his muscular arms, each of his big fingers covered with a number of rings'[919] loomed in the entrance. He was the first black man Christian had ever seen. With his old great-aunt Olga Kroseberg, a cousin and her three small children, and his sister holding her crying baby, they faced the American down. But only inquiring whether there were any German soldiers in the house, the American turned and left.

There was a total curfew. No one was allowed to leave their homes. But starvation was imminent and Christian was forced to scavenge for food. Near town he found a grain barge sunk in the Weser by the withdrawing Germans. Filling a baby carriage with waterlogged grain and tapioca found in the nearby mill, the family lay the grain out in the courtyard of the Krosberg family home to dry and then spent hours pulverizing it by hand with a coffee grinder to make bread. Combined with the tapioca, it provided food for some weeks.[920]

Christian's aunt Olga told the fifteen-year-old boy to take her bicycle to Essen to find his father. Since Rose had never been able to cook, they presumed that he was still living at the family home with the old couple that looked after him.

Travelling illegally by back roads to avoid roadblocks and check points, Christian reached Essen and found his father working in the garden behind the family home.[921] His father looked at him for a long, long while as if he had 'never expected to see any of his family again'.[922] Thereafter Christian stayed with his father in Essen. Sometime between July and October 1945 Gerd join them from his POW camp in Holland. Christian and Gerd found work in the city clearing bricks from bombed-out buildings.[923]

The house was crowded. In August and September 1945, thousands of German refugees had fled from the rape and pillage in the Russian zone in the East. What civic authority remained in Essen-Heisingen ordered that they be housed with the local population. The whole upstairs of the Rose family home in Essen, with its five bedrooms and two bathrooms, was given over to the Eastern refugees. Stovepipes poked out of the bedroom windows. The Roses made do on the first floor. Hans Rose slept in the living room, under a huge Claus Bergen painting of *U 53*, a reminder of that other unsuccessful war.

The Roses used the laundry room in the basement for showers, as the bathrooms above were reserved for the refugees. The old couple and three or four of their relatives lived in servants' quarters in the attic.[924] Between twenty and twenty-four people lived in the house.[925] One of the women could do no more than walk around with a constantly glazed look in her eyes; she had been multiply raped by Russian soldiers. Another was shunned by the other refugees; she had been forced to prostitute herself for food for her family.[926]

In 1958 Rose would write, 'only he will become a good European who is a good German.'[876] In the immediate aftermath of Germany's defeat in 1945 Hans Rose read Christian British author George Warwick Deeping's best-selling novel *Sorrell and Son*. Rose was a nationalist, but he wasn't nationalistic.

In 1945 starvation and the freezing winter cold stalked the Roses. Gerd Noormann, one of Hans Rose's old *U 53* crewmen, arranged to find a milk sheep for his old captain. Son Gerd picked the animal up by train and then walked her eight kilometres back to the family house. They named her Mini. She was a precious resource and had to be guarded from theft at all times. The Roses arranged to have her covered and in the autumn she gave birth to two lambs; one for the owner of the ram and one for the Roses, providing them with fresh meat. Over the next several years Mini, who was milked twice a day by everyone including Hans Rose,[927] provided the Roses with two lambs a year, wool for 'itchy socks'[928] and fertilizer for the garden. Ultimately, she graced the table herself.

To help combat the cold the Roses relied upon the small seam of coal that traversed their back yard. Over the course of 1945-6 the Roses became backyard miners, digging a shaft where they would crawl down to the seam to hack away at the coal. They would continue surreptitiously mining the seam, even after the British occupied their home.[929]

Occupation and Expulsion

Towards noon one day in September 1945 a group of British soldiers arrived at the Rose residence.[930] The British made a list of all the furnishings and belongings in the house, and then announced that the house had been requisitioned for use by the British Governor of the German coal industry and his family. The Rose family and the other occupants of the house were given four hours to vacate the premises, ordered to take only their personal clothes with them.

Fortunately, the British neglected to itemize the contents of the attic, where many of the Rose family belongings had been stored to make room for the Eastern refugees. Working like demons, Christian, Gerd, and their father Hans Rose moved everything they could from the house to a hidden location in the back yard garden. Paintings hanging on the walls, including those by Claus Bergen, were replaced with prints. Good furniture and carpets were replaced by less valuable pieces. The family silver was secured. A considerable number of belongings were surreptitiously removed. Christian recalled never having worked so hard in his life.[931] The Rose family home would only be returned to them in 1952.

In the five years following the expulsion Hans Rose and sons Gerd and Christian successively lived in three different locations. In the winter of 1945/46 they were homeless and spent a very miserable time.[932] Christian recalls:

> My brother and I moved into an unfinished room with big windows but without any glass, no floor and unfinished walls, no electricity. My father was put into a small summer garden cottage with an outhouse, no bath, but one small room with a bed, table dresser and two chairs; luckily it had a small kitchen with a working water tap. The house keeper got a room in the village... We all met in the cottage during the day and disbursed at night.[933]

They did whatever they could to survive. Christian surreptitiously tapped into a power line to steal electricity.[934] Cousins from Niagara Falls in America helped, sending them care packages whose contents were eked out over weeks.[935]

The second location was a small two-room bungalow the Roses built on a tiny lot in the spring of 1946. The three men scavenged materials from a war-damaged army barracks between Witten and Hagen. Rose purchased it by selling the family silver and some valuable carpets. With postwar inflation between 1945 and 1947 running 7 marks for a single cigarette, 100 marks for a pound of butter, non-essentials like Rose's fine carpet only garnered 500 marks.[936] Around the cabin, they grew turnips, carrots, beets, and peas, which Mini fertilized.[937]

The men also used some of the panels from the barracks to fix up a small summer garden cottage located on one of the other plots. Referred to as 'the barracks', Rose would live in this third location from 1947 until his retirement in 1950.

Conditions were difficult for the three men living in the barracks. Hans Rose, now sixty-two, was working as hard as his sons. He was emaciated and weighed perhaps ninety pounds. Nonetheless, throughout this period, Rose maintained the credo that had guided him throughout his life; first to survive himself, then to ensure the survival of his family (and the house-keeper), and finally, to help those in the community around him. Conditions were so bad that he had little energy or resources to expend outside of his family. Christian found that this period in 1946 and 1947 marked the first time that his father treated his sons as equals.[938]

This new-found equality is a telling reflection of Rose's struggle for survival and the transformation it imposed upon him. Rose's sense of duty kept him sane throughout his life and particularly during the two periods of collapse: duty to *Volk*, to family, to community, to the nation, to the navy. He lived his life by the motto to which he pledged himself and his fiancée in August 1912: 'forever undaunted'.[404] But the defeats and the raw struggle for individual survival after the war caused him to shed some of his command style and build a new relationship with his sons.

With economic shock treatment, conditions had begun to improve by the autumn of 1948. It was the time of the 'return to normality'.[939] Reich Marks were exchanged for the new Deutsche Marks at a rate of 10 to 1, wiping out any savings Germany's middle class still possessed. In the western zones everyone was given forty Marks and required to declare all real-estate. In the initial conversion 90% went to the state while the original owners retained 10%. They had five years to buy back 51% of their own properties to regain full possession. Hans Rose would sell off a considerable portion of his assets to secure his core properties.[940]

As normalcy gradually returned, intellectual pursuits could be revived. Christian recalled renewed conversations about Goethe, Schiller and Thomas Mann. Hans Rose rejoined *ETUF*, the Essen Gymnastics and Fencing Club, whose patron, Gustav Krupp the armament baron, he knew personally. Since Rose was now not only a leading citizen of Essen and a national war hero but had also been a past captain of one of Krupp's own U-boats, Rose became an occasional visitor to Krupp's huge *Villa Hügel* home outside of Essen. At home, as 'a diversion from the struggle to survive',[941] Rose began his ultimately unsuccessful quest to redesign the family's heraldic crest.

Hans Rose's children were now all adults and pursuing their own lives. Helga had married Schimanski. Gerd was pursuing a degree in architecture at the Karlsruhe Technical Institute.[942] And Christian, now eighteen, had moved out of the family home to live on his own in town: 'My father decided that I was not academic and therefore should go into a trade. I was signed up as a textile apprentice at Cramer & Meermann in Essen.'[943]

Four years later, a day after his twenty-second birthday, Christian emigrated to Canada. The night before he left Winterberg, his father counseled him: 'Son, before you get on the ship make sure you have a full belly and keep it full until you get off.'[944]

Rose's Second Family

In 1948, Hans Rose, now living alone with his housekeeper, began the search for a second wife. Once again, he was very particular regarding the social implications of his choice. A first candidate from the von Raishop family did not ultimately meet his approval. And Rose called off relations with a second woman when, after asking his son Christian's opinion, the latter found her and her son unsatisfactory. Christian recalls that his father was 'not asking permission, he was asking for my opinion, asking for my acquiescence. My father was very democratic.'[945]

Professionally and militarily, Hans Rose kept his distance; the importance of rank and discipline being self-evident. Social roles were to be maintained. But when it came to his family and to his friends, Hans Rose had become both much more inclusive and more democratic. Stepson Rudolf Brickenstein asserts: 'Rose was not a democrat before WWII. He became a democrat after the war.'[946]

While staying on holiday at a pension in Winterberg, Rose renewed an old friendship with the Brügmann family. It was not the first time that Rose had met Theodora Brügmann Brickenstein. While he and Anne-Marie were vacationing at the house of a local forester in January 1918, they visited *Hubertushof*, signed the family register and met Theodora, then only thirteen years old. Years later, Theodora would tell her son Hans-Joachim that as a young girl, she was very impressed by 'the former naval hero and *Pour le Mérite* recipient Hans Rose'.[947]

On 29 January 1949, almost exactly six years after the death of his first wife Anne-Marie, Hans Rose, sixty-three, married his second wife Theodora. Known to her family as 'Mutti' and to Rose as 'Dorle' and 'Dorchen',[948] Theodora was forty-four. She was an intelligent, well-educated widow almost twenty years his junior who had first married in 1923 when she was eighteen. At a stroke, Rose embraced a second family comprised of the five of Theodora's six children who survived the war that had also claimed her first husband Rudolf Brickenstein. Over time the couple developed a deep respect for each other and spent the remaining twenty years of his life peacefully together. Hans-Joachim was convinced that in the end the relationship between Theodora and Hans Rose was a romance.

In the early years of their marriage times remained lean. It was a challenge just to find sufficient food. For their marriage, Theodora had to take in Rose's suit with safety pins. For much of the first year of their marriage, until his retirement in 1950, Rose lived in the 'barracks' in Essen, and only saw his wife on the weekends. When he visited her, they would hole up in a single small room in *Hubertushof*, heated with a coal stove.

Germany's population was resilient; stepson Peter Brickenstein:

> With the fruits of the year's investments they built a tile stove to heat the entire house. Rose couldn't stand the noise the workman was making and insisted on moving out. So, it being winter, Mutti found him a room in a hotel five hundred metres away. One day walking along to the hotel with Mutti he slipped and fell into the gutter. The Winterbergers asked Mutti whether she was trying to get rid of her husband after so short a time.[949]

Setting aside the everyday realities, Theodora and Rose reinstituted the *Hubertushof* reading circle to stimulate themselves intellectually. It had been this reading group that had first brought Hans Rose to *Hubertushof* at the end of WWI.[950]

In school during the decade following the war the Brickenstein children were shown movies about the concentration camps. They came home to talk about it with their parents and they asked Hans Rose, 'How could you allow this to happen?' Rose replied, 'We thought they were only work camps.'[951] He went on to explain that of course there had been no reporting, and that they had been part of the segment of society whose privileges cut them off completely from the realities. Hans-Joachim recalled: 'Hans Rose told us to open our eyes and face the realities of the world.'[952]

In September 2007 the authors had the good fortune to be able to visit and interview Hans Rose's three surviving stepchildren, Rudolf, Peter and Hans-Joachim, at the beautiful family manor, *Hubertushof*, in Winterberg, nestled in the North Rhine-Westphalia mountains. The interviews demonstrated a mature appreciation of their stepfather.

Rudolf recalled Rose's attitude towards fear; telling his stepson: 'Fear opens your mind. Fear helps you see clearly. The man that does not have fear is stupid... I've soiled my pants in dangerous situations.'[953]

Peter commented: 'Hans Rose knew how to tell a risqué story. He was after all a sailor. But he had the gift of knowing exactly where the line was between risqué and unacceptable.'[954]

Hans-Joachim recalled: 'Rose was as true a gentleman as you can find. A woman responds to that. [But] my mother was used to making her own decisions. So there were of course the occasional conflicts.'[955]

Hans-Joachim, the youngest and only nine when Hans Rose married his mother, recalled that it was his stepfather's belief that inculcating the young with ideals was a question of survival: 'What you learned from the old generation is not the rights that you have, but your duties.'[956]

Despite their advanced years, all three men, the youngest then sixty-seven years old, the oldest seventy-eight, all used the fond diminutive '*Väterchen*', meaning 'daddy', whenever they spoke of Hans Rose. In 2014 grandson Andreas recalled 'I can remember him only as a white-haired, but very impressive man. Impressive but not frightening!'[957] Peter was left with a similar impression:

> Rose was very strict with us... I was eleven when my mother married Hans Rose. Hans-Joachim was nine. Our mother asked us if we would approve. We said 'absolutely not' but he won us over by the strength of his character.[958]

Rose appears to have been a substantially different sort of father with his second family; much more engaged with his stepchildren. Hans-Joachim Brickenstein revered his birth father but was surprised at how solicitous this second father, Hans Rose, was: 'In those days one didn't let one's children look into one's personal affairs ... [yet] Rose was such a nice man.[959]

Rose actively supported his stepsons in school. On one occasion a pin awarded Hans-Joachim was taken away without explanation. In the Spating School students learned how to command by punishing the lower class men. Hans-Joachim surmised that the pin was taken away because he had somehow stood up against some upper classman's misdeed. He wrote to his stepfather in Winterberg from the school in northern Germany. In short order Hans Rose arrived at the school and spoke with the director, who was a minister. Years later Rose told Hans-Joachim: 'It wasn't a very comfortable conversation for the director.'[960] The pin was re-awarded to Hans-Joachim several days after Rose left.

Peter Brickenstein recalled:

> Once I got knocked on the nose by the director of my school. He bloodied my nose. He didn't like me and I didn't like him. Hans Rose went to see the director at the school, grabbed him by the front, lifted him off his feet and said 'never again!'[961]

When the authors shared their transcripts of the stepchildren's interviews with Rose's birth son Christian, he commented:

> It seems that my father was two fathers – one for his real family and an entirely other father for his second family. Of course the times and the circumstance had changed drastically during his life-time.[962]

The times and circumstances had changed, but so too had the man. Rose had been able to recalibrate his parenting to be less authoritarian and more empathetic. As mature adults all three of Rose's stepchildren demonstrated an abiding appreciation of and love for their stepfather, while both Helga and Christian maintained more ambivalent feelings about him. Hans Rose seems to have been unable to find the language necessary to transform his relationships with them. In 1958 Rose sent Christian a reworked speech by General Admiral Herman Boehm, telling his son that 'the speech provides a glimpse of how we "old people" think.'[963]

Rose considered the speech, 'What We Learned From the Sea', so important that he intended ending his autobiography with it. Destined for members of the German Navy, it is near Arthurian in its articulation of Rose's chivalric code of honour, and lists the duties that bound him and his crewmates together:

> Reciprocal CONSIDERATION was one of the first duties which the sea taught us. I believe there is only one other profession which provides the same kind of training: that of the collier, the miner deep under the earth...
>
> HELPFULNESS, COURAGE, PRUDENCE and DETERMINATION were needed. All of these the sea taught us...
>
> CHARACTER is built through the storms of the world, as the sea has taught us.
>
> ... [nautical] tender training was essential for developing a SENSE OF RESPONSIBILITY.
>
> ... the sea not only taught us active WILL POWER, and sparkling LOVE OF LIFE, we also learned to submit to the command of those senior to us, though not without silent grumbling. OBEDIENCE too, we learned from the sea.
>
> ... that the subordinate looks up to his superior, that he gladly accepts him as something higher. As such he wants to admire him. The superior, however, must in turn be more knowledgeable and be more ACCOMPLISHED all around. COMPOSURE too, we learned from the sea...
>
> Over and over again we faced new challenges and new problems. Over and over again we had to learn to adapt. How our understanding broadened in the interaction with foreigners and foreign cultures. We learned to appreciate them, we learned that all events can be interpreted from different points of view. We learned to include foreign reactions, viewpoints, to develop a fuller understanding of the world around us. The sea taught us JUDGMENT...
>
> The sea also taught us REVERENCE. Reverence growing out of the realization of the limits of our knowledge, as well as our capabilities. The deeper we felt, the more serious and prudent we became. For this too, thank you, surging sea.
>
> ... through the grace and rigour of the sea we grew into what Goethe considered the highest good of mankind – the sea developed our human PERSONALITY.[876]

The language used is Rose's language; one who fails to see the world through the eyes of his son, and so remains inaccessible to him. Honour makes a poor father if not tempered by understanding and a willingness to instruct children why honour is important and how day-by-day one personifies these romantically articulated concepts. Hans Rose had changed his view on parenting by learning from his mistakes. But he was unable to articulate this important change in himself to Christian in order to help heal the rupture with his son. Tragically for Christian, who always felt that his father had marginalized him, the transformation of his father into a more loving and nurturing parent for his second family seems only to have rubbed more salt into the wound.

As the 1950s advanced and Hans Rose entered the eighth decade of his life, his routine settled into a peaceful family life and the social affairs of a retired war hero. He became a German elder statesman. He participated in the annual meetings of the *Ordre Pour le Mérite* holders. There were visits to such pillars of German society as Gustav Krupp and Frederick Augustus III of the house of Hohenzollern. For years, ever the sailor, Rose remained an active member of the *Baldeneyseeverein ETUF* sailing squadron in Essen. His first love remained the navy, and as long as he lived, he was a member of the German Navy Federation and honorary member of the Navy Federation Essen 188. He also remained active within the Naval Officers Association and the Naval Officer's Mess, Essen. Old naval friends and colleagues were frequent visitors to *Hubertushof*.

In the 1950s Hans Rose devoted considerable attention to preparing his autobiography, creating several short versions and a number of substantial chapters for a major work. But he never finished the longer version. Rose it seems had lost the need to polish his reputation and define his place in history. At the same time, nowhere in his copious writing will one find any sort of introspection or judgement about his role, nor of his beliefs, even though his life experience caused him to modify many of them over time.

His stepsons would remember that Rose got up unbelievably early in the morning to mow the lawn, frequently dressed in nothing more suitable than his undershirt tucked into his long underwear, and a pair of shorts over everything. Mutti was not amused. But as Peter pointed out, 'he was able to laugh at himself.'[964] Rose's love for garden work remained. Once, eager to disassemble all the pathways around the house and build new ones on the steep slopes, he fell down with a wheelbarrow full of stones. Peter found him, and Rose warned him 'Never tell Mutti.'[965]

Rose made wine in the basement out of currants (cassis), which turned out quite sour. But after his death the family opened a bottle and found it had aged to a sweet liqueur. To the end of his days, Rose adored eating oysters with fine wines, often consuming a dozen at a sitting. He had Wehr & Karl August Immich, who had vineyards, send him crates of wines.

Rose remained chivalrous around women. Peter remembered that 'You couldn't imagine an occasion when he didn't stand up, kiss the lady's hand, and open the door for her.'[966] To tweak Mutti's nose, Rose would tip his hat in front of the hat shop.

Regardless of status, everyone was equally welcome in the house. Whether the guest was General Admiral Boehm or boatswain Geoden, all were treated with the same politeness.

At the same time he remained patrician. In the mid-1960s, shortly after the birth of his grandson Nicholas, Hans Rose made one of only two visits to Christian's family in Canada. Christian's wife, Margaret, was sent out to buy a bottle of wine. At dinner he raised the wine glass to his nose, inhaled the aroma of the wine, set the glass down on the table and pointedly pushed it away from his place setting – it was not adequate.

Rose enjoyed telling jokes. Among his favourites, an anti-fascist one:

Hitler, Göring & Goebbels are driving by a farm and run over the farmer's dog. The three men decide that someone must go tell the farmer that they have killed his dog. Neither Hitler, nor Göring are too enthusiastic about the job. Finally, Goebbels says that he'll do it. He walks in to the farm house and in no time walks out again, saying that everything is all right. Hitler and Göring are astonished and ask him how he did it. It was simple he says, 'I walked in and said "*Heil Hitler – der Hund ist tod*" [*Heil* Hitler! The dog is dead] and the farmer went "Hallelujah" and thanked me.'[967]

As he became older Rose became very cautious with his money. He had a trust fund set up after his death called 'Greetings from Valhalla'. It was something to remember him by.

In his mid-seventies, Rose made a trip to Bretagne in north-western France. The romantic in the man, and his fascination with all things harkening back to the age of the free-roaming Viking warrior race, found renewed, peaceful expression:

I have always craved the opportunity to actually visit the mysterious Brittany. That was only recently possible. I took away with me two indelible impressions of this strange country: first the menhirs, of which more than a thousand rise to the heavens near Carnac...

The second was the incessant murmuring and whispering. The whole country is dreamy and quaint as are sagas, dreams and remembrances. They find their pictorial expressions in the five point star, the Druid's foot, the Gothic pentagram.[968]

In 1964, the year before Friedrich Wilhelm, the latest Prince of the House of Hohenzollern died, Rose combined that memory with his appreciation of the proper order of things. Having created a small carpet 'depicting the menhirs in the morning glow, while above them, the five point star pours its light over the heavens', he presented it to the Prince with the statement:

As long as I can remember, I have tried to loyally fulfil my duty to the fatherland. Repeatedly, destiny has brought me into contact with the House of Hohenzollern. I was always treated uncommonly kindly. I have therefore decided to lay this carpet at your feet in the true sense of the term, as a sign of my ongoing thankfulness. Please cast a glance on it occasionally. May it bring you and your house everlasting luck. That is my heart's desire.[969]

Rose's loyalty and abiding respect for the monarchy, however anachronistic, remained steadfast. It was the gesture of a Samurai for his lord.

Chapter 25
Coda

Leaving a salutation in *U 53*'s Guest Book, 15 April 1918, Franz Krapohl wrote:

> Some day when the bells of freedom once more ring out across free German territory, when German ships again sail to the remotest shore ... your name will be praised in glory. You of undaunted courage, in night and day, in storm and bad weather, sank the enemy's goods and armour. By helping smash the strangling iron ring placed 'round the German heart' you've erected your eternal monument within the German nation.
>
> The student for his venerable master[970]

On 6 December 1969, St. Nicholas Day, at the age of 84, fifty-two years to the day after Hans Rose sank the American destroyer *Jacob Jones*, he passed away asleep in his bed in the family home, *Hubertushof*.

Hans Rose would have approved of his own funeral; it was almost a state affair. The casket with its honour guard of four officers of the *Bundesmarine*, the two cadets holding displays of his medals, the adoring soliloquies from fellow veterans, all these were a fitting farewell to a great and gallant warrior, an icon of the best tradition of the German military.

FUNERAL OF HANS ROSE December 1969. [Rose Family Archive]

Representing the Federal Defence Ministry, retired submariner *Fregattenkapitän*, Commander Gerhard Glattes declared:

> I say goodbye to Captain Rose in the name of those who once wore the blue uniform and who were closely connected to him in the fifty years since WWI.
>
> To all of us, Hans Rose always was a paragon, a motivation, and a good comrade, who was there for each and every one of us. He gave us much through his enthusiasm for the Navy and his deployment, wherever this was necessary. We take leave from him with many thanks.[971]

Representing The knighthood of the Order of *Pour le Mérite*, Captain z. See a.D. Walther Forstmann, the second most successful U-boat Ace of WWI, bade farewell to his comrade-in-arms:

> Hans Rose exemplified the authentic soldier's existence, by always setting himself the highest standards.
>
> In no career is the power of character of more importance than in that of the soldier. Hans Rose had long-term commands on torpedo- and U-boats. Here the Commander lived in close proximity with his crew and acquired an authoritative reputation through mastery, performance and exemplary leadership. [Quoting Rose] 'I always let the men know that I depended on them, and that they could depend on me. We were one large family. Authority does not develop out of nothing. It does not depend on "gold braid".'...
>
> We the Knights of the Order of *Pour le Mérite*, take leave with the promise that we will keep him in our comradely memory. For it is indeed true to say: 'I had a wonderful comrade, there is no better.'[972]

Finally, addressing those grieving at the Mourning Hall of the Essen Honour Cemetery, Rear Admiral Hermann Boehm, fellow crew-mate from the class of 1903 and supreme commander of the German Navy in occupied Norway, concluded:

> Today, we his comrades and friends are in deep sorrow over the loss of Hans Rose – but a proud sorrow. Proud because he was one of us, one of the best in terms of character and mastery, including such virtues as preparedness; courage; a chivalrous attitude in warfare; exemplary fellowship and warm humanity. 'You will not find a better one' as the song of the 'Good Comrade' puts it.
>
> As a fitting epitaph for Hans Rose's life, I would like to close my remarks by quoting Freiherr von Stein: 'Because death is inevitable, we should be brave!' Valour determined his life, his actions in war, as well as his attitudes towards survival and life's purpose. We, his comrades and friends will retain his image in our hearts, as long as our old hearts continue beating.[973]

Hans Rose – Contemporary Knight

Hans Rose, member of the crew of 1903, served the German Navy honourably in both World Wars. His undeniable skill, determination, bravery, aggressiveness, and tactical intelligence were complemented by sheer good luck which allowed him to survive the vicissitudes of war. He wielded his considerable martial talents with a chivalrous determination to extract what decency is possible in time of war. This made him a formidable warrior, the fifth most successful U-boat ace of WWI, and its foremost ace during the convoy period. At the same time it earned him the admiration of friend and foe alike. Both as a military teacher and a front-line commander Rose was the personification of the German military doctrine of *Auftragstaktik*. There is no doubt that Rose deserved his reputation for 'gallantry and daring'.[974]

By temperament a somewhat aloof patrician with an idealistic, romantic, and sentimental view of life, his public persona was motivated both by a sense of *noblesse oblige* and the gift of a certain theatricality. He saw himself as a modern German knight, and he relished and enthusiastically embraced his role as a commander of men, and later his public role as a national hero. He acted both out behind a modest facade that hid a considerable aggressiveness. He was well served by his gifts as an actor and speaker. His sense of service as well as his gifts as a teacher, albeit somewhat paternalistic, of the men under his command, motivated both his public and private persona. This sense of service drove his perception of family, civic duty and his gallantry towards women, made him a respected member of his community, and ultimately defined his view of what it meant to be German.

Philosophically Rose was a Social Darwinist with a 'profound consciousness of rights and equality above all'. Politically he was a pan-Germanic narrow nationalist with idealist social democratic standards. The combination of his 'my country right or wrong' nationalism and romantic idealism, his authoritarian temperament and choice of a military career, clouded his judgement and facilitated his flirtation with fascism during the interwar period, especially prior to *Kristallnacht* in 1938. It also allowed him, for a time, to place his considerable prestige and leadership ability in the service of a regime that ultimately espoused social ideals antithetical to his own and profoundly destructive to the nation he so loved. While he privately abhorred and condemned anti-semitism, on at least two occasions between 1934 and 1938, at a time when the Nazis were consolidating their police state, Rose courageously opposed the machinations of the *Marine SA* against the German church and denounced attacks upon friends and colleagues.

Prior to 1939 Rose was swept up by the populist nationalism of the Nazi Party and its programs, which restored economic prosperity to Germany. After *Kristallnacht* Rose, while ever bound to follow the orders of his leaders, nonetheless surreptitiously distanced himself from its worst manifestations in a period of descent into the police state. But it was only towards the end of WWII that he lost all confidence in Nazism. Still, though he embraced much of the populist Nazi platform, and remained an ardent and narrow nationalist through most of the war, his actions while in uniform were decidedly un-Nazi. This is especially the case during the three years that he was Sea Commander in occupied Norway, where, somewhat insulated by his role as a senior naval officer, he was able to keep the Gestapo and the SS at arm's-length.

Despite his philosophical shortcomings Hans Rose was, in the best sense of the word, a knight, who served his beloved navy and country with tremendous honour and distinction.

In 1958, Rose, ever the sailor, wondered:

> Is it presumptuous to ask in retrospect whether the sea is angry with us? Too late –
> we have to live with our destiny. We must not despair, or lose our belief in Germany's
> and Europe's future. The purpose of our erstwhile profession was to protect the life
> of our nation, if necessary by bearing arms. This purpose has now passed from our
> generation. What remains for us to do is a more modest task: to help the younger
> generation not only in crafting their own livelihood, but also to convey those
> soldierly values that remain unchanged even though they may take on new forms.[876]

Rose took up the mantle of knighthood and with it a romantic, idealistic
and archaic understanding of human interactions and the nature of conflicts
and conflict resolution. His sense of duty, honour, perseverance and strength
of character gave him the capacity to survive forty of the most difficult
years demanded of any generation. Yet he paid a price. His credo made him
undeniably successful as a warrior but its inflexibility became a barrier to
success in the fluid environment of civilian business and occasionally even in
the military. His perception of always acting from a position of moral probity
allowed him to rationalize an authoritarian command style which was neither
nurturing nor effective in his first family. The very high standards he set for
himself also exacted an emotional toll in depression and self-doubt.

Becoming a truly modern knight required learning how to bow to context,
becoming a more modern man; less patrician, less judgmental, less patronizing.
It required shedding some ideas of hierarchy. Doing so requires self-awareness;
a gift Rose only exhibited when he changed the way he interacted with his
second family. Rose appears to have been unaware of just how rigid he was.
Greater empathy would have made him less of a loner.

Deep losses often make one more human – if they don't drive you mad. Rose had
enough strength of character not to be destroyed both by what he lived through and
the failure and loss of so much that he believed in and loved. At the conclusion of
his autobiography, Rose returned once again to Goethe, quoting the poem *Tasso*:

> Hope springs eternal,
> And in all situations hope is better than despair.
> For who can calculate what is possible?[876]

The month before he died, physically weak, but mentally lucid,[975] Rose
requested that his far-flung family join him one last time under one roof. The
family, including Christian and all his family from Canada, gathered around at
Hubertushof to be with him in the days preceding his death.

That year the world had been riveted by news of the Apollo moon missions.
Christian was excited to share the latest news with his father. Pete Conrad and
Alan Bean had just made man's second successful landing on the moon. His
father thought about it, but did not share his son's enthusiasm, commenting
'this is beyond the confines of my time.'[976] For Hans Rose the romantic, the
moon was not a thing to be conquered. The moon was in the realm of the Gods
and Man had not walked upon it, he had trampled there.

Appendix – Stepping Aboard *U 53*

U 53 IN HARBOUR (probably Kiel or Wilhelmshaven). Note the towing cable shackled to the side of the hull to port of the conning tower. [Bibliothek für Zeitgeschichte Stuttgart]

Hans Rose's *U 53* was one of six submarines, *U 51* to *U 56*, of common design built by the *Germaniawerft* shipyard in Kiel. The *U51*-class boats represented state-of-the-art in U-boat technology at the start of WWI. These six submersibles measured 65.2m (213ft 11in) long. On the surface they displaced 715 tons and required 3.6m (11ft 10in) of draught, while submerged with their ballast tanks full, they displaced 902 tons. They could safely submerge to a depth of 50 metres (164 feet.)

For weeks at a time these U-boats would be home to crews of thirty-five men. A pressure hull protected the living space. It was divided into a row of five watertight compartments, each with its own emergency air supply.[977] Midship, the control station with the conning tower above, and the control room (the *Zentrale*) below comprised watertight compartment *Three*. Watertight compartment *Five* (in the boat's stern) and compartment *One* (closest to

MAN DIESEL TYPE S6V 45-42 NON-EXHAUST-SIDE When powering the U51-class boats this side of the motor faced the central corridor. The boats were equipped with mirrored pairs. [MANroland AG, VMM/Rolle, Museum und Historisches Archiv]

the bow) were the two torpedo chambers. Immediately aft of the conning tower, in watertight compartment *Four* were two chambers; the forward one housing the diesel engines, the aft chamber the great electric motors. The primary living quarters of the crew were located just forward of the conning tower in watertight compartment *Two* although some crewmen bunked in the torpedo chambers. The bank of 210 enormous batteries was located below deck in compartment *Two*.

To optimize their surface sea-keeping qualities, the boats were double-hulled and their outer hulls resembled the hull of a surface ship with its sharp tapered bow and more rounded stern. The boat's graceful 'whaleback' hull shape was formed from the fuel bunkers and diving tanks which sandwiched the central pressure hull to starboard and port and gave the U-boat its full 6.44 m (21ft 2in) beam.

Abaft, between and just aft of the boat's two bronze propellers was the ship's vertical rudder. Attached to the diving tanks, two on each side, a pair close to the bow and the other pair close to the stern, were the hydroplanes (the horizontal diving rudders), which drove the U-boat to the depths and brought her to the surface again.

An almost flat deck inboard of the boat's whaleback was nearly fifty metres long, providing 'a large area for work and recreation'.[978] At the bow it sheered upwards slightly to better slice through the water. Along the centre-line of the deck, one for each of the watertight compartments *One*, *Two*, *Four* and *Five* were four hatchways.

A permanent fore and aft antenna for the radio was rigged from bow to stern, rising over the top of the conning tower and above the periscopes when in their lowered positions. This antenna structure served the additional purpose of protecting the guns, conning tower and periscopes of floating obstructions, mines or nets encountered when running submerged. When the U-boat did not have to be ready for a crash dive it was possible to extend the receiving range of the U-boat's radio telephony to 2000 miles[979] by raising a pair of radio masts mounted outboard.

Armament

Permanently mounted on deck were two guns, one forward and one aft. Along with torpedoes, and hand-set explosive charges, they comprised the U-boat's armament. The *U51*-class boats were rated to carry eight 50 cm. (19.685in) torpedoes.[980] Torpedoes were an extremely sophisticated and expensive weapon. At the beginning of the war a single torpedo cost about 40,000 Goldmarks. At that time, the annual pay for a Leutnant zur See like Hans Rose was 900 Goldmarks, while Grand Admiral von Tirpitz drew a salary of 30,000 Goldmarks.[981] When he could, Hans Rose, sank his targets using other means.

- 1 burned to the waterline
- 15 sunk with explosive charges
- 33 sunk by 10.5 cm. shells
- 50 sunk by torpedo

'The Iron World Around Us'

The U-boat's conning tower was forged from Friedrich Krupp's nickel steel. To protect against enemy artillery, the bridge platform walls were about 75 mm (3in) thick. The upper portion of the conning tower 'shaped like a chariot'[982] with its' high forward part acting as a shield from wind and spray rose only 2.82 m (9ft 4in) above deck. In heavy weather, if the lookouts weren't attached to the tower with cables, they could be washed overboard and lost. In addition, the relatively low height of the conning tower permitted the lookouts a relatively short vision horizon of 6.25 km (3.88 miles.)

Three periscopes protruded from the conning tower superstructure. The principal periscope to the rear, used during submerged attacks, was fitted with a second six magnification eye-piece adjusted by a lever on the outside of the tube. When the U-boat was surfaced it could be used to extend the submarine's vision horizon to about 10.73 km (6.66 miles.) The second periscope atop the conning tower, having its centre of field of vision in the zenith, was used primarily to look for aircraft.[983] The third periscope was set at the forward end of the conning tower leading to the control room, and was auxiliary, for the use principally by the Chief Engineer.

Crewmen reached the conning tower from the deck by climbing up a steel-rung ladder at its rear from the main deck to the *oberdeck*. The bridge platform, with ample space for a half-dozen men, was shaped roughly like a horse-shoe, with its prongs facing backward around a raised central dais containing the circular hatch at its forward end, and ventilation, air-intake and exhaust manifold behind it. The rear of the conning tower was open, protected only by a steel hand-rail under which the men ducked when mounting the conning tower from the deck. Forward of the chariot-like protective coaming, on the exposed top of the forward portion of the conning tower a ship's wheel permitted steering outside under calm conditions.

Because of the U-boat's low freeboard, the only access to the submersible kept open in anything but the calmest seas was the circular hatch in the top of the conning tower. Climbing through the hatch and entering the conning tower, crewmen descended eight iron rungs at the rear of the cramped control station above the control room. Three men had their stations here. At the forward end of the control station the helmsman stood at the second of the boat's three wheels directly below the one outside. His only direct line of sight for navigation was provided by six small heavy glass viewports paired forward and aft, and singly to port and starboard. Directly behind him, if necessary, a crewman could stand at the secondary periscope. Typically this space 'was occupied by the 1st Officer in charge of diving controls, torpedo firing controls and telegraphs to the engine room.'[984] The station for the Captain at the primary periscope was directly behind that of the secondary periscope. The Captain stood on a platform that raised and lowered automatically with the periscope. This made it considerably more comfortable to use than the secondary periscope since the primary periscope's eye-piece was always at the same height relative to the platform the Captain stood on.

Located directly behind the radio compartment, the captain's 'office' was an equally small three-sided space comprised of a desk, seat, and lockers for navigational instruments, charts, and a small library. It was open to the central passage. Across the central corridor, on the boat's port side was the Captain's bunk. Together they comprised the Captain's 'cabin', the privacy of which was secured at either end by nothing more than curtains that stretched across the central corridor. The next room forward was the officer's wardroom; a relatively large chamber with three 0.46m- (18in)-wide berths for officers and guests. A temporary central table could be set up where the U-boat's central corridor bisected the chamber. Bergen described it as 'small but cosy, with its homelike wooden panelling, in such refreshing contrast to the iron world around us'.[985]

A small door closed the wardroom off from the rest of the boat forward. Beyond it, on the port side, two lavatories separated the officer's wardroom from the additional crew quarters in the forward section of compartment *Two*. The larger 'Water Cabinet' (WC), reserved for the officers, was 'nicely fitted'.[986] Located across from them, on the starboard side of the boat, was the electric galley with an electric range, coppers, cooking utensils and a freshwater pump. The crew space forward of the galley and the lavatories was divided into two sections separated by a door. The section closer to the *Zentrale* was reserved for deck officers and like the marginally larger wardroom held three bunks and a temporary central table amidships. The second section closer to the boat's bow contained double bunks for eight crewmen but no table. Lockers for each crewman were located below the lower bunks. The upper iron-framed bunks folded flush against the wall when not in use.

Between the galley and lavatories in compartment *Two*, a steel-runged ladder led from the escape chamber up to the forward access hatch sandwiched between two small storage closets.

The remainder of the crew bunked in two bunks right astern in watertight compartment *Five*, and in four bunks forward in the fo'c's'le in watertight compartment *One*. Their quarters were extremely cramped. There were twenty-one bunks in the U-boat. Fourteen of them were reserved for crewmen, seven for officers or senior ratings. Since the latter had their own bunks, twenty-eight members of the crew had to share the remaining fourteen bunks or used hammocks.

Propulsion

The engine rooms of the U51-class boats were located in watertight compartment *Four* immediately aft of the control room. Each of the U-boat's two power trains was comprised of a diesel motor, electric motor, high pressure air compressor, drive shaft, and the propeller. The room directly behind the control room housed the U-boat's two six-cylinder, four-cycle 1,200 hp MAN diesel engines.

The diesels could drive the boat to a top speed of 17.1 knots on the surface. With a fuel capacity of 103 tons, and operating at an economical speed of 8 knots, they gave the U-boat a theoretical range of 9,400 nautical miles. They could also drive the electric motors as generators to recharge the huge battery bank below the floor boards in compartment *Two*. Telegraph controls from the control room dictated five speeds forward and three reverse.

When the diesels were disengaged, the power train was driven by the electric motors located behind a rectangular door in the bulkhead that divided compartment *Four*. Powered by the 210-unit battery bank, these two 600 hp. electric motors could drive the U-boat to a top speed of 9.1 knots submerged. At a more economical 5 knots, this gave the U-boat a submerged range of 55 nautical miles.

Sources and Bibliography

[ACR] "278th Armored Cavalry Regiment." Wikipedia. Wikimedia Foundation, 20 Jan. 2014. Web. 29 Jan. 2014. <http://en.wikipedia.org/wiki/278th_Armored_Cavalry_Regiment>.

[AGSU53] Knight, A. M., Commandant, Naval Station, Narragansett Bay, R.I. (1916, October 7). Subject: Arrival of German Submarine U 53 [Letter to Navy Department (Operations)]. United States National Archives, Washington, D.C.

[AH] Fest, J. C. Hitler, Trans. Winston R. and Winston, C. London: Harcourt, Brace and Company, 1974.

[AK] Manchester, William. The Arms of Krupp 1587-1968. New York: Bantam Books, 1970. Print.

[ALP] Rose, Hans. Ein Lebensbild (A Life Portrait) Trans. Christian Rose with corrections by Dr. Gertrude J. Robinson. Autobiography, Rose family archives, Quadra Island, British Columbia, Canada, begun circa 1951, possible rewrite 1968. Copy donated to Wehrgeschichtliches Ausbildungszentrum Marineschule Mürwik.

[APL] "Odessa." Wikipedia. Wikimedia Foundation, 27 Jan. 2014. Web. 27 Jan. 2014. <http://en.wikipedia.org/wiki/Odessa>. citing Alexander Puskin, letters

[AR <date>] Rose, Andreas. "Subject." Email to Markus F. Robinson. (date of email).

[ARAGS] The National Archives of the UK (TNA): ADM 137/4143. Assessment of results of attacks on German Submarines for 20.8.16.

[AT] Rose, Hans. Auftauchen! – Kriegsfahrten von U 53. Essen: Essener Verlagsanstalt, 1939. Print.

[AW] Mann, Chris and Jörgensen, Christer. Hitler's Arctic War: The German Campaigns in Norway, Finland and USSR 1940-1945. New York: St. Martin's Press, 2002. Print.

[AWR] Bracher, Karl Dietrich. Die Auflösung der Weimarer Republik; eine Studie zum Problem des Machtverfalls in der Demokratie. Berlin: Ring-Verlag, 1978. Print

[BBI] Rose, Hans. "Die Männer von Backbord Eins – zweites Buch – In aller Welt Haro." Autobiography. Rose family archives, Winterberg, Germany. circa 1950s. Copy donated to Wehrgeschichtliches Ausbildungszentrum Marineschule Mürwik.

[BBIV] Rose, Hans. "Die Männer von B.B.I. – Viertes Buch Verworrene Jahre: Haro." Autobiography. Rose family archives, Winterberg, Germany, 1960. Copy donated to Wehrgeschichtliches Ausbildungszentrum Marineschule Mürwik.

[BGBG] Carr, William Guy. By Guess and by God; the Story of the British Submarines in the War. Garden City, NY: Doubleday, Doran &, 1930. Print.

[BJ1] Brickenstein, Hans-Joachim. Personal interview. September 6-8, 2007, Winterberg, German

[BJ2 <date>] Brickenstein, Hans-Joachim. "Subject." Email to Markus F. Robinson. (date of email).

[BKN] Weir, Gary E. *Building the Kaiser's Navy: The Imperial Naval Office and German Industry in the von Tirpitz Era, 1890–1919.* Annapolis: Naval Institute Press, 1992. Print.

[BM <date>] Molter, Bernd. "Subject." Email to Markus F. Robinson. (date of email).

[BP] Brickenstein, Peter. Personal interview. 6-8 Sept. 2007. Winterberg, Germany.

[BPSSF] Rose, Wickliffe. Brittany Patrol: *The Story of the Suicide Fleet.* New York: W.W. Norton & Company, Inc., 1937. Print.

[BR1] Brickenstein, Rudolf. Personal interview. 6-8 Sept. 2007. Winterberg, Germany.

[BHJ1] Brickenstein, Hans-Joachim. Personal interview. 6-8 Sept. 2007. Winterberg, Germany.

[CB] "Claus Bergen." *Wikipedia.* Wikimedia Foundation, 05 July 2014. Web. 11 May 2014. <http://en.wikipedia.org/wiki/Claus_Bergen>.

[CFAD] DeMello, A. (n.d.). Regarding U 53 radio transmission [Letter to Lieut. C.G. Moore]. Washington Navy Yard Archive.

[CHHR] "Document Numbers 1-12 19 June 1914–28 June 1914." Gooch 1-12. (30325) No. 7. Sir H. Rumbold to Sir Edward Grey. (Received July 6.) Berlin, July 3, 1914. Captain Henderson to Sir H. Rumbold, Confidential, Berlin, July 3, 1914. British Documents on the Origins of the War, 1898-1914, List of Documents: Vol. XI – Items 1–299. Web. 21 Jan. 2014. <http://net.lib.byu.edu/estu/wwi/1914m/gooch/1-12.htm>.

[CODP] McLean, Iain, and Alistair McMillan. *The Concise Oxford Dictionary of Politics.* Oxford: Oxford UP, 2009. Print.

[CR1] Rose, Christian. Personal interview. 30 Sept. 2003. Quadra Island, British Columbia, Canada.

[CR2] Rose, Christian. Personal interview. 14 Feb. 2004. Quadra Island, British Columbia, Canada.

[CR3] Rose, Christian. Personal interview. 8 Oct. 2005. Quadra Island, British Columbia, Canada.

[CR4] Rose, Christian. Personal interview. 10 Sept. 2006. Quadra Island, British Columbia, Canada.

[CR5] Rose, Christian. Personal interview (telephone). 4 Jul. 2004. Quadra Island, British Columbia, Canada.

[CR6 <date>] Rose, Christian. "Subject." Email to Markus F. Robinson. (date of email).

[CRALS] Rose, Christian. *"A Life Story of Chris Rose."* Autobiography, 7 Oct. 2010. Rose family archives, Quadra Island, British Columbia, Canada.

[CS] Greig, I. T. (december 1984). The Convoy System and the Two Battles of the Atlantic (1914-18 and 1939-45). *The South African Military History Society, Military History Journal,* 6(4).

[CTR] Evans, Richard J. *The Coming of the Third Reich.* New York: Penguin, 2004. Print.

[CU53] Long, W. (october, 1966). The Cruise of U 53. *U.S. Naval Institute Proceedings,* 86-95. [#764, 86: Proceedings V 1 U6 v92:7-12 1966] (NIP-WL)

[DE] Cummins, C. L. Jr., and E. Diesel. *Diesel's Engine. – 1: From Conception to 1918.* Wilsonville, Or.: Carnot, 1993. Print.

[DEW] Kielmansegg, Peter. *Deutschland Und Der Erste Weltkrieg.* Frankfurt Am Main: Akademische Verlagsgesellschaft Athenaion, 1968. Print.

[DGJ] Jeffrey, D. G., Commander. (n.d.). *Transcript of broadcasts given over Canadian radio 1930s RE; War at Sea, 1914-8, especially anti-submarine warfare.* Manuscript, Folio 73/81/1, Imperial War Museum Archives. (anti-submarine section completely missing)

[DGSO] The National Archives of the UK (TNA): ADM137/3840 1916/1917. Dossier of German Submarine officers. Includes photographs and newspaper articles regarding Walther (*U 52*) and Rose (*U 53*)

[DJE] Rose, Hans. "Das Junge Europa," article/speech. Trondheim, Norway, 3 Apr. 1943. Rose family archives, Winterberg, Germany. Copy donated to Wehrgeschichtliches Ausbildungszentrum Marineschule Mürwik.

[DK] Lohmann, Walter, and Hans H. Hildebrand. *Die Deutsche Kriegsmarine 1939-1945.* (3 Vols). Bad Nauheim: Verlag Hans-Henning Podzun, 1956–1964. Print.

[DMS] Duncan, F. (april, 1965). Deutschland – Merchant Submarine. U.S. *Naval Institute Proceedings.*

[DORA1] "DORA 1." Wikipedia. Wikimedia Foundation, 18 Dec. 2013. Web. 28 Jan. 2014. <http://en.wikipedia.org/wiki/DORA_1>.

[DOS] Bejski, Dr. Moshe, *Days of the Shoah*, translated by Rochel Semp Edited by Fay and Julian Bussgang

[DOSWW] Kurowski, Franz. *Deutsche Offiziere in Staat, Wirtschaft Und Wissenschaft*: Bewährung Im Neuen Beruf. Herford Und Bonn: Maximilian, 1967. pp. 144-151 Print.

[EBS] Akermann, Paul. "Encyclopaedia of British Submarines 1901-1955", limited edition of 500, copy 137 in the Royal Navy Submarine Museum archives, Gosport, England

[EG] "Geschichte." Geschichte. ETUF Essen. Web. 21 Jan. 2014. <http://www.etuf.de/geschichte/>.

[EV] "Essener Verlagsanstalt." Wikipedia. Wikimedia Foundation, 24 Dec. 2013. Web. 25 Feb. 2014. <http://de.wikipedia.org/wiki/Essener_Verlagsanstalt>.

[EWC] Oliver, J. E. (Ed.). (2005). Oliver, J. E. (Ed.). (2005). Encyclopedia of World Climatology. Encyclopedia of Earth Sciences Series, (XX), 854.

[FTB] Funerary Testimony Rear Admiral Hermann Boehm, December 6, 1969 Copy donated to Wehrgeschichtliches Ausbildungszentrum Marineschule Mürwik.

[FTF] Walther Forstmann, Funerary Testimony Captain z. See a.D. Forstmann (in the Honorary Cemetery of Essen Dec.11, 1969 Copy donated to Wehrgeschichtliches Ausbildungszentrum Marineschule Mürwik.

[FTG] Glattes, Gerhard. *Funerary Testimony by d.R. Glattes in honor of Captain z. See a.D.Hans Rose.* Essen, 11. Dec. 1969. Rose family archives, Winterberg, Germany. Copy donated to Wehrgeschichtliches Ausbildungszentrum Marineschule Mürwik.

[FWJ] Joch, F. W. (n.d.). Autobiography of F.W. Joch. Manuscript, Robinson family archives, Guelph, Ontario, Canada. Copy donated to Wehrgeschichtliches Ausbildungszentrum Marineschule Mürwik.

[GAB] "German AB-aktion in Poland." Wikipedia. Wikimedia Foundation, 18 Jan. 2014. Web. 28 Jan. 2014. <http://en.wikipedia.org/wiki/German_AB-aktion_in_Poland>. citing Maria Wardzynska "Byl rok 1939 Operacja niemieckiej policji bezpieczenstwa w Polsce" IPN Instytut Pamieci Narodowej, 2009 ISBN 978-83-7629-063-8, and Meier, Anna "Die Intelligenzaktion: Die Vernichtung Der Polnischen Oberschicht Im Gau Danzig-Westpreußen" VDM Verlag Dr. Müller, ISBN 3-639-04721-4 ISBN 978-3639047219

[GD] Feldman, Gerald D. *The Great Disorder: Politics, Economics, and Society in the German Inflation, 1914-1924.* New York: Oxford University Press, 1997. Print.

[GDPT] *"German Denazification Panel Testimonials: Hans Rose. 22a Essen-Heisingen, Nordschleswigstrasse 55. 23. Dezember 1946, Translated testimonies."* copy of original. Rose family archives, Winterberg, Germany. Copy donated to Wehrgeschichtliches Ausbildungszentrum Marineschule Mürwik.

[GDTK] Doerries, Reinhard R., and Michael Wala. *Gesellschaft Und Diplomatie Im Transatlantischen Kontext: Festschrift F,r Reinhard R. Doerries Zum 65. Geburtstag.* Stuttgart: F. Steiner, 1999. Print.

[GHSF] Scheer, Reinhard. *Germany's High Sea Fleet in the World War.* London: Cassell, Limited, 1920. Print.

[GSM] Alboldt, E. (1926). *Gutachten des Sondersachverständigen Marinesekretärs a.D. Alboldt Die Ursachen des Zusammenbruchs der Marine* (Rep.).

[GWS] Hough, Richard. *The Great War at Sea, 1914-1918.* Oxford: Oxford University Press, 1983. Print.

[GWT] *German War Trials. Report of Proceedings before the Supreme Court in Leipzig (with Appendices).* London: H.M. Stationary Office, 1921. Print.

[GWVH] GERMAN WAR VESSEL HERE – U.53 Under Sea Fighter Creates a Stir – WAS HERE FOR THREE HOURS – Reason of Visit and Destination Unknown. (1916, October 10). *Newport Herald.* Newport, Rhode Island, USA

[H5] The National Archives of the UK (TNA): ADM173/2584. Section of interest, 7/10/1916 – 7/18/1916. Log of H.M. Submarine no. H5 Commenced June 4th 1916, Finished July 29th, 1916, Cromwell Varley Captain.

[H5RP] Varley, C., Captain. (n.d.). Report of Proceedings of Submarine H5 between 7/10/16 and 7/16/16. Typescript, ADM137/3745, Public Records Office, Kew, England.

[HAB] Kershaw, Ian. *Hitler: A Biography.* New York: W.W. Norton & Company, 2000. Print.

[HF] "Hans Frank Www.HolocaustResearchProject.org," Frank, Hans, speech delivered at Berlin University, November 18, 1941. Hans Frank Www.HolocaustResearchProject. org. Holocaust Education & Archive Research Team, Web. 21 Jan. 2014. <http://www.holocaustresearchproject.org/ar/frank.html>.

[HH] Fröhle, Claude und Hans- Jürgen Kühn. *Hochseefestung Helgoland – Eine militärgeschichtliche Entdeckungsreise.* Vol. 1, 1891-1922. Herbolzheim: Fr^hle-K.hn Verlagsgesellschaft, 1999

[HI] "Weimar Germany." Weimar Germany, The 1923 hyperinflation. Alpha History. Web. 21 Jan. 2014. <http://alphahistory.com/weimargermany/1923-hyperinflation/>.

[HN] Nelson, Horatio. "Letters and Dispatches of Horatio Nelson." Letters and Dispatches of Horatio Nelson. The War Times Journal, n.d. Web. 22 Apr. 2014. <http://www.wtj.com/archives/nelson/1805_10c.htm>.

[HO] Homer, *The Odyssey*, 10th Book. Trans. Shewring. Oxford: Oxford University Press, 1980. Print.

[HR To: <correspondent>, <date>] Rose, Hans, correspondence

[HRFW] Rose, Hans. speech to Friedrich Wilhelm. 1964. Rose family archives, Winterberg, Germany. Copy donated to Wehrgeschichtliches Ausbildungszentrum Marineschule Mürwik.

[HRH] Rose, Hans. "*Heldengedenken*", speech delivered in Norway between 1940-1943. Rose family archives, Winterberg, Germany. Copy donated to Wehrgeschichtliches Ausbildungszentrum Marineschule Mürwik.

[HRV] Rose, Hans. "*Vereidigung*", speech delivered in Norway between 1940-1943. Rose family archives, Winterberg, Germany. Copy donated to Wehrgeschichtliches Ausbildungszentrum Marineschule Mürwik.

[HW] Irving, David. *Hitler's War.* New York: Viking Press, 1977. Print.

[JGH] "Johann Gottfried Herder." Wikipedia. Wikimedia Foundation, 16 Jan. 2014. Web. 19 Jan. 2014. <http://en.wikipedia.org/wiki/Johann_Gottfried_Herder>.

[JPR] Polonsky, A., *The Jews in Poland and Russia*, Volume III, 1914 to 2008, (2012), containing speech by Frank to his senior officials, 16 Dec 1941, repr. in: Office of Chief Counsel for Prosecution of Axis Criminality, OCCPAC

[JTP] "Josef Terboven." Princeton University. N.p., n.d. Web. 28 Jan. 2014. <http://www.princeton.edu/~achaney/tmve/wiki100k/docs/Josef_Terboven.html>.

[KA] Mielke, O. (1958). UnterseeBoot U 53 – Kurs Amerika. *SOS-Schicksale Deutscher Schiffe*, Nr. 143. M.nchen

[KN] Groos, Otto (volumes I to V) and Gladish, Walther (volumes VI and VII). *Der Krieg in der Nordsee 1914-1918.* vol 1, Appendix 2. Berlin: E.S. Mittler, 1920–1965. Print.

[KZS <volume>] Spindler, Arno. *Der Krieg Zur See, Der Handelskrieg Mit U-Booten.* Berlin: E.S. Mittler & Sohn, 1932. Print. Volumes I, II, III of five, unpublished English translation commissioned by the British Admiralty, National Maritime Museum Library, Greenwich, London

[LAUC] compiled from "List of All U-boat Commanders." The Men of the U-boats. Uboat.net, n.d. Web. 28 Jan. 2014. <http://www.uboat.net/men/commanders/index. html>.

[LWM] "Lofoten War Museum – Occupation." Lofoten War Museum – Occupation. Lofoten War Museum, Lofoten Norway, n.d. Web. 28 Jan. 2014. <http://www. lofotenkrigmus.no/e_okkupasjon.htm>.

[LUM] O'Sullivan, Patrick. *The Lusitania: Unraveling the Mysteries*. Dobbs Ferry, NY: Sheridan House, 2000. Print.

[MFT] Jameson, William S. *The Most Formidable Thing; the Story of the Submarine from Its Earliest Days to the End of World War I*. London: Rupert Hart-Davis, 1965. Print.

[MLT] "Martial Law in Trondheim in 1942." Wikipedia. Wikimedia Foundation, 11 Dec. 2013. Web. 28 Jan. 2014. <http://en.wikipedia.org/wiki/ Martial_law_in_Trondheim_in_1942>.

[MP] Stärk, Hans. Marineunteroffizierschule Plön/Holstein. Ein Betrag zur Geschicte der Unteroffizierausbildung in der Marine. Selbstverlag des Verfassers (self published by the author), 1974. Print.

[MTU53] Petersen, C. (n.d.). Meine Tauchfahrt auf "U 53" – Deutschland – Amerika (USA) – Deutschland – 7.600 sm., 17. September bis 28. Oktober 1916. Unpublished manuscript, [Das] U-Boot-Archiv, Cuxhaven-Altenbruch. Unpublished diary in the possession of his son Günther Petersen

[NWWII] Dagre, Tor. "Norway and World War II." Norwegian Ministry of Foreign Affairs, 1995. Web. 21 Jan. 2014. <http://odin.dep.no/odin/engelsk/norway/ history/032005-990466/>. & <http://www.b24.no/background.htm>.

[NYT 7/10/1916, 2] 'German U-Boat Reaches Baltimore Having Crossed Atlantic in 16 Days; Has Letter From Kaiser to Wilson, 'Lake Threatens to Libel Craft', 'Hints at Regular Undersea Service'. (1916, July 10). *New York Times*, p. 2.

[NYT 7/11/1916, 2] 'Giant U-Boat Held to be a Trader; Unarmed and Brings Only Dyestuffs; Captain Tells of Trip; More Coming', 'To Finish U-Boat Inspection Today', *New York Times*, July 11, 1916, p.2

[NYT 7/12/1916, 3] 'Navy Experts Say Giant Submarine is Merchantman', 'Germany Jubilant at U-Boat Exploit', *New York Times*, July 12, 1916, p.3

[OGNS] Price, H. B., Commanding Officer U.S.S. Melville, Newport, Rhode Island. (1916, October 7). Subject: Observations on the German Naval Submarine No. 53 [Letter to Commander, Destroyer Force, Atlantic Fleet], United States National Archives, Washington, D.C. pp. 2-3

[PAM] Memmesheimer, Paul Arthur. Personal interview (telephone). 26 Nov. 2013.

[PGL] "Pan-German League." Wikipedia. Wikimedia Foundation, 01 Nov. 2014. Web. 29 Jan. 2014. <http://en.wikipedia.org/wiki/Pan-German_League>.

[PH] "Kiel Week 2009" dp-forum News 2009/Fall by DP Sailcloth Technology. N.p., n.d. Web. 28 Jan. 2014. <http://www.dimension-polyant.com/en/pdf/DP_Forum_2009_2. pdf>.

[R40] Beesly, Patrick. *Room 40: British Naval Intelligence 1914-1918*. San Diego: Harcourt, Brace Jovanovich, 1982. Print.

[RDT] Herzog, Bodo & Schomaekers, Günter, *Ritter der Tiefe Graue Wölfe, Die erfolgreichsten U-Boot-Kommandanten der Welt des Ersten und Zweiten Weltkrieges*, München, Wels: Verlag Welsermühl, 1965. Print.

[RGG] Reuth, Ralf Georg. *Goebbels*. Wien: Verlag Fritz Molden, 1990. Print.

[RH] Schimanski, Helga Rose. Personal interview (telephone). 5 Oct. 2005.

[RM] Rose, Margarite. Personal interview. 30 Sept. 2003. Quadra Island, British Columbia, Canada.

[ROI] Larimer, M. W., Lieutenant (j.g.) U.S.N. (1916, November 6). Subject: Report of inspection, German Naval Submarine ?U 53?, 3 [Letter to Commander, Destroyer Force, Atlantic Fleet]. United States National Archives, Washington, D.C.

[RPCI] *Record of Proceedings of a Court of Inquiry convened on board the U.S.S. Melville, Base No. Six, to inquire into the loss of the U.S.S.* Jacob Jones, *December 6, 1917,* (n.d.). Manuscript, United States National Archives

[RTRSJJ] From: Naval Attache, London, To: Director of Naval Intelligence. Date: 2/20/1930 RE: Radio Traffic relative to sinking of *Jacob Jones*, United States National Archives

[SA] Scientific American. (April 1899)

[SAD] Smith, Anthony D. (2010). Nationalism. Cambridge, England, UK; Malden, Massachusetts, USA: Polity Press. ISBN 0-19-289260-6.

[SAH] The National Archives of the UK (TNA): ADM137/3902 REF 1665. Extract from an unsigned Letter from New York addressed to Sir Arthur Herbert, 1 Hill Street, Knightsbridge. Dated 26.10.16

[SAN] Smith, Anthony D. *Nationalism.* Cambridge, England, UK; Malden, Massachusetts, USA: Polity Press, 2010. Print.

[SCMS] Folio 53548-1001, Ministry of Shipping, *The System of Convoys for Merchant Shipping in 1917 and 1918*, National Maritime Museum, Greenich, England 940.414 1

[SLH] "*The Salt Lake Herald*, March 08, 1908, News Section, Page 2, Image 2 About The Salt Lake Herald. (Salt Lake City, Utah) 1870-1909," "Germany's New Naval Monster" and the subtitle "Other Giant Battleships Being Constructed." News about Chronicling America RSS. Library of Congress, Chronicling America – Historic American Newspapers, Image provided by University of Utah, Marriott Library. Web. 21 Jan. 2014. <http://chroniclingamerica.loc.gov/lccn/sn85058130/1908-03-08/ed-1/seq-2/%3bwords=GERMANYS+NEWNAVALMONSTER>.

[SNL] "Hirden." Store Norske Leksikon. N.p., n.d. Web. 28 Jan. 2014. <http://snl.no/Hirden>.

[SNPP] Borgoyne, A. H. (1901). *Submarine Navigation: Past and Present: A Scientific Quarterly*, London

[SNS <chapter>: <page>] Rose, Hans. "*Der Seekommandant: Nordische Skizzen,*" 223-page manuscript submitted to publisher F. Bruckmann Verlagm, 5 Nov. 1941. Copy donated to Wehrgeschichtliches Ausbildungszentrum Marineschule Mürwik.

[SSR] Gleaves, A., Commander, Destroyer Force Atlantic Fleet, U.S.S. Birmingham, Flagship, Newport, Rhode Island. (1916, October 7). Subject: Visit of German Submarine U 53 to Newport, R.I., 7 October 1916 – Second Supplementary Report [Letter to Commander in Chief, Atlantic Fleet]. United States National Archives, Washington, D.C.

[SSS] SIX SHIPS SUNK BY GERMAN SUBMARINE – U 53 Leaves Newport on Errand of Destruction Off Nantucket Lightship – SURVIVORS BROUGHT HERE BY DESTROYERS, CARED FOR AND SENT TO NEW YORK BY WICKFORD LINE, WARFARE PURSUED DURING THE NIGHT – Nine Ships, Three Unidentified, Destroyed by Germans – British Cruisers Off Nantucket Early This Morning – CRASH IN WHEAT VALUES – WAVE OF SELLING – THE KANSAN AT BOSTON – DANIEL SENDS REPORT. (1916, October 9). *The News*, p. 1. Newport, Rhode Island, USA

[STB] Hoar, Allen. *The Submarine Torpedo Boat: Its Characteristics and Modern Development.* Van Nostrand: New York, 1916. Print.

[SUJJ1] Bagley, D.W., From: Com. D.W. Bagley, U.S.N. (Comdg. Off. U.S.S. *Jacob Jones*), To: Force Commander, Subject: Torpedoing and sinking of U.S.S. *Jacob Jones*, by enemy submarine, 6 December, 1917, United States National Archives

[SUJJ2] Bagley, D.W., From: Lt. Com. D.W. Bagley, To: Force Commander, Subject: Sinking of U.S.S. *Jacob Jones*, Date: 10 December, 1917, United States National Archives

[TG <date>, <page>] *The Guardian*, Guardian Unlimited – online website – Guardian Unlimited © Guardian Newspapers Limited 2002

[TLA] Rose, H. Captain, (December 1, 1926). With U 53 to America. II. *The Living Age*, 421-427.

[TN] "Trondheim." Wikipedia. Wikimedia Foundation, 18 Jan. 2014. Web. 28 Jan. 2014. <http://en.wikipedia.org/wiki/Trondheim>.

[TWCV2] Churchill, Winston. *The World Crisis: 1915*, Vol. II. New York: Scribner's, 1928. Print.

[U51D] Depositions (From R.M.A. – (Shipyard Department) File VI-8-1-174, Issue 10, U 51, Ärztlicher Bericht btr. Untergang U 51) (n.d.). Manuscript, Admiralstab D. Marine, Bundesarchiv Militararchiv, Kriegstagebuch U.51, Kptl. Rumpel. vom 19.2.16 bis 14.7.16 Bd. 1.

[U52R] Walther, Hans, *Reminiscences of U 52*, (personal memoir of U 52 by Captain Hans Walther, presented to F.W. Joch, unpublished, Markus F. Robinson family archives). Copy donated to Wehrgeschichtliches Ausbildungszentrum Marineschule Mürwik.

[U53GB] *U 53 Gästebuch* (*U 53 Guest Book*). 19 May 1916. Visitors Log of the U 53 containing remarks (5/19/1916 – 4/15/1918) by those visiting the U-boat. Original in the Rose family archives, Winterberg, Germany. Markus Robinson Personal Archive. Copy donated to Wehrgeschichtliches Ausbildungszentrum Marineschule Mürwik.

[U53KTBI] U/22/61612, PG/U/22/61612, *855 KTB (Kriegstagebuch) U 53 BD 1: 22.4.1916 – 31.5.1917*, U 53 War Diary Vol. I, Bundesarchiv – Militärarchiv, Freiburg, Germany

[U53KTBII] U/22/61613, PG/U/22/61612, *855 KTB (Kriegstagebuch) U 53 BD 2: 1.6.1917 – 16.9.1918*, U 53 War Diary Vol. II, Bundesarchiv – Militärarchiv, Freiburg, Germany

[UBS] Bergen, Claus. *My U-boat Voyage*, in Neureuther, Karl, Claus Bergen. *U-boat Stories: Narratives of German U-boat Sailors*. Trans. Sutton, Eric. London: Constable, 1931. Print.

[UCT] Rose, H. (1923, May 13). U-Boat Commander Tells How USS Jacob Jones Was Torpedoed. *The Sunday Star*, p. 3., Washington D.C., USA

[UJ] Jürgens, Ursula, Die Segelriege in ETUF e.V. (the Yacht section in ETUF (Essen Turn- und Fecht Verein). pp. 161-162, Essen, Germany

[UP] Hill, A. J. *Under Pressure: The Final Voyage of Submarine S-Five*. New York: Free, 2002. Print.

[UST] *Unser Schwerster Tag – Our Most Difficult Day – A Conversation between Captain Rose and Watch-Officer Esch of U 53* transmitted on the Westdeutschen Rundfunk on 11/7/1933. Rose family archives, Winterberg, Germany. Copy donated to Wehrgeschichtliches Ausbildungszentrum Marineschule Mürwik.

[UW] Gray, Edwyn. *The Underwater War; Submarines, 1914-1918*. New York: Charles Scribner's Sons, 1972. Print.

[VA] von Arnim, *Captain von Arnim's Account of ex-Sultan Abdul Hamid II's Rescue from Istanbul to Salonika: A Secret Mission*, Nov. 2, 1912, Rose Family Archives. Copy donated to Wehrgeschichtliches Ausbildungszentrum Marineschule Mürwik.

[VAS] Sims, William Sowden, and Burton Jesse Hendrick. *The Victory at Sea*. Garden City, NY: Doubleday, Page & Co., 1920. Print.

[VBH] Haffner, Sebastian. Von Bismarck zu Hitler: Ein Rückblick. München: Kindler Verlag, 1987

[VGSU53] Gleaves, A., Commander, Destroyer Force Atlantic Fleet, U.S.S Birmingham, Flagship, Newport, Rhode Island. (1916, October 7). Subject: Visit of German Submarine U 53 to Newport, R.I., 7 October 1916 [Letter to Commander in Chief, Atlantic Fleet]. United States National Archives, Washington, D.C.

Sources and Bibliography

[VTTT] Rose, Hans. "Von Tampen, Torpedoes und Tausenderlei – Erinnerungen eines Seeoffiziers – Um das Tägliche Brot." Autobiography, circa 1950s. Rose family archives, Winterberg, Germany. Copy donated to Wehrgeschichtliches Ausbildungszentrum Marineschule Mürwik.

[WDBDN] Hubatsch, W. 1960. "Weserübung:" Die Deutsche Besetzung von Dänemark und Norwegen 1940. 2nd Ed. Band 7: Studien und Dokumente zur Geschichte des Zweiten Weltkriegs. Göttingen: Musterschmidt Verlag.

[WRH] Unspecified, Agent (1916, October 31). [Letter to Captain W.R. Hall, C.B. Ad.C. Director of Intelligence Division, Admiralty War Staff, Admiralty, Whitehall, S.W.]. United States National Archives, Washington, D.C. Private correspondence

[WWLS] Rose, Hans. Rose version of General Admiral Herman Boehm's speech "What We Learned from the Sea", presented June, 1958 on the 55th anniversary of the Navy Academy Class of 1903. Rose family archives, Winterberg, Germany. Copy donated to Wehrgeschichtliches Ausbildungszentrum Marineschule Mürwik.

Endnotes

Acronyms reference the Sources and Bibliography section above.

Introduction

[1] MFT: frontispiece, [2] MFT: frontispiece, [3] SCMS, [4] AK: 336, [5] AK: 336, [6] GSM: 93, [7] BGBG: ix, [8] HR To: Christian Rose, 9/21/1943, [9] CR1

Chapter One

[10] U53KTBII: 6.12.17 5:35pm, [11] BPSSF: 135, [12] UCT, [13] SUJJ2: 1, [14] RPCI, [15] SUJJ1: 5, [16] SUJJ1: 3, [17] RPCI: 12, [18] UCT, [19] UCT, [20] UCT, [21] UCT, [22] UCT, [23] U53KTBII, [24] UCT, [25] UCT, [26] UCT, [27] CFAD, [28] UCT, [29] U53KTBII: 6.12.17, 7:40 pm, [30] U53KTBII: 6.12.17, 9:50 pm, [31] SUJJ2, [32] UCT, [33] GWT: 12-13, [34] GWT: 3, [35] RTRSJJ: 1, [36] VAS: 127-128

Chapter Two

[37] SNPP: 5, [38] SA, [39] UW: 12, [40] STB: 15, [41] AK: 25, [42] BKN: 52, [43] MFT: 13-14, [44] LUM: 60, [45] UP: 55-56, [46] WWLS, [47] KN, [48] DMS: 70, [49] NYT 7/10/1916, 2, [50] AK: 259, [51] NYT 7/10/1916, 2, [52] NYT 7/11/1916, 2, [53] NYT 7/11/1916, 2, [54] NYT 7/12/1916, 3, [55] NYT 7/12/1916, 3, [56] NYT 7/12/1916, 3

Chapter Three

[57] AT: 57, [58] AT: 58, [59] AT: 58-59, [60] CU53: 87, [61] CU53: 87, [62] AT: 58-59, [63] AT: 60, [64] ALP: 6, [65] AT: 63, [66] AT: 61, [67] U53KTBI: 70, [68] CU53: 88, [69] CR3, [70] CU53: 88, [71] CU53: 87, [72] RDT: 175-176, [73] EWC, [74] AT: 66, [75] RDT: 176, [76] U53KTBI: 6.9.17 9.20pm, [77] MTU53 9/18/1917, [78] AT: 68-69, [79] KA: 9, [80] AT: 68-69, [81] RDT: 176, [82] AT: 68-69, [83] AT: 68-69, [84] DE: 648, [85] EV, [86] CU53: 89, [87] U53KTBI: 21.09.16, [88] CU53: 88, [89] CU53: 88, [90] AT: 71, [91] AT: 69, [92] AT: 75, [93] U53KTBI: 9/23/1916 11am, [94] AT: 73-74, [95] AT: 73-74, [96] AT: 47-75, [97] AT: 75-76, [98] AT: 76, [99] RDT: 176-177, [100] KZS III: 239, [101] AT: 76-77, [102] AT: 77-78, [103] U53KTBI: 9/28/1916, [104] AT: 78-79, [105] CU53: 88, [106] AT: 69, [107] KA: 11, [108] AT: 70,[109] KA: 11, [110] CU53: 89-90, [111] CU53: 89, [112] CU53: 89, [113] CU53: 89, [114] AT: 85-86, [115] ALP: 7, [116] RDT: 177-178, [117] RDT: 178-179, [118] AT: 87, [119] AT: 87-88, [120] CU53: 90, [121] AT: 91, [122] AT: 91, [123] CU53: 90, [124] CU53: 90, [125] CU53: 90

Chapter Four

[126] RDT: 178-179, [127] AT: 93, [128] CU53: 91, [129] AT: 93, [130] RDT: 179-180, [131] RDT: 179-180, [132] AT: 95, [133] AT: 96, [134] AT: 97, [135] CU53: 92, [136] WRH, [137] AGSU53: 2, [138] AGSU53: 2, [139] OGNS, [140] SAH, [141] AGSU53: 3, [142] SAH, [143] ROI: 3, [144] WRH: 2, [145] GWVH, [146] GWVH, [147] GWVH, [148] GWVH, [149] GWVH, [150] GWVH, [151] GWVH, [152] GWVH, [153] GWVH, [154] OGNS: 1, [155] AGSU53: 2, [156] VGSU53, [157] OGNS: 1, [158] ROI: 4, [159] WRH, [160] SSR, [161]RDT: 179-180, [162] RDT: 180, [163] AT: 100, [164] TLA: 421, [165] SSS, [166] TLA: 424, [167] CU53: 93, [168] CU53, [169] SSS, [170] SSS, [171] SSS, [172] SSS, [173] TLA: 424, [174] SSS, [175] SSS, [176] TLA: 424, [177] TLA: 424, [178] TLA: 425, [179] TLA: 424, [180] TLA: 425-426, [181] TLA: 425, [182] TLA: 425, [183] TLA: 425, [184] MTU53 10/22/1916, [185] AT: 114, [186] AT: 114, [187] CU53: 95, [188] AT: 116, [189] AT: 116, [190] TLA: 426, [191] TLA: 426, [192] SSS

Chapter Five

[193] ALP: 22, [194] BBI: 38, [195] SAD: 41, [196] ALP: 1, [197] CR6: 5/25/2013, [198] CR2, [199] CR2, [200] CR6: 9/26/2005, [201] CR2, [202] BR1, [203] AR: 9/20/2005, [204] CR2, [205] CR6 8/17/2007, [206] CR6 5/3/2012, [207] BHJ1, [208] CR1, [209] CR2, [210] BR1, [211] BJ1, [212] CR1, [213] BBI: 60-62, [214] CR4, [215] ALP: 2-3, [216] CR2, [217] CR6 2/12/2011, [218] CR1, [219] RH, [220] BP

Chapter Six

[221] ALP:1, [222] DGSO: Association to aid shipwreck survivors, [223] ALP: 2, [224] ALP: 2, [225] ALP: 2, [226] BBI: 1, [227] BBI: 2, [228] BBI: 2, [229] BBI: 2, [230] BBI: 2, [231] BBI: 3, [232] BBI: 6, [233] BBI: 3, [234] BBI: 4, [235] BM 8/15/2012, [236] BBI: 10, [237] BBI: 10, [238] BBI: 10, [239] BBI: 10, [240] BBI: 11, [241] BBI: 11, [242] BBI: 11, [243] BBI: 5, [244] BBI: 7, [245] BBI: 3, [246] BBI: 6, [247] BBI: 9, [248] BBI: 9, [249] BBI: 9, [250] BBI: 9, [251] BBI: 9, [252] BBI: 10, [253] BBI: 9, [254] BBI: 12, [255] ALP: 2-3, [256] ALP: 2-3, [257] BBI: 11, [258] BBI: 12, [259] ALP: 7,[260] CR6 7/26/2012, [261] BBI: 12, [262] BBI: 12, [263] BBI: 13, [264] BBI: 34, [265] BBI: 13, [266] BBI: 13, [267] BBI: 14, [268] BBI: 14, [269] BBI: 17, [270] BBI: 17, [271]BBI: 20, [272] BBI: 21, [273] BBI: 22, [274] BBI: 23, [275] BBI: 24, [276] BBI: 26, [277] BBI: 30, [278] BBI: 30, [279] BBI: 31, [280] BBI: 31, [281] BBI: 31, [282] BBI: 34, [283] BBI: 34, [284] SLH, [285] BBI: 35, [286] BBI: 35, [287] BBI: 37, [288] BBI: 37, [289] BBI: 35, [290] BBI: 35, [291] BBI: 36, [292] BBI: 35, [293] BBI: 35, [294] BBI: 38, [295] BBI: 37, [296] BBI: 37, [297] BBI: 37, [298] BBI: 37, [299] BBI: 37, [300] BBI: 36, [301] BBI: 42

Chapter Seven

[302] BBI: 38, [303] BBI: 38, [304] BBI: 38, [305] BBI: 38, [306] BBI: 38, [307] BBI: 39, [308] BBI: 39, [309] BBI: 39, [310] BBI: 39, [311] BBI: 39, [312] BBI: 40, [313] BBI: 40, [314] BBI: 40, [315] BBI: 42, [316] BBI: 41, [317] BBI: 41, [318] BBI: 41, [319] BBI: 41, [320] BBI: 41, [321] BBI: 41, [322] BBI: 41, [323] BBI: 41, [324] BBI: 43, [325] BBI: 43, [326] BBI: 43, [327] BBI: 43, [328] BBI: 43, [329] BBI: 43, [330] BBI: 43, [331] BBI: 44, [332] BBI: 44, [333] BBI: 44, [334] BBI: 43, [335] BBI: 43, [336] BBI: 43, [337] BBI: 44, [338] BBI: 44, [339] BBI: 44, [340] BBI: 46, [341] BBI: 46, [342] BBI: 46, [343] BBI: 45, [344] BBI: 45, [345] BBI: 47, [346] BBI: 46, [347] BBI: 47, [348] BBI: 48

Chapter Eight

[349] BBI: 46, [350] ALP: 3, [351] BBI: 80-82, [352] HRV, [353] BBI: 49-50, [354] BBI: 49-50, [355] BBI: 57-58, [356] BBI: 57, [357] BBI: 83-84, [358] BBI: 132-133, [359] BBI: 141, [360] BBI: 66-68, [361] BBI: 69-72, [362] BBI: 83-84, [363] BBI: 83-84, [364] BBI: 132, [365] BBI: 137, [366] BBI: 133, [367] BBI: 50, [368] BBI: 50-53, [369] BBI: 53-54, [370] BBI: 54-56, [371] BBI: 57-58, [372] BBI: 57-58, [373] BBI: 53-54, [374] BBI: 58-60, [375] BBI: 74, [376] BBI: 135-137, [377] BBI: 85, [378] BBI: 58-60, [379] VTTT: 38, [380] BBI: 49-50, [381] BBI: 49, [382] BBI: 60-62, [383] BBI: 75-77, [384] BBI: 75-77, [385] BBI: 84, [386] BBI: 135-137, [387] BBI: 81-82, [388] BBI: 80, [389] BBI: 87, [390] BBI: 83, [391] BBI: 132-133, [392] CR6 10/5/2005, [393] CR6 5/10/2004, [394] BBI: 49-50, [395] BBI: 130, [396] BBI: 131, [397] BBI: 131-132, [398] BBI: 137-139, [399] BBI: 75-77, [400] BBI: 57-58, [401] BBI: 60-62, [402] BBI: 67, [403] BBI: 72-73, [404] BBI: 75-77, [405] BBI: 86, [406] APL, [407] BBI: 63-64, [408] BBI: 65, [409] BBI: 66, [410] BBI: 65-66, [411] BBI: 68, [412] BBI: 69-72, [413] BBI: 74, [414] BBI: 77, [415] BBI: 77, [416] BBI: 77, [417] BBI: 77-78, [418] BBI: 79-80, [419] BBI: 79-80

Chapter Nine

[420] BBI: 53-54, [421] BBI: 80, [422] BBI: 86-89, [423] BBI: 86-89, [424] VA: 2, [425] VA: 2-4, [426] VA: 5, [427] VA: 12, 15, [428] BBI: 134, [429] VA: 18, [430] BBI: 89, [431] BBI: 92, [432]BBI: 100-101, [433] BBI: 110, [434] BBI: 113-114, [435] BBI: 122, [436] BBI: 124, [437] SSR, [438] BBI: 128-130, [439] BBI: 131, [440] BBI: 133-135, [441] BBI: 137-138, [442] BBI: 139-140, [443] BBI: 141, [444] BBI: 141, [445] BBI: 142, [446] BBI: 143

Chapter Ten

[447] BBI: 144, [448] BBI: 144, [449] ALP: 3, [450] PH, [451] GHSF: 10, [452] FWJ: 40, [453] CHHR, [454] TG 6/29/1914, [455] FWJ: 40, [456] BBI: 144-145, [457] ALP: 3-4, [458] CU53: 88, [459] CU53: 88, [460] BM 1/13/2014, [461] ALP: 4, [462] ALP: 5

Chapter Eleven

[463] R40: 87[464] GWS: 30, [465] TWCV2: 280, [466] CS

Chapter Twelve

[467] HH: 8, [468] DGJ, [469] UBS: 1-2, [470] UBS: 159, [471] FWJ[472] UBS: 5, [473] AT: 22-23, [474] AT: 23-24, [475] AT: 27-28, [476] H5: 1-9, [477] H5RP 7/18/1916, [478] AT: 28-30, [479] U51D: 28, [480] U51D: 28, [481] U51D: 29, [482] U51D: 29, [483] U51D: 29, [484] U51D: 29, [485] U51D: 25, [486] AT: 30, [487] U52R: 1-6, [488] U52R: 1-6, [489] AT: 35-42, [490] AT: 44-50, [491] AT: 50-51, [492] AT: 53, [493] AT: 50, [494] AT: 50, [495] AT: 53, [496] ARAGS 8/20/1916, [497] GDTK: 79-80, [498] GDTK: 80, [499] GDTK: 80, [500] GDTK: 89, [501] TLA: 427., [502] CU53: 95, [503] TLA: 424, [504] CU53: 95, [505] TLA: 427, [506] CU53: 95, [507] TLA: 427, [508] TLA: 421

Chapter Thirteen

[509] AT: 123, [510] AT: 123, [511] AT: 124, [512] AT: 123, [513] GHSF: 158, [514] AT: 126, [515] AT: 125-127, [516] AT: 128-129, [517] AT: 134-137, [518] AT: 129-134, [519] AT: 147-148, [520] AT: 141, [521] ALP: 10-11, [522] AT: 143, [523] ALP: 11-12, [524] AT: 143, [525] ALP: 12, [526] AT: 137-141, [527] KZS IV: 64

Chapter Fourteen

[528] UBS: 5-6, [529] UBS: 3-4, [530] UBS: 5, [531] CR1, [532] CB, [533] UBS: 6, [534] UBS: 11-13, [535] UBS: 13, [536] UBS: 6-7, [537] UBS: 10-11, [538] UBS: 8-9, [539] UBS: 10, [540] UBS: 14-16, [541] UBS: 17, [542] UBS: 17-18, [543] UBS: 19-22, [544] UBS: 22-26, [545] UBS: 27, [546] UBS: 26-27, [547] UBS: 29-30, [548] UBS: 30-34, [549] AT: 282, [550] UBS: 35-36, [551] UBS: 41-44, [552] UBS: 44-45, [553] UBS: 47-50, [554] UBS: 50-51, [555] UBS: 51-52, [556] UBS: 54-56, [557] U53KTBII: 20

Chapter Fifteen

[558] VAS: 1-2, [559] VAS: 3-4, [560] VAS: 3, [561] VAS: 3, [562] VAS: 6-7, [563] SCMS: 1, [564] HN, [565] SCMS: 1, [566] VAS: 8, [567] SCMS: 2-3, [568] SCMS: 3, [569] SCMS: 4, [570] SCMS: 6, [571] SCMS: 7, [572] SCMS: 8, [573] SCMS: 5, [574] SCMS: 18, [575] AT: 151, [576] AT: 151-155, [577] AT: 178-180 [578] SCMS: 9, [579] AT: 160-165, [580] AT: 167-175, [581] AT: 174-175, [582] AT: 175-176, [583] AT: 177-178, [584] U53KTBII: 23.11.17 8:30 AM, [585] UCT, [586] UCT, [587] UCT, [588] UCT

Chapter Sixteen

[589] AT: 219, [590] U53KTBII: 2/20/1918, [591] U53KTBII: 2/11/1918, 4:00 pm, [592] AT: 219-220, [593] AT: 220-224, [594] AT: 225-226, [595] ALP: 9-10, [596] DGSO, [597] U53KTBII: 2/4/1918, [598] AT: 238-250, [599] AT: 250-252, [600] UST, [601] AT: 266, [602] AT: 272-273, [603] AT: 267, [604] AT: 268, [605] AT: 269, [606] AT: 270, [607] AT: 271, [608] AT: 280-282, [609] U53KTBII: 28/6/1918 10:35, [610] AT: 282-283, [611] U53KTBII: 8/7/1918, [612] U53KTBII: 8/7/1918 4:05 AM, [613] U53KTBII: 8/7/1918 5:00 AM, [614] AT: 288-291, [615] AT: 292-293

Chapter Seventeen

[616] AT: 294, 296, [617] CR6 6/6/2013, [618] AT: 296, [619] AT: 297-298, [620] VAS: 222, [621] AT: 301, [622] ALP: 17-18, [623] AT: 301, [624] CR6 4/14/2013, [625] AT: 302, [626] AT: 303, [627] ALP: 18, [628] AT: 303, [629] RDT: 186-187

Chapter Eighteen

[631] GD: 148, [630] VBH: 177-178, [632] DEW: 681, [633] VTTT: 1-2, [634] VTTT: 3-4, [635] VTTT: 5-6, [636] CTR: 88, [637] VTTT: 4-5, [638] VTTT: 9, [639] VTTT: 9, [640] VTTT: 11-12, [641] ALP: 19, [642] VTTT: 11-12, [643] VTTT: 23, [644] VTTT: 23, [645] VTTT: 24-25, [646] ALP: 18, [647] ALP: 18, [648] CTR: 105, [649] HI, [650] VTTT: 38, [651] VTTT: 13-14, [652] ALP: 19, [653] ALP: 19, [654] VTTT: 28, [655] ALP: 19, [656] VTT: 29 , [657] UCT, [658] ALP: 19, [659] ALP: 19, [660] ALP: 19, [661] ALP: 19, [662] ALP: 19-20, [663] ALP: 19-20[664] ALP: 20-21, [665] ALP: 20, [666] VTTT: 32, [667] ALP: 21, [668] VTTT: 38, [669] ALP: 21, [670] ALP: 21, [671] ALP: 21, [672] ALP: 19, [673] HAB: 128, [674] VTTT: 19, [675] VTTT: 41, [676] VTTT: 20, [677] CR6 8/17/2007, [678] VTTT: 41, [679] VTTT: 41-42, [680] VTTT: 41-42, [681] VTTT: 48, [682] CRALS: 4, [683] VTTT: 49, [684] VTTT: 51, [685] VTTT: 53-55

Chapter Nineteen

[686] ALP: 21, [687] VTTT: 36, [688] VTTT: 37, [689] VTTT: 38, [690] VTTT: 37, [691] VTTT: 38, [692] VTTT: 38, [693] CR1, [694] AWR: 565, [695] CTR: 235, [696] VTTT: 57, [697] VBH: 216-220, [698] CTR: 264-265, [699] VTTT: 57-58,

[700] VTTT: 58, [701] VTTT: 56, [702] VTTT: 56, [703] CR6 2/14/2013, [704] VTTT: 58-61, [705] VTTT: 62-63, [706] CR1, [707] VTTT: 71-73, [708] CTR: 279-307, [709] CR5, [710] RGG: 210, [711] CTR: 293-294 & 306, [712] CR6 10/8/2005, [713] CRALS: 4, [714] AH: 397-399, [715] AH: 405, [716] CTR: 382, [717] VTTT: 78, [718] CTR: 460-461, [719] VTTT: 64, [720] VTTT: 71-73, [721] VTTT: 72, [722] VTTT: 72, [723] VTTT: 74, [724] VTTT: 75, [725] AH: 433-434, [726] VTTT: 72, [727] VTTT: 73

Chapter Twenty

[728] RH, [729] BBIV, [730] CR1, [731] CR6 3/3/2013, [732] ALP: 22, [733] BP, [734] CR1, [735] CR1, [736] CR1, [737] CR1, [738] CR1, [739] CRALS: 9-10, [740] CR6 10/5/2005, [741] BP, [742] RH, [743] CR6 10/5/2005, [744] BP, [745] BR1, [746] GDPT, [747] GDPT, [748] DOSWW: 149, [749] DOSWW: 148, [750] DOSWW: 151, [751] PAM, [752] PAM, [753] CRALS: 5, [754] VTTT: 81, [755] CRALS: 5-6, [756] CRALS: 7, [757] CR1, [758] RM, [759] CR1, [760] BP, [761] CR6 8/20/2007, [762] UJ, [763] VTTT: 75, [764] VTTT: 80-81, [765] CRALS: 8, [766] CR2, [767] VTTT: 85, [768] VTTT: 86, [769] VTTT: 87-88, [770] VTTT: 87

Chapter Twenty-One

[771] HRV, [772] BBIV: 52-53, [773] BBIV: 55, [774] RH, [775] MP, [776] DK, [777] DK, [778] CRALS: 10, [779] CRALS: 10, [780] CRALS: 10, [781] RH, [782] CR1, [783] HF, [784] JPR: 434, [785] DOS, [786] GAB, [787] CR1, [788] MP, [789] CR6 10/5/2005, [790] CRALS: 12, [791] CRALS: 11, [792] CRALS: 12, , [793] AW: 7, [794] SNS 2: 1-4, [795] SNS 2: 16-19, [796] SNS 2: 21-23, [797] SNS 2:21, [798] SNS 2: 22-23, [799] SNS 2: 22-23, [800] SNS 2: 19, [801] NWWII, [802] LWM, [803] SNS 4: 3, [804] SNS 6: 1-2, [805] SNS 6: 1-2, [806]WDBDN

Chapter Twenty-Two

[807] ALP: 23-24, [808] BR1, [809] ALP: 27-28, [810] ALP: 23, [811] ALP: 23, [812] TN, [813] DORA1, [814] HW, [815] MLT citing Lilleeng, Sverre (2007-05-08). "Unntakstilstand i Trondheim". Trondheim: Byavisa., [816] SNL, [817] MLT, [818] JTP, [819] RH, [820] BR1, [821] CR6 9/12/2005, [822] CR6 9/24/2005, [823] CR1 , [824] CR1, LAUC, [825] SNS 13, [826] SNS 13, [827] SNS 18, [828] SNS 18: 1-2, [829] SNS 13: 14-15, [830] SNS 13, [831] SNS 13: 5-7, [832] SNS 13: 16-17, [833] ALP: 23, [834] SNS 18: 3-4, [835] SNS 18: 7, [836] SNS 18: 8-9, [837] SNS 20: 2, [838] SNS 20: 5, [839] SNS 20: 5, [840] SNS 20: 6, [841] SNS 20: 8, [842] SNS 20: 10-11, [843] SNS 20: 13, [844] SNS 20: 14, [845] SNS 20: 12-14, [846] SNS 20: 15, [847] SNS 20: 16, [848] SNS 20: 18, [849] ALP: 24-26, [850] ALP: 24-26, [851] BR1, [852] ALP: 26, [853] SNS 17: 7-8, [854] SNS 17: 14, [855] SNS 21: 1, [856] SNS 21: 2-3, [857] SNS 21: 6, [858] SNS 21: 12-14, [859] SAN: 41, [860] JGH, [861] JGH, [862] SAN: 41, [863] PGL

Chapter Twenty-Three

[864] ALP: 27-29, [865] HO, [866] SNS 13: 1, [867] SNS 13: 1 unless otherwise stated, all future quotes in this section are drawn from Vom Morgenstern und Tautropfen, [868] CR6 9/24/2005, [869] DJE Unless otherwise attributed, all other quotes in this section are from the same source, [870] CODP, [871] JGH, [872] JGH, [873] BM 3/7/2008, [874] HRH, [875] JGH, [876] WWLS, [877] ALP: 23-24, [878] VTTT, [879] RH, [880] ALP: 29, [881] CR6 9/24/2005, [882] BR1, [883] ALP: 26, [884] ALP: 26, [885] ALP: 29, [886] ALP: 29, [887] BP, [888] BJ1, [889] ALP: 27

Chapter Twenty-Four

[890] CR6 5/3/2013, [891] CR6 5/2/2013, [892] BBIV: 53-55, [893] CRALS: 12, [894] CRALS: 12, [895] HR To: Christian Rose, 9/21/1943, [896] CR6 10/5/2005, [897] CR6 10/5/2005, [898] RH, [899] CR6 5/5/2013, [900] RH, [901] RH, [902] RH, [903] CRALS: 21, [904] CRALS: 22, [905] CRALS: 21, [906] CRALS: 22, [907] ALP: 22, [908] CRALS: 20, [909] CR2, [910] BR1, [911] ALP: 22, [912] GDPT, [913] CR4, [914] CRALS: 24, [915] CRALS: 24, [916] CRALS: 24, [917] CR6 5/16/2013, [918] ACR, [919] CRALS: 25, [920]CR4, [921] CR6 5/17/2013, [922]CR4, [923]CR4, [924] CR1, [925] CR6 5/2/2013, [926]CR4, [927] CR6 8/17/2007, [928]CR4, [929] CR4, [930]CR4, [931] CR6 5/17/2013, [932] CR6 5/17/2013, [933] CR6 10/5/2005, [934] CR6 8/17/2007, [935] CR6 8/17/2007, [936] CR4, [937] CR4, [938] CR4, [939] CR4, [940] CR4, [941] CR6 9/21/2005, [942] CR6 5/19/2013, [943] CRALS: 27, [944] CRALS: 31, [945] CR4, [946] BR1, [947] BJ2 5/21/2013, [948] CR6 3/27/2009, [949] BP, [950] BJ1, [951] BJ1, [952] BJ1, [953] BR1, [954] BP, [955] BJ1, [956] BJ1, [957] AR 4/18/2014, [958] BP, [959] BJ1, [960] BJ1, [961] BP, EG, [962] CR6 11/25/2007, [963] HR To: Christian Rose, 5/17/1958, [964] BP, [965] BP, [966] BP, [967] BR1, [968] HRFW, [969] HRFW

Chapter Twenty-Five

[970] U53GB: 14, [971] FTG, [972] FTF, [973] FTB, [974] CU53: 87, [975] CRALS: 54, [976] CR6 9/12/2005

Appendix

[977] ROI: 4, [978] SSR: 2, [979] OGNS: 2-3, [980] OGNS: 3, [981] BM 1/16/2014, [982] ROI: 1, [983] SSR: 1, [984] WRH: 1, [985] UBS: 14-16, [986] OGNS: 3-4 #7

Index

For the sake of readability, no italic has been used. Individuals are listed by nationality under Personalities.